THE EMERGING MINORITIES IN AMERICA

THE EMERGING MINORITIES IN AMERICA

A RESOURCE GUIDE FOR TEACHERS

Contributions of significance
which members of minority groups
have made to the historical and
cultural development of the
United States of America

A man bleeds, suffers, despairs
not as an American or a Russian
or a Chinese,
but in his innermost being
as a member of a single human race.

ADLAI E. STEVENSON
1963

ABC-CLIO INC.

Santa Barbara, California
Oxford, England

Library of Congress Catalog Card No. 72-77550
ISBN Clothbound Edition 0-87436-092-7
Printed and bound in the United States of America

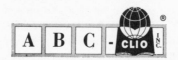

American Bibliographical Center-Clio Press
Riviera Campus, 2040 Alameda Padre Serra
Santa Barbara, California

European Bibliographical Center-Clio Press
30 Cornmarket Street
Oxford OX1 3EY, England

CONTENTS

FOREWORD

THE EMERGING MINORITIES IN AMERICA, a guide for teachers, is a step in the direction of developing positive attitudes on the part of all children toward themselves and toward each other. As simple as this may sound it is, after all, one of the central roles of the school. An attempt has been made here to document contributions by members of cultures other than the culture which those who belong to it call dominant.

Purely for purposes of convenience, the information put down here is arranged by cultural groups. This is a kind of segregation in itself, but none is intended. It is appropriate to point out here that these people are Americans first and members of their ethnic group second. It is the hope of those who have compiled these data that society will move in the direction that we may soon become one people and that we may all become an amalgam of the best characteristics of all cultures.

No greater single challenge confronts education today than that of achieving with students a realistic and humanistic attitude toward the variety of subcultures which make up the mainstream of the citizens of the United States. No challenge is more demanding nor more significant to our national health. It is a part of the preservation of our human and natural environment since our ecology includes us all.

Many people have contributed to this document. A special place is included to record their names. We are deeply grateful for their involvement and participation. Particular appreciation is expressed to Mr. George R. Monroe, former Assistant Superintendent, Instructional Services, who encouraged and nurtured creative leadership in education at all times and who gave support to the development of this document. Recognition is given to the work of Mrs. Ruth J. Smith, Coordinator of Compensatory Education, who conceived the idea for this project and motivated the action. Special credit is given to Mr. Eleazar Ruiz, Coordinator of Child Welfare and Attendance Services, who served as the overall chairman of the various working committees and who coordinated the development of this publication. Recognition is also given to Mrs. Charlotte D. Davis, Coordinator of Library Services, who gave yeoman service throughout and who edited the final document. Appreciation is expressed to Dr. Edith P. Stickney, Librarian, University of California, Santa Barbara, who arranged and edited the information contained herein as it was being developed.

It is the hope of those who have labored cooperatively to produce this document that teachers will find it useful in meeting and solving some of the most pressing problems of our times.

SOPHIE E. SCHNITTER
Assistant Superintendent,
Curriculum and Instructional Services

PREFACE

CONCERNS OVER THE NEEDS of minority youth have assumed top priority in our educational planning. Many different approaches have been devised to meet these needs. One of the more successful approaches has been the documentation of the contributions of minority group members to the cultural and historical development of our country. This publication is the direct result of the efforts of the County Schools Office staff to fulfill this need in Santa Barbara county.

A task force approach was utilized in developing the materials for this publication. Some forty teachers, students and administrators participated. Of this number, twenty-four stayed with the project through its entirety and completed the research activities required.

The major goal of the project was to develop reference materials which will help teachers to establish positive attitudes toward minority groups. Essentially, the content has been organized to provide an historical perspective of each ethnic group, biographical sketches of key individuals within these groups, and brief descriptions of contributions made by the individuals.

Users of the book will also find a rather extensive bibliography of sources and other references. As a final facilitative effort, two appendices have been included which provide a historical reference by ethnic group or individual and another list giving a breakdown by subject or occupational classification.

Hopefully, this publication will, in some small way, help teachers and children gain positive insight and understanding of the role and contributions of minority groups and individuals in our society.

LORENZO DALL'ARMI
Santa Barbara County
Superintendent of Schools

June 27, 1972

ACKNOWLEDGEMENTS

THE EMERGING MINORITIES IN AMERICA, a teachers' resource guide, has been prepared by a county-wide committee with representation from school districts, the Santa Barbara County Schools Office, and members of the community. Their names are listed below in grateful appreciation for the time and effort each devoted to extensive research and writing. A special note of thanks is extended to the administrators of the participating school districts for authorizing released time during regular school days for general committee meetings. These meetings were essential in providing project continuity throughout the year, in coordinating the research, and developing the format.

COMMITTEE RESEARCH TEAMS

Afro American; Co-Chairmen: ROLAND ANDERSON and MRS. SELENA PEDERSEN
    ROLAND ANDERSON, Teacher, Santa Maria School District
    MRS. CONSTANCE BELFILS, Librarian, Montecito Union School District
    MRS. LOUCILE HECKMAN, Librarian, Santa Barbara School District
    MRS. SELENA PEDERSEN, Member, Governing Board, Cold Spring School District
    MRS. RUTH J. SMITH, Coordinator, Compensatory Education, Santa Barbara County Schools
    DR. EDITH P. STICKNEY, Librarian, University of California, Santa Barbara

Asian American; Chairman: MRS. SEMA ENGLISH
    JO ANN BAKER, Teacher, Santa Maria School District
    MRS. CHARLOTTE D. DAVIS, Coordinator, Library Services, Santa Barbara County Schools
    MRS. SEMA ENGLISH, Teacher, Goleta Union School District
    MRS. MADELINE REED, Member, American Association of University Women, Santa Barbara, California

Indian American; Chairman: WALTER L. McCULLEY
    MRS. JEAN E. ANTHONY, Coordinator, Instructional Services, Santa Barbara County Schools
    COLONEL ROBERT BARAY, U.S. Army (Retired), Vandenberg Air Force Base, Lompoc, California
    CHARLES HURLBUT, Principal, Lompoc Unified School District
    MRS. BARBARA JOHNSON, Teacher, Los Olivos School District
    WALTER L. McCULLEY, Superintendent, Cold Spring School District
    SOPHIE E. SCHNITTER, Assistant Superintendent, Curriculum and Instructional Services, Santa Barbara County Schools
    ED ZIMMERMAN, Teacher, Santa Ynez Valley Union High School District

Mexican American; Chairman: HECTOR SAMANIEGO
  JOSEPHINE COSTANTINI, Principal, Carpinteria Unified School District
  MRS. ELIZABETH BOWDON, Reading Teacher, Carpinteria Unified School District
  RAYMOND DUTCHOVER, Teacher, Vista del Mar Union School District
  JOHN ROMO, Teacher, Goleta Union School District
  ELEAZAR RUIZ, Coordinator, Child Welfare and Attendance, Santa Barbara County Schools
  HECTOR SAMANIEGO, Teacher, Lompoc Unified School District
  REYES VILLALPANDO, English as a Second Language Teacher, Santa Barbara School District

CONSULTANTS

Consultants who made presentations to the committee were a significant source of inspiration. They offered suggestions and made recommendations as the project proceeded through its various phases. The committee is indebted to them for their participation and service.

DR. RUDY ACUÑA, Chairman, Mexican American Studies Department, San Fernando Valley State College, Northridge, California
COLONEL ROBERT R. BARAY, U.S. Army (Retired), Vandenberg Air Force Base, Lompoc, California
J. QUENTIN MASON, Coordinator, Intergroup Relations, Sequoia Union High School District, Redwood City, California
STEVEN MURATA, Student, University of California, Santa Barbara, California
MARGO TAM, Student, University of California, Santa Barbara, California

An additional note of thanks is extended to Paul Jillson, Director of Curriculum; to Jack Stoltz, Coordinator of Educational Broadcasting; to the members of the clerical staff; to Mrs. Jeanne Rassuli, student; and to Rubye Ballard, Black Studies Librarian, University of California, Santa Barbara, and the personnel of the Reference Departments of the library of the University and of the Santa Barbara Public Library.

INTRODUCTION

THE EMERGING MINORITIES IN AMERICA has been prepared as a specific reference and resource guide for teachers. It is designed to provide assistance in curriculum development through incorporation into the curriculum of the cultural and historical contributions of minority groups. In essence, it will aid the teacher in developing and enhancing a very significant two-part educational process

1   in providing minority students with personal models from their own ethnic cultures with whom they can identify, thereby assisting students in the enhancement and development of more positive self-concepts.

2   in providing students from the dominant Anglo-American culture with factual data about ethnic minority groups which in many instances, heretofore, have not been a significant part of school curricula.

The committee devoted a great deal of time and effort in the development of criteria which were used as guidelines in the selection of the entries. In general, the criteria required that

1   the contribution or achievement must have directly affected the state or national population in regard to its history or culture.

2   the contribution or achievement
    a   must have been significant to a particular ethnic group,
    b   must have furthered the cause of the minority group,
    c   must have been made or gained in spite of various obstacles.

The committee is keenly aware of the fact that there may be other ethnic minority members who could equally well have been included but whose names do not appear. And too, there are uncounted others who make their contributions unheralded and unsung. However, it was the committee's intent to prepare a resource guide which contains representative members of minority groups in America who meet the criteria previously cited. It obviously is not an all-inclusive publication. Nonetheless, the committee looks upon this publication as a very important first step. President Kennedy was fond of quoting an old Chinese proverb, which says that if we are to walk a thousand miles, we must take the first step.

The teachers' guide is divided into five parts. The first four parts contain biographical data for selected members of each of the following minority groups: Afro Americans, Asian Americans, Indian Americans, and Mexican Americans.

Each part consists of four sections:

1   Historical Perspective. An overview of the minority group in relation to the majority group within the American culture.

2   Biographical Summaries. Specific information regarding name, birthdate, education, and a brief statement of *significance* followed by a biographical sketch. Each entry is keyed in the

upper right hand corner of the narrative to provide the teacher with the source of information.

3 Bibliography of Sources Used. Key sources documenting the information in the Biographical Summaries.

4 Other References. Additional reading.

Part Five includes two appendices:

Appendix A. A quick reference to identify the members of each minority group in specific historical periods as listed below:

  1400–1700: Exploration and Colonial Period
  1770–1860: Revolutionary War to Civil War
  1861–1878: Civil War and Reconstruction Period
  1879–1919: Late 19th and Early 20th Centuries
  1920–1940: Between the World Wars
  1941–1970: World War II to the Present

Appendix B. A list of the members of minority groups in alphabetical order by subject or occupational classification.

Teachers are encouraged to make opportunities available for students to find in their own communities the members of minority groups who have made significant contributions.

TEACHING STRATEGIES

OVERVIEW

A few pertinent concepts and learning activities are briefly suggested here for the implementation of this guide. These are not all-inclusive by any means nor have they been given grade level allocations. It will, therefore, be the task of each teacher at each grade level or groups of teachers in each district to adjust, develop and expand the concepts and learning activities. The levels of understanding, the unique needs and the interests of the students concerned will be the determining guidelines.

Other considerations in the implementation of this guide will be:

1   *the development of overall goals and performance objectives*
2   *the establishment of operative plans for evaluation*
3   *the identification of pertinent concepts*
4   *the choice of teaching strategies*
5   *the careful selection of appropriate teaching materials.*

Studious consideration must be given to the material found in this guide for its realistic inclusion in the curriculum at each grade level from kindergarten through high school and for its sequential development. The determination of curricular allocations for the study of minorities and their social and economic concerns cannot be left to chance. The California Education Code in Sections 7604, 7700, 8553, and 8576 requires that California elementary and secondary schools include courses of instruction on the contributions of minority groups in the economic, political and social development of California and the United States. Logical inclusion in the curriculum for such studies may be as a part of the social sciences program. Other curricular areas such as literature, music, art, science, mathematics, health and physical education offer many opportunities for enrichment experiences.

SUGGESTED CONCEPTS TO BE DEVELOPED

1   All people of the earth are classified into racial groups, namely, mongoloid, negroid, and caucasoid.
2   People of all races are more alike than they are different.
3   The racial grouping of the people of the earth is based on observed physical differences in color of skin, texture and color of hair, and shape of the eyes, nose, and lips.
4   No single trait marks one race from another.
5   No scientific fact supports the statement that the people of one race are inherently superior to the people of other races.

6   The observed physical differences which identify the race to which people belong have been developed through time because of evolutional and environmental conditions.
7   Physical differences influenced by evolutional and environmental conditions are found among all living things.
8   Members of the different racial groups have been crossing and recrossing since the origin of mankind.
9   There are no "pure" races today.
10 It is difficult to group most people by race alone.
11 People throughout the world have common needs, the attainment of which varies in difficulty and mode from culture to culture (example: food).
12 The way people live is significantly dependent on the environment in which they find themselves and on their level of technology.
13 Each racial group is made up of many different cultures resulting from geographic location, social institutions, level of technology, economic development, and political strivings.
14 People of all races and of cultures and sub-cultures within each race develop mores, customs, laws, and institutions unique to their particular needs.
15 Environment and the level of technology influence the level of civilization of a people.
16 People of one cultural group are influenced by people of other cultural groups with whom they come in contact.
17 All people have an identity through their culture and through their individual uniqueness as a member of that culture.
18 People of all races and cultures have made significant contributions to mankind.
19 An understanding of the people of another race, their culture, customs, mores, beliefs, and traditions tends to bring about better relationships.
20 A clash of cultures may result from differences in ideologies, customs, beliefs, mores, and economic and political strivings.
21 People of all races have culturally significant heritages.
22 Cultural differences within a society can be a strength and an asset.
23 Most people strive for their conception of the good life, i.e., social, economic, and personal improvement.
24 Self esteem is nurtured through equal opportunities, equal rights, and responsible citizenship.
25 Prejudices often arise because of conflicting social and cultural differences.
26 Prejudice is an attitude stemming from a lack of understanding, a lack of knowledge, or an unwillingness to accept known differences.
27 Social and cultural differences can be a challenge to understanding rather than a barrier.
28 The basic rights for which all people strive are equated with responsibilities.

SUGGESTED LEARNING ACTIVITIES FOR STUDENTS

The learning activities listed here are a challenge to the teacher's ingenuity to make the necessary modifications for the students of his/her particular grade level. The modification made will depend largely on the level of understanding, the unique interests, the abilities and the skills of the students involved. The learning activities for any student or group of students regardless of age should be relevant, vital, and a stimulation to thinking and feeling.

The choice of the teaching strategy—the catalyst to effective learning—is vitally important to setting the stage for the learning act. The teacher as the strategist plans the kind of activities that will stimulate research, critical thinking, and inquiry on the part of students. The short biographies of the members of the different ethnic groups entered in this guide offer many possibilities. At any grade level a biography may lead to a discussion of the underlying issues prompted by the social, economic, and political conditions of the time, or by the striving of the individual or of his group. The biographical content may motivate such activities as simulations, games, role playing or socio-dramas. This type of learning involvement brings the student face-to-face with the feeling level—the route to the internalization of learning. The need for further research may also be stimulated.

Room environment and the access to many kinds of learning materials are crucial elements to the success of the strategy that is being planned by the teacher. Another element is the teacher's knowledge of the understandings that the students bring to the learning situation and how they actually feel about the people to be studied.

The first activity in the following listing can be used at any grade level. It is an excellent activity to give the teacher the necessary knowledge for the kind of curricular planning that includes student involvement. It is a means for immediate discussion and a challenge to the development of critical thinking.

The activities listed have no particular order or sequence. They are merely suggestions to the teacher, and are not all-inclusive.

1 Choose one of the ethnic groups, Afro, Asian, Indian or Mexican American, and quickly list views and understandings on the blackboard as fast as they come as a matter of information. Examine views and understandings for classification. Suggest appropriate titles for each category. Discuss the categories and through committee action develop research plans to verify category listings and titles. Regroup and/or discard if necessary and do more extensive research. (To the teacher: This activity may take several days or weeks. Information gathered may give clues for directions to be taken in the study and may open a variety of areas for depth study, for simulations, and for bringing students to higher levels of thinking. Tape recordings of discussions could be useful for evaluation of concepts, understandings, and attitudes as the study progresses.)

2 Begin to develop a bulletin board of news items about one or more of the four ethnic groups. Search the items for words and phrases that would indicate bias, prejudice or discrimination. Compare these to the views and understandings listed in Number One above. Discuss and rewrite some of the articles in a way to bring out the facts without bias or prejudice. (To the teacher: A tape recording could be made as a means of evaluating attitudes and understandings as the study progresses.)

3 Begin to develop a bulletin board of pictures from current magazines that depict ethnic group situations. Create captions for each. Choose one of the pictures and write a short paragraph about what it means to you. Plan and carry out discussions, simulations and research. (To the teacher: This activity may very well take several days or weeks. Aspects may be a source for extended depth study and for later evaluation of attitudes and understandings.)

4 View a film and/or listen to a story about a major contribution to society today by a member of one of the ethnic groups. Discuss, then plan committee action for research in depth about one or more members of one or several ethnic groups. Plan ways in which research information is presented to the class. (To the teacher: A tape recording could be made for realigning direction, if necessary, and for evaluating attitudes and understandings as the study progresses.)

5 View a film and/or listen to a news broadcast about the concerns of ethnic groups today. Discuss and make plans to research facts and to simulate pertinent aspects in order to understand underlying issues and to arrive at reasonable solutions. (To the teacher: Tape recordings and/or video taping could be useful in helping students analyze simulation techniques and individual and group understandings.)

6 Organize a plan for the study of an ethnic group in any period of history. Discuss and list possible sources of information such as books, films and resource people.

7 Simulate a significant event in the history of one of the ethnic groups. List and discuss impressions and conclusions. Research in depth to verify and extend understandings. (To the teacher: A tape recording and/or video tape could be made for immediate analysis of simulation techniques, future references and for evaluation of attitudes and understandings as the study progresses.)

8 List the issues involved in movements or events related to one or more of the ethnic groups. Discuss their significance and simulate actions involved in order to arrive at possible solutions. (To the teacher: Record the discussion on tape to analyze for direction in continued planning and as a means of evaluating attitudes and understandings as the study progresses.)

9 Make a list of the different kinds of work found in your community today. Discuss the importance of each to the community and why such a variety is necessary. Include in your discussion the kinds of abilities that are necessary to do the work and the amount of education required. Develop categories and titles for each, then discuss whether ethnic background is or should be a job requirement. Support your views with research on the contributions made by members of different ethnic groups to each category. (To the teacher: A period of several days or even several weeks may be necessary for this activity which could very well open additional avenues for action and study.)

10 Develop a mural tracing the historical role of one of the ethnic groups in the development of the United States. Discuss elements depicted and support with facts and further research.

11 List areas of human endeavor such as medicine, science, literature, the arts, politics, entertainment and sports. Through committee action plan to research each area for contributions made by members of ethnic groups. Discuss the significance to society, in time and place, of the contribution made in each area. List the eminent individuals who made contributions in each area. Develop a class book, bulletin board or mural to show some of the interesting discoveries made through research. (To the teacher: This activity may continue over a period of time and several of the areas may lead to other activities. Evaluations in attitudes and understandings may be made by recording the discussions on tape and comparing these with tapes made earlier in the study.)

12 Study the art forms of one or more of the ethnic groups. Compare and contrast with the art forms of other ethnic groups.

13 Trace and discuss the influence of the art of any one of the ethnic groups on life today; for example, architecture, dress, and customs.

14 Sing the songs and learn the dances of one, or more than one, of the ethnic groups. Show how these have influenced our life today.

15 Listen to or read stories written by members of one or more of the ethnic groups. Discuss the underlying motivation of the author and simulate some of the actions involved in the issues.

16 Examine the folk tales of one or more of the ethnic groups and discuss the possible reason for their development, their significance to the culture itself and their influence on other cultures.

17 Examine the literature of one or more of the ethnic groups. Discuss its significance and its contribution to the field of literature.

18 Develop a bulletin board or a mural or a class book illustrating the influences and/or contributions through the arts of one or more of the ethnic groups.

19 Invite members of an ethnic group to talk to your class about their art, music, and/or literature.

20 Research to find the areas of contributions made by members of one or more of the ethnic groups. Invite members of the ethnic group to discuss particular contributions.

21 Write a story about an event in your life or a reaction you may have to ethnic group issues as if you were a member of another ethnic group. (To the teacher: This activity may be used for evaluating attitudes and understandings, particularly if earlier efforts were made to document discussions.)

22 Visit a church or a social affair of one of the ethnic groups. Discuss your impressions with your class members. Invite members of the group you visited to talk to the class about questions that may have been raised. Rediscuss with your class members. (To the teacher: This activity may be used to evaluate attitudes and understandings particularly if earlier efforts were made to document discussions.)

23 Invite a member of an ethnic group to participate with you in the services of your church or a social affair. Write a brief paragraph about your experiences or share it with your classmates. (To the teacher: This activity may be used to evaluate attitudes and understandings particularly if discussions were recorded on tape earlier in the study.)

PART ONE

AFRO AMERICANS

. . . A world I dream where blacks or whites,
Whatever race you be,
Will share the bounties of the earth
And every man is free . . .
Where wretchedness will hang its head
And joy, like a pearl,
Attend the needs of all mankind
Of such I dream—our world!

LANGSTON HUGHES

AFRO AMERICANS

BIOGRAPHICAL SUMMARIES

HENRY AARON
  (Baseball   46*)
  Born: 1934, Mobile, Alabama
  Education: High School
  Significance: *Major league baseball player*
  Henry Aaron began playing professional
baseball out of high school in 1952. He started
with the Indianapolis Clowns of the Negro
American League, but soon signed with the Milwaukee Braves. Aaron has the highest lifetime
batting average among active players and challenges Willy Mays for second place in lifetime
home runs.

ROBERT S. ABBOTT
  (Journalism   32)
  Born: 1870, St. Simons Island, Georgia
  Died: 1940
  Education: Hampton Institute, Virginia;
    Kent Law School, Chicago
  Significance: *Founder of the* Chicago
    Defender, *a widely read activist
    newspaper*
  Robert Abbott opened his first newspaper
office in his landlady's dining room, after practicing law in the Midwest. He sold the first copies on foot, during the depths of racial
inequalities in 1905. He attacked injustice in his
editorials and spurred Negroes to migrate north
to seek improved living conditions. His newspaper had reached half a million circulation by the
1920's.

*These numbers refer to the *Bibliography of Sources
Used,* found at the end of this section.

SAMUEL CLIFFORD ADAMS, JR.
  (Government   46)
  Born: 1920, Waco, Texas
  Education: B.A. and M.A., Fisk
    University, Nashville, Tennessee;
    Ph.D., University of Chicago; London
    School of Economics
  Significance: *International educational
    project leader*
  Samuel Clifford Adams joined government
service in 1954 as an education adviser in Indo-
china. He headed the education divisions of the
United States Operations Missions in Saigon
and Phnom Penh to 1957. He was then transferred to Nigeria and in 1962 became the
Agency for International Development's mission director in Mali. He was at the State Department's Foreign Service Institute for four
years until the President appointed him ambassador to Niger in 1968.

ALVIN AILEY
  (Entertainment, Dancing   46)
  Significance: *Founder of the Alvin Ailey
    American Dance Theater*
  Alvin Ailey's American Dance Theater is
one of America's most important cultural as-
sets. Ailey consolidated the group between 1958
and 1961, and uncommonly successful tours of
Australia and Southeast Asia in 1962 and of
Europe in 1965 seconded the enthusiastic re-
sponse of home audiences.
  Ailey was a star athlete in high school in Los
Angeles in the late 1940's. Stints in several col-
leges were interspersed with dance instruction

and work with Lester Horton, Hanya Holm, and Martha Graham. He also studied acting in those years and has appeared in musical shows, e.g., *House of Flowers* (1954) and *Jamaica* (1957), and in a dramatic role in *Tiger, Tiger, Burning Bright* on Broadway.

FERDINAND LEWIS ALCINDOR, JR.
(KAREEM ABDUL JABBAR)
(Basketball   46)
Education: B.A., University of California, Los Angeles
Significance: *Professional basketball player*

Kareem Abdul Jabbar (Lew Alcindor) led Power Memorial High School in New York to three straight city championships and seventy-one consecutive victories. The most sought-after high school basketball player since Wilt Chamberlain, Alcindor decided on the University of California at Los Angeles, where his team won three straight national championships. He was drafted by the Milwaukee Bucks of the National Basketball Association in 1969 and has been a major factor in turning that team into a regular championship contender in the years since.

IRA ALDRIDGE
(Acting, Music   40)
Born: 1807, New York
Died: 1867
Education: African Free School
Significance: *Dramatic actor on international stages*

Ira Aldridge was a great Negro actor who had to go to Europe to earn fame. Being accepted there, he played before huge crowds. Later, he became a British citizen. He is famous for his roles in *Othello* and other Shakespearean plays. Aldridge was also a singer. He died before he had an opportunity to perform in the United States.

RICHARD ALLEN
(Religion, Public Relations   1)
Born: 1760
Died: 1831

Significance: *Leadership in religious freedom movement*

Richard Allen was the founder in 1787 of the African Methodist Church, the oldest and largest institution among Negroes. On April 14, 1787, Allen and several other Negroes formed the Free African Society whose purpose was the improvement of the social and economic conditions of free Negroes. In the reaction which followed the end of the Revolutionary War, Negroes were discouraged from worshipping at churches with white congregations. One Sunday in November, 1787, Allen and several of his friends rebelled against the increasing restrictions of segregation that were imposed upon their right to worship in St. George's, one of Philadelphia's leading Methodist churches. Using the Free African Society as his foundation, Allen led an exodus of Negroes from the church and set about organizing a new denomination, the African Methodist Episcopal Church.

In less than two years, Allen and his group had constructed a new church called "Bethel." Philadelphia Negroes joined it. In 1816 he was a prime mover in calling together sixteen independent Negro Methodist congregations from different states and organizing them into one group. Allen was elected as the first bishop of this new denomination and thus began a career of preaching and church organization.

Allen seemed to have a natural gift for organization. As a slave he made enough money as a wood cutter and wagoner to buy his own freedom and that of his brother in 1783. Converted to Christianity while a slave, Allen used the first years of his freedom to preach the gospel to Negroes in and around Pennsylvania.

COLONEL ALLENSWORTH
(Military   5)
Died: 1914
Education: Roger Williams University, Nashville, Tennessee
Significance: *Founder of California colony for Negroes*

Colonel Allensworth, born a slave, was educated at Roger Williams University in Nashville, Tennessee. He was appointed by the

American Baptist Association to travel and lecture to children after his Army duty.

Allensworth served in the Civil War, Spanish-American War, and the Philippine Insurrection. He was chaplain of the 24th Infantry of Negro soldiers. He also had charge of a school for enlisted men. After retirement from the Army, he moved to Los Angeles. He organized a company for Negro colonization in California. Land was purchased in Tulare County and the town site named Allensworth. The town was founded in 1908 and was governed by Negroes.

His private library was left to the Mary Dickinson Memorial Library in Allensworth. He was killed accidentally in September, 1914.

MARIAN ANDERSON

(Music 46)
Born: 1902, Philadelphia, Pennsylvania
Education: Studied with Giuseppe
  Boghetti
Significance: *Concert Artist*

Marian Anderson began singing in a church choir, and her Philadelphia church helped her raise a fund for a year's study with Giuseppe Borghetti. After several years of private instruction and singing tours of southern colleges, she attempted a concert at Town Hall in New York. That concert (1925) was poorly received, but she subsequently won a major competition for young singers, which led to an appearance with the New York Philharmonic Orchestra. Nevertheless, American concert opportunities were limited so she had to go to Europe, where, aided by several fellowships, she spent much of her time between 1929 and 1935. She returned to the United States a star, and by 1941 she was one of America's highest paid concert and recording artists.

In 1939 the Daughters of the American Revolution denied her the stage of Constitution Hall in Washington, D.C. and provoked a national scandal. Her memorable appearance singing from the steps of the Lincoln Memorial on Easter Sunday drew an audience of 75,000 people that same year.

Marian Anderson was the first Negro to sing at the Metropolitan Opera. She has garnered awards and honorary degrees (24) from many American states and cities and half a dozen foreign countries. She was a member of the U.S. delegation to the 13th session of the United Nations General Assembly.

LOUIS ARMSTRONG

(Music, Jazz 39)
Born: 1900, New Orleans, Louisiana
Died: 1971
Significance: *Jazz musician*

Louis Armstrong grew up surrounded by jazz. He was given a cornet from the Waif's Home and started playing. Later he switched to the trumpet. He moved around a lot, made money, made friends, and played the best he knew how, and his best was very good. When he was twenty-two, he was writing music. He met Lil Hardin, a jazz pianist, whom he married.

Armstrong played in New York and Europe. A new interest in jazz developed in Europe as a result. Armstrong's was a major—perhaps the major—influence in molding the jazz style of the swing era. In later years he became something of an elder statesman of jazz and traveled abroad a good deal, often under State Department sponsorship.

ARTHUR ASHE

(Tennis 46)
Born: 1943, Richmond, Virginia
Education: University of California, Los
  Angeles
Significance: *Champion tennis player*

Arthur Ashe learned to play tennis at the Richmond Racket Club, which had been formed by local Negro enthusiasts. Dr. R. W. Johnson sponsored Ashe's tennis career, spending thousands of dollars and much time with him.

By 1958, Ashe had reached the semi-finals in the under-fifteen division of the National Junior Championships. In 1960 and 1961, he won the Junior Indoors Singles title.

In 1961 Ashe entered the University of California at Los Angeles on a tennis scholarship. Since then he has beaten most of the world's top players. The coach of the Australian Davis Cup team once called Ashe "the most promising player in the world today, and the biggest single threat to our ... supremacy." By 1966 Ashe was the third ranked amateur in the United States; he won the national clay court championships in 1968 and the United States National Championship in 1970.

CRISPUS ATTUCKS

(Military   49)
Born: 1723
Died: 1770
Significance: *First casualty in Boston Massacre*

Crispus Attucks was an American who shared the popular hatred of the British troops in the City of Boston. On the night of March 5, 1770, the bell in the meeting house rang out, calling the people together. A fight between British Redcoats and Boston citizens broke out over an unimportant incident. Hearing cries, the people, armed with rocks and clubs, ran to face the Redcoats who stood with drawn bayonets.

Attucks, a seaman who worked on the docks where the heavily-taxed British merchandise was unloaded, called out above the noise of the crowd: "The way to get rid of these soldiers is to attack the main guard. Strike at their roots." Encouraged by his words, the townspeople began their fight for freedom. The Redcoats, following the orders of their officers, fired into the crowd. Attucks was the first to fall. Three others fell. This tragedy was known as the "Boston Massacre." It so aroused the citizens that they demanded and secured the removal of the British Lieutenant-Governor and the King's Council. This was the first round in what was to become the American Revolution.

The bodies of these martyrs to the cause of American Independence lay in state in Faneuil Hall where tribute was paid by hundreds of people. The martyrs were buried in a single grave. Later a monument was erected on Boston Common to honor these patriotic heroes.

PEARL BAILEY

(Music, Acting   46)
Born: 1918, Newport, Virginia
Significance: *Singer, actress, entertainer*

Pearl Bailey made her professional debut working in small clubs around Philadelphia, where she moved with her family in 1933. She subsequently developed her unique style as a band singer with Cootie Williams and Count Basie. By 1941 she performed as a single with engagements at the Vanguard and Blue Angel in New York, and she toured with U.S.O. shows throughout World War II. She won the Donaldson Award for her role in *St. Louis Woman* in 1946 as the year's most promising new personality. Movies and hit records followed. A major role in *Carmen Jones* (1954) was immediately followed by star billing in *House of Flowers* on Broadway.

She continues as a headliner in night clubs and on television, and she was awarded a special Tony Award for her work in *Hello Dolly!* in 1967–68.

JOSEPHINE BAKER

(Music, Dancing   46)
Born: 1906, St. Louis, Missouri
Significance: *Singer, promoter of international brotherhood*

Josephine Baker became Bessie Smith's maid at fifteen. She soon rose from maid to performer with Bessie Smith's company, leaving for a job in the chorus line of *Shuffle Along* in New York. She later had small parts in two other Broadway shows and in 1925 was chosen to go to Paris with the Revue Negre. Her debut at the Champs Elysees Theater created a sensation. The jazz rhythms she introduced quickly swept the Continent and eventually earned her top billing at the Folies Bergere.

In World War II she worked as a nurse with Air Auxiliary of the Free French Forces and entertained to raise money for war relief. She won two decorations for her wartime services and returned to the Folies until she retired in 1956. She has adopted eleven children from various countries and devoted herself to fostering understanding among peoples.

JAMES BALDWIN

(Literature   12)

Born: 1924, New York City
Education: DeWitt Clinton High School,
New York City
Significance: *Contemporary author*

James Baldwin was the first of nine children. His father, an authoritarian, was a minister. James became a minister at fourteen, preaching in a store-front church. After high school, he left the church, his family, and Harlem. He met and was encouraged by Richard Wright. He won the Eugene F. Saxon Trust Award for his novel, *Go Tell It On The Mountain,* published in 1953. He spent almost ten years, from 1948, in Paris, where he developed objectivity about himself and his background. His writing became more militant after his return to America. He treats subjects hitherto avoided and not in the mainstream of literature. His religious inheritance is apparent in the conviction and emotion of his writing rather than in its content.

Baldwin's publication's include: *Giovanni's Room* (1965); *Another Country* (1963); *The Fire Next Time* (1964); *Blues for Mr. Charley* (1964); *Going To Meet the Man* (1965); and *Tell Me How Long the Train's Been Gone* (1968).

BENJAMIN BANNEKER
(Astronomy, Mathematics   7, 46, 53)
Born: 1731, Maryland
Died: 1806
Education: Diploma, Integrated private
school, Maryland
Significance: *Publisher and scholar*

Benjamin Banneker's maternal grandmother, an Englishwoman who manumitted and married one of her slaves, attended to Banneker's early education herself and enrolled him in a private integrated school for a time. He early demonstrated special mathematical and mechanical aptitudes and constructed what was probably the first clock built in the colonies, a wooden affair that worked effectively for many years.

About 1773 he began making astronomical calculations for almanacs. Eventually he sold the farm he inherited from his father to pursue his scientific interests. In 1791 he began publish-ing an almanac which was well received and which continued to appear until 1802. His famous letter to Jefferson in defense of the intellectual capacities of Negroes was published as a prefatory note to the almanac. He published studies of bees and the cycles of locust plague, and proposed a "Plan for a Peace Office for the United States," which contained the notion of a league of nations.

He was named to the Capitol Commission and helped Major Pierre Charles L'Enfant in surveying the site for the new federal city of Washington, D.C.

RICHMOND BARTHÉ
(Sculpture   7, 46)
Born: 1901, Bay St. Louis, Mississippi
Education: Art Institute, Chicago, Illinois
Significance: *Sculptor*

Richmond Barthé was of mixed Creole stock and grew up in New Orleans. He studied at Chicago's Art Institute, where in 1928 an instructor turned him from painting to sculpture. Early commissions, including a bust of Toussaint L'Ouverture, led to a one-man show in Chicago and a Rosenwald grant to pursue his studies in New York. In 1936 the Whitney Museum purchased three of Barthé's works, and by that time he had held six one-man shows in New York. His work has been exhibited in several major American museums, including the Metropolitan Museum of Art in New York. He was the first Negro to receive a commission for a bust to be included in New York University's Hall of Fame. In 1947 he was on a committee of artists to help modernize the sculpture in Catholic churches in the United States.

His forty years of creativity, teaching, and lecturing have made him America's most famous Negro sculptor. He is the only Negro sculptor to hold membership in the National Academy of Arts and Letters.

WILLIAM (COUNT) BASIE
(Music, Jazz   46)
Born: 1904, Red Bank, New Jersey
Significance: *Jazz musician and band
leader*

William (Count) Basie's band became the first American jazz band to play a royal command performance for the Queen of England and the first Negro band to play at the Waldorf Astoria, both in 1957. For twenty years before that, however, Basie's band had been a major force in American music.

During the early 1920's, Basie toured in vaudeville. Stranded in Kansas City, he joined Walter Page's Blue Devils and in 1935 formed his own band. A Kansas City radio announcer soon dubbed him "Count." Basie brought his group to New York City in 1936. Within a year, he was an established figure in the jazz world. The Basie trademark was a rhythm section featuring Basie's own crisp piano. Except for two years when he had a small group, Basie has always led a big band, surviving changing fashion virtually unscathed.

EBENEZER D. BASSETT
   (Government, Diplomacy   1)
   Born: 1833, Litchfield, Connecticut
   Died: 1908
   Education: Wesley Academy, Wilbraham,
      Massachusetts; Connecticut Normal
      School; Yale University, New Haven,
      Connecticut
   Significance: *Diplomatic service*
Ebenezer D. Bassett served as the first Negro officially representing the United States abroad. Appointed by President Ulysses S. Grant in 1869 as minister-resident to Haiti, Bassett set a high standard of achievement. With honor to himself and satisfaction to his country, he filled the position for eight years, which was as long as the combined terms of his white predecessors.

Although relations between the United States and Haiti were relatively stable but tense, Haiti and Santo Domingo were having serious difficulties. At this time, the United States was considering annexing Santo Domingo, and Haitians' awareness of this created strong anti-American feelings. In addition to these problems, the Haitians were faced with serious internal difficulties. Bassett was expected to carry out United States policy and to keep his country informed of developments on the is-

land. Bassett's dispatches to Hamilton Fish, then Secretary of State, and others, indicated a firm grasp of political developments in his host country. Appraisals of Bassett's work unanimously agree that he did the best job possible in the rather tense atmosphere of the early 1870's. As a maneuver in diplomacy, his appointment could hardly have been wiser, for the Haitians accepted Bassett with a confidence his predecessors never enjoyed.

Additional evidence of Bassett's success as a diplomat may be seen in the fact that after he completed his assignment in 1877, he was appointed as consul general *from* Haiti to the United States, a post he held for ten years. In 1888, Bassett returned to Haiti to live as a private citizen. While there he collected materials, which were subsequently published in a *Handbook of Haiti,* printed in French, English, and Spanish. In recognition of this work he was named a member of the American Geographical Society and of the Connecticut Historical Society. (From Russell L. Adams, *Great Negroes Past and Present.* Chicago: Afro-Am Publishing Co., Inc., 1967.)

ANDREW J. BEARD
   (Invention   46)
   Significance: *Railroad car invention*
In 1897 Andrew J. Beard sold his design for an automatic railroad coupler for $50,000. His system, called the "Jenny coupler," replaced manual coupling, which required the dropping of a metal pin as two cars crashed together—a split-second operation which not infrequently produced crushed limbs and bodies. The invention of the "Jenny coupler" has saved the lives of countless railroad men.

JAMES P. BECKWOURTH
   (Exploration   7)
   Born: 1798, Virginia
   Died: 1867
   Significance: *Historic mountain man*
James P. Beckwourth was born in Virginia, one of thirteen children of a white officer in the Revolutionary Army, and a Negro slave woman. After the war, the family moved to an

area known as the Beckwourth Settlement near St. Louis. He was apprenticed to a blacksmith. When he was about eighteen, he ran away to Galena, then went to New Orleans. He returned to St. Louis and joined an expedition commanded by General Henry Ashley, connected with the Rocky Mountain Fur Company. He became an excellent trader, learned to be a good hunter and became an Indian fighter and scout. He had the ability to make friends with the Indians.

During the 1820's and 1830's, the heyday of mountain men and the fur trade, Beckwourth became a legendary figure, like his friends Jim Bridger and Kit Carson. The Indians respected him so highly that he was accepted into their tribes, first by the Blackfeet and later the Crows. He took the daughter of a chief for a wife and set up a fur trading post among the Blackfeet. He was always able to protect himself. Twice, he saved General Ashley's life, once from a charging buffalo, again from a swirling river.

In 1844 he discovered the pass through the Sierra Nevada to California and the Pacific Ocean that still carries his name. He became the chief scout for Fremont's exploring expedition in the Rockies in 1848. Later he established a store and trading post in the Sierra Nevada in the Feather River Valley and worked as a guide for wagon trains crossing the mountains to California. He then moved back to Missouri, but in 1864 he was back in the West to participate in the Cheyenne War, and he finally settled in Denver, Colorado. The story is told that when he died the Crow Indians buried him in their ancestral graveyard so he could always be with them. The small town of Beckwourth, California, is a living memorial to this early mountain man. A plaque marks the location of his trading post.

HARRY BELAFONTE, JR.

(Music, Acting   46)
Born: 1927, New York City
Education: Public School
Significance: *Singer, actor, composer*
Harry Belafonte moved to the West Indies when he was eight years old, but returned to New York five years later. He joined the Navy in 1944. Back in civilian life, Belafonte worked as a janitor until he became interested in a dramatic career. For a time, he studied at Stanley Kubrick's Dramatic Workshop, but he soon switched his primary interest to singing.

Returning to New York from a Florida engagement, he opened a restaurant in Greenwich Village to support himself while he studied folk singing. The restaurant failed, but Belafonte's folk-singing career was underway. In 1953, he won acclaim in *John Murray Anderson's Almanac* on Broadway. The following year he starred in the movie, *Carmen Jones* and, in 1955 in Broadway's *Three for Tonight.*

Belafonte has headed a number of troupes which have served to showcase numerous young talents, including the South African singer Miriam Makeba.

LERONE BENNETT

(Journalism   46)
Born: 1928, Clarksville, Mississippi
Education: Morehouse College, Atlanta, Georgia
Significance: *Author and editor*
Lerone Bennett, senior editor of *Ebony* since 1958, has been a journalist all his working life and has published poetry and fiction as well as works in history and biography. He edited school papers in both high school and college and joined the Atlanta *Daily World* after graduation from college. He became *World* city editor in 1952 after three years and moved to the Johnson Publishing Co. as associate editor of *Jet* and *Ebony* in 1953.

Bennett's published titles include *Before the Mayflower: A History of the Negro in America, 1619–1964; Black Power U.S.A.* (1967), a history of Reconstruction; *What Manner of Man* (1964), a biography of Martin Luther King; and *Negro Mood,* a volume of essays.

MARY MCLEOD BETHUNE

(Education   32)
Born: 1875, Mayesville, South Carolina
Died: 1955

Education: Scotia Seminary, North
Carolina; Moody Bible Institute,
Chicago
Significance: *Leadership in education and
public service*

Mary McLeod Bethune founded Bethune-
Cookman College at Daytona Beach, Florida,
in 1904, with one dollar and fifty cents and five
pupils. Her work demonstrated much foresight
and dynamic leadership. She has received many
honors, including the Medal of Merit from the
Republic of Haiti and the NAACP's Spingarn
Award.

Mrs. Bethune was the founder of the National Council of Negro Women and served as
the director of the American Red Cross in the
State of Florida. For many years, she served as
president of the Association for the Study of
Negro Life and History.

Under President Franklin D. Roosevelt she
served as director of the Negro Affairs Division
of the National Youth Administration, and as a
consultant to the founding conference of the
United Nations. After the President died, Mrs.
Roosevelt presented his cane to Mrs. Bethune in
recognition of her work. She used the cane until
her death.

DAVID H. BLACKWELL
(Mathematics 24)
Education: Ph.D., University of Illinois
Significance: *Teacher and researcher in
mathematics*

Dr. Blackwell has been a fellow at the Institute for Advanced Study at Princeton University in New Jersey. He has published many
original articles in the field of mathematics and
has served as consultant in the United States
Navy Department. In the last decade, Dr.
Blackwell was professor of mathematics at San
Jose State College in San Jose, California.

HENRY BLAIR
(Invention 46)
Significance: *Invention of labor-saving
machinery*

Henry Blair is thought to be the first Negro
to receive a United States patent. His corn har-
vester is recorded in the registry of the Patent
Office for 1834. In 1836, he patented a cotton
planter. Uniquely in the early records of the
Patent Office, Blair, a resident of Maryland, is
identified as "a colored man."

JULIAN BOND
(Politics, Civil Rights 11)
Born: 1940, Nashville, Tennessee
Education: George School, Pennsylvania;
Morehouse College, Atlanta, Georgia
Significance: *Civil Rights leader and a
Georgia State Legislator*

Julian Bond, son of the president of Lincoln
University, attended the nearby George School,
a Quaker prep school, where he was the only
Negro. There he developed his appreciation for
nonviolence. Bond entered Morehouse College
but left during his senior year to work full time
for the Atlanta *Inquirer.* He also became communications director of the Student Nonviolent
Coordinating Committee (SNCC).

In 1965 Bond was elected to the Georgia
House of Representatives from the Atlanta district. He was prevented from taking his seat for
a full year because of objections by fellow legis-
lators to his outspoken opposition to the American military operations in Vietnam. The
prominence he gained through that unsought
martyrdom was immeasurably swelled by his
conspicuous role as a successful insurgent delegation leader and Vice Presidential nominee at
the Democratic National Convention in
Chicago in 1968.

Bond was reelected to the Georgia legislature
where he introduced a bill to legalize rent strikes
and another to raise the minimum wage to two
dollars an hour. He is a member of the House
Committee on Education, Insurance, and State
Institutions and Property. He is effective as an
ombudsman for his people, responding to their
grievances in many local civic matters. Bond
has served as co-chairman and executive board
member of the National Conference for a New
Politics, and is a member of a number of boards
including the Southern Regional Council, the

NAACP Legal Defense and Education Fund, the Voter Education Project, the Martin Luther King, Jr. Memorial Center, and the Delta Ministry Project of the National Council of Churches. He is married and the father of four children.

ARNA BONTEMPS
    (Literature, Library Science   48)
    Born: 1902, Alexandria, Louisiana
    Education: B.A., Pacific Union College,
       Angwin, California; M.A., University
       of Chicago
    Significance: *Poet, anthologist, author*

Arna Bontemps has been one of the most productive Negro writers in the 20th century. He was the son of a brick mason and a school teacher. His family moved to Los Angeles when he was three years old. He worked his way through college at a variety of jobs. He is the recipient of two Rosenwald Fellowships (1938–39, 1942–43), and was also a Guggenheim Fellow in 1949–50. He went to Harlem and became involved in the Negro Renaissance. In 1924 his poetry was published in *Crisis.* He won first prize for his poetry in a *Crisis* contest in 1927, the *Opportunity* short story prize in 1932 for "Nocturne at Bethesda," and the Alexander Pushkin award in 1926 for "Golgotha is a Mountain." He was head librarian at Fisk University from 1943 to 1965 and Director of University Relations from 1965 to 1968. He is a prolific writer of fiction and non-fiction for both adults and children.

EDWARD WARNER BRICE
    (Government   32)
    Born: 1916, Hallboro, North Carolina
    Education: B.A., Tuskegee Institute,
       Tuskegee, Alabama; Ph.D., University
       of Pennsylvania
    Significance: *Government service*

Dr. Brice, a high-ranking federal official in the field of education, has held a number of important positions in the federal government. He was chief of the education division of the United States Operations Missions to Liberia and to Nepal between 1952 and 1958, and served as director of the adult education branch and specialist in fundamental and literacy education 1958–66.

Dr. Brice served as an assistant to G. Mennen Williams, Assistant Secretary of State for African Affairs, with a special assignment as public affairs officer at the United States Embassy in Monrovia, Liberia. Previously he was dean of education extension and professor of graduate education at South Carolina State College.

Dr. Brice has received eighteen awards, citations, and honorary degrees from foreign governments, the United States government, and domestic and foreign universities. He is the author of eight books, including three textbooks. He was also the chief architect of UNESCO's world experimental literacy program.

ANDREW FELTON BRIMMER
    (Economics   46)
    Born: 1926, Newellton, Louisiana
    Education: B.A., M.A., University of
       Washington; Delhi School of
       Economics; University of Bombay;
       Ph.D., Harvard University,
       Cambridge, Massachusetts
    Significance: *An outstanding economist*

Andrew Brimmer was appointed to the Board of Governors of the Federal Reserve System in 1966, capping a distinguished career as a professional economist, educator, and government official.

He was a Fulbright fellow in India (1951–52), a staff economist with the New York Federal Reserve Bank (1955–58), and taught at Michigan State University and the Wharton School. He was appointed Deputy Assistant Secretary of Commerce in 1963 and Assistant Secretary for Economic Affairs in 1965.

He is a trustee of Tuskegee Institute and has served in advisory capacity for Harvard, Princeton, and Atlanta Universities. He has received numerous important awards and is the author of several books and many articles for professional journals.

EDWARD W. BROOKE
    (Politics   42)
    Born: 1919, Washington, D.C.
    Education: B.S., Howard University,
        Washington, D.C.; LL.B., Boston
        University Law School, Massachusetts
    Significance: *First Negro U.S. Senator
        since Reconstruction*

Edward Brooke was reared in a middle-class Negro neighborhood in Washington, D.C. While at Howard University he was in the R.O.T.C. With the attack on Pearl Harbor, he was called into service and assigned to the all-Negro 366th Combat Infantry Regiment at Fort Devens, Massachusetts. Among his varied duties he was assigned to defend enlisted men in courts martial. He soon found himself looking forward to the study of law, his father's profession. He then served in General Mark W. Clark's Fifth Army in the bitter campaign in Italy. He received a Bronze Star and served as liaison officer with the Italian patriots behind the lines. In Italy, he met his future wife, whom he married in 1947.

Upon the completion of his law degree in 1950, he ran for State Representative from Roxbury's 12th ward but was defeated. In 1952, he ran for judge of the General Court in the 12th ward and again lost by a narrow margin. During the next eight years, he cemented his position as a highly qualified lawyer and as an activist in civic affairs. The Junior Chamber of Commerce named him, along with John F. Kennedy, one of Boston's "outstanding young men." He was elected to membership on sixteen boards of trustees, including Boston University and the Opera Company of Boston, which he later headed. In 1960, he ran for secretary of State in Massachusetts. Though Brooke lost again, he polled over a million votes, despite the fact that he was a Republican in a state where Democrats outnumber Republicans two to one, he was an Episcopalian in a predominantly Catholic state, and a Negro in a state where the black population number less than three percent.

Brooke was appointed chairman of the Boston Finance Commission. In this office he exposed the graft and corruption in the city. Next he ran against great odds and was elected state attorney general. In this position he made it clear that he represented all the people, saying: "The moment I become a specifically Negro attorney general I cease to do justice to my office and in fact I squander whatever effectiveness I might have in advancing civil rights." He refused to identify as Black, not from a sense of shame, for he is extremely proud of his heritage, but because he considers himself part of a society as much his as anyone's.

When Senator Saltonstall decided not to run again, Brooke announced his candidacy and won by sixty-two per cent of nearly two million votes cast. *The New York Times* hoped, editorially, that people would "forget his race and notice his public usefulness."

GWENDOLYN BROOKS
    (Literature   48)
    Born: 1917, Topeka, Kansas
    Education: Wilson Junior College
    Significance: *Pulitzer Prize Winner*

Gwendolyn Brooks became known as a poetess at thirteen when her first poem was accepted for publication. By seventeen she was a frequent contributor to local newspapers. Many of her poems were printed in the *Chicago Defender.* After graduating from junior college, her first job was with a phony "spiritual advisor," where she refused to cooperate and was fired. However, in this work she learned much about the problems of the poor and ignorant. She then attended classes at the Southside Community Art Center and did newspaper and office work. She entered a poem in competition and won the Eunice Tietjen Award from *Poetry* magazine in 1949. She won four awards in three consecutive years from the Midwest Writers Conference, and was selected by *Mademoiselle* magazine as one of the "Ten Women of the Year" in 1945. She was made a fellow of the American Academy of Arts and Letters in 1946, and was awarded a $1,000 prize. She won two Guggenheim Fellowships in 1946 and in 1947, and received the Pulitzer Prize for poetry in 1950 for *Annie Allen.*

Miss Brooks, with other leading American poets, was invited by President John F. Kennedy to read at a poetry festival at the Library of Congress. She lectures at colleges and universities. Much of her effort is directed toward the development of creative writing by children.

CHARLOTTE HAWKINS BROWN
    (Education   32)
    Born: 1883, Henderson, North Carolina
    Died: 1961
    Education: State Normal School, Salem,
        Massachusetts; Wellesley College,
        Massachusetts
    Significance: *School founder*

Charlotte Hawkins was raised and educated in Cambridge, Massachusetts, but she made annual visits to North Carolina with her parents. She completed her education with the aid of Alice Freeman Palmer and returned to North Carolina, to take a teaching position with the American Missionary Association near Sedalia. The association was forced to close the school in 1902. Miss Hawkins recognized the urgent need and determined to continue instruction on her own; she worked without salary, and with the cooperation of the churches and the people of the community she completed the first year. She returned north to raise money (partly by public readings from the works of Paul Laurence Dunbar), and in 1904 she was able to build the first building of the Palmer Memorial Institute. After fire destroyed the school's wooden building in 1917 it was replaced with several brick buildings.

She married Edward S. Brown in 1911 and continued as president of the institute until 1952 and as its finance director until 1955. She was president of the North Carolina Federation of Women's Clubs, and vice president of the National Association of Colored Women. She also maintained a busy lecture schedule.

JAMES BROWN
    (Music, Entertainment   46)
    Born: ca. 1930, Augusta, Georgia

Significance: *Exponent of big-beat "soul" music*

James Brown's style, made up of frenzied wails and intricate dance steps, has taken him to the top in the field of popular soul music. Annoyed by the American public's neglect of its native "down-home" music, Brown organized his own troupe to tour the country. With a forty-man ensemble he played on the road for 340 days in 1965 and grossed over a million dollars. He has made numerous television appearances. In recent years he has invested a great deal of time and money in the promotion of business for the black community. Because of his concern for the morale of the black serviceman fighting abroad, he took members of his troupe to Vietnam as a personal goodwill gesture.

His hit songs include "Please, Please, Please," "It's a Man's World," and "I Feel Good."

JIM BROWN
    (Football   7, 46)
    Born: 1936, St. Simon Island, Georgia
    Education: Manhasset High School, Long
        Island, New York; Syracuse
        University, New York
    Significance: *Football player*

Jim Brown was an outstanding competitor in high school in baseball, basketball, track and field, football, and lacrosse. At graduation he had a choice of over forty college scholarships as well as professional offers from the Boston Braves and the New York Yankees. He chose Syracuse University, where he was an All-American in both football and lacrosse. He declined to compete in the decathlon in the Olympic Games of 1956 because it conflicted with his football schedule. In 1957 he entered professional football with the Cleveland Browns. He paced Cleveland to a division championship and was a unanimous choice for Rookie of the Year. Thereafter he was all-league fullback virtually every season and was voted "back" of the decade. In 1966 he retired from football to devote his time to the improvement of Negro business and to a screen career.

STERLING BROWN
(Literature 19)
Born: 1901, Washington, D.C.
Education: A.B., Williams College; A.M.,
   Harvard University, Cambridge,
   Massachusetts
Significance: *Poet and philosopher*
Sterling Brown's poetry first appeared in
Harlem Renaissance periodicals. His work was
best known in the thirties. He taught at Namassas, Virginia Seminary and College, at Fisk University, at Lincoln University, and for thirty
years at Howard University. He was editor of
Negro Affairs for the Federal Writers Project
from 1936 to 1939, and a staff member of the
Myrdal study of the Negro in 1939. It was in
this year that Brown was awarded a Guggenheim Fellowship for creative writing. In 1941
Brown and other associates published *The Negro Caravan: Writings by American Negroes.* It
is a comprehensive anthology of all literary
types representing the expression of the Negro,
from Phillis Wheatley and Jupiter Hammon to
Richard Wright.

WILLIAM WELLS BROWN
(Literature 7)
Born: 1816, Lexington, Kentucky
Died: 1884
Education: Studied medicine
Significance: *Historian*
William Wells Brown's mother was a slave
and his father was a white slave holder. Early in
life, Brown was taken to St. Louis and hired out
on a steamboat. Then he was employed by the
editor of the *St. Louis Times.* Again he hired
out on a steamboat. In 1834, he escaped to Ohio
with the intention of going to Canada. He was
sheltered by a Quaker and assisted other fugitive slaves. From 1843 to 1849 he was an anti-slavery lecturer. He was also interested in
temperance, women's suffrage, and prison reform. In 1849, he visited England and represented the American Peace Society at the Peace
Congress in Paris. He stayed abroad until 1854.
Although Brown studied medicine, his reputation rests largely on his ability as a historian and
writer of fiction. Brown was the author of *The*
Black Man, His Antecedents, His Genius and
His Achievements (1863) and *The Negro in the*
American Rebellion (1867).

BLANCHE K. BRUCE
(Politics 23)
Born: 1841, Farmville, Virginia
Died: 1898
Significance: *United States Senator*
Blanche K. Bruce was elected to the United
States Senate in 1875, the only Negro to be
elected to a full term until the election of Edward Brooke, Republican from Massachusetts,
in 1966. He had been born a slave in Virginia.
When the Civil War came, he escaped from St.
Louis to Hannibal, Missouri, and established a
school for Negroes. After the war he studied in
the North for several years. In 1869, he went to
Mississippi, entered politics and worked up
through a succession of offices from tax collector to sheriff and superintendent of schools.

In the Senate he introduced a number of bills
to improve the conditions of Negroes. He succeeded in having some pension bills passed, but
his chief work was with the committee on manufactures, education and labor, as well as pensions. As chairman of the select committee on
the Freedmen's Bank, he conducted a thorough
investigation of the causes for its failure. His
wide range of interests as a lawmaker is seen in
the introduction of bills on the Geneva award
for the Alabama claims, another for aid to education and railroad construction, and one for
the reimbursement of depositors in the Freedmen's Bank. It was in the forty-first Congress,
in 1869, that Negroes, three of them, first made
their appearance in the federal legislature. In
the next Congress there were five. The peak was
reached in the forty-third and forty-fourth Congresses when seven sat in the House of
Representatives.

CHARLES WESLEY BUGGS
(Life Science 51)
Born: 1906, Brunswick, Georgia
Education: A.B., Morehouse College,
   Atlanta, Georgia; M.S., Ph.D.,

University of Minnesota, Minneapolis,
Minnesota

Significance: *Medical research*

Dr. Charles Wesley Buggs has been head of
the Department of Microbiology at the College
of Medicine, Howard University, Washington,
D.C., since 1958. At the University of Minnesota, he was a Shevlin Fellow in bacteriology.
He then taught biology at Dover State College,
at Dillard, and at Wayne State. He is a member
of the honor society of science, Sigma Xi, and
of a number of scientific societies. In 1949, he
made a special study for the United States Office
of Education on Pre-medical Education for
Negroes. He has written significant articles on
antibiotic therapy and others dealing with the
value of chemotherapy in the treatment of com-
pound fractures and on penicillin and skin
grafting.

ED BULLINS

(Literature   33)

Significance: *Playwright*

Ed Bullins is the co-founder of Black Arts
West in San Francisco's Fillmore District. This
is a counterpart of LeRoi Jones' Black Arts
Repertory Theater/School in Harlem. He is a
member of the Black Arts Alliance, helping
LeRoi Jones in film-making in San Francisco
and Los Angeles. He is a resident playwright of
the New Lafayette Theater in Harlem.

RALPH JOHNSON BUNCHE

(Government, Diplomacy   1)

Born: 1904, Detroit, Michigan

Died: 1972

Education: A.B., University of California,
    Los Angeles; M.A., Ph.D., Harvard
    University, Cambridge, Massachusetts;
    LL.D., Boston University;
    post-doctoral study, Northwestern
    University; London School of
    Economics, England; University of
    Capetown, Johannesburg, South Africa

Significance: *Diplomatic service*

A diplomat and United Nations mediator,
Dr. Ralph Johnson Bunche's forty-odd degrees
and one Nobel Prize are eloquent testimony to
the contribution he made to America and to
world peace. He graduated Magna Cum Laude
from the University of California and won the
Tappan Prize at Harvard University for the best
doctoral dissertation in the social sciences. He
was one of America's most honored Negroes.

After a career at Howard University which
paralleled his academic advancement, Dr.
Bunche was named chairman of Howard's Po-
litical Science Department in 1937, and a year
later he joined the Swedish economist, Gunnar
Myrdal, to begin a comprehensive study of the
American Negro, published in 1945 as *An
American Dilemma.*

By 1942 he was at work in the Office of Strategic Services as a research analyst of material
relating to Africa. By 1946, he had advanced to
the position of Associate Chief of the State Department's Dependent Areas section. Already a
foreign affairs adviser of growing reputation,
Dr. Bunche left the State Department for the
Trusteeship Division of the United Nations. In
quick succession, he was head of the United
Nation's Trusteeship Department and personal
representative of the United Nations' Secretary
General in the extremely dangerous Arab-
Israeli dispute. Following the assassination of
the United Nations' Palestine Mediator in 1947,
Dr. Bunche was named acting mediator and
achieved an historic settlement of the Palestine
question.

In 1949 Dr. Bunche was awarded the Spingarn Medal and, in 1950, he received the Nobel
Prize for Peace. Other honors and offers came
to him, including a professorship at Harvard
University, the presidency of the City College of
New York and the post of Assistant Secretary
of State. However, Dr. Bunche remained with
the United Nations and became its Under Secretary General. He went to the Congo in 1960 as
the United Nations' special representative during the turmoil there.

The achievements of Dr. Bunche are based
on an extraordinary personal ability and hard
work. His father was a poor Detroit barber; his
mother an amateur musician. Both parents died
before Dr. Bunche reached his teens and he
found himself living in California with his

grandmother and several aunts. When he won an athletic scholarship to the University of California, he paid his other expenses by working as a campus janitor. Friends and neighbors raised money for his living expenses for one year after he won a tuition scholarship to Harvard. From this point onward, Dr. Bunche depended on determination and his own resources.

(From Russell L. Adams, *Great Negroes Past and Present.* Chicago: Afro-Am Publishing Co., Inc., 1967.)

HARRY T. BURLEIGH
    (Music   46)
    Born: 1866, Erie, Pennsylvania
    Died: 1949
    Education: National Conservatory of
        Music
    Significance: *Concert artist*
Harry T. Burleigh began singing in local choirs and then won a scholarship to the National Conservatory of Music, where he studied with Anton Dvorak. Later he taught at the conservatory. He became baritone soloist at St. George's Church in New York in 1894 and at Temple Emanuel in 1900. Burleigh's concert tours included appearances before royalty and several American presidents. He composed several hundred songs, but he is perhaps best known for his transcriptions of Negro spirituals, which he pioneered on the concert stage.

GODFREY CAMBRIDGE
    (Entertainment   46)
    Born: ca. 1925, New York
    Education: Hofstra College, Hempstead,
        New York
    Significance: *Stage and motion picture
        performer*
Born in New York, Godfrey Cambridge attended grammar school in Nova Scotia. After finishing school, he studied acting, subsequently making his Broadway debut in *Nature's Way.* He was featured in *Purlie Victorious,* both on the stage and on the screen. He has also appeared off-Broadway in *Lost in the Stars, Take A Giant Step,* and *The Detective Story.* He won

the Obie Award for the season's most distinguished performance in *The Blacks,* 1960–61.

Cambridge has appeared frequently on television as a comedian. His material is drawn from the contemporary racial situation. He has also performed in many television dramatic roles. In 1965, he played in *A Funny Thing Happened on the Way to the Forum* in stock.

ROY CAMPANELLA
    (Baseball   46)
    Born: 1921, Philadelphia, Pennsylvania
    Significance: *Baseball player*
Roy Campanella began playing semi-pro baseball with the Bacharach Giants. In time, he became part of the hectic life of Negro professional baseball, touring the United States in buses with the Baltimore Elites during the summer, and playing winter ball in Latin America.

Campanella was signed by the Dodgers in 1946. Two years later, Branch Rickey delayed Campanella's debut with the Dodgers by deciding instead to break the color barrier of the American Association at St. Paul, Minnesota. Before the season was over, however, Campanella went to Brooklyn. Over the next eight years, the Dodger star played with five National League pennant winners and one world championship team.

In January of 1958, his career as a player was ended by an automobile accident which left him paralyzed. Today, he is a sports commentator.

ELMER SIMMS CAMPBELL
    (Art   1)
    Born: 1908, St. Louis, Missouri
    Education: Chicago Art Institute, Illinois
    Significance: *Commercial artist*
While in high school, E. Simms Campbell was editorial cartoonist for the school paper. He broke into commercial art in his home town of St. Louis where he was told that it was a waste of time for a Negro in his youth to try to make a living in commercial art. Confident of his own ability, Campbell went to New York. With the help of other cartoonists, he began free-lancing. *Esquire* quickly spotted his talent and signed him to a long-term contract. Advertising agen-

cies sought his talents and soon he was turning out annually more than 500 finished cartoons.

During the thirties and forties, his cartoons symbolized sophisticated humor. A syndicated cartoon appearing in hundreds of newspapers, ads for some of the nation's leading manufacturers, and numerous cartoons in *Esquire* magazine bear the signature E. Simms Campbell.

Little publicity has been given the fact that Campbell has illustrated children's books and exhibited serious paintings. Campbell's skill has earned him a place in *Current Biography,* in *We Have Tomorrow,* in *Who's Who* and other biographical works. He and his wife now make their home in Switzerland. With the vigor of a beginning artist he continues to meet the heavy demands of his syndicate and magazine contracts.

STOKELY CARMICHAEL
(Civil Rights   46)
Born: 1941, Trinidad, West Indies
Education: Howard University,
    Washington, D.C.
Significance: *Leadership in the civil rights movement*

Stokely Carmichael was among the founders of the Student Nonviolent Coordinating Committee (SNCC) and became its national chairman in 1966. He had been the organization's field secretary in Alabama and a major organizer of the Lowndes County Freedom Organization. He was arrested twelve times in the course of his work for SNCC. His election to its chairmanship marked a turning point for the organization away from doctrinaire nonviolence and toward a more revolutionary line. He introduced the term Black Power to the American public during the Meredith March through Mississippi in 1966. He subsequently parted with SNCC and left the United States. Married to Miriam Makeba, he has resided in Africa for several years.

GEORGE WASHINGTON CARVER
(Physical Science, Agriculture   49)
Born: ca. 1860, Diamond Grove,
    Missouri

Died: 1943
Education: Simpson College, Iowa; M.A.,
    Iowa Agricultural College, Ames,
    Iowa
Significance: *Scientific research and development*

Born a slave, George Washington Carver never knew his mother or father. As a baby he had been stolen by raiders, but the plantation owner, Moses Carver, managed to ransom the infant by trading a race horse for him. The Carvers brought him up and gave him their name. He worked as a farm hand to support himself while attending a one-room school. He was then determined to go to college. After several rejections, he was accepted by Simpson College in Indianola, Iowa, as its first Negro student. Here he made an outstanding record. After gaining a master's degree, he was elected to the faculty of the Iowa Agricultural College as its first Negro faculty member, but he soon left for Tuskegee Institute at the urging of Booker T. Washington.

Dr. Carver's great desire was to show the people of the South that they could diversify their crops and not have to depend on single money crops such as cotton, tobacco, and rice. He was a patient researcher, and developed some three hundred products from the peanut, such as dyes, plastics, soap, ink, and many others now in common use. He traveled through the Alabama countryside to bring his knowledge to farmers of both races. Henry Ford provided a laboratory in which Dr. Carver might expand his work and visited him there regularly. His students remember the great scientist as a kindly teacher who "would never embarrass you or get angry in public." Many years before Dr. Martin Luther King asked his followers to meet hatred with love, Dr. Carver had said, "No man can drag me down so low as to make me hate him."

For many years Dr. Carver worked for the United States Government. Once he was called before Congress and given fifteen minutes to explain his work, as no one thought that talk about peanuts or sweet potatoes need take longer. His talk was so interesting to the Congressmen that they allowed him almost two hours. Many of his findings were published by the Department of Agriculture for the use of farmers everywhere. Dr. Carver received many honors. In 1917 he was made a Fellow of the Royal Society of Arts in London, and in 1923 was awarded the coveted Spingarn Medal. In 1939 he was the winner of the Theodore Roosevelt Medal for Distinguished Research in Agricultural Chemistry. In 1941 the University of Rochester conferred on him the degree of Doctor of Science. During his later years he used his life savings of $33,000 to establish the George Washington Carver Foundation for Agricultural Research.

Dr. Carver never married. At his death President Franklin D. Roosevelt and Vice-President Henry A. Wallace led the nation in paying respect to this great scientist. The farmland near Diamond Grove where he was born and raised is now maintained as a national monument by the United States Government.

HORACE ROSCOE CAYTON
(Government, Economics   28)
Born: 1903, Seattle, Washington
Education: A.B., University of
    Washington; University of Chicago,
    Illinois
Significance: *Social scientist and author*
Horace Cayton was a deputy sheriff in Seattle, Washington, from 1929 to 1931. He was research assistant in political science at the University of Chicago from 1931 to 1933, in sociology from 1933 to 1934, and in anthropology from 1936 to 1937. From 1934 to 1935 he was special assistant to the Secretary of the Interior in Washington, D.C. At Fisk University he was instructor of economics and labor from 1935 to 1936. He held a Rosenwald Fellowship from 1937 to 1939, and in 1940 he became director of the Parkway Community House in Chicago.

He was United Nations correspondent for the Pittsburgh *Courier* (1952–54) and a staff member with the office of the New York City Welfare Commissioner, the City College of New York, and the Langley Porter Clinic (1957–60). He has been associated with the University of

California in various administrative positions since 1961.

In 1945 his *Black Metropolis* (written with St. Clair Drake) won the Anisfield-Wolf Award for the year's best book on human relations. This book was included in the Stromberg collection of Negro literature and was cited by the New York Public Library as the outstanding race relations book of the year. Cayton has also been a columnist for the Pittsburgh *Courier* and a book reviewer for the *New York Times.*

WILT CHAMBERLAIN
(Basketball   46)
Born: 1936, Philadelphia, Pennsylvania
Education: University of Kansas
Significance: *Professional basketball
    player*
By the time Wilt Chamberlain entered high school, he was already six feet eleven inches tall, two inches short of his present height. Chamberlain is seven feet tall, and he is strong, graceful, and agile. He has run a quarter-mile in forty-seven seconds, put a sixteen-pound shot fifty-five feet, and high-jumped six feet ten inches. When he graduated from high school, he had his choice of seventy-seven major colleges. He chose the University of Kansas, but left after his junior year with two years of All-American honors behind him. In 1959 he joined the Philadelphia Warriors of the National Basketball Association.

In his rookie season, with fourteen games left, Chamberlain had already broken the existing full-season league scoring and rebounding records. Before the year was out, he had set eight new NBA records. He continued to dominate the sport with the San Francisco Warriors and the Philadelphia 76ers. His success has continued since he joined the Los Angeles Lakers.

RAY CHARLES
(Jazz   7, 46)
Born: 1934, Georgia
Significance: *Jazz musician and recording
    artist*
Ray Charles, blinded at six, received his first musical training at the School for the Blind in

St. Augustine, Florida. At fifteen he quit school to work professionally. Two years later he organized a trio, and in 1954 organized a larger rhythm and blues group. He made his first record in 1957 and since then he has been one of America's most popular jazz instrumentalists, pianists, and blues singers.

CHARLES WADDELL CHESTNUTT
(Literature   1)
Born: 1858, Cleveland, Ohio
Died: 1932
Significance: *Writer of novels of social consequence*

When Charles Waddell Chestnutt was fourteen years old, he was a bookkeeper in a white saloon in North Carolina. He began teaching at sixteen and was principal of the State Normal School for Negroes at Fayetteville when twenty-two. He worked for Dow Jones in New York City; he then went to Cleveland, Ohio, where he was a commercial and legal stenographer and court reporter. Having read law privately, he passed the Ohio bar exam with high scores and was admitted to the bar in 1887. He wrote many essays and articles for periodicals. He was first published in *Atlantic Monthly* in 1881. He received the Spingarn Medal in 1928 for "pioneer" work in literature. Involved personally in the blurred color line, he wrote impartially and realistically about miscegenation and mob violence. Called a "voluntary Negro," he dealt with intra-racial prejudice and achieved a balance between literary technique and social concern. He was the author of *The Conjure Woman* (1899), *House Behind Cedars* (1901), and other novels.

KENNETH BANCROFT CLARK
(Psychology   10, 32)
Born: 1914, Panama Canal Zone
Education: B.A., M.S., Howard
    University, Washington, D.C.; Ph.D.,
    Columbia University, New York
Significance: *Youth leader, psychologist*

Kenneth Clark's mother raised her children in New York City, where she helped organize a union in the sweatshop where she was a seamstress. While a university student, Clark was deeply influenced by one of his teachers, Dr. Ralph Bunche. After his studies in experimental psychology were completed, he took part in the study of the American Negro problem headed by the Swedish economist, Gunnar Myrdal. He then taught psychology at Hampton Institute and held a fellowship from the Julius Rosenwald Fund. In 1941 and 1942 Dr. Clark served on the research staff of the Office of War Information, traveling around the country to study the morale of the Negro population. Since 1942 he has been on the faculty of the College of the City of New York. In 1960 he was the first Negro in the history of the College to receive a permanent appointment as professor.

In 1950 Dr. Clark prepared a psychological report showing that school segregation mars the development of white as well as Negro students. This report the United States Supreme Court cited in its history-making decision of May, 1954, declaring segregation in public schools unconstitutional.

In 1962 he organized the Harlem Youth Opportunities Unlimited (HARYOU), a preventive program aimed at reducing the number of unemployed youngsters, school dropouts, and juvenile delinquents. One recommendation in its 1964 report was a "reading mobilization year."

In his book, *Prejudice and Your Child,* published in 1955, Dr. Clark analyzed the effects of racial discrimination upon Negro and white children and proposed certain remedies. He has also written for popular and scholarly journals and has held a number of federal, state, and city posts. In 1950 he was on the fact-finding staff of the Mid-Century White House Conference on Children and Youth. In an interview published in the *New York Times* magazine (August 25, 1963) Dr. Clark summed up the goal of the American Negro, saying: "Negroes want what other human beings want—respect, dignity, the opportunity to grow and to be evaluated in terms of their worth as individuals. The term equality means to every thoughtful Negro exactly what it says. Equality is not qualifiable." He was recognized for his invaluable service to various committees of the United States Riot Commission as he appeared as a witness during the 1967 hearings.

WILLIAM MONTAGUE COBB
   (Anthropology   51, 53)
   Born: ca. 1910, Washington, D.C.
   Education: A.B., Amherst College,
      Massachusetts; M.D., Howard
      University, Washington, D.C.; Ph.D.,
      (Case) Western Reserve University,
      Cleveland, Ohio
   Significance: *Medical care leader*
William Montague Cobb did his internship at Freedmen's Hospital in Washington, D.C., with further postgraduate work at Washington University in St. Louis, Missouri. Among the scholarships and fellowships he received was the Rosenwald Fellowship for study of skeletal aging, 1941 to 1942. He participated in track and boxing in high school and college.

He has received many professional honors for his contributions to the field of medicine for his research in attacking the myths related to racial characteristics, and for his comprehensive research in exposing the inadequacies of medical facilities for the minority citizens of the District of Columbia. He also led the fight to open the facilities of the municipally owned Gallinger Hospital to students, interns, and faculty members of Howard University.

Dr. Cobb is the past president of the Anthropological Society, Washington, the American Association of Physical Anthropologists, and the National Medical Association and past vice-president of the American Association for the Advancement of Science. His numerous publications are on the development of graphic methods of learning anatomy, research on the physical anthropology of the American Negro, research on cranio-facial union in mammals and man, studies in age changes in the adult human skeleton, and the relationship between medical care and the situation of the Negro.

ALVIN COFFEY
   (Exploration   5, 17)
   Born: 1822, St. Louis, Missouri

   Died: 1902
   Significance: *California pioneer*
Alvin Coffey's grandfather, a Kentuckian, was an officer under Andrew Jackson in the battle for New Orleans. Coffey went to California from Missouri during the Gold Rush in 1849. He opened a laundry in Red Bluff, California, and earned $1,500 to purchase his freedom and that of his wife and three children. He also farmed near Red Bluff for many years. He was the only non-white member of The Society of California Pioneers in San Francisco. He gave money to help found the Home for the Aged and Infirm Colored People at Beulah, California, and was its first resident.

NAT "KING" COLE
   (Music, Acting   46)
   Born: 1919, Montgomery, Alabama
   Died: 1965
   Education: High School
   Significance: *Pianist, band-leader and
      singer*
Nat "King" Cole grew up in Chicago where his father was a minister. He played the piano and organ in his father's church, formed his own band in high school, and worked with other small groups.

When his touring company failed in Los Angeles, he found work in small clubs in that city. In 1934 the drummer in his quartet failed to appear one night, and the King Cole Trio was born. In 1943 he recorded and sold more than half a million copies of his own composition, "Straighten Up and Fly Right." In succeeding years he recorded one hit after another. His career also included several acting roles in the movies.

JOHN COLTRANE
   (Jazz   46)
   Born: 1926, Hamlet, North Carolina
   Significance: *Jazz experimentalist*
John Coltrane was the son of a tailor who played several musical instruments as a hobby. Music became a dominant force in Coltrane's life when he was eighteen years of age.

He played with a small group in Philadelphia, with the United States Navy band in Hawaii, and with a rhythm and blues group. By the 1950's, however, he was working with some of the greats of contemporary jazz and began to formulate the new sound for which he is famous. The music which Coltrane created continues to be controversial. He used the tenor saxophone to produce harsh sounds not easy for many listeners to appreciate. His dissonant experimentation is still a major influence in American jazz.

FANNY M. JACKSON COPPIN
  (Education   32)
  Born: 1836, Washington, D.C.
  Died: 1913
  Education: Rhode Island State Normal
    School, Bristol, Rhode Island; Oberlin
    College, Ohio
  Significance: *Educational leadership*
Fanny M. Jackson Coppin served for over 30 years as principal of the Institute for Colored Youth, later the Cheyney Training School for Teachers. She later joined her husband Bishop Levi J. Coppin as a missionary in South Africa.

Fanny Jackson was born into slavery. After an aunt purchased her freedom she lived in New England with relatives. An interested employer aided her to matriculate at Oberlin College in 1860. Freedmen began to flood into Ohio in the last months of the Civil War, just as she was completing her studies. Her experience in teaching literacy classes for them convinced her that the education of her people should be her life's work. She went to Philadelphia as a teacher at the Institute for Colored Youth, and in 1869 became its principal. She greatly expanded the school's curriculum, especially in the direction of industrial training.

She published *Hints on Teaching* and an autobiography, *Reminiscences of School Life.*

BILL COSBY
  (Entertainment   46)
  Born: ca. 1935, Philadelphia,
    Pennsylvania
  Education: Temple University,
    Philadelphia, Pennsylvania
  Significance: *Actor, comedian*
Bill Cosby dropped out of high school to join the Navy, obtaining his high school diploma while in the service. After his service, he entered Temple University where he played football and tended bar at night. He left Temple in 1962 to pursue a career in show business. He began in small clubs around Philadelphia and in New York's Greenwich Village. Within two years, he was playing the top nightclubs around the country, and making television appearances on major shows.

Cosby is the first Negro actor ever to star in a network television series, *I Spy,* in a racially neutral role. He is also the first Negro to win an Emmy. In recent years he has returned to school and devoted much of his time to educational projects, including *The Electric Company* on television.

PAUL CUFFE
  (Business   7, 32)
  Born: 1759
  Died: 1817
  Significance: *Shipbuilder and leader of*
    African resettlement movement
Paul Cuffe was one of the most outstanding Negroes searching for economic independence and group self-respect during the post-Revolutionary War period. Early in his life he developed an interest in commerce. When he was sixteen he worked on a whaling vessel. In the following year, during his second voyage, he was captured by the British and detained in New York for three months. During the war he and his brother refused to pay taxes in Massachusetts on the grounds that they were denied the franchise. Shortly thereafter Massachusetts passed a law allowing free Negroes liable to taxation all the privileges belonging to other citizens.

In 1780, Cuffe began to build ships of his own and to engage in commerce. As profits mounted, he expanded his sea-going activities and built larger vessels. He began with small, open boats of less than ten tons. By 1806, he owned one large ship, two brigs, and several smaller vessels, and considerable property in houses and land. After joining the Society of Friends, he became deeply interested, along with many other Quakers, in the welfare of Negroes and wanted to engage in some activity that would improve their lot.

In 1811, he went to Sierra Leone in his own vessel to investigate the possibilities of taking free Negroes back to Africa. The War of 1812 prevented the fulfillment of his plans. In 1815, however, he took thirty-eight Negroes to Africa at an expense of three or four thousand dollars. He learned, as colonizers of a later day were to learn, that the expense of taking Negroes back to Africa was so great as to be prohibitive.

COUNTEE CULLEN
(born COUNTEE PORTER)
    (Literature   1)
    Born: 1903, New York City
    Died: 1946
    Education: New York University, New
        York; M.A., Harvard University,
        Cambridge, Massachusetts
    Significance: *Poet and teacher*
Countee Cullen was reared by a Methodist minister, a political and racial activist, who gave him his last name. He was recognized in high school for his poetry and won the Witter Bynner poetry prize in 1925. He was elected to Phi Beta Kappa at New York University. He published *Color* when he was twenty-one. He is also the author of *One Way to Heaven*. In 1927, he received the Harmon Foundation Gold Medal for literature and became a leader of the Harlem Renaissance in the twenties. He was assistant editor of *Opportunity* and *Journal of Negro Life.* Having spent two years in France on a Guggenheim Fellowship, he returned to New York and dedicated the rest of his life to teaching.

Cullen collaborated with Arna Bontemps in dramatizing the latter's *God Sends Sunday.* Known as the "gentle poet," he wrote in the classical idiom adapted to protest themes and new ideas. He wished to be known as an "American poet" and represented the peak of Negro poetry of his time.

ULYSSES GRANT DAILEY
    (Medicine   46)
    Born: 1885, Donaldsonville, Louisiana
    Died: 1961
    Education: M.D., Northwestern
        University Medical School, Chicago,
        Illinois; postgraduate work: Paris,
        Berlin, London, and Vienna
    Significance: *Founder Dailey Hospital
        and Sanitarium, Chicago*
Ulysses Grant Dailey, after his graduation in 1906, served for four years as assistant to the distinguished Negro physican, Dr. Daniel Hale Williams, at Provident Hospital, in Chicago. His name came to be widely known in the fields of anatomy and surgery.

For many years, Dr. Dailey was an associate editor of the *Journal of the National Medical Association.* He traveled around the world in 1933, under the sponsorship of the International College of Surgeons, of which he was a Founding Fellow. In 1951, and again in 1953, the State Department sent him to Pakistan, India, Ceylon, and Africa.

BENJAMIN O. DAVIS, JR.
    (Military   16)
    Born: 1912
    Education: U.S. Military Academy, West
        Point, New York
    Significance: *Highest ranking Negro in
        U.S. military history*
A career officer from West Point, Captain Benjamin O. Davis, Jr. led the 99th Pursuit Squadron when it was sent to North Africa early in 1943. These men were trained in a flying school for blacks at Tuskegee Institute. Before the war ended, 600 had been trained and 88 had won the Distinguished Flying Cross. After the 99th had been in combat for almost a year, participating in almost 500 combat missions and nearly 4,000 sorties against the enemy, it was transferred in December 1943 to the newly formed 332nd Fighter Group, an all-black organization. Under the command of Captain Davis,

who later was promoted to major and then to lieutenant colonel in a single day, the 332nd Group won acclaim in many engagements. The 332nd flew more than 15,500 missions and nearly 11,000 sorties in the Mediterranean Theater of Operations. No bomber under its protection was lost to an enemy plane. Colonel Davis personally flew 60 missions, including those against the oil fields of Romania. He won the Legion of Merit on three occasions, the Distinguished Flying Cross, and the Air Medal with four oak leaf clusters. He received the Silver Star for gallantry in action while leading a squadron of P-51 fighter planes against airfields in the south of Germany.

After the war, Davis became the first black general officer in the U.S. Air Force. He was also the first black to command an air base, Godman Field in Kentucky. Davis was later promoted to Major General. On April 16, 1965, President Johnson promoted him to Lieutenant General, named him Chief of Staff of U.S. Forces in Korea, and Chief of Staff of the United Nations Command in Korea. In 1970, Davis retired early and took the position of Director of Public Safety in Cleveland, Ohio, to head the Cleveland police and fire departments, but he resigned the position six months later.

MILES DAVIS
    (Jazz   46)
    Born: ca. 1923, St. Louis, Missouri
    Education: Juilliard School of Music,
        New York
    Significance: *Jazz trumpet player*
Miles Davis has played a major role in effecting the transition from the hard aggressive stance of bop to the softer, more subtle shadings of cool jazz. In the early 1940's, he sat in with his idols Charlie Parker and Dizzy Gillespie when they passed through St. Louis with Billy Eckstine's band. In 1945, his father sent him to the Juilliard School of Music in New York; he was soon working the 52nd Street music clubs with Parker and Coleman Hawkins. He toured with the bands of Billy Eckstine and Benny Carter. Davis has been an important jazz presence since 1950.

OSSIE DAVIS
    (Acting   46)
    Born: 1917, Cogdell, Georgia
    Education: Howard University,
        Washington, D.C.
    Significance: *Motion picture and
        television actor*
Ossie Davis and his wife Ruby Dee have won a secure place in the American theater. Together or separately, the Davises have also performed successfully on television, in movies, and in cabarets. Davis grew up in Waycross, Georgia. Alain Locke of Howard University suggested that he try for an acting career in New York. His first role was in *Jeb* in 1946. He met Miss Dee in that play, and two years later they were married.

After appearing in the movie, *No Way Out,* Davis won Broadway roles in *No Time for Sergeants, Raisin in the Sun,* and *Jamaica.* In 1961, he and Miss Dee starred in *Purlie Victorious,* which Davis wrote. Davis' other movies include *The Cardinal* and *Shock Treatment.* He has written a number of TV scripts, and has appeared in several television series, including *The Defenders, The Nurses,* and *East Side, West Side.* He directed the motion picture *Cotton Comes to Harlem.*

SAMMY DAVIS, JR.
    (Entertainment, Music   46)
    Born: 1925, New York City
    Significance: *Versatile entertainer*
Sammy Davis, Jr. first appeared professionally at the age of four in vaudeville with his father and the Will Mastin Trio. Two years later he made his movie debut with Ethel Waters in *Rufus Jones for President.* When he entered the Army in 1943 he was assigned to writing, directing and producing camp shows. After his discharge he rejoined the trio, which had reached the big time with a successful Hollywood appearance in 1946.

Davis continued to the top of show business, with hit records, numerous films and Broadway shows, notably *Mr. Wonderful* (1956) and, more recently, *Golden Boy.* He played the part of Sportin' Life in the movie version of *Porgy and Bess* in 1959. He has also had his own network television series. He has written a best selling autobiography, *Yes, I Can.*

WILLIAM LEVI DAWSON
(Music   1)
Born: 1898, Anniston, Alabama
Education: Tuskegee Institute, Alabama;
    Washburn College, Topeka, Kansas;
    Institute of Fine Arts, Kansas City,
    Missouri; Chicago Musical College,
    Illinois; American Conservatory of
    Music, Chicago, Illinois
Significance: *Director of Music at
    Tuskegee Institute*

William Levi Dawson is an eminent composer whose works have brought pleasure to thousands of music lovers. He was not allowed to take part in one of his own graduation exercises in 1927 because of his color and had to secure special permission to attend a concert featuring his work in Birmingham, Alabama, for the same reason.

Dawson ran away from home to attend Tuskegee Institute. There he took a job caring for the band instruments and learned to play most of them. He studied under Felix Borowski at the Chicago Musical College and under Adolph Weidig at the American Conservatory. At the same time he earned his living playing in Chicago bands, training Negro church choirs, and occasionally playing the trombone with the Chicago Civic Orchestra—its only Negro member during that time.

Among his many compositions are "I Couldn't Hear Nobody Pray," and "Talk About a Child That Do Love Jesus, Here Is One." His most notable symphonic work is *Negro Folk Symphony No. 1,* which premiered at Carnegie Hall under conductor Leopold Stokowski in 1934. For many years, William Dawson was Director of Music at Tuskegee Institute, and he made the institute choir one of the nation's finest. Following retirement from active direction of the choir in 1955, Dawson was sent to Spain by the U.S. State Department to train Spanish choral groups in the singing of Negro spirituals.

Dawson has a deep and abiding love for spirituals. He has enhanced their natural beauty with the discipline and training of the devoted professional.

(From Russell L. Adams, *Great Negroes Past and Present.* Chicago: Afro-Am Publishing Co., Inc., 1967.)

OSCAR DEPRIEST
(Politics   46)
Born: 1871, Florence, Alabama
Died: 1951
Significance: *First Negro congressman of
    the 20th century*

Oscar DePriest was the first Negro to win a seat in the U.S. House of Representatives in the 20th century, and the first to be elected from a Northern state, serving from 1929 to 1935. His election was in part attributable to the large-scale migration of Negroes to urban areas in the North.

DePriest moved to Kansas with his family at the age of six. He completed business and book-keeping classes there before running away to Dayton, Ohio.

He arrived in Chicago in 1889 and became a painter and decorator. He soon turned to real estate and amassed a fortune. He won Republican backing in 1904 in a successful bid for the office of Cook County Commissioner. He was re-elected in 1906.

He was chosen as an alternate delegate to the Republican Convention of 1908 but saw his political ambitions largely thwarted until 1915, when he became Chicago's first Negro alderman. In the 1920's, he aligned himself with a number of conflicting interests, some of which cut across party lines. In 1928, he was a candidate for Republican committeeman, and a delegate to the Republican National Convention and won his seat in Congress in a race occasioned by the sudden death of the incumbent, whom he had supported.

He was the unofficial spokesman for the eleven million Negroes in the United States during this period and faced a formidable challenge in the profound political and economic transformation that occurred during the Depression.

Though sincerely desirous of improving conditions for the Negro, he found himself in a difficult partisan position and shifted his support from Republican to Democratic candidates on the local level. In 1934, he was defeated by Arthur Mitchell, the first Negro Democrat elected to Congress.

DePriest returned to his real estate business. He was again an alderman from 1943 to 1947.

JAMES DERHAM

(Medicine   6)
Born: 1762, Philadelphia, Pennsylvania
Significance: *Recognized as first Negro physician in America*

James Derham, a slave, learned the art of medicine while serving as an assistant to his physician master. In 1788, he was one of the top physicians in New Orleans. Dr. Benjamin Rush, a leading doctor of the day, said: "I have conversed with him upon most of the acute and epidemic diseases of the country where he lives. I suggested some new medicines to him, but he suggested many more to me."

DEAN DIXON

(Music   1, 32)
Born: 1915, Manhattan, New York
Education: B.S., Juilliard School of Music, New York; M.A., Columbia University, New York
Significance: *Orchestra conductor*

Dean Dixon was exposed to classical music by his parents. As a small boy, he was regularly taken to Carnegie Hall. While he was still in high school, Dixon formed his own amateur orchestra at the Harlem YMCA. On the basis of a successful violin audition, he was admitted to Juilliard.

The Dean Dixon Symphony Society, which he had formed in 1932, began to receive financial support from the Harlem community in 1937. In 1941, at the request of Eleanor Roosevelt, Dixon gave a concert at the Heckscher Theater. He was later signed by the musical director of NBC to conduct the network's summer symphony in two concerts. Two months after the NBC concerts, he made his debut with the New York Philharmonic. He was the first Negro and, at twenty-six, the youngest musician ever to conduct the New York Philharmonic Orchestra.

JACOB DODSON

(Exploration   5)
Significance: *Member of Fremont's expeditions*

Jacob Dodson was a free Negro and a servant of Fremont's father-in-law, Senator Thomas Hart Benton. He volunteered to accompany Fremont's expedition and was with him when the Klamath Lakes were discovered.

He made an historic horseback ride in 1847, when he and Fremont completed a round trip between Los Angeles and Monterey, California, a distance of 840 miles, in seventy-six hours of riding in eight days.

AARON DOUGLAS

(Art   46)
Born: 1899, Topeka, Kansas
Education: B.F.A. University of Nebraska, Lincoln; M.F.A. Columbia University
Significance: *Painter of the "Negro Renaissance"*

Aaron Douglas was one of perhaps a dozen Negro artists to achieve recognition before 1940. He illustrated James Weldon Johnson's *God's Trombones: Seven Negro Sermons in Verse.* The angular figures and mystical light patterns he employed were used in his later murals with even greater effectiveness. He has exhibited in the Brooklyn Museum, among others, and in 1936 was the only Negro artist to exhibit at the Findlay Gallaries in New York City. His murals can be found in the Fisk University Library, Bennett College, and the Countee Cullen branch of the New York Public Library. They deal mostly with themes from American Negro history and culture. He has illustrated books authored by Alain L. Locke, Langston Hughes, and Countee Cullen. He traveled through the southern states and in Haiti on a Rosenwald grant. At the invitation of President John F.

Kennedy in 1963 he attended the centennial celebration of the Emancipation Proclamation.

FREDERICK DOUGLASS
(Civil Rights   19)
Born: 1817, Tuckahee, eastern shore of
Maryland
Died: 1895
Significance: *Orator and champion of civil rights*

Frederick Douglass was born a slave. He became the most prominent Negro of his time. He lived on Colonel Edward Lloyd's plantation until he was 10 years old, then moved to Baltimore. He was taught to read by his master's wife. He escaped from Maryland in 1838, went to New York, married, and gained his freedom legally in 1846. He became famous as an anti-slavery orator and writer, championing Negroes' emancipation, enfranchisement, vocational training, military privileges, and rights as laborers. He also fought for women's rights, temperance, and the working class in England, Scotland, and Ireland. Douglass was the greatest Negro orator of his time. In 1847 he began his own weekly, *The North Star,* which he continued until 1863. He was the author of *Narrative of the Life of Frederick Douglass* (1845); *My Bondage and My Freedom* (1835); and *The Life and Times of Frederick Douglass* (1881). He served as Recorder of Deeds in Washington and as Resident Minister and Consul General to Haiti.

THOMAS E. DOWNS
(Architecture   44)
Born: ca. 1915, Los Angeles, California
Education: University of Southern
California, Los Angeles
Significance: *Architect and master planner*

Thomas E. Downs, architect, was associated with the architectural firm of Daniel, Mann, Johnson, and Mendenhall in Los Angeles prior to becoming an architect with the State of California. He has been with the State Office of Architecture and Construction for over eight years. He developed the master plan for the California State College campus at Hayward, California, the Transportation Center in Sacramento, and most recently, the master plan for the visitors' center at the Oroville Dam in Oroville, California.

CHARLES R. DREW
(Medicine   2, 49, 51)
Born: 1904, Washington, D.C.
Died: 1950
Education: A.B., Amherst College,
Massachusetts; M.D., McGill
University Medical School, Montreal,
Canada
Significance: *Medical education, pioneer in blood transfusion research*

Charles R. Drew combined scholarship with exceptional athletic ability. He was captain of varsity teams at both Amherst and McGill. He was among the top hurdlers in the country and rated as one of the football greats of his time. As director of athletics at Morgan State College in Baltimore, Maryland, from 1926 to 1928, he developed many athletes who later became outstanding athletic coaches.

At McGill University, he won first prize in physical anatomy, two fellowships in medicine, and honors in athletics. He became an instructor in pathology at Howard University School of Medicine.

After several years of postgraduate work at Columbia College of Physicians and Surgeons, where he wrote a thesis on "Banked Blood: A Study in Blood Preservation," he became director of the first Blood Transfusion Association, supplying plasma to the British forces, 1940–41. His report of this British project guided later developments in this kind of work for the U.S. Army and the Allies. When in 1941, the American Red Cross set up blood donor stations to collect blood plasma for the armed forces, Dr. Drew was appointed director of the project.

After organizing this work, he resigned to become chairman of the surgery department at Howard University. He was an examiner, American Board of Surgery, 1942–1950, and in 1944 he was a member of the American-Soviet Science Commission. Besides banked blood, he was recognized as an authority in surgical shock and in fluid balance in surgery. His great ability as surgeon and as teacher has opened new vistas for Negroes in the field of surgery. In 1944, he was awarded the Spingarn Medal by the National Association for the Advancement of Colored People.

WILLIAM EDWARD BURGHARDT DuBois
(Civil Rights, Literature   32)
Born: 1868, Great Barrington,
    Massachusetts
Died: 1963
Education: Fisk University, Nashville,
    Tennessee; Harvard University,
    Cambridge, Massachusetts
Significance: *Civil Rights*

Dr. William DuBois believed that the salvation of his race required equality in educational opportunity as a prerequisite to full equality. DuBois graduated with honors from Fisk University and Harvard University, and later studied in Europe. He started teaching in 1894 at Wilberforce University in Ohio, later to move to the University of Pennsylvania and then to Atlanta University.

In the early years of the twentieth century the Niagara Movement, a group of Negro intellectuals under the leadership of Dr. DuBois, organized a program to promote full citizenship for Negroes. The last meeting of the Niagara Movement was held in 1908 in Oberlin, Ohio. It was absorbed into a broader and more powerful organization, the National Association for the Advancement of Colored People (NAACP), dedicated to the achievement of civil rights and the elimination of discrimination. The first national officers were all white with the exception of Dr. DuBois, who was named director of publicity and research. He was the editor of the organization's publication, *The Crisis*. The NAACP launched a campaign to suppress lynching and one to seek greater police protection.

Dr. DuBois' numerous books include *The Suppression of the Slave Trade* (1896); *The Philadelphia Negro* (1899); *The Souls of Black Folk* (1903); *John Brown* (1909); *Quest of the Silver Fleece* (1911); *The Negro* (1915); *Darkwater* (1920); *Black Reconstruction* (1935); *The Gift of Black Folk: Then and Now* (1939); *Dusk of Dawn* (1940); *Color and Democracy* (1945); *The World and Africa* (1947); *In Battle for Peace* (1952); and a trilogy, *Black Flame* (1957–1961).

Dr. DuBois emigrated to Africa in 1961 and continued his writing and publishing, working especially on a massive Encyclopaedia Africana, a longtime dream.

EDWARD R. DUDLEY
(Law   32)
Born: 1911, South Boston, Virginia
Education: Johnson C. Smith University,
    Charlotte, North Carolina; Howard
    University, Washington, D.C.; LL.B.
    St. John's Law School, Brooklyn, New
    York
Significance: *Legal and diplomatic service*

Edward R. Dudley taught in Virginia rural schools and was in real estate in New York for three years before he took his law degree in 1941. After a year of private practice he became an assistant in the New York State Attorney General's office. Subsequently he was a member of the legal staff of the National Association for the Advancement of Colored People, a job he returned to on two later occasions (1947–48, 1954). In 1945 he was appointed counsel to the governor of the Virgin Islands.

The American legation in Liberia was raised to an embassy in 1948, and Dudley was appointed ambassador. He was the first Negro of ambassadorial rank in the United States Foreign Service. That appointment broke a State Department policy which had restricted Negroes to lower diplomatic posts. He continued as ambassador until 1953.

He was appointed to the Domestic Relations Court of the City of New York in 1955 and became Manhattan Borough President in 1961. In 1965 he was elevated to a seat on the New York State Supreme Court.

PAUL LAURENCE DUNBAR
(Literature   1)

Born: 1872, Dayton, Ohio
Died: 1906
Significance: *Writer and poet*

Paul Laurence Dunbar's mother was a slave in a cultured home in Kentucky. Her talent for narration was apparently inherited by her son. His father, much older, was a Civil War soldier. Dunbar's ability was discovered in high school. Although the only Negro in his class, he was class poet, president of the literary society, and editor of the school paper and yearbook. He was unable to attend college. His early poems were published on a homemade press by the Wright Brothers, his early friends. The only job he could find was as an elevator operator at a hotel where he sold his home-printed books to friends. At this time he also wrote poetry for newspapers. Later his verse and prose were published in magazines and eventually in collections.

He used folk material and minstrel tradition. The influence of Robert Burns is evident in his writing. He wrote romantically, avoiding social issues. He wrote lyrics, many of which were set to music. He also worked for a time at the Library of Congress. He is the author of *Sport of the Gods, Lyrics of the Hearthside,* and *Folks in Dixie.*

TODD DUNCAN
  (Acting, Music   46)
  Born: 1903, Danville, Kentucky
  Education: Butler University,
    Indianapolis, Indiana; M.A., Columbia
    University, New York
  Significance: *Singer, actor and teacher of
    music*

Todd Duncan has taught at Howard University since 1931, occasionally taking time out to work in the theater or in concerts.

On the strength of a single performance in New York of an all-Negro version of the opera *Cavalleria Rusticana,* George Gershwin auditioned him and he won the role of Porgy in *Porgy and Bess.* He subsequently sang the same part in two revivals of the play. He was featured on Broadway in *Cabin in the Sky* and in the motion picture *Syncopation.* In his concerts he sings German, French, and Italian songs.

KATHERINE DUNHAM
  (Dancing   1, 46)
  Born: 1910, Chicago, Illinois
  Education: M.A., University of Chicago,
    Illinois
  Significance: *Exponent of primitive dance
    in modern choreography*

Katherine Dunham excelled in athletics and music in high school and financed her education at the University of Chicago by giving dance lessons. In 1936–37 she did field work in the West Indies, first with a project sponsored by Northwestern University, then on a Rosenwald Fellowship. This study provided the basis for the unique dance forms she has since developed, blending Broadway traditions with Afro-Cuban rhythms and forms. She began to perfect these styles with the WPA Federal Theater in Chicago in the late thirties.

She appeared in *Cabin in the Sky* (1940) and several other films. She appeared as guest artist with both the San Francisco and Los Angeles Symphony Orchestras and made several appearances at the Hollywood Bowl. She established her own dance company in 1945, with which she toured the United States, Mexico, and Europe. She is the author of several articles and books.

JEAN BAPTISTE POINTE DUSABLE
  (Exploration   49)
  Born: ca. 1745, Haiti
  Died: 1818
  Education: Boarding school for boys near
    Paris, France
  Significance: *Pioneer trader and founder
    of Chicago*

Pointe DuSable lived in New Orleans as a youth. In constant danger of being imprisoned or sold into slavery, he escaped up the Mississippi River in a small boat with a close friend and an Indian guide. He lived with the Indians near the trading post of St. Louis and then in Illinois near Peoria. He was an excellent businessman, in the manner of his French forebears, and left many records and legal documents about himself throughout the Northwest Territories. He built a trading post on the north branch of the Chicago River near Lake Michigan in 1772. He enlarged his house and brought his family and a band of Potawatomi Indians to settle in the area. His daughter was born there, the first recorded birth in the settlement. Later the Indians used to say, "The first white man in Chicago was a Negro!"

He was highly respected by missionaries, trappers, hunters, and explorers, who made DuSable's trading post, now Chicago, their stopping-off place. The Potawatomis once proposed him as their chieftain. He was also the friend of the great Ottawa chief, Pontiac, and of Daniel Boone.

The bill of sale of his holdings is recorded in the Wayne County Building in Detroit and proves DuSable's claim as founder of Chicago. A bronze plaque at the corner of Dearborn Street and Wacker Drive indicates the site of his house, the first permanent dwelling in Chicago.

EDWARD KENNEDY (DUKE) ELLINGTON
(Music   46)
Born: 1899, Washington, D.C.
Education: Pratt Institute, Brooklyn,
    New York
Significance: *Pianist, composer, and
    orchestra director*
Duke Ellington evidenced his musical talent early—he played the piano at seven, composed his first song at seventeen, and began appearing professionally at eighteen. He was interested in architecture and was offered a scholarship at Pratt Institute, but soon forsook school for professional music making. He brought his band to New York in 1923 and was booked into a five-year run at the Cotton Club in Harlem in 1927. Films, records, radio, and international tours followed; he and his band have been consistently popular from the Cotton Club days, through the annual Carnegie Hall concerts of 1943–50, to his victories in Downbeat and critics' polls in the late sixties.

Ellington has pioneered many important developments in jazz and popular music in the years since he won the New York School of Music's annual award for best musical composition for "Creole Rhapsody" in 1933. He was the first to use the human voice instrumentally in big band jazz arrangements. He introduced a miniature concerto form to back his band's excellent soloists. He played one of the first college jazz concerts in 1940. His extended jazz compositions, including "Black, Brown, and Beige" (1943) and "Liberian Suite" (1948) added a new dimension to popular music. He conceived and presented at San Francisco's Grace Cathedral and New York's St. John the Divine Cathedral Church a concert of sacred music in the jazz idiom. The nearly one thousand songs he had produced have included an unmatched number of enduring standards of American popular music.

The Ellington bands' personnel—Ben Webster, Cootie Williams, Johnny Hodges, Oscar Pettiford, and many, many others—is among the most impressive in jazz history.

RALPH ELLISON
(Literature   12)
Born: 1914, Oklahoma City, Oklahoma
Education: Tuskegee Institute, Alabama
Significance: *Writer*
Ralph Ellison experienced injustices but felt no innate inferiority while growing up. Oklahoma had been a state only a short time, and although segregated, had no tradition of slavery. Ellison had an early interest in jazz and classical music. He discovered the "Renaissance Man" concept while in high school. After studying musical composition at Tuskegee, he moved to New York to study sculpture. He met Richard Wright and began publishing in *New Masses* and *The Negro Quarterly.* His early work showed his interest in left-wing politics, but he was too individualistic to join any group. His later work stresses the recognition of the Negro identity. He was sponsored but not influenced by Richard Wright. He was definitely influenced by T. S. Eliot and James Joyce, however. His *Invisible Man,* an autobiographical odyssey, has been called the "most distinguished single work" published in America

since 1945. It won the National Book Award in 1952. He is known to be a painstaking craftsman.

James A. Emanuel

(Literature   19)

Born: 1921, Alliance, Nebraska

Education: B.A., Howard University, Washington, D.C.; M.A., Northwestern University, Evanston, Illinois; Ph.D., Columbia University, New York

Significance: *Poet and teacher*

As a teenager, James Emanuel worked on ranches and farms, operated an elevator, managed a C.C.C. canteen and held other jobs. He became confidential secretary to General Benjamin O. Davis, Sr. in Washington, D.C., and served in the South Pacific. He worked for the Civil Service Department in Chicago. He also taught in a Y.M.C.A. secretarial school in Harlem. Since 1957 he has been an assistant professor of literature at City College of the City University of New York. He was a visiting professor of American literature at the University of Grenoble in France.

His poems have been published in *Ebony, Phylon, Negro Digest, Midwest Quarterly, The New York Times, Freedomways,* and many other magazines. He also appears in anthologies such as *Sixes and Sevens* (London) and *La Poesie Negro Americaine* (Paris). Emanuel is also the author of *Dark Symphony: Negro Literature in America* (1968).

Esteban

(Exploration   41)

Born: 1498 or 1499, Azamor, Morocco

Significance: *Explorer of what is now the American Southwest*

Esteban, sometimes called Estevanillo, or Estevanico, was about thirty when he joined the expedition of Panfilo de Narvaez, a Spanish explorer, in 1527. The expedition was shipwrecked off the coast of Florida. Esteban, Alvar Nunez Cabeza de Vaca, and two others survived. For eight years they wandered among the tribes. All became "medicine men." Esteban became familiar with Indian customs and characteristics and learned to speak a number of Indian languages. He traveled with Cabeza de Vaca across Texas and Mexico to the Gulf of California, finally returning to Mexico City in 1536.

In Mexico City, Esteban served under the Viceroy of Spain for three years. One account states that he was a slave of Hernando de Alarcon, but no other mention is made of his being a slave, although almost every Spanish explorer had Negro slaves in their expeditions.

In 1539, Esteban left Mexico City with Fray Marcos de Niza. He went ahead with a party of Indians into the land of the Zuñis in search of the Seven Cities of Cibola. He was killed by the Indians before the Spaniards arrived at the Zuñi settlement. When they heard what had happened to Esteban, the Spaniards returned to Mexico City.

James Carmichael Evans

(Engineering   3, 51)

Born: 1900

Education: B.S., M.S., Massachusetts Institute of Technology, Boston, Massachusetts

Significance: *Government service in science*

From 1943, until his retirement James Carmichael Evans was a professor of electrical engineering at Howard University. He was administrative assistant to President Roosevelt from 1937 to 1942, and from 1941 to 1943 was vocational training associate, Council of National Defense, Washington, D.C. He then became a civilian aide to the Secretary of War, 1943–47, and civilian assistant to the Secretary of Defense in 1949.

In 1926 he was the recipient of the Harmon Award in science for research in electronics. He is a member of many scientific societies and the author of many monographs on training and placement in technical fields. His fields of research are electronics preceding radar, magnetism and electronic magnetic applications, and ionized fluids. He is the holder of a patent on the integration of exhaust gases to prevent icing on aircraft.

JAMES FARMER
    (Civil Rights, Government   46)
    Born: 1920, Marshall, Texas
    Education: B.S., Wiley College, Marshall,
        Texas; Howard University,
        Washington, D.C.
    Significance: *Leadership in the Civil
        Rights Movement*

James Farmer, one of the founders of the Congress of Racial Equality (CORE), served as the national director until 1966. CORE was the first American Negro protest organization which used the Gandhian technique of nonviolence and passive resistance. CORE staged its first successful sit-in demonstration in 1942 at a restaurant in Chicago's Loop.

James Farmer was very active during the 1950's in the civil rights struggle. He has also served as a commentator on radio and television for programs sponsored by the United Auto Workers in Detroit. Like many civil rights leaders, James Farmer spent time in jail (forty days in 1961) for his activities. Farmer and CORE were major participants in the famous March on Washington in 1963. He is the author of *Freedom, When?* CORE is also known for the introduction of the Freedom Rides. CORE's activities sparked the legal fight which yielded the 1960 Supreme Court decision outlawing segregated bus terminals.

CATHERINE FERGUSON
    (Community Service   32)
    Born: ca. 1850, aboard a schooner en
        route from Virginia to New York City
    Significance: *Work with homeless and
        destitute children*

Catherine (Katy) Ferguson was born a slave. Her mother was sold when Katy was eight, and they never saw each other again. She was freed at sixteen and married at eighteen. Both her children died in infancy. Thereafter, she devoted her life to orphaned children.

She conducted regular Sunday sessions of religious instruction in her home and gathered neglected children both black and white. Her Sunday class was moved to basement quarters in the Murray Street Church, beginning forty years' association with the Murray Street Sabbath School. She continued to invite "her" children to her home on Fridays and on Sunday afternoons. In the course of those years, she provided a foster home for nearly fifty children, twenty of them white. A home for unmarried mothers founded in 1920 was named in her honor.

ELLA FITZGERALD
    (Jazz   46)
    Born: 1918, Newport News, Virginia
    Significance: *Jazz singer*

Ella Fitzgerald was picked out of an amateur contest at Harlem's Apollo Theater by Chick Webb in 1934, and a year later cut her first record; "A Tisket, A Tasket" (1938) brought her commercial success and a wide and appreciative public. She has been the premier female singer in American jazz and popular music ever since. Her occasional film appearances include *Let No Man Write My Epitaph.* She tours Europe annually. She has a remarkable ability to use her voice as an instrument, effortlessly improvising on melody and rhythm with unmatched subtlety and clarity.

T. THOMAS FORTUNE
    (Journalism   18)
    Born: 1856, Mariana, Florida
    Died: 1928
    Education: Stanton School; Howard
        University, Washington, D.C.
    Significance: *Editor and publisher*

After the Civil War, Thomas Fortune's father was active in Reconstruction politics. Thomas went to New York in 1879 and worked in the composing room of the *Weekly Witness.* He became editor of *The Rumor,* which was later called the *New York Globe.* Although influential, the paper suspended publication in 1884. He then became editor and publisher of the New York *Freeman.* Fortune was one of the first Negroes on the editorial staff of a white daily, the *New York Evening Sun.* Later he

published the *New York Age* until 1905, when
he sold his interest. He joined the staff of Booker
T. Washington's National Negro Business
League. Eventually he broke with the league,
but continued to write articles.

JOHN HOPE FRANKLIN
  (History 7)
  Born: 1915, Rentiesville, Oklahoma
  Education: A.B., Fisk University,
    Nashville, Tennessee; M.A., and
    Ph.D., Harvard University,
    Cambridge, Massachusetts
  Significance: *Historian of the*
    Reconstruction Period
John Hope Franklin has taught at the North
Carolina College at Durham, Howard University, Brooklyn College, and the University of
Chicago. Franklin is one of the leading Reconstruction revisionist historians. He followed W.
E. B. DuBois' example in *Black Reconstruction*
in reevaluating the social position and political
performance of the post-Civil War southern Negro. In 1943 he published his study of the status
of the Negro in North Carolina in pre-Civil War
times, *The Free Negro in North Carolina.* His
other works are: *From Slavery to Freedom*
(1947), *The Militant South* (1956), *Reconstruction After the Civil War* (1961), and *The Emancipation Proclamation* (1963). Dr. Franklin, an
eminent contemporary scholar, is Chairman of
History Department at the University of
Chicago.

E. FRANKLIN FRAZIER
  (History, Sociology 7, 23)
  Born: 1894, Baltimore, Maryland
  Died: 1962
  Education: Howard University,
    Washington, D.C.; University of
    Chicago, Illinois
  Significance: *Writer and teacher*
E. Franklin Frazier taught in the sociology
department of Howard University and occa-
sionally at Columbia University. He was a Gug-
genheim Fellow in 1940–41, president of the
American Sociological Society in 1948, and ex-
pert on race for UNESCO. He is best known for

his book, *Black Bourgeoisie.* His *The Negro in
the United States* was first published in 1949
and in a revised edition in 1957. Of this book
Dr. Louis Wirth of the University of Chicago
wrote in his preface:

The present study treats the Negro in his
interaction with the larger American society
of which he is a part. Professor Frazier has
adopted a broad sociological perspective and
has found that by portraying the experiences
of the Negro in the context of his own community and institutions and the more inclu-
sive American community and its
institutions, it is possible to reveal with
greater realism and balance the actual life of
the Negro and of America . . . A mature or-
dering and integration of the most important
work that has been done so far to provide
understanding of the life of the Negro people
in America and of minorities on the road to
integration. The emphasis . . . is not upon the
formulation of broad social policies but upon
the meticulous analysis of social processes
. . . (He furnishes us) with an authentic and
richly documented account of our record so
far.

Frazier has also written *The Negro Church
in America* and *Race and Culture Contacts in
the Modern World.*

After the Harlem riots of 1935, an interracial
Committee on Conditions in Harlem was appointed by Mayor LaGuardia. This Committee,
which Frazier headed, studied the causes of the
riot and concluded that the lawlessness was provoked by "resentments against racial discrimination and poverty in the midst of plenty."

DEBORAH GANNET
  (Military 49)
  Significance: *Soldier throughout the*
    Revolutionary War
Deborah Gannet of Massachusetts was anxious to help America gain its independence from
the British. Accordingly, when the call went out
for "all able-bodied men to come to the aid of
their country," she signed up. She disguised herself as a man and joined a Massachusetts regi-

ment under the name of Robert Shurtliff. She exhibited extraordinary heroism and served throughout the war without revealing her sex. When the war was over and won, Deborah applied to the Massachusetts legislature for military compensation as a consideration for her service. She was granted a retroactive pension of thirty-four pounds a year. Deborah Gannet was cited for discharging the duty of a "faithful gallant soldier, and at the same time preserving the virtue and chastity of her sex, unsuspected and unblemished," and was honorably discharged from the service.

MIFFLIN WISTER GIBBS
(Law   36)
Born: 1823, Philadelphia, Pennsylvania
Died: ca. 1901
Education: Oberlin College, Ohio
Significance: *Newspaper publisher and diplomat*
Mifflin Gibbs began as a bootblack in San Francisco, but later became one of the publishers of *Mirror of the Times,* the first Negro newspaper in California.

He moved to Victoria, British Columbia, where he studied law. Then he moved to Little Rock, Arkansas. He also worked with Frederick Douglass in the anti-slavery movement. He was elected a judge and later became U.S. Consul to Madagascar from 1897 to 1901.

ALTHEA GIBSON
(Tennis   46)
Born: 1927, Silver, South Carolina
Education: Florida Agricultural and Mechanical College, Tallahassee, Florida
Significance: *Tennis champion*
Althea Gibson, raised in Harlem, won the Department of Parks Manhattan Girls' Tennis Championship while still in elementary school. She first received professional coaching in 1942 at the interracial Cosmopolitan Club and the following year won the New York State Negro girls' singles title. In 1948 she graduated to the Women's Division which she dominated for the next ten years.

At Florida A&M University in Tallahassee (1949–53) she played tennis and basketball for four years. In 1950 she became the first Negro to play at Forest Hills, and the next year the first Negro to play at Wimbledon. In 1957 she won the Wimbledon singles crown, receiving a hero's welcome upon her return to New York. Retired from tennis she has married, been engaged in public relations work in industry, and undertaken a career in professional golf.

DIZZY GILLESPIE
(Jazz   46)
Education: Lauringburg Institute, North Carolina
Significance: *Jazz musician*
John Birks Gillespie, whose father was a musician, was a scholarship student at Lauringburg Institute in North Carolina, where he studied trombone, trumpet, and music theory. He played with the Teddy Hill, Cab Calloway, and Mercer Ellington big bands in the late thirties. With his own bands and small groups in the forties, Gillespie, in company with Charlie Parker and Thelonius Monk, led the revolution in jazz called bop. A showman as well as a consummate technician, Gillespie played Carnegie Hall—that almost obligatory symbol of respectability achieved—and, often under State Department aegis, he has toured Europe, the Middle East, Africa, and Latin America.

SHIRLEY GRAHAM
(Music, Literature   46)
Born: 1904, Indianapolis, Indiana
Education: A.B., M.S., Oberlin College, Ohio; Sorbonne, France
Significance: *Author and composer*
While she was in college, Shirley Graham wrote and composed the musical play, *Tom-Tom,* in 1932. After studying composition at the Sorbonne, she returned to America to teach first at Morgan State and later at Tennessee State University. While associated with the Chicago Federal Theater, she designed, directed, and composed the music for *Little Black Sambo* (1937), and *The Swing Mikado* (1938). Her play, *Dust to Earth,* was produced at the

Yale School of Drama in 1941 when she was there as a Rosenwald fellow. She held a Guggenheim grant in 1947. She also won the Julian Messner Award and the Anisfield Wolf Prize. Three of her biographical histories are *Dust to Earth, There Was Once A Slave,* and *Your Most Humble Servant.*

LORENZO JOHNSTON GREENE
  (History   32)
  Born: 1899, Ansonia, Connecticut
  Education: B.A., Howard University,
    Washington, D.C.; M.A., Ph.D.,
    Columbia University, New York
  Significance: *Authority on the history of
    the Negro people in Colonial America*
Lorenzo Johnston Greene began his academic career as assistant to Carter G. Woodson, aiding in the collection of materials for *The Negro Wage Earner* (1932). In 1933 he went to Lincoln University in Jefferson City, Missouri, as an instructor in history. His authoritative study of the early history of the Negro in the United States, *The Negro in Colonial New England, 1620–1776,* was published in 1942. Since then he has published frequently in scholarly journals. He edited the *Midwest Journal* and was president of the Association for the Study of Negro Life and History.

DICK GREGORY
  (Entertainment   46)
  Born: 1932, St. Louis, Missouri
  Education: Southern Illinois University,
    Carbondale, Illinois
  Significance: *Comedian and civil rights
    advocate*
Dick Gregory won the Missouri state championship in the mile run in 1951 and again in 1952. He secured a track scholarship to Southern Illinois University, where he was named the outstanding athlete in 1953. He left college for the Army where he served in the Special Services and performed as a comedian. After his discharge he reenrolled at SIU and worked at odd jobs in Chicago until 1960 while trying to establish himself as a professional comedian. A television appearance and a fill-in in 1961 at the Chicago Playboy Club led to national recognition. Gregory was among that small group of comics whose introduction of racial and political material found a large and enthusiastic public in the early sixties.

Gregory lent his name and his resources to the civil rights movement, and in recent years has tended to prefer the college platform to the nightclub stage as a forum for the message he conveys. He has published several books, among them his autobiography, *Nigger* (1964).

PRINCE HALL
  (Community Service   32)
  Born: 1735, Barbados, British West
    Indies
  Died: 1807
  Significance: *Civil rights leader*
Prince Hall organized the first Masonic lodge among Negroes in America. In 1775 he and a group of free Negroes in Boston were inducted into the Masons, and in 1787 they obtained a charter from the English Grand Lodge as African Lodge No. 459, with Hall as master. In succeeding years an African Grand Lodge was organized and lodges were established in Philadelphia and Rhode Island. After Hall's death the name of the national organization was changed to the Prince Hall Grand Lodge.

Hall was born in Barbados and moved to Boston in 1765, where he eventually established himself as a property holder, a Methodist minister, and a leader of the small community of free Negroes. In the Revolution he successfully petitioned to join the American armies, which had originally refused to enlist Negroes. Always an abolitionist and defender of the rights of Negroes, Hall petitioned the Massachusetts legislature to support the cause of emancipation, led a successful effort to get the city of Boston to provide schools for Negro children, and campaigned for protection of free Negroes from being kidnapped into slavery.

W. C. HANDY
  (Music   31, 46)
  Born: 1873, Florence, Alabama
  Died: 1958

Education: Kentucky Musical College
Significance: *"Father of the Blues"*

W. C. Handy was a cornettist and band leader in the 1890's, but he is most famous as a music publisher and songwriter, largely in the blues form. He thought of his hard times and composed accordingly, including symphony pieces. He said, "Life is like this trumpet; if you don't put anything in it, you don't get anything out of it." He owned the Pace and Handy Music Company in Memphis, Tennessee. His most famous compositions are "St. Louis Woman," "Careless Love," "Beale Street Blues," and "Memphis Blues."

LORRAINE HANSBERRY
    (Literature   46)
    Born: 1930, Chicago, Illinois
    Died: 1965
    Education: Chicago Art Institute, Illinois;
        University of Wisconsin, Madison,
        Wisconsin; Guadalajara, Mexico
    Significance: *Playwright*

Lorraine Hansberry was interested in theater in high school. She studied art at various institutions. While living in Greenwich Village she wrote *Raisin in the Sun,* as a reaction against the Negro stereotype. It opened on Broadway in 1959, a time not propitious for productions with Negro themes. The show was produced, directed, and acted by Negroes. Later it was translated and performed abroad, and eventually became a motion picture starring Sidney Poitier. Her play, *The Sign in Sidney Brustein's Window,* is an example of integration in the arts. She was one of only ten Negro playwrights in thirty-five years to have works produced on Broadway, and one of only two with more than one production.

RICHARD B. HARRISON
    (Acting   46)
    Born: 1864, Canada
    Died: 1935
    Significance: *Actor and dramatic reader*

Richard B. Harrison moved to Detroit as a boy and worked as a waiter, porter, and handyman, attending the theater as often as possible.

He studied drama in Detroit and he made his professional debut in Canada. For thirty years, Harrison entertained Negro audiences with dramatic readings from Shakespeare, Poe, Kipling, and Paul Laurence Dunbar. He was on the faculty of North Carolina Agricultural and Technical State College in 1929 when he was chosen for the part of "De Lawd" in *Green Pastures.* Harrison performed as "De Lawd" 1,656 times. He won the 1930 Spingarn Medal and was awarded several honorary degrees.

WILLIAM H. HASTIE
    (Law, Government   32)
    Born: 1904, Knoxville, Tennessee
    Education: Amherst College,
        Massachusetts; J.D., Harvard
        University Cambridge, Massachusetts
    Significance: *Judicial and governmental
        service*

William H. Hastie was the first Negro appointed to the federal bench (1937) and has served with distinction as judge of the Third U.S. Circuit Court of Appeals since 1949.

Hastie left private practice in 1933 to become assistant solicitor in the Department of Interior. He impressed Interior Secretary Harold Ickes, and in 1937 he was appointed to the U.S. District Court for the Virgin Islands. In 1939 he became dean of the Howard University Law School, where his former law partner, Charles H. Houston, was engaged in a major improvement program.

Hastie took a leave of absence (1940) from his academic duties to serve as a civilian aide in the War Department, charged with overseeing policy with regard to Negro servicemen. Hastie resigned in 1942, frustrated in attempts to accelerate integration of the armed forces. He was named Governor of the Virgin Islands in 1946, moving from there to the appeals court.

COLEMAN HAWKINS
    (Jazz   46)
    Born: 1904, St. Joseph, Missouri
    Died: 1969
    Education: Washburn College, Topeka,
        Kansas

Significance: *Jazz saxophonist*

Coleman Hawkins innovated the use of the tenor saxophone in American jazz. He learned to play the saxophone when he was nine, having already studied piano and cello. He toured with Mamie Smith's Jazz Hounds in 1922 and in 1923 joined Fletcher Henderson's band. He was with Henderson for ten years and toured Europe for five years. He returned to the United States in 1939, organized his own band, and recorded his first and biggest commercial hit, "Body and Soul."

Hawkins was more receptive than many of his contemporaries to the bop experimentation of the forties and offered support and encouragement to Dizzie Gillespie and Charlie Parker and other "boppers." He was still winning Downbeat and Playboy polls in the early sixties, and with the rise of the soul sound, his warm full style won him a new generation of admirers.

BOB HAYES

> (Track, Football   46)
> Born: 1942, Jacksonville, Florida
> Education: Florida Agricultural and
>   Mechanical College, Tallahassee,
>   Florida
> Significance: *Track champion and*
>   *professional football player*

Bob Hayes is one of professional football's most dazzling performers as a split end and flanker back for the Dallas Cowboys of the National Football League. Hayes still holds three world sprint records and has been labeled "the world's fastest human." At the 1964 Olympics in Tokyo, Hayes won two gold medals in sprint competitions. He first captured the national track spotlight in 1961 by equalling the then world record of 9.3 seconds for the 100-yard dash. Two years later, he set a new record (9.1 seconds) for this distance at the National AAU championships in St. Louis, Missouri.

ROLAND HAYES

> (Music   1, 46)
> Born: 1887, Curryville, Georgia
> Education: Fisk University, Nashville,
>   Tennessee

Significance: *Concert artist*

Roland Hayes's early concert successes broadened the opportunities available to other Negro singers such as Paul Robeson and Marian Anderson. Hayes said of his early years, "It was as natural for me to sing as to breathe." He chanced to hear some recordings by the great tenor Caruso and from that moment he determined to become a professional singer.

Hayes was born of former slave parents. After his father's death his mother kept the family together. The Hayes children were sent to school in rotation—one worked while the others studied. Roland attended the Fisk University's preparatory department, while working as a servant and appearing in concerts. He left a tour with the Fisk Jubilee Singers in Boston and remained there to study voice. By 1916 he was ready for concert bookings and with little encouragement, he undertook his own management and soon achieved success.

He was the first Negro to give a recital in Boston's Symphony Hall (1917). While in Europe he gave a command performance before George V. There followed a highly successful European tour, and his blend of folk songs, spirituals, operatic arias, and lieder soon became a staple of concert stages in the United States and abroad. After achieving financial success, Hayes insisted on low admission prices so that the poor of all races could hear him. His farewell concert (1962) at Carnegie Hall in New York on his 75th birthday was the pinnacle of a grand career.

LEMUEL HAYNES

> (Religion, Military   1, 32)
> Born: 1753, West Hartford, Connecticut
> Died: 1833
> Education: Studied theology, Greek and
>   Latin
> Significance: *Early American Christian*
>   *leader*

Lemuel Haynes was ordained a Congregational minister in 1780 and was pastor to white congregations in various parts of New England. Haynes was also one of several Negroes at Lexington and Concord and accompanied Ethan Allen at the capture of Fort Ticonderoga.

Haynes was abandoned in infancy and grew up in the home of Deacon David Rose of Granville, Massachusetts. Rose was nearly blind and he assigned his young servant the task of reading to the family on Saturday evenings from the sermons of noted clerics. Once Haynes surprised the deacon by reading an excellent sermon he had written himself. The incident led to private instruction in Latin and Greek and his eventual ordination. His second pastorate was in the leading church of Torrington, Connecticut, where the power of his oratory overcame the disgruntlement of some members. He subsequently served other white congregations in New England, including churches in Manchester, Vermont, and Granville, New York. He took an active part in the "Great Awakening" of religion in America at the turn of the century and preached many revival sermons for both the Vermont and Connecticut Missionary Societies.

JAMES AUGUSTINE HEALY

(Religion, Education   1)
Born: 1830, Macon, Georgia
Died: 1900
Education: Franklin Park Quaker School, Burlington, New York; Holy Cross College, Washington, D.C.
Significance: *Leadership in the Catholic Church*

Bishop James Augustine Healy, the mulatto son of a Georgia planter and his household servant, was the first Catholic bishop of African descent in the United States. For twenty-five years, Bishop Healy presided over the diocese of Maine and New Hampshire. Under him sixty-eight mission stations, eighteen parochial schools and fifty church buildings were erected. The number of Catholic communicants more than doubled. The Church recognized Bishop Healy's work by making him Assistant to the Papal Throne, a rank just below that of Cardinal.

Bishop Healy had received the best possible training for his post. For over a decade he was assistant to Bishop John Fitzpatrick of Boston,

who had appointed him chancellor and "deputized him to handle most of the routine business of the diocese. This included keeping the bishop's account books, taking care of the official correspondence with other bishops, with the sixty-one priests of the diocese, with the many seminarians in American and foreign seminaries and with the religious orders of men and women working in the diocese."

Bishop Healy had been pastor of St. James Church on Boston's southeast end amidst the Irish where he performed his office during the various epidemics of typhoid, pneumonia and tuberculosis. The Boston Irish were at first reluctant to accept him but eventually overcame their reservations and came to recognize him as a true priest.

(From Russell L. Adams, *Great Negroes Past and Present.* Chicago: Afro-Am Publishing Co., Inc., 1967.)

JOSIAH HENSON

(Civil Rights   32)
Born: 1789, Maryland
Died: 1883
Education: Taught to read by one of his own sons
Significance: *Agent for the Underground Railroad*

Josiah Henson's life is presumed to have been the model for Harriet Beecher Stowe's *Uncle Tom's Cabin,* and Miss Stowe wrote an introduction for an 1858 edition of Henson's autobiography, originally published in 1849.

Henson was born in Maryland; both his parents were sold when he was a child. After many years of well-behaved servitude, he was entrusted with delivering other slaves to Kentucky, and he remained there for three years. In Kentucky he attempted to purchase his freedom, but learned that he was to be sold to New Orleans instead. Thereupon he escaped to Ohio and then to Canada with his wife and two children. Once free, he became an active and ardent abolitionist. He was an agent of the Underground Railroad, helped to found the British-American Manual Labor Institute of Canada, and traveled to England on at least three occasions in support of the abolitionist cause. The narrative of his life, in various editions and under several titles, eventually sold well over 100,000 copies.

MATTHEW ALEXANDER HENSON
   (Exploration   1, 29, 49)
   Born: ca. 1867, Charles County,
     Maryland
   Died: 1955
   Education: Only several years of formal
     education
   Significance: *Explorer with Admiral
     Peary*

Matthew Henson was born on a farm in Charles County, Maryland. He was orphaned early and at the age of eleven ran away from his stepmother, going to Washington where he became a dishwasher. He then became a cabin boy at thirteen on the ship, *Katie Hines.* The Captain encouraged him to read, write and to study navigation.

While working at a naval supply shop in New York City, Henson met Robert Peary, a naval engineer. Henson and Peary developed a close friendship. Henson became Peary's right-hand man on geographical expeditions to Central America and Greenland for the United States Navy. He had an unusual capacity to understand and appreciate new and different ideas and was a person who learned easily to do the variety of work needed on an expedition. Henson developed knowledge of all aspects of navigation. He overhauled and stored supplies, rearranged sledges, traded with Eskimos, did carpentry, made sledges, and built igloos. He lived with Eskimos and learned their language and way of life. One winter their ship was locked on ice at the Russian harbor of Murmansk. Henson learned Russian, hunted wolves, and learned how to drive sleighs. He became an expert on the Arctic, its winds and weather.

Between the ages of twenty-five and forty-two, Henson maintained the mutual goal with Peary of reaching the North Pole, making seven unsuccessful attempts. Between expeditions, Peary lectured widely while Henson became a consultant to the American Museum of Natural History in New York on Arctic geography. One of his duties was to mount Arctic animals true to their natural habitat of the far North. In 1908, Peary and Henson set out for what they felt would be their last trip. Peary determined the precise point of the Pole, and on April 7, asked Henson to place the American flag on the spot. He was then the first man to set foot on the North Pole.

Henson was decorated by Congress and received a gold medal from the Chicago Geographical Society. A building on the campus at Dillard University in New Orleans is named for him. On April 6, 1954, Henson received the last of his many decorations on the 45th anniversary of the discovery of the North Pole. The presentation was made by President Eisenhower at the White House. He had married in 1907 and had adopted an orphan boy, Kudlooktoo. He lived to be 88 and died in New York City.

JULIUS HAMINGTON HOLDER
   (Community Service   51)
   Born: 1917, Port of Spain, Trinidad,
     West Indies
   Education: State University of New
     York; Harvard University School of
     Design, Cambridge, Massachusetts;
     A.B., Benedict College, South Carolina
   Significance: *City planner*

Julius Holder came to the United States in 1921 and was naturalized in 1925. He went to high school in New York City with further education in drafting and design, in landscape and ornamental horticulture, and in landscape design. He has held positions in planning for the City of Ventura and for the Counties of San Luis Obispo and of San Mateo, all in California.

In 1967 Holder was responsible for writing the first phase program for a master plan for the Los Angeles shoreline. His present position is with the Urban Village Corporation in Los Angeles, a non-profit organization in research and development of cooperative housing for low income people. A resident of Santa Barbara, California, Holder is a member of the Santa Barbara Housing Authority, and is on the vestry (governing board) of Trinity Episcopal Church in Santa Barbara.

BILLIE HOLIDAY
(Jazz   46)
Born: 1915, Baltimore, Maryland
Died: 1959
Significance: *Jazz singer*
Billie Holiday ("Lady Day") wrote "I've been told that nobody sings the word 'hunger' like I do. Or the word 'love.' Maybe I remember what those words are all about. Maybe I'm proud enough to *want* to remember Baltimore and Welfare Island, the Catholic Institution and the Jefferson Court Market, the sheriff in front of our place in Harlem and the towns where I got my lumps and scars."

Billie Holiday commenced her singing career in 1929 at the age of 15 in Harlem night clubs. Her reputation was established in the thirties and her unique gift was demonstrated in the classic "Strange Fruit" and the evocative "God Bless the Child," which expressed the depth of her personal alienation.

Her later life was scarred by drug addiction and frequent bouts with the law. Her autobiography relates the agony of her addiction and the effects of drugs and alcohol, ". . . all they can do is kill you . . . the long, slow, hard way." She died in Metropolitan Hospital in New York City.

JEROME HEARTWELL HOLLAND
(Diplomacy, Education   51)
Born: 1916, Auburn, New York
Education: B.S., M.S., Ph.D., Cornell
    University, Ithaca, New York
Significance: *Educator and diplomat*
Jerome Holland was the son of a domestic-gardener-handyman in Auburn, New York, one of thirteen children. He began working for his father at the age of eight and soon learned that education was the most available escape from poverty. He worked his way through Cornell with honor grades. Whatever discrimination he suffered, he is not anxious to discuss it. A husky six-footer, he was twice an All-American end at Cornell and was elected in 1965 to the Football Hall of Fame.

Dr. Holland was an instructor in sociology and physical education at Lincoln University from 1939 to 1942. He then spent a number of years in personnel work and in 1947 became Professor of Sociology at Tennessee Agricultural and Industrial College in Nashville, Tennessee. In 1960 he became president of Hampton Institute in Virginia. In January, 1970, he was appointed United States Ambassador to Sweden. He is chairman of the board of Planned Parenthood-World Population of Greater New York. He is the author of *Black Opportunity* (1969).

JOHN HOPE
(Education   1, 32)
Born: 1868, Augusta, Georgia
Died: 1936
Education: Worcester Academy,
    Massachusetts; M.A., Brown
    University, Providence, Rhode Island
Significance: *Higher-education system leader*
John Hope began his teaching career at the Roger Williams University in Nashville. He was then transferred by the American Baptist Home Mission Society to the Atlanta Baptist College, or Morehouse College, as a teacher of Latin and Greek. He became the assistant to the president and, upon the resignation of Dr. George Sale in 1906, was appointed acting president, and a year later, president.

As early as 1904, in an article published in *Voice of the Negro,* Hope voiced his concern over the number of schools trying to operate in Atlanta as separate units. His dream of bringing these colleges—Morehouse, Spelman, Clark, Morris Brown, and Gammon Theological Seminary—into a unified system of education in Atlanta was partially realized in 1929. Morehouse, Spelman, and Atlanta University agreed to affiliate and function as members of the Atlanta University system. Each college kept its own administration, but facilities were shared. Atlanta University became the center of graduate study, while Spelman and Morehouse concentrated on developing excellent undergraduate training. Later, Clark University and Morris Brown became affiliated.

John Hope, along with W. E. B. DuBois, objected to the philosophy of compromise of Booker T. Washington. He became one of the most active supporters of the National Association for the Advancement of Colored People. He served on the Commission on Interracial Cooperation and the Georgia State Council of Work among Negro Boys. He was also an active member of the Association for the Study of Negro Life and History, serving as one of its officials. In 1929, he received the Harmon Award in education. He was awarded the Spingarn Medal, posthumously, in 1936.

LENA HORNE

(Acting, Music 46)

Born: 1917, Brooklyn, New York

Significance: *Stage, motion picture, television performer, and career in singing*

Lena Horne began her career in the Cotton Club chorus line in 1933. She worked as a dancer with Noble Sissle and as a singer with Charlie Barnett. She went to Hollywood where she was the first Negro woman ever to sign a term contract in motion pictures. Among her films are *Cabin in the Sky, Stormy Weather* (both, 1943), and *Meet Me in Las Vegas* (1956). In 1957 she starred in the musical *Jamaica,* which innovated interracial casts in Broadway shows. Her most popular recordings are "Stormy Weather," "The Lady is a Tramp," and "Mad About the Boy."

LANGSTON HUGHES

(Literature 48)

Born: 1902, Joplin, Missouri

Died: 1967

Education: Lincoln University; Columbia University, New York

Significance: *Black poet laureate of our age*

Langston Hughes' early life was spent in Kansas with his mother, where he was influenced by the theater and his grandmother's stories. He discovered books in Cleveland and was encouraged by Effie Power at the public library. At Central High he was on the track team and the honor rolls, and also wrote for *The Belfry Owl,* the school newspaper. While spending summers with his father in Mexico, he tutored wealthy families in English. He was encouraged by Carter Woodson, in whose office in Washington, D.C. he worked, and by Vachel Lindsay, the poet. At various times he worked as bus boy, clerk, cafe bouncer and office boy. He lived in Haiti, Mexico, France, Italy, and Russia.

With Countee Cullen, he became one of the "twin stars" of the Harlem Renaissance. He was the recipient of many prizes and honors including the Witter Bynner prize (1926), a Guggenheim Fellowship (1935), a Rosenwald Fellowship (1941), a grant from the American Academy of Arts and Letters (1947), the Anisfield-Wolf Award (1953), the Spingarn Medal (1960), and the Catholic Dove Award at Cannes.

Hughes was awarded honorary doctorates in literature from Howard University and Western Reserve University.

He wrote a weekly column for *The New York Post,* using a literary spokesman called "Jesse B. Simple," later the basis of five prose volumes. He lectured at many schools and colleges. Although famous in the 1920's, he was not supported by his writings until after 1930. He remained a very prolific and versatile writer of prose and poetry, fiction and non-fiction. He wrote for young people as well as adults. Not only did he write for the theater himself, but he provided lyrics for William Still, Elmer Rice, Meyerowitz, and Kurt Weill. His plays were translated and performed abroad, and his poetry was translated into nineteen languages and dialects. His works included *Ask Your Mama* (poetry); *Not Without Laughter* (novel); *Scottsboro Limited* (play); and *The Story of the Negro* (non-fiction).

EARLE HYMAN

(Acting 7, 46)

Born: 1926, North Carolina

Significance: *Shakespearean actor*

Earle Hyman has appeared in several Broadway productions and over 100 television programs. He was also with the American Shakespeare Festival at Stratford, Connecticut, for five years. He made a trip to Europe in 1957 and was charmed by Norway. He returned to America determined to learn Norwegian and to that end studied Shakespeare in translation, especially the role of Othello. The director of the national theater in Bergen, Norway, invited him to play Othello there. He accepted and enjoyed a substantial success, returning two years later to do *Emperor Jones.*

Hyman is the third foreigner and first American honorary member of the Society of Norwegian Artists. A bust of him in the role of Othello stands in the Bergen theater.

BOSE IKARD

(Ranching   16)

Born: 1847, Noxubee County, Mississippi

Died: 1929

Significance: *Pioneering cowboy*

Bose Ikard was born to slavery and brought to Texas with the Ikard family when he was five years old. There he learned to farm, manage cattle, and fight Indians. In 1866, Oliver Loving, a pioneer cattlemen, took him on the trail. He helped break the Goodnight-Loving trail and rode it for four years, finally returning to Texas with Goodnight in 1889 where he bought a farm. Goodnight said of him that he "surpassed any man I had in endurance and stamina. There was a dignity, a cleanliness and reliability about him that was wonderful." He also said of Ikard: "He was my detective, banker and everything else in Colorado, New Mexico and the other wild country we traveled together . . . he was the most skilled and the most trustworthy man I ever knew."

Ikard is buried at Weatherford, Texas, under a marker: "Served with me four years on the Goodnight-Loving Trail, never shirked a duty or disobeyed an order, rode with me in many stampedes, participated in three engagements with Comanches, splendid behavior. C. Goodnight."

Some say that Bose Ikard was the greatest trail hand who ever lived.

JESSE JACKSON

(Civil Rights   37)

Born: 1942, Greenville, South Carolina

Education: University of Illinois, Urbana, Illinois; North Carolina Agricultural and Technical State University, Greensboro, North Carolina; Chicago Theological Seminary, Illinois

Significance: *Ministry and Civil Rights leadership*

Reverend Jesse Jackson at the age of twenty-seven was probably the most powerful Negro in Chicago. He is not a complex personality, but he seems to have several personalities which fit together loosely as if events have come too quickly and fame crowded too closely. He is a new breed of Baptist minister, "the most secular that walks." In 1963 he criticized the strategy and slow pace of protest marchers in Greensboro and was challenged to do better. Almost daily for a month he led marches, followed by picketing and sit-ins. He succeeded in desegregating downtown Greensboro, North Carolina, and gained statewide recognition for the achievement. He became president of the North Carolina Intercollegiate Council of Human Rights.

MAHALIA JACKSON

(Music   46)

Born: 1911, New Orleans, Louisiana

Died: 1972

Significance: *Gospel singer*

Mahalia Jackson, the outstanding gospel singer of our day, as a child had to sneak away from her religious household to hear Bessie Smith at a New Orleans theater. At 16 she went to Chicago to sing in churches and to work as a hotel maid until she saved enough to open her own beauty shop. She made her first record in 1934, but her 1945 hit, "Move On Up a Little Higher," brought her national fame. Within a few years, she acquired an international following; a successful Carnegie Hall concert in 1950 was followed by a European tour in 1952. In

1958 she recorded "Black, Brown, and Beige" with Duke Ellington. She was a favorite of many foreign chiefs of state, was received by the Pope, and sang several times for Presidents Kennedy and Johnson.

She expanded her musical repertoire, initially limited to gospel, but continued to insist that she was not a jazz singer. Her billing, "The World's Greatest Gospel Singer," was entirely justified.

WALLER JACKSON
    (Exploration   7, 27)
    Born: ca. 1800, Boston, Massachusetts
    Significance: *First Negro miner in California*

Waller Jackson came to California from Boston via the Horn. He became a miner at Downieville, California. He was a servant on John C. Fremont's fourth expedition. Gold was discovered on Fremont land, and Jackson was permitted to mine enough for the $1,700 needed to buy his family out of slavery. He then returned to Missouri and disappeared from history.

LAWRENCE JOEL
    (Military   16)
    Born: ca. 1926, Winston-Salem, North Carolina
    Significance: *Congressional Medal of Honor winner*

Lawrence Joel, an army medic, Specialist 6, was shot twice as he treated wounded men of a platoon that had been ambushed by Viet Cong near Bien Hoa in November, 1965. Joel, a high school dropout, had been raised by a foster family from the age of eight. He already had a long military career behind him when he went to Vietnam at the age of thirty-nine. He was the first black in Vietnam to win the Congressional Medal of Honor for an action that he survived.

Joel acknowledged, as any honest soldier would, that he was "afraid" when his platoon of the 503rd Infantry, 173rd Airborne Brigade, was pinned down by the enemy on a routine search-and-destroy mission. When the firing began, he wasn't even sure who the targets were, but, taking no chances, he ducked behind a small rock.

"Soon it got real quiet," Joel said, "I could hear men holler 'Medic' all around. I was afraid to go out there and some other men said, 'We'll go out and get them for you.' But I knew that was my job. I made a dash to reach one man and got shot in the leg."

During twenty-four hours that followed his initial wound, he was shot a second time and saw twelve men of his forty-man unit killed and fifteen wounded. Throughout the long and deadly night Joel crawled over the battlefield, patching up wounds, administering plasma and morphine, and applying mouth-to-mouth resuscitation without ever being quite sure whether his patient was dead or alive. His legs swelled as his own wounds went unattended, and, although his pain was almost more than he could bear, he gave himself only one shot of morphine for fear that any more of the drug would render him incapable of caring for his buddies. He was among the last to be evacuated the following day.

Joel was embarrassed when the president presented him with the Medal of Honor and called him a very brave soldier with "a special kind of courage." Joel responded modestly to all the attention he had received, saying, "I do not wear this medal for Lawrence Joel. I wear it for every American and for all the soldiers who died."

(From Phillip T. Drotning, *Black Heroes in our Nation's History.* © Phillip T. Drotning. Reprinted by permission of Doubleday & Company, Inc.)

CHARLES SPURGEON JOHNSON
    (Government, Education   10, 11, 32)
    Born: 1893, Bristol, Virginia
    Died: 1956
    Education: B.A., Virginia Union University, Richmond, Virginia;
        Ph.D., University of Chicago, Illinois
    Significance: *Government service*

Charles Spurgeon Johnson, after serving as an enlisted man in World War I, joined the Chicago Commission on Race Relations, and in

1921 became director of the National Urban League in New York. His first book, *Negro in Chicago* (1922), has been acclaimed as a landmark in social research. In 1923 he founded *Opportunity,* the Urban League's journal of Negro Life. His association with Fisk University began in 1928, when he became Director of the Department of Social Science and Professor of Sociology, and later President.

Johnson held many distinguished positions, among them the director of racial relations of the Julius Rosenwald Fund. He was a member of a three-man League of Nations commission sent to Liberia to investigate charges of slavery. After World War II, he became a member of the educational mission sent to Japan by the U.S. Department of State at the request of General Douglas MacArthur. Later in 1946, President Truman appointed him delegate to UNESCO for its first meeting in Paris. Johnson authored *Shadow of the Plantation* (1934), *Growing up in the Black Belt* (1941), *Patterns of Negro Segregation* (1943), *To Stem This Tide;* and *Into the Mainstream: Best Practices in Race Relations in the South* (1947).

HENRY JOHNSON
   (Military   16, 46)
   Born: 1897
   Died: 1929
   Significance: *World War I hero*

Henry Johnson was a member of the all-Negro 369th Infantry Regiment, the first American Negro unit under fire in World War I. He was awarded the French Croix de Guerre for repelling a German patrol, an incident emblazoned across the front pages of American newspapers as "Henry Johnson's War." The regimental colors were also decorated with the Croix de Guerre for action in the Champagne region in 1918.

JACK JOHNSON
   (Boxing   12, 46)
   Born: 1878, Galveston, Texas
   Died: 1946
   Significance: *First Negro heavyweight champion*

John Arthur Johnson won the heavyweight championship from Tommy Burns in Sydney, Australia, in 1908. There had been Negro champions in the lower divisions before that date, and Tom Molineaux had fought unsuccessfully for the heavyweight championship almost a full century earlier, but the white world had never before been confronted with the symbolic fact of a black heavyweight champion of the world. Immediately there was a public clamor for a capable white challenger—a "White Hope." James J. Jeffries, the undefeated former champion, was lured out of retirement and met Johnson in Reno, Nevada in 1910. Johnson knocked him out in fifteen rounds.

Johnson's win over Jeffries was a racial victory. Negroes celebrated; segments of the white society were outraged by Johnson's defiance of traditional racial roles and moral conventions.

Johnson's only subsequent fight in the United States was stopped by the police. He was convicted under the Mann Act and fled to Europe in 1913. Johnson earned more than $600,000 in his career, but, dogged by controversy, unable to get respectable fights, and unwilling to give up the fast life he was used to, he was a poor man when he signed to meet Jess Willard in Havana, Cuba, in 1915 for $30,000. He lost the bout and his title by a knockout in twenty-six rounds. In 1931, at 53, he returned briefly to the ring for a barnstorming tour of the United States.

JAMES WELDON JOHNSON
   (Literature, Civil Rights   48)
   Born, 1871, Jacksonville, Florida
   Died: 1938
   Education: B.A., Atlanta University,
      Georgia; M.A., Columbia University,
      New York
   Significance: *Teacher, author and
      diplomat*

James Johnson passed a comfortable childhood in Florida. He taught in Negro rural schools during the summer to earn money for his own education. The first Negro to pass a written examination for the bar, he practiced law and taught school. After moving to New

York, he wrote musical comedies with his brother and was professor of Creative Literature at Fisk University. He became editor of *The Daily American,* the first Negro daily in America. He also edited *New York Age* and ran a popular column in it for ten years. In 1922, he published the anthology, *Book of American Negro Poetry.*

After writing about the United States Marines in Haiti, Johnson made the United States occupation a campaign issue. His essays on the roots of Negro literature and music came out in the 1920's. Having joined the NAACP in 1916, he became its field secretary (1916-1920), and executive secretary (1920-1930). He worked to pass the Dyer Anti-Lynching Bill in 1921. Active in politics, a supporter of Teddy Roosevelt, he fought "lily-white" primaries. He served as consul to Nicaragua and Venezuela. At Fisk University, the Adam K. Spence Chair of Creative Literature was established for him. He was awarded the Spingarn Medal in 1925. Johnson was the author of *The Autobiography of an Ex-Colored Man* (fiction).

JOHN HAROLD JOHNSON
(Journalism 1)
Born: 1918, Arkansas City, Arkansas
Education: University of Chicago,
    Illinois; Northwestern University,
    Evanston, Illinois
Significance: *Successful magazine
    publisher*
John Johnson was brought to Chicago by his mother in 1937. In high school he became editor of the school paper and yearbook, and president of the student council. While attending college he worked for a life insurance company. In 1942, he started the *Negro Digest* on a $500.00 loan. He became the founder, president, publisher and editor of the Johnson Publishing Company. Its publications, *Ebony, Jet, Negro Digest,* and *Tan,* have combined circulation of almost two million. Mostly through *Ebony,* he is responsible for the growing employment of Negro models in the advertising media. *Jet* is one of the most successful small magazines in the country. The company moved into hard

cover books in 1963 by publishing works of authors discovered by or connected with Johnson publications. *Negro Digest,* which uses white contributors, became famous with a series by Eleanor Roosevelt, "If I Were a Negro."

JOSHUA JOHNSON
(Painting 12)
Born: 18th Century
Significance: *Earliest known Negro
    portrait painter*
Joshua Johnson, in 18th century Maryland, was a Negro artist. He painted portraits of many of the rich white people of the state. These paintings were characterized by a kind of decorativeness often seen in rococco and baroque paintings. An oil, "Mrs. Andrew Beckford Bankson and Child" done about 1780, shows mother and daughter bedecked with jewels, sedately poised on what might have been a piece of Sheraton furniture. Johnson's painting is considered outstanding in American primitive art.
(From Marion E. Brown, "The Negro in the Fine Arts," in *The American Negro Reference Book,* John P. Davis, ed. © 1966 Prentice-Hall, Inc. Reprinted with permission of the publisher.)

MALVIN GRAY JOHNSON
(Painting 1)
Born: 1896, Greensboro, North Carolina
Died: 1934
Education: New York Academy of
    Design
Significance: *Symbolic abstractionist
    painter*
Malvin Gray Johnson ranks high in the estimation of historians of the Negro in art. In *The Negro in American Culture,* Margaret Just Butcher declared that some of his works are among the most significant commentaries on the American Negro scene. Alain Locke felt that Johnson caught better than most artists the sardonic humor and mystical pathos in the moods of the Negro. In interpretative paintings such as "Swing Low, Sweet Chariot" and "Roll, Jordan, Roll," Johnson attempted to treat the spirituals in terms of abstract symbolism. These

and similar works were regarded as technical advances in the handling of Negro thematic material. During the last years of his life Johnson turned to genre subjects, painting a brilliant series of watercolors of urban and rural Negroes. "Dixie Madonna," "Ruby," "Brothers," "Red Road," and "Convict Labor," all works from his final period, are believed to be typical of his best efforts.

Johnson's work was shown in several of the Harmon Exhibits in 1929 and the early thirties. In 1931, the Anderson Gallery displayed some of his work. He won the Otto H. Kahn prize for painting in 1929.

(From Russell L. Adams, *Great Negroes Past and Present.* Chicago: Afro-Am Publising Co., Inc., 1967.)

MORDECAI WYETH JOHNSON
  (Education, Oratory   1)
  Born: 1890, Columbus, Tennessee
  Education: A.B., Morehouse College,
    Atlanta, Georgia; M.S.T., Harvard
    University, Cambridge, Massachusetts;
    D.D., Gammon Theological Seminary,
    Atlanta University Center, Georgia
  Significance: *University president*

Mordecai Johnson, as president of Howard University in Washington, D.C., became a near-legendary figure in his own lifetime. Under Dr. Johnson, Howard University, which was founded in 1867 in an abandoned dance hall and beer saloon, changed from a cluster of second-rate departments to nationally approved units of distinction. The school of law is pre-eminent in the area of civil rights. Johnson's oratorical ability won him acclaim even while in high school and was quite evident at Morehouse and Harvard, where in 1922 he attracted national attention with a commencement speech entitled "The Faith of the American Negro."

Before assuming the presidency of Howard University in 1926, Dr. Johnson had been a successful Baptist minister in Charleston, West Virginia. Prior to this he had taught economics and history at his alma mater, Morehouse College. He had also served as student secretary with the national office of the Young Men's Christian Association.

When Dr. Johnson came to the University at the age of thirty-six, many people questioned his ability. When he retired thirty years later, he was acknowledged as the great president of the school. The faculty had tripled; salaries had doubled. Congressional appropriations which support the school had increased to $6,000,000 annually. Freedmen's Hospital was turning out half of the Negro physicians in the country. The University's physical plant was valued at $34,000,000.

Dr. Johnson was active in numerous religious and governmental bodies, including a presidential commission for the study and review of conditions in Haiti and the Virgin Islands. He was a member of the Advisory Council of the National Youth Administration and a member of the National Advisory Council on Education.

In addition to many honorary degrees, Dr. Johnson is one of the few Negroes who has won the Spingarn Medal (1929) for his contribution to the progress of the Negro during the previous year.

(From Russell L. Adams, *Great Negroes Past and Present.* Chicago: Afro-Am Publishing Co., Inc., 1967)

RAFER JOHNSON
  (Track   46)
  Born: 1935, Hillsboro, Texas
  Education: University of California, Los
    Angeles
  Significance: *Olympic gold medal winner*

Rafer Johnson holds the Olympic record (set in 1960) for points scored in the decathlon, considered to be the toughest test of all-around athletic ability in the world of sports. Johnson competed in his first decathlon in 1954, while attending the University of California at Los Angeles, where he was also president of the student body.

In spite of a knee injury in the 1956 Olympics at Melbourne, Australia, Johnson competed in the event, and finished second to Milt Campbell, another American Negro who was the first of his race to win an Olympic decathlon. Competing in Moscow in 1958, Johnson shattered the world record with a total of 8,302 points. Two years later, at the Olympics in Rome, Johnson won the decathlon gold medal with 8,392 points.

CLARA JONES

    (Library Science   38)
    Born: 1913, St. Louis, Missouri
    Education: B.A., Spelman College,
      Atlanta, Georgia; University of
      Michigan, Ann Arbor, Michigan
    Significance: *Leadership in library service*

Mrs. Clara Jones, Director of the Detroit Public Library, has had library experience at Atlanta University, Dillard University in New Orleans, and Southern University Library in Baton Rouge, Louisiana. At Baton Rouge she taught prospective school librarians. In Detroit, her first assignment was as a children's librarian, and then as adult librarian in Home Reading. Following this, she was young adult librarian in a public branch library, chief of division in charge of three branches, and department chief of a department at a single branch. Late in 1968, she was assigned as library neighborhood consultant, with the mission of establishing and improving communications with the library's public.

In February, 1970, Mrs. Jones was appointed director of the Detroit Public Library, the first woman and also the first black person to be appointed to this position.

JAMES EARL JONES

    (Acting   46)
    Born: 1931, Tate County, Mississippi
    Education: B.A., University of Michigan,
      Ann Arbor, Michigan
    Significance: *Actor*

James Earl Jones' triumph in the film and stage presentations of *The Great White Hope,* followed more than a decade of work in a broad range of the New York theater and in movie roles. After finishing college and service in the Army, Jones received his diploma at the American Theater Wing in 1957 and appeared in the

off-Broadway production of *Wedding in Japan* in the same year. He subsequently appeared in some 20 stage productions, Shakespearean, modern, and avant-garde, and on television and in movies. He won an Obie in 1962 for his work off-Broadway and a Tony in 1969 for *Great White Hope.*

JOHN JONES

    (Business   32)
    Born: 1817, North Carolina
    Died: 1879
    Significance: *Abolitionist Movement
      Leader*

John Jones was born free and learned to read and write while serving an apprenticeship in tailoring. He and his wife moved to Chicago in 1845, and he opened a tailor shop which he built into a thriving and profitable business. The money he earned was used to finance an attack on Illinois' "Black Laws." His reform efforts continued through the Civil War; he served two terms on the Cook County Board of Commissioners and was instrumental in abolishing segregation in the Chicago schools.

JOHN JONES

    (Business   5)
    Born: 1829, Lexington, Kentucky
    Died: 1881
    Significance: *San Francisco port steward*

John Jones moved to Palmyra, Missouri, at the age of six, living there until he was sixteen. He studied as much as he could, but the opportunity for education was meager. In 1846, at the beginning of the Mexican-American War, he went with the army to Mexico. He returned in 1847 to St. Louis and worked on a river steamer. In the fall of 1849, he went to Sacramento. He became a steward in a club in San Francisco. Senator Broderick took him to Washington as his valet and confidential servant. In 1855, Jones was given stewardship of a steamer going from San Francisco to Sacramento. Later he became port steward of a fleet of ships. He worked for the abolition of colored schools in the State of California. He was elected captain of the Brannan Guards, a soldier company. Jones was noted for his oratory.

LE ROI JONES

(Literature   4)
Born: 1934, Newark, New Jersey
Education: A.B., Howard University,
    Washington, D.C.; Rutgers University,
    New Brunswick, New Jersey;
    Columbia University, New York
Significance: *Poet, author, and playwright*

Le Roi Jones traveled in Africa, the Middle East, and Europe during two years with the Strategic Air Command. He taught poetry and writing at The New School and was a lecturer on theater arts at Columbia. He founded and directed the Black Arts Repertory Theater and School in Harlem, and later The Spirit House Movers and Players, to promote consciousness of black culture. He has written on jazz for *Downbeat, Metronome, Jazz* and *Jazz Review.* His poetry has been published in *Nation, Poetry, Harper's,* and the *Negro Digest,* and his articles in *Negro Digest* and *Evergreen Review.*

He has done editorial work on many publication. He was editor of *The Moderns* (1963) and *Four Young Lady Poets* (1962). He is the author of *Dutchman* (1963), *Black Art* (1966) and co-editor of *Black Fire* (1968).

VIRGINIA LACY JONES

(Education, Library Science   32)
Born: 1912, Cincinnati, Ohio
Education: Hampton Institute, Virginia;
    M.S., University of Illinois, Urbana,
    Illinois; Ph.D., University of Chicago,
    Illinois
Significance: *Leader in library science*

Virginia Lacy Jones attended the University of Illinois as a General Education Board fellow. On becoming a librarian, she worked at Louisville Municipal College in Kentucky, Hampton Institute in Virginia, and Prairie View State College in Texas. At Atlanta University she served first as cataloger and then as director of the School of Library Service.

Dr. Jones has published two books, *U.S. Government Publications on the American Negro, 1916-1937* and *Problems of Negro Public School Library Service in Selected Southern Cities,* and many articles.

PERCY JULIAN

(Physical Science   17, 53)
Born: 1898
Education: A.B., DePauw University,
    Indiana; A.M., Harvard University,
    Cambridge, Massachusetts; Ph.D.,
    University of Vienna
Significance: *Scientific research*

Percy Julian has been awarded twelve honorary degrees and an impressive list of scholarships and fellowships. He is a member of Phi Beta Kappa and Sigma Xi honor societies and a trustee of five universities. From 1936 to 1953 he was director of research for the Soya Products Division of the Glidden Company. From 1953 to 1964 he was president of the Julian Laboratories in Chicago. He perfected a soya protein for use in coating paper. In 1935, he synthesized a drug used in the treatment of glaucoma. His research includes work on indoles, amino acids, and the soybean. The method he perfected eventually lowered the cost of sterols from which cortisone is derived, thus enabling millions of people suffering from arthritis to obtain relief at a price within their means.

ERNEST E. JUST

(Life Science   7)
Born: 1883, Charleston, South Carolina
Died: 1941
Education: A.B., Dartmouth College,
    New Hampshire; University of
    Chicago, Illinois
Significance: *Biological research*

Ernest E. Just was educated in the public schools for Negroes in Orangeburg, South Carolina. He worked his way to New York in 1900 and was accepted at Kimball Academy. After graduation from Dartmouth with high honors, he became professor of zoology at Howard University, Washington, D.C., where he remained the rest of his life. He was awarded the first Spingarn Medal by the N.A.A.C.P. in

1915. His important treatises on chromosome makeup in animals and cellular theory gave him a considerable academic reputation. He has published papers on experiments with protoplasm showing how living cells take up and hold water. Dr. Just also conducted research in marine biology for the United States Government at Woods Hole, Massachusetts. He was the author of *General Cytology* (1924), *Biology of the Cell Surface* (1939), and *Basic Methods for Experiments on Eggs of Marine Animals* (1939).

CORETTA (SCOTT) KING
(Civil Rights, Music   35)
Born: ca. 1930, Heiberge, Alabama
Education: B.A., Antioch College, Ohio; New England Conservatory of Music, Boston, Massachusetts
Significance: *Humanitarian work and leadership in civil rights*

Coretta Scott King was born on her grandfather's farm outside Marion, Alabama. She and her elder sister, Edythe, became active in music while attending Lincoln High School, a school for all black students with an integrated faculty, in Marion, Alabama. Edythe was accepted by Antioch College, Yellow Springs, Ohio, as the first black student to attend on a completely integrated basis. Coretta, too, attended Antioch College, where she majored in elementary education and began to study music seriously. In 1951 she enrolled in the New England Conservatory of Music in Boston. While there, she met Martin Luther King, Jr. They were married by his father in Marion, Alabama on June 18, 1953.

In 1964, Mrs. King began to give freedom concerts as a fund raising effort for the Southern Christian Leadership Conference (SCLC), an organization in which she has become very active since her husband's death. In 1969, she was given honorary degrees by Boston University and Marymount Manhattan College. She also received the Antonio Telsrinelli Prize for humanitarian work given by the Italian Academia del Linci. In March of 1969, she became the first woman to speak at a regular service in St. Paul's Cathedral in London. She was in England to visit the organizers of the Martin Luther King Foundation which works for racial understanding in Britain.

MARTIN LUTHER KING, JR.
(Religion, Civil Rights   12)
Born: 1929, Atlanta, Georgia
Died: 1968
Education: B.A., Morehouse College, Atlanta, Georgia; B.D., Crozer Theological Seminary, Chester Pennsylvania; Ph.D., Boston University, Massachusetts
Significance: *Civil rights leader, Nobel Prize winner*

Dr. Martin Luther King, Jr. organized the Southern Christian Leadership Conference (SCLC) in 1957. He was awarded the Nobel Prize in 1964. In the spring of 1968 he was assassinated. In his dozen years before his death he was a dominant figure in the Afro Americans' struggle for equality.

He was named outstanding member of his graduating class at Crozer and won the J. Lewis Crozer fellowship for his subsequent study. He accepted his first pastorate at the Dexter Avenue Baptist Church in Montgomery, Alabama, and there his name first reached the headlines in connection with the year-long bus boycott in 1956. As president of the Montgomery Improvement Association, which coordinated the boycott, Dr. King convened a meeting of Southern Negro leaders which resulted in the formation of the SCLC, of which he also became president. The SCLC remained the organizational vehicle for Dr. King's leadership of the movement of nonviolent direct mass action for civil rights.

In 1960 he became co-pastor, with his father, of Ebenezer Baptist Church in Atlanta, where the SCLC was headquartered. In succeeding years he inspired, coordinated, led, directed, and advocated nonviolent demonstrations throughout the South—supporting fair hiring practices, political equity, and desegregation of public facilities. His "I have a dream" speech was the centerpiece of the 1963 March on Washington. It symbolized King's national constituency and the movement he personified.

The establishment of Operation Breadbasket in Chicago (1966) conceptually and geographically broadened Dr. King's crusade. The Negroes' economic disabilities in the United States eventually occupied a central place in the Black struggle and King's efforts moved beyond the boundaries of the South. He was killed in Memphis, Tennessee, where he had come to support the demands of striking sanitation workers.

ELIZABETH DUNCAN KOONTZ

(Education, Government   32)

Born: 1919, Salisbury, North Carolina

Education: B.S., Livingstone College, North Carolina; M.A., Atlanta University, Georgia; Columbia University, New York; University of Indiana, Bloomington, Indiana; North Carolina College, Durham, North Carolina

Significance: *Educational leader*

Elizabeth Duncan Koontz was the first Negro president of the National Education Association (NEA) and since 1969 has been director of the Women's Bureau in the Labor Department and delegate to the United Nations Commission on the Status of Women. She taught in the schools of Landis, Winston-Salem, and Salisbury, North Carolina. She served two terms as president of the local teachers association, and was president of the North Carolina Association of Classroom Teachers (1958-62), president of the NEA classroom teachers department (1965-66), and NEA national vice-president (1967-68) before her election to the presidency for the year 1968-69.

DAVID LAMSON

(Military   16)

Significance: *Revolutionary war leader*

David Lamson was chosen by a group of old men who had been left in Menotomy, Massachusetts, to lead the capture of a British supply train on April 19, 1775. Lamson was a mulatto who had served in the French and Indian War of 1754-1763 and a man of bravery and determination. He placed his old men behind a bank of earth and stones. As the wagon trains appeared, he ordered his men to their feet, took aim at the horses, and ordered the grenadiers to surrender. When the British whipped up their horses, Lamson's men opened fire. Several men and horses were killed. Thus the black veteran and his elderly army had captured the first British troops and the first supplies in the American Revolution. Later, Lamson tramped off at Washington's call for service to help drive the British from Boston with the capture of Dorchester Heights in March of 1776.

LEWIS HOWARD LATIMER

(Invention, Engineering   34)

Born: 1848, Chelsea, Massachusetts

Died: 1928

Significance: *Pioneering electrical inventions*

Lewis Latimer, born of a poor family in Boston in 1848, sold copies of Garrison's *The Liberator* on the streets to help support his family and also to further the cause of emancipation. When he was sixteen, he joined the United States Navy serving aboard the U.S.S. *Massasoit* during the Civil War. After the war, he began work as an office boy in a Boston company of patent lawyers. He rose to the position of chief draftsman for the firm.

Sometime around 1876, Latimer met Alexander Graham Bell. It was Latimer who executed the drawings and assisted in preparing the applications for Bell's telephone patents. Later he joined the United States Electric Lighting Company at Bridgeport, Connecticut. With the noted Hiram S. Maxim, he invented an incandescent electric light and supervised the building of manufacturing plants in New York, Philadelphia, and Canada.

From 1884 he worked for Thomas Edison. He was a member of the Edison Pioneers, a group of people who had worked with Edison before 1885. In 1890, he wrote a book, explaining the use and workings of the electric light. He was the company's star witness in patent cases that reached the courts. When he died in 1928, the Edison Pioneers published a statement in which they outlined his life, saying:

He was of the colored race, the only one in our organization ... Broadmindedness, versatility in the accomplishment of things intellectual and cultural, a linguist, a devoted husband and father, all were characteristic of him and his genial presence will be missed from our gatherings.

HUDDIE LEDBETTER
(Music   46, 7)
Born: 1888, Mooringsport, Louisiana
Died: 1949
Significance: *Contributor to the world of folk music*

Huddie Ledbetter (Leadbelly) was the self-educated son of a former slave. He grew up in Texas where he learned to play accordion and guitar. He served seven years for murder in the twenties and was again jailed for attempted homicide in the early thirties. After his parole in 1934 he was discovered by folklorist Alan Lomax, who took him north to appear in concerts and to record for the Library of Congress. Among his best known songs are "Good Night, Irene" and "On Top of Old Smoky." His musical interpretations helped spark worldwide interest in American folk music.

JAMES LEWIS
(Government   1)
Born: 1832, Wilkinson County, Mississippi
Significance: *Military and governmental service*

James Lewis is one of the least known and appreciated figures who achieved prominence in Louisiana during the Reconstruction. At various times, he was Surveyor-General for New Orleans; a colonel in the Second Regiment of the State Militia; collector for the New Orleans Port; a naval officer; and superintendent of the United States Bonded Warehouse in New Orleans. He was also administrator of police and administrator of public improvements for New Orleans.

At the outbreak of the Civil War, he was serving as steward aboard a Confederate ship; on hearing of the Emancipation Proclamation,

Lewis jumped ship and made his way to New Orleans, which had just fallen into the hands of the Union. Lewis persuaded the commanding officer to allow him to raise two companies of colored volunteers.

In 1864 Lewis resigned his commission and joined the Freedman's Bureau as a traveling agent, setting up schools for ex-slaves. This work turned out to be more dangerous than soldiering. He was appointed to the post of United States Inspector of Customs, making him the first Negro in Louisiana to hold a Federal appointive office.

He was appointed Colonel of the Second Regiment of the State Militia in 1870. In the same year, he was elected administrator of police and shortly afterwards, administrator of public improvement for New Orleans. The latter post was regarded as one of the most important in the city government.

JULIAN LEWIS
(Medicine   3)
Born: 1891
Education: Ph.D., University of Chicago, Illinois; M.D., Rush Medical College, Chicago, Illinois
Significance: *Medical research*

Dr. Julian Lewis has had a distinguished career as a pathologist and physician. From 1927 to 1945, he was associate professor of pathology at the University of Chicago. He was director of research at Provident Hospital, in Chicago (1945-1952), and since 1952, pathologist at St. Catherine Hospital, in East Chicago, Indiana, and at St. Margaret Hospital, in Hammond, Indiana. He had a Guggenheim fellowship for study at Basel, Switzerland in 1926-27. Dr. Lewis was the recipient of the Rickett's prize in 1915 and the Benjamin Rush medal in 1917. His fields of research are immunity and cancer.

ALAIN LEROY LOCKE
(Literature   1)
Born: 1886, Philadelphia, Pennsylvania
Died: 1954
Education: A.B., Harvard University; Ph.D., Oxford University, England

Significance: *Author and the first black Rhodes Scholar*

Alain Leroy Locke, after returning to the United States from Oxford in 1912, was engaged to teach philosophy and education at Howard University, becoming a full professor in 1917. He served in this capacity through 1953. He also taught at Fisk University in 1927; the University of Wisconsin from 1945 to 1946; the New School of Social Research in 1947; and the College of the City of New York in 1948. He was an Inter-American exchange professor to Haiti in 1943. Dr. Locke was a leading participant in the Harlem Renaissance. His writing is original in a controversial field. He tended to spend himself in encouraging others. His best work, *The Negro in American Culture,* was finished after his death by Margaret Butcher in 1956.

RAYFORD LOGAN
   (History   9, 26)
   Born: ca. 1915, Washington, D.C.
   Education: A.B., Williams College, Massachusetts; Ph.D., Harvard University, Cambridge, Massachusetts
   Significance: *Civil rights leader*

Rayford Logan became a professor of history at Howard University in 1938. He edited *What the Negro Wants* in 1944. He was also the editor of the *Journal of Negro History,* and author of *Diplomatic Relations of the United States with Haiti* (1941), *The Negro and the Post-War World* (1945), and *The Negro in American Life and Thought: The Nadir, 1877-1901* (1954). This last volume places race relations in a national rather than a regional context. At one time, Dr. Logan was consultant to the Coordinator of Inter-American Affairs. He also served as consultant to the NAACP in fighting segregation cases. He was a co-drafter of the anti-discrimination bill in the Selective Service Act. In 1965, he wrote *Betrayal of the Negro.*

LOUIS EMANUEL LOMAX
   (Journalism   46)
   Born: 1922, Valdosta, Georgia
   Died: 1970
   Education: Paine College, Augusta, Georgia; American University, Washington, D.C.; Yale University, New Haven, Connecticut
   Significance: *Author and journalist*

Louis Lomax was a newspaperman from 1941 to 1958. From 1958 to 1969, he was a newscaster for WNTA-TV and freelance writer. Many of his published articles have received recognition. He was the author of *The Reluctant African* (1960), and *The Negro Revolt* (1962). In 1961, he received the Anisfield-Wolf Award.

JOE LOUIS
   (Boxing   46)
   Born: 1914, Chambers County, Alabama
   Significance: *Heavyweight boxing champion*

Joe Louis was the world heavyweight champion for nearly twelve years, from 1937 to 1949. He defended his title in twenty-five fights— more than all of the eight champions who preceded him.

His parents were sharecroppers in Alabama, but Louis grew up in Detroit. He won fifty out of fifty-nine amateur bouts (forty-three knockouts) before turning professional in 1934. He fought former champion Primo Carnera in 1935 and knocked him out in six rounds.

Louis won a split decision from Jersey Joe Walcott in 1947 and knocked him out in a rematch in 1948, then announced his retirement. He later lost to Ezzard Charles and to Rocky Marciano.

JOHN R. LYNCH
   (Government   1)
   Born: 1847, Concordia Parish, Louisiana
   Died: 1939
   Significance: *United States Congressman during Reconstruction*

John R. Lynch was one of the few Negro Congressmen during the Reconstruction era to be elected three times to Congress from Mississippi as a Republican. Lynch was elected to the 43rd, 44th, and 47th Congresses but served only two full terms. His last election to the 47th Congress in 1877, the end of the Reconstruction era, was contested, and he was not allowed to take his seat. There is some belief that the state defrauded him of his rightful term.

Nevertheless, Lynch remained active in public life. He was chairman of the Mississippi Republican State Executive Committee from 1881 to 1889, and near the close of his political career, was appointed fourth auditor of the Treasury in the Navy. In 1898, he was appointed as paymaster in the regular army and served until his retirement in 1911.

The success of Lynch's self-education can be seen in the following excerpt from a speech made after the Civil War in which he stresses the patriotism of the Negro:

> They were faithful and true to you there; they are no less so today. And yet they ask no special protection as a race. They feel that they purchased their inheritance, when upon the battlefields of their country, they watered the tree of liberty with the precious blood that flowed from their loyal veins. They ask no favors, they desire and must have, an equal chance in the race of life.

(From Russell L. Adams, *Great Negroes Past and Present.* Chicago: Afro-Am Publishing Co., Inc., 1967.)

JACKIE (MOMS) MABLEY

(Entertainment 56)

Born: ca. 1900, North Carolina

Significance: *Comedienne*

Jackie (Moms) Mabley was born Loretta Mary Aiken in North Carolina. She entered show business as a teenager with the team of Buck and Bubbles. She developed her own comic character, a world-weary old woman in funny hat and droopy stockings. Her routine is a mixture of sass, folk wisdom, and sly insight.

After almost fifty years as a favorite of Negro audiences, she caught the attention of a broader public and her first record album, "Moms Mabley at the U. N.," was a commercial success. It was followed by "Moms Mabley at the Geneva Conference" and others.

THURGOOD MARSHALL

(Law 42)

Born: 1908, Baltimore, Maryland

Education: Lincoln University, Chester, Pennsylvania; Howard University Law School, Washington, D.C.

Significance: *Member of the United States Supreme Court*

Thurgood Marshall's mother was a teacher and his father a dining car waiter on the Boston and Ohio Railroad. One of his school experiences was with an all-white faculty with an all-black student body. His application for the law school at the University of Maryland was rejected on the basis of color. After law school at Howard University, he joined a firm in Baltimore where he specialized in civil rights cases. He won a "breakthrough" in educational segregation when he defended a Negro who, like Marshall, had been refused admission to the University of Maryland Law School.

In 1935, he was asked to become a lawyer for the NAACP under the chief counsel, Charles Houston, who had been dean of the Law School at Howard University when Marshall was a student there. When Houston went into private practice, Marshall succeeded him and a year later became director-counsel of the NAACP Legal Defense and Educational Fund. Marshall was not primarily a Negro spokesman but a constitutional lawyer. He felt it was now his duty to make the Supreme Court reflect the real America in a series of civil rights cases involving the "equal protection" clause of the 14th Amendment. For some years, the NAACP filed a suit every time a Negro was denied an education available to whites. In 1945, the NAACP decided that segregation should be their main target. They began with cases in the graduate schools. In 1950, two successful cases resulted in more than a thousand black students' being admitted to white graduate schools.

Then came the cases that originated from suits in four states—Kansas, South Carolina, Virginia and Delaware—that bear collectively the name of Oliver Brown, the father of an eight-year-old girl who was not permitted to attend an elementary school in Topeka within five blocks of her home because it was reserved for white students. She had to walk a long route through railroad yards in order to take a bus to a Negro school twenty-one blocks away. Brown and the parents of the other aggrieved black children asked the courts to enjoin the states from continuing school segregation. In three of the states, the federal courts refused. Thus the stage was set for appeals of all cases to the Supreme Court of the United States. Marshall had to demonstrate that segregated education, no matter how designed and how expensive, was basically unequal. To do this, he brought in a group of psychologists to provide evidence of the effects upon children of forced isolation in a segregated community in which the segregated school was the worst offender. After prolonged hearings and further study, the Supreme Court unanimously agreed that "separate educational facilities are inherently unequal."

In 1961, Marshall was appointed to a federal judgeship. Four years later, President Johnson asked him to take the job of Solicitor General, third-ranking position in the Department of Justice, with a cut in salary and tenure at the President's pleasure instead of for life. He was the government's chief appellate lawyer before the Supreme Court. Two years later, he was appointed to the Supreme Court to fill the vacancy caused by the resignation of Tom C. Clark. He was confirmed by an overwhelming majority of the Judiciary Committee and finally by the whole Senate.

JAN ERNEST MATZELIGER
    (Invention   25)
    Born: 1852, Paramaribo, Surinam or
        Dutch Guiana
    Died: 1889
    Significance: *Inventor of shoe
        manufacturing equipment*
The shoe-lasting machine invented by Jan Matzeliger, a Negro from Surinam, revolutionized the shoe industry and made Lynn, Massachusetts, the "shoe capital of the world."

Matzeliger found employment in the government machine works of Surinam at the age of ten. Eight years later, he migrated to the United States, settling at first in Philadelphia, where he worked in a shoe factory and learned the trade. He then left for New England, settling permanently in Lynn.

The Industrial Revolution had resulted in the invention of a number of machines to cut, sew, and tack shoes, but none had been perfected to last a shoe. Seeing this, Matzeliger lost little time in designing and patenting just such a device. Matzeliger's patent was subsequently bought by Sydney W. Winslow who established the United Shoe Company, a multimillion dollar concern. The continued success of this business brought about a fifty percent reduction in the price of shoes across the nation, doubled wages, and improved working conditions for millions of people dependent on the shoe industry for their livelihood. After his death in 1889, Matzeliger was awarded a gold medal by the Pan-American Exposition of 1901. There is a statue of him in Lynn.

DOROTHY MAYNOR
    (Music   46)
    Born: 1910, Norfolk, Virginia
    Education: Hampton Institute, Virginia;
        B. Mus., Westminister Choir College,
        Princeton, New Jersey
    Significance: *Leading concert singer*
Dorothy Maynor made her debut to critical acclaim at New York's Town Hall in 1939. Since then, she has appeared as a soloist with almost every major orchestra in the United States and has made concert tours in Europe, Canada, and Latin America. After graduating from college in 1935, she studied voice in New York. For four years she directed a choir and taught before she felt ready for her New York debut. She received support from Serge Koussevitzky, conductor of the Boston Symphony Orchestra. Miss Maynor has made several recordings for RCA Victor and has been a guest artist on both radio and television.

WILLIE MAYS
    (Baseball   46)
    Born: 1931, Fairfield, Alabama
    Significance: *Baseball player*

Willie Mays entered professional baseball in 1948 with the Birmingham Black Barons, his father's team. He signed with the N.Y. Giants in 1950, and was brought up to the major leagues in 1951, when he was National League's Rookie of the Year. After serving two years in the Army he returned to the Giants and led them to the world championship in 1954. He was the National League's Most Valuable Player that year, with 41 home runs and a batting average of .345. After the Giants moved to San Francisco, Mays continued his phenomenal hitting and led his team to a pennant in 1962. His exploits in the field are no less remarkable than his strong and timely hitting, and in 1963 *Sport* magazine named him "the greatest player of the decade."

ELIJAH McCOY
(Invention   46, 7)
Born: 1884, Canada
Died: 1928
Significance: *Inventor of automatic lubricating devices*
In 1872 Elijah McCoy moved from Canada to Ypsilanti, Michigan, where he worked as an inventor. He was granted numerous patents during his lifetime, most of them relating to lubricating appliances for machinery. Perhaps his most useful device was the "drip cup," which regulated the flow of lubricant to moving parts of heavy machinery, making it unnecessary to stop a machine to oil it.

The expression "the real McCoy" came from his inventions for lubricating railroad cars; without the "McCoy" mark on them devices for lubricating were considered incomplete. He also devised inventions related to telegraphy and electricity.

HATTIE McDANIEL
(Acting   46)
Born: 1898, Wichita, Kansas
Died: 1952
Significance: *First Negro to win an Oscar*
In 1931, Hattie McDaniel had made her way to Hollywood. After a slow start, during which time she supported herself as a maid and washer woman, she gradually began to get more and more movie roles. She received the Academy of Motion Picture Arts and Science's 1940 award for the year's best supporting actress in *Gone With the Wind* for her portrayal of a "mammy."

DORIE MILLER
(Military   46)
Born: 1919, near Waco, Texas
Died: 1943
Education: High School
Significance: *World War II hero*
Dorie Miller was a messman aboard the U.S.S. *Arizona* when the Japanese attacked Pearl Harbor. He manned a machine gun and brought down four of the attacking planes. He remained a messman and was killed in the South Pacific in December of 1943. He was awarded the Navy Cross and commended for "distinguished devotion to duty, extreme courage, and disregard of his personal safety during the attack."

ARTHUR W. MITCHELL
(Politics   46)
Born: 1883, Chamber County, Alabama
Education: Columbia University, New York; Harvard University, Cambridge, Massachusetts
Significance: *Civil rights leader*
The 1934 victory of Arthur W. Mitchell, the first Negro Democrat ever elected to Congress, symbolized a major shift in the pattern of Negro voting sentiment in the United States which had persisted from Reconstruction. Oscar DePriest, the man whom he defeated, was the last Negro Republican to serve in the House.

By 1939, Mitchell founded Armstrong Agricultural School in West Butler, Alabama, and he had become a wealthy landowner and a lawyer, with a thriving practice in Washington, D.C. When he left the nation's capital that year, it was with the avowed purpose of entering politics and becoming a representative from Illinois.

Mitchell's most significant victory on behalf of civil rights came, not in the legislative chamber, but in the courts. In 1937, he had brought suit against the Chicago and Rock Island Railroad after having been forced to leave his first-class accommodations en route to Hot Springs, Arkansas, and sit in a "Jim Crow" car. He argued his own case before the Supreme Court in 1941, and won a decision which declared Jim Crow practices illegal.

GEORGE F. MONROE

(Postal Service   27)

Significance: *Pony Express rider and stagecoach driver*

George Monroe was a Pony Express rider from Merced to Mariposa, California. From 1868 to 1886, he drove stagecoaches to Yosemite Valley. An expert driver, he was chosen to drive President U. S. Grant into Yosemite Valley in 1879. Monroe Meadow in Yosemite National Park is named for him.

SCIPIO MOOREHEAD

(Painting   7, 12)

Born: 18th century

Significance: *Colonial artist*

Scipio Moorehead is said to be the first formally trained Negro artist in colonial America. His known work was inspired by the classics. This inspiration resulted in two paintings. One of them was a work based on the legend of Damon and Pythias. The other, a painting entitled "Aurora," inspired the poetess Phillis Wheatly to write a poem entitled "To S. M., A Young African Painter, on Seeing His Works."

(From Marion E. Brown, "The Negro in the Fine Arts," in *The American Negro Reference Book,* John P. Davis, ed. © 1966 by Prentice-Hall, Inc. Reprinted with permission of the publisher.)

GARRETT MORGAN

(Invention   46)

Born: 1877, Paris, Kentucky

Died: 1963

Significance: *Inventor of gas inhalator, automatic stop sign*

Garrett Morgan sold his first invention, an improvement on the sewing machine, for $150.00. His reputation was made by his invention of a gas inhalator. The value of his invention was first recognized during a successful rescue operation at the site of a tunnel explosion that trapped several men in the Cleveland Waterworks some 200 feet below the surface of Lake Erie. Morgan, his brother, and two other men wearing inhalators descended into the smoke- and gas-filled tunnel and saved several of the men from asphyxiation. Orders for the Morgan inhalator soon began to pour into Cleveland from fire companies all over the nation. During World War I, the inhalator was transformed into a gas mask used by combat troops.

Having established his reputation with the gas inhalator, Morgan was able in 1923 to command a price of $40,000 from the General Electric Company for his automatic traffic signals.

E. FREDERICK MORROW

(Government, Finance   46)

Born: 1909, Hackensack, New Jersey

Education: Bowdoin College, Brunswick, Maine; Law School, Rutgers University, New Brunswick, New Jersey

Significance: *Political, economics and banking leader*

E. Frederick Morrow was working on the public affairs staff of the Columbia Broadcasting System when he joined General Eisenhower's presidential campaign staff in 1952. He became adviser on business affairs to the Secretary of Commerce and worked in close liaison with Congress from 1953 to 1955. In 1955 President Eisenhower appointed him an Administrative Assistant, the first Negro on the White House staff.

Morrow had earlier been business manager for the National Urban League's official journal, subsequently became field secretary for the National Association for the Advancement of Colored People, and served as a Major in the Army during World War II. When the Eisenhower Administration left office, Morrow became vice-president of the African-American Institute, whose function is to improve American economic and cultural relations with the nations of Africa. Later, he became an assistant vice-president with the Bank of America. He is the author of *Black Man in the White House* (1963).

FERDINAND MORTON

(Jazz   46)
Born: 1885
Died: 1941
Significance: *Jazz soloist, composer and arranger*

Ferdinand (Jelly Roll) Morton was a pianist in New Orleans from 1902 and lived in California from 1917 to 1922. With a band called "Morton's Red Hot Peppers," between 1926 and 1930 he cut a series of records which brought him nationwide fame. Among the many controversial aspects of Morton's life was his claim that he had "invented jazz in 1901." When jazz fashions changed in the 1930's, Morton's popularity declined. In 1938, he made a number of recordings for the Library of Congress, playing and singing and narrating the major incidents of his life and career.

CONSTANCE BAKER MOTLEY

(Law, Civil Rights   46)
Born: Connecticut
Education: Columbia University Law School, New York
Significance: *Judicial service*

Constance Baker Motley was appointed by President Johnson to the United States District Court for Southern New York, the nation's first Negro woman federal judge.

While still a law student at Columbia University, Mrs. Motley began working with the NAACP Legal Defense and Education Fund, beginning an association that was to make her famous as a defender of civil rights. After receiving her law degree, she became an associate counsel for the NAACP.

WILLARD MOTLEY

(Literature   46)
Born: 1912, Chicago, Illinois
Died: 1965
Significance: *Novelist*

Willard Motley grew up in a middle-class Chicago neighborhood. Most of his books deal with poverty rather than race. It was not known professionally that he was a Negro.

He is the author of *Knock on Any Door,* a book on juvenile delinquency made into a film starring Humphrey Bogart and *We Fished All Night* (1951), a book dealing with the impact of World War II on youth. *Let No Man Write My Epitaph,* a sequel to his first book, was also filmed. His last book, *Let Noon Be Fair* (1966), was published a year after his death in Mexico City.

HUGH NATHANIEL MULZAC

(Merchant Marine   49)
Born: 1886, British West Indies
Education: Swansea Nautical College, South Wales
Significance: *First Negro to become captain of a U.S. Merchant Marine Liberty Ship*

Hugh Mulzac was still in his teens when he signed up for his first sea voyage. At twenty-five, he came to the United States and became a citizen. He studied navigation and wireless techniques in New York at the Shipping Board School and earned his second mate's license for both steam and sailing vessels. In World War I, he carried war materiel to the Allies and in 1920 received his master's papers from the steamboat inspectors. As there were few opportunities for Negroes at that time, he took any work available. In 1922, he became captain of a ship of Marcus Garvey's Black Star Line.

At the beginning of World War II, Mulzac helped ship war materiel to the British in Egypt since he could not get an assignment from the United States Shipping Administration because of his color. After pressure from a Negro organization and the passage of President Roosevelt's Fair Employment Practices Act, Mulzac became the captain of a Liberty ship, the *Booker T. Washington,* launched in California. This ship was the first in the Merchant Marine Service to have an integrated crew and a Negro captain. Later three other such ships had Negro masters.

ISAAC MYERS

(Labor, Government   32)

Born: 1835, Baltimore, Maryland
Died: 1891
Education: Private school
Significance: *Pioneer in organized labor movement*

Isaac Myers was a journeyman ship caulker in Baltimore in 1865, when Negro longshoremen and mechanics faced discriminatory layoffs. He raised ten thousand dollars, borrowed thirty thousand more, established a shipyard, won a government contract worth fifty thousand dollars, and paid off his note within five years. His yard was entirely owned and staffed by Negroes.

Incensed at the anti-Republican and anti-Negro political and organizational program of the National Labor Union (NLU), Myers organized the Colored National Labor Union and became its president. He sent agents throughout the country to organize local and state affiliates and to reenforce Negro support for the Republican Party.

Myers was appointed an agent-at-large for the Post Office Department in 1870, founded a weekly newspaper, the *Colored Citizen,* in 1880, organized the Maryland Colored State Industrial Association in 1888, and along the way also promoted the establishment of a retirement home for African Methodist Episcopal ministers.

EFFIE LEE NEWSOME

(Literature, Library Science   48)
Born: 1885, Philadelphia, Pennslyvania
Education: Wilberforce University, Ohio; Oberlin College, Oberlin, Ohio; University of Pennsylvania, Philadelphia, Pennsylvania
Significance: *Poet and librarian*

Effie Newsome's father was a minister of the African Methodist Episcopal Church. She spent a bookish, pleasant childhood enjoying art, music, and the out-of-doors. At five, she began writing, "a novel of four pages and three chapters." After college, she married a minister. She became head of the Children's Library in the Department of Education in Central State College, Wilberforce University. She has also worked in the public library. Carter Woodson spurred her on to a writing career by asking her to send poems to *The Negro History Bulletin.* Her *Gladiola Garden,* a collection of children's verse, was published by the Association for the Study of Negro Life and History. She is also the author of *Come Ye Apart.*

FREDERICK O'NEAL

(Acting   46)
Born: 1908, Brookville, Mississippi
Education: New Theater School, American Theatre Wing, New York City
Significance: *Award winning actor*

In 1927 Frederick O'Neal and some friends in St. Louis founded the Ira Aldridge Players, the second Negro acting group in America, and during the next decade he played in thirty of that group's productions. In 1937 he went to New York and in 1940 founded the American Negro Theater, which under his direction has nourished succeeding generations of Negroes in the theater.

O'Neal starred in *Anna Lucasta* and later appeared in several other Broadway productions. In the 1944-45 season he won two awards for the best supporting performance by an actor on Broadway. He has also appeared in numerous television programs. Among his films are *Pinky* and *The Man With the Golden Arm.* O'Neal became president of Actors' Equity in 1964 and is active in union affairs, including memberships in the AFL-CIO's civil rights committee and the American Arbitration Association.

ESTELLE MASSEY OSBORNE

(Health   46)
Born: 1901, Palestine, Texas
Education: Prairie View Agricultural and Mechanical College, Texas; Nursing School of City Hospital #2, St. Louis, Missouri; B.S. and M.A., Columbia University, New York
Significance: *Leader in public health nursing*

After taking her master's degree in 1931, Estelle Massey Osborne became educational director at Freedman's Hospital in Washington, D.C., and subsequently director of nursing at Phillips Hospital in St. Louis and consultant to the National Nursing Council for War Service (1942-46). Her appointment as assistant professor in nursing education at New York University (1945) made her NYU's first Negro woman faculty member. She joined the staff of the National League for Nursing in 1954, and became its associate general director in 1960. She retired in 1966. She has been active in the Urban League and the National Association for the Advancement of Colored People and has held numerous directorships in national health organizations. The Estelle Massey Scholarship was established at Fisk University in her honor.

JESSE OWENS
  (Track   46)
  Born: 1913, Danville, Alabama
  Education: Ohio State University,
    Columbus, Ohio
  Significance: *Olympic track champion*
Jesse Owens was the son of a sharecropper and worked in the cotton fields as a child. The family moved to Cleveland and his father became a steel worker. In 1934 Owens entered Ohio State University where he made track history. He set world records in three events (the 220 yard dash, the 220 yard low hurdles, and the broad jump) in one day while representing Ohio State in the Big Ten Conference championships in 1935. In the 1936 Berlin Olympiad Jesse Owens won an unprecedented four gold medals. Adolf Hitler's subsequent refusal to present Owens his trophies created an international furore. The incident only added to Owens' fame.

SATCHEL PAIGE
  (Baseball   46, 7)
  Born: 1904, Mobile, Alabama
  Significance: *Major league pitcher*
Satchel Paige was familiar to the sporting world long before Jackie Robinson broke the color barrier in organized baseball. His almost legendary feats in Negro baseball were repeated in the occasional exhibition games he played against major league players. In 1933 he bested Dizzy Dean's team in a 1-0 shutout and later Joe Dimaggio referred to him as "the best pitcher I ever faced."

In 1946 he led the Kansas City Monarchs to the Negro World Series championship, pitching 64 consecutive scoreless innings, and 93 innings in which he allowed but two runs. In 1948, in his forties, he finally reached the major leagues and contributed six victories in Cleveland's pennant drive. He was named to the American League's All-Star squad in 1952 while pitching for the St. Louis Browns.

CHARLIE (BIRD) PARKER
  (Jazz   46)
  Born: 1920
  Died: 1955
  Significance: *Jazz musician*
Charlie (Bird) Parker's influence on the development of jazz has been felt on the whole spectrum of jazz ideas. A series of records with Dizzy Gillespie's rhythm section in 1945 marks the beginning of the bop movement. Although Parker's innovations met with a great deal of opposition from traditional jazz musicians and critics, a host of younger musicians followed his lead, and he is now universally revered.

GORDON ROGER PARKS
  (Graphic Arts   1)
  Born: 1912, Fort Scott, Kansas
  Significance: *Prize-winning photographer,*
    composer, author
Gordon Roger Parks had a varied career after leaving high school, working as a waiter, lumberjack, piano player, bandleader and semiprofessional basketball player. In 1937, he chose photography as a career. He moved to Chicago where he was inspired and influenced by artists of the South Side Community Art Center. Here he was provided a darkroom in which to work, and eventually given a one-man exhibit by David P. Ross, director of the gallery. As a result of this show he won a Rosenwald Fellowship, the first awarded for photography. He later

became a member of the Farm Security Administration.

In 1949 he was engaged by *Life* magazine as a staff photographer which meant assignments in every part of the world. Parks feels that a great photograph is as timeless as a great painting because it captures and records the world as it is. He was named "Magazine Photographer of the Year" in 1961. He has also received honors in the Art Directors Show and in the News Pictures of the Year competitions.

Parks considers himself a "week-end composer." He has written several musical compositions, including "First Concerto for Piano and Orchestra, which was performed in 1953, and three piano sonatas, performed in Philadelphia in 1955. He wrote one book on photography, and also *The Learning Tree* published in 1963 and *The Choice of Weapons in 1966.*

(From Russell L. Adams, *Great Negroes Past and Present.* Chicago: Afro-Am Publishing Co., Inc., 1967.)

ROSA PARKS
   (Civil Rights   8)
   Born: 1913
   Significance: *Leader in nonviolent
      movement for civil rights*

Ordered to give her seat on a Montgomery, Alabama, city bus to a white passenger, Rosa Parks refused. Upon her arrest, Montgomery Negroes refused to ride buses. The date was December 1, 1955. Before the bus boycott had ended, all passengers regardless of race could sit wherever they chose. Mrs. Parks' refusal marked the beginning of the nonviolent civil rights movement.

BILL PICKETT
   (Ranching   16)
   Born: Texas
   Died: 1932
   Significance: *Star rodeo performer*

Bill Pickett attained fame as a hand on the famous 101 Ranch in northeastern Oklahoma. During the early 1900's this famous ranch was also the home of one of the most successful wild west and rodeo shows of the time. Pickett was one of the show's star attractions. In an early performance in New York's Madison Square Garden, Pickett and Will Rogers took their horses over the hurdle and into the grandstand. In a famous show in Mexico City, Pickett said he could throw two steers in the time it would take two bullfighters to throw one. No one accepted the challenge, but 5,000 pesos was bet that Pickett couldn't hold on to a fighting bull for five minutes. During this event it became apparent that the officials had no intention of ringing the bell, and after six minutes 101 Ranch hands rode into the arena to call time.

Pickett's career, and the show, ended abruptly in London in August, 1914. War had come to England, and under a national emergency order all the troupe's stock except six horses and a wagon were commandeered.

PINCKNEY BENTON STEWART PINCHBACK
   (Politics   13)
   Born: 1837, Macon, Georgia
   Died: 1921
   Education: High school, Cincinnati, Ohio
   Significance: *Reconstruction period
      political leader*

Pinckney Benton Stewart Pinchback was the son of a white Mississippi planter and Eliza Stewart, who had been a slave. He was born free because his mother had been emancipated by the father of her children, who sent them to Ohio to be educated. In 1848 he became a cabin boy and then a steward on the riverboats. In 1862, running the blockade at Yazoo City, he reached New Orleans, which was already in possession of the Union forces. He enlisted, and raised a company of Negro volunteers, known as the Corps d'Afriques, but resigned his commission in September, 1863, because of difficulties over his race. Subsequently he was authorized to raise a company of Negro cavalry.

At the close of the war, he threw himself into Louisiana politics. Shrewd, energetic, and aggressive, he represented the typical Negro politician of the Reconstruction Period. In 1868 he won a seat in the State Senate, where he was elected president pro tempore. He became, by virtue of that office, lieutenant-governor at the death of the mulatto incumbent in 1871. For the brief period from December 9, 1872 to January 13, 1873, he filled the gubernatorial office. Though he had been nominated for governor by his wing of the Republican Party in 1872, he consented, in the interest of party harmony, to accept the place of congressman-at-large on the Republican ticket. He was declared elected but he was never seated because his Democratic opponent contested and ultimately won the seat. Although elected Senator by the Louisiana Legislature in January 1873, the election was contested, and Pinchback was finally denied the seat after a contest of three years. The last office in his public career was that of surveyor of customs in New Orleans, to which he was appointed in 1882.

FRANK EDWARD PINDER

(Agriculture 51)

Born: 1911, Key West, Florida

Education: B.S., Florida Agricultural & Mechanical College, Tallahassee, Florida

Significance: *Foreign agricultural specialist*

Frank Edward Pinder was a county agricultural agent from 1933 to 1940. He then worked for the United States Department of Agriculture for three years, first as a cooperatives specialist, then as agriculturist. As senior agricultural production specialist with the Foreign Economic Administration, he was assigned to Liberia in 1944. In 1946 he became the agricultural attache at the American legation in Liberia, and in 1947 the head agricultural specialist with the United States Economic Mission in Liberia. In 1950 the United States Department of State presented him with the Meritorious Service Award and cited him for his outstanding contributions to the important work of the Department and the Foreign Service.

RILEY LEROY PITTS

(Military 16)

Significance: *First officer of his race to win the Medal of Honor (posthumously)*

On October 31, 1967 Captain Riley Leroy Pitts was leading his company in an assault on a strongly entrenched enemy unit. They were under enemy fire from three sides when Pitts picked up a grenade taken from a captured Vietcong and threw it at a machine gun bunker. The grenade rebounded into the midst of his men. Without hesitation, Pitts threw himself on the grenade, but miraculously it did not explode. His respite from death was brief, however. A short time later, Pitts moved from the cover of the dense jungle foliage in order to direct the attack more effectively, and in this exposed position he was fatally wounded.

President Johnson commented, when he awarded the Medal of Honor to Pitts' widow, Mrs. Eula M. Pitts of Oklahoma City, "what this man did in an hour of incredible courage will live in the story of America as long as America endures—as he will live in the hearts and memories of those who loved him."

SIDNEY POITIER

(Acting 46)

Born: 1924, Miami, Florida

Significance: *Academy award winning actor*

Sidney Poitier was brought up in the Bahamas and returned to the United States in 1939. After the attack on Pearl Harbor he enlisted and served four years in the Army. Poitier auditioned for acting roles in Frederick O'Neal's American Negro Theater in New York. After an initial failure he was accepted and received acting lessons in exchange for performing backstage chores.

He made his first movie in 1950. He has since become the most sought after Negro movie star in America. In 1964 he won an Academy Award for his starring role in *Lilies of the Field.* He also starred in Lorraine Hansberry's *Raisin in the Sun* on Broadway in 1959. Among his successful films are *Cry, the Beloved Country, The Defiant Ones, Porgy and Bess, Guess Who's Coming to Dinner,* and *For Love of Ivy.* He repeated his stage success in *Raisin in the Sun* on the screen.

POMPEY

(Military   49)
Born: 18th century
Significance: *Revolutionary War service*

Pompey was the slave of a patriotic farmer in the Hudson River Valley. Stony Point was a strategic fort on the Hudson, taken by the British after the Americans had occupied it and erected a blockhouse. The British fortified it even more strongly. In 1779 General Washington was determined to retake Stony Point in spite of the extreme difficulties. The slave Pompey had become a favorite of the British garrison and crossed regularly between the British and American lines. The British soldiers had no idea that he was reporting regularly to the Americans. Accordingly, when the day of the battle came, the American General Wayne had the countersign for entry to the garrison obtained through Pompey. The skirmish was quickly over, with gold and silver medals awarded to officers and men. Pompey was quickly forgotten. Only his master rewarded his service to America by giving him a horse and never exacting any more labor from him.

SALEM POOR

(Military   16)
Born: 18th century
Significance: *Revolutionary War*
    battlefield conduct

Salem Poor was an ex-slave who fought at Lexington, Concord, and Bunker Hill. There are no specific accounts of his service with Colonel Frye's regiment at Bunker Hill, but it must have been extraordinary, because Colonel Prescott and thirteen of his officers petitioned the Continental Congress in Poor's behalf. The officers wrote: "In justice to the character of so brave a man . . . we declare a Negro man called Salem behaved like an experienced officer, as well as an excellent soldier." The officers left to Congress the decision as to what reward was due. He continued in Washington's command to endure the bitter winter at Valley Forge, shoeless and half-starved, and then to fight at White Plains.

ADAM CLAYTON POWELL, JR.

(Politics, Civil Rights   7, 46)
Born: 1908, New Haven,
    Connecticut
Died: 1972
Education: A.B., Colgate University,
    New York; M.A., Columbia
    University, New York; D.D., Shaw
    University, North Carolina; LL.D.,
    Virginia University, Charlottesville,
    Virginia
Significance: *Author and*
    Congressman

In the 1930's, Adam Clayton Powell, Jr. was active along with his father in organizing relief in Harlem and campaigning for broadened job opportunities for Negroes. He succeeded his father as pastor of the Abyssinian Baptist Church in 1937. In 1941 he was elected to the New York City Council, and in 1945 to the U.S. House of Representatives. He was noted in the Congress as a civil rights leader and personally desegregated Congressional facilities as well as restaurants and theaters in Washington, D.C.

In Congress Powell initiated legislation which would deny federal funds to projects which discriminated against Negroes; suppress discrimination in the armed forces; and establish the right of Negro journalists to sit in Congressional press galleries. In 1960 he became Chairman of the House Committee on Education and Labor and subsequently steered nearly 50 important social welfare bills through Congress.

Powell was excluded from his House seat in 1967 for allegedly using public funds for personal purposes. Although the investigating committee recommended censure, a fine, and loss of seniority he was denied his seat and a special election was held to fill it. Powell did not campaign, but he received 74% of the vote cast nonetheless.

He was decorated by the government of Ethiopia in 1954. He published several books, among them *Is This a White Man's War?* (1942), *Stage Door Canteen* (1944), *Marching Blacks* (1945), and *Adam Clayton Powell* (1960).

LEONTYNE PRICE
(Music   46)
Born: 1927, Laurel, Mississippi
Education: College of Education and
    Industrial Arts, Wilberforce, Ohio
Significance: *Lyric operatic soprano*

Leontyne Price, lyric soprano, began her career by appearing in a revival of Virgil Thomson's *Four Saints in Three Acts* on Broadway in 1952. She played Bess in the revival of *Porgy and Bess* in the same year, and toured with it in Europe under State Department sponsorship.

In 1957 she sang in *Aida* with the San Francisco Opera. Engagements followed at Vienna, London's Covent Garden, and in Verona. She appeared in *Il Trovatore* which opened the new Salzburg Festival House in 1960. In the same role she made her Metropolitan Opera debut in 1961. In 1966 she opened the Metropolitan Opera season in the role of Cleopatra in Samuel Barber's *Antony and Cleopatra.*

JOSEPH HAYNE RAINEY
(Politics   7, 46)
Born: 1832, Georgetown, South Carolina
Died: 1887
Significance: *First Negro Congressman*

Joseph Rainey was drafted by Confederate authorities in 1862 to work on the fortifications of Charleston. He escaped to the West Indies, not returning to his native state until after the war.

In 1867 he became a member of the executive committee of the newly formed Republican Party of South Carolina, and the following year was a delegate to the state constitutional convention. He was elected to a seat in the State Senate. In 1870 he entered the U.S. House of Representatives where he continued to serve until 1879. He was the first Negro in the House of Representatives.

While in Congress he fought for legislation to enforce the Fourteenth Amendment, which was ratified in 1868. He also fought for equal access for Negroes to public accommodations, on one occasion refusing to leave a hotel dining room until forcibly ejected.

A. PHILIP RANDOLPH
(Labor, Civil Rights   8)
Born: 1889, Crescent City, Florida
Significance: *Leader for fair labor
    practices*

Early in his adult life, A. Philip Randolph urged workers to fight for better working conditions. He was also interested in equal job opportunities for people of all races. During World War II he persuaded the government to issue an order forbidding any industry holding defense contracts to discriminate in hiring. Randolph is perhaps best known as the long-time leader of the Brotherhood of Sleeping Car Porters. He was the first Negro vice-president of the AFL-CIO.

JAMES T. RAPIER
(Politics, Labor   7, 46)
Born: 1837, Florence, Alabama
Died: 1882
Education: Montreal College, Canada;
    University of Glasgow, Scotland;
    Franklin College, Nashville, Tennessee
Significance: *Legislative leader in the
    Negro cause*

James T. Rapier was born of free parents. His father, a white planter, provided a tutor for him and sent him to Canada and Scotland for his education. Reputedly trained as a lawyer, he never practiced but became a successful cotton planter.

He became involved in the politics of his native Alabama after the Civil War, helping to found the state Republican Party and serving as the state party's vice president and as a delegate to the 1867 constitutional convention. He was interested in organizing urban and rural workers and chaired the first state Negro labor convention. He founded the Montgomery *Sentinel* to promote the unity of the Negro community and improve understanding between the two races in Alabama.

Rapier was elected to the U.S. House of Representatives in 1872 and worked for the passage of the Civil Rights Act of 1875 and for firm enforcement of earlier legislation. His political career was limited to one term. He then served as United States Internal Revenue Officer for Alabama until his death.

GEORGE W. REED, JR.

(Physical Sciences   3)
Born: 1920, Washington, D.C.
Education: B.S., Howard University, Washington, D.C.; M.S., Ph.D., University of Chicago, Illinois
Significance: *Research in nuclear physics and geocosmochemistry*

George W. Reed, Jr., has been Associate Chemist at the Argonne National Laboratory since 1952. His work deals with the abundance of the chemical elements and theories of the origins of the elements. Four of the important papers of which he is co-author are: "Uranium, Helium and the Ages of Meteorites," "Uranium and Barium in Stone Meteorites," "Determinations of Concentrations of Heavy Elements in Meteorites by Activation Analysis," and "Mercury in Chondrites." He was one of the principal investigators working on lunar samples.

WILSON R. RILES

(Education   44)
Born: 1917, Alexandria, Louisiana
Education: B.A., M.A., Arizona State College, Flagstaff, Arizona
Significance: *Leadership in education at state level*

Dr. Wilson R. Riles, a World War II veteran, taught elementary school for fourteen years. He came to California in 1954 as Pacific Coast executive secretary of the Fellowship of Reconciliation. He joined the State Department of Education in 1958 as a consultant and executive secretary of the Commission on Equal Opportunities in Education. Dr. Riles promoted fair hiring practices in schools and became chief of the Bureau of Intergroup Relations. He served as the state's first director of Compensatory Education until 1969, receiving national recognition. In 1969 he was appointed Deputy Superintendent of Public Instruction. In 1970 he waged a successful campaign for the position of State Superintendent of Public Instruction. Dr. Riles was awarded an honorary doctorate,

LL.D., from Pepperdine College, Los Angeles for his public service in education.

A partial listing of Dr. Riles' civic involvement includes membership on the National Advisory Committee on the Teacher Corps, the National Education Association Task Force on Urban Education, the Advisory Board on Educational Tuition and the Voucher System for Harvard University. He was chairman of President Nixon's Task Force on Urban Education, having served President Lyndon Johnson in a similar capacity.

NORBERT RILLIEUX

(Invention, Engineering   1, 7, 46)
Born: 1806, New Orleans, Louisiana
Died: 1894
Education: Engineering in Paris
Significance: *Inventor of labor-saving devices*

Norbert Rillieux's father was a wealthy engineer and plantation owner. His mother was a slave on the plantation. His father recognized his intelligence and sent him to school in Paris. There he became an instructor in applied mechanics at the Ecole Central at twenty-four (1830). While there, he published a series of papers on steam engine mechanics, and began work on the triple-effect evaporator for sugar refining which was first installed in 1845 and received a patent in 1846. Rillieux' process greatly reduced production costs in the refining process and provided a superior quality of sugar. The "Rillieux system" rapidly spread to sugar factories throughout the U.S. South and the Caribbean.

Rillieux returned from France to become the most famous engineer in Louisiana. Frustrated by the increasing inhibitions placed on men of his color in Louisiana, Rillieux returned to France in 1854. He secured a scholarship and worked for ten years with the Champollions in deciphering Egyptian hieroglyphics. Eventually, he returned to invention, and in 1881 he perfected the application of his process to the refining of beet sugar. The principle has since spread to numerous other products.

FRANCES E. RIVERS
   (Law, Civil Rights   32)
   Born: 1893, Kansas City, Kansas
   Education: Yale University, New Haven,
      Connecticut; Columbia University Law
      School, New York
   Significance: *Judiciary service*
Francis E. Rivers earned Phi Beta Kappa
honors at Yale but couldn't find work in New
York and enrolled in Columbia University Law
School. He was admitted to the bar in 1922 and
again began the frustrating round of prospective
employers. He had gone to work part-time for
the post office when Jonah Goldstein, a prominent New York lawyer, heard of him and hired
him. He opened his own practice in 1925 and
plunged into Republican politics in Harlem,
winning election to the New York legislature in
1929. In 1937 he joined the Manhattan district
attorney's staff under Thomas Dewey. In 1943,
Governor Dewey appointed him to the New
York Municipal Court bench. Judge Rivers led
the assault on the color line in the American Bar
Association and won the endorsement of all
parties in court elections after 1953. He continued on the bench until he retired in 1963. He
was named chairman of President Kennedy's
special committee on civil rights and in 1965
was appointed president of the NAACP Legal
Defense and Education Fund.

ELBERT R. "DOC" ROBERTSON
   (Invention   7)
   Born: ca. 1865
   Died: 1925
   Significance: *Inventions for railroads and
      building construction*
Elbert R. Robertson spent years in litigation
with railroad companies over patent rights on
his inventions. In Nashville, Tennessee, he had
invented the chilled groove wheel, used by all
railroads. Although it was patented, he maintained that it had been stolen by a white man
who sold it to the Chicago Railway Company.
The United States Supreme Court finally decided in his favor and awarded him thirteen
million dollars in royalties. In addition to the
chilled groove wheel, Robertson invented the

third rail used by elevated railways in various
cities, and a mold in which concrete pillars were
made for building foundations.

PAUL ROBESON
   (Acting, Music   1, 46)
   Born: 1898, Princeton, New Jersey
   Education: Rutgers University, New
      Brunswick, New Jersey; Columbia
      University, New York
   Significance: *Athlete, actor, singer and
      scholar*
Paul Robeson attended Rutgers on an athletic scholarship. While there he excelled in
sports and scholarship. He was selected to the
Walter Camp All-American team in football in
1918, starred in three other sports, won Phi
Beta Kappa honors, and delivered the senior
commencement address in 1919. He subsequently financed his graduate education in law
at Columbia University by playing professional
football. Eugene O'Neill saw him perform in an
amateur theatrical production, and he secured
parts in *Taboo, All God's Chillun Got Wings,*
and *Emperor Jones.* Incidental to his role in
Emperor Jones he sang for the first time from
a professional stage.
   Emperor Jones was followed by an over-
whelmingly successful Greenwich Village concert of spirituals and other Negro music in 1925.
He then toured the United States and Europe
and repeated his earlier successes on an even
larger scale. His appearances in *Show Boat,
Porgy and Bess* and his Broadway performance
in *Othello* (1943-44) led to unrestrained praise
from critics and public alike. He achieved a similar success as a recording artist.
   Robeson's incomparable voice and stage talent made him a star of first rank until after
World War II. Following the war his political
sympathies for the Soviet Union alienated large
segments of his American public. During the
late forties and until his return to the United
States in 1963 he spent much of his time abroad,
in the Soviet Union and England.

BILL ROBINSON
   (Dancing   46)

Born: 1878, Richmond, Virginia
Died: 1949
Significance: *"King of the Tap Dancers"*

Bill (Bojangles) Robinson was raised by his grandmother, a former slave. At the age of eight he supported himself by dancing in the street for pennies and working as a stable boy.

In 1887 he toured with a show called *The South Before the War* and the following year moved to Washington, D.C., to work in the stables again. He entered vaudeville in 1896 and was successful on the Keith circuit until its demise in the Panic of 1907. In 1927 he starred in *Blackbirds* on Broadway, and in 1932 he had top billing in the first all-Negro talking movie, *Harlem Is Heaven.* In Hollywood he performed with Shirley Temple in *The Little Colonel, The Littlest Rebel,* and *Rebecca of Sunnybrook Farm.* In all he made fourteen movies.

JACKIE ROBINSON

(Baseball   7, 46)
Born: 1919, Cairo, Georgia
Education: University of California, Los
    Angeles
Significance: *Broke the color barrier in
    big league professional baseball*

Jack Roosevelt Robinson was raised in Pasadena, California. He starred in baseball, football, and track at UCLA (1939-41), and left school in his junior year to play professional football. He served in the Army and was commissioned a Lieutenant during World War II. He played baseball for the Kansas City Monarchs of the Negro leagues in 1945. Branch Rickey of the Brooklyn Dodgers then made a deliberate decision to broach the color line in professional baseball by offering Robinson a contract. Robinson spent two seasons with the Dodgers' Montreal farm team and in 1947 moved up to the parent club, the first Negro to play with a modern major league baseball team. When Robinson retured in 1956 after a distinguished baseball career, segregation in major professional sports had all but disappeared. He was inducted into the baseball Hall of Fame in 1962.

Since his retirement from baseball, Robinson has pursued a successful career as a food company executive in New York and has been influential in the Republican Party and state and national politics.

MOSES RODGERS

(Engineering   27)
Born: ca. 1800, Missouri
Died: 1890
Significance: *Pioneer in California mining*

Moses Rodgers, a well-known mining engineer, was born a slave. He was a "49er." He became a miner in Hornitos, twenty-five miles from Merced, California. He owned a group of mines near Quartzburg and was a partner in the Sweet Vengeance mine in Brown's Valley. He became known as one of the best engineers and metallurgists on the Pacific Coast and his services were much in demand.

EDWARD ROSE

(Exploration   21)
Born: Late 1700's
Significance: *Guide and Indian interpreter*

No one knows where Ed Rose was born. The earliest record of him is 1806. In the next two decades he played a leading role in most of the important expeditions to the Rocky Mountains. It was said that his ancestory included Negro, white, and Cherokee. He was muscular, thick set, but of good height. His nose had been slashed in an accident or fight. The Indians called him Cut Nose.

In 1807 he ascended the Missouri River with Manuel Lisa to the mouth of the Yellowstone. In 1809 he went with Ezekial Williams, and in 1811 with Wilson Price Hunt. The trappers built Fort Lisa on the Yellowstone River. Rose learned the language of the Crow Indians. He was the interpreter for the Atkinson-O'Fallian expedition to Yellowstone in 1823. Washington Irving wrote about Rose in *Astoria* and in *Adventures of Captain Bonneville.* He was considered a first-rate trail blazer and mountain man, guide and interpreter. He was made a Crow chief. He was buried on the banks of the Missouri nearly opposite the mouth of the Milk River.

CARL ROWAN

(Diplomacy, Government   46)

Born: 1925, Ravenscroft, Tennessee

Education: Tennessee Agricultural and
    Industrial State University, Nashville;
    B.A., Oberlin College, Ohio; M.A.,
    University of Minnesota, Minneapolis,
    Minnesota

Significance: *Journalist and diplomat*

Carl Rowan received his early college education at Tennessee Agricultural and Industrial
State University just prior to World War II. He
was one of the first fifteen Negroes commissioned in the Navy during the war. Following
the war he returned to Oberlin College (Ohio)
for his B.A., and to the University of Minnesota
for an M.A. in journalism.

He became a staff writer for the *Minneapolis
Tribune* in 1950 and soon established himself in
the field. President Kennedy appointed him
Deputy Assistant Secretary of State for Public
Affairs (1961) and Ambassador to Finland
(1963) and later became director of the United
States Information Agency. In that position he
became the first Negro to sit on the National
Security Council. After his resignation from the
USIA in 1965 he commenced a syndicated col-
umn in Washington, D.C. for the Chicago *Daily
News.*

His several books include the autobiographical *South of Freedom* (1953), *The Pitiful and
the Proud* (1956), *Go South to Sorrow* (1957),
and *Wait Till Next Year* (1960), the biography
of Jackie Robinson.

WILMA RUDOLPH

(Track   46)

Born: 1940, St. Bethlehem, Tennessee

Education: Burt High School,
    Clarkesville, Tennessee; Tennessee
    State University, Nashville, Tennessee

Significance: *World record setting
    sprinter*

Wilma Rudolph is the only American
woman athlete to win three Olympic gold medals (Rome, 1960)—despite a childhood illness
that left her unable to walk properly until she
was eight years old. She starred in basketball
and track in high school. She entered America's
most important training center for women athletes, Tennessee Agricultural and Industrial
State University, in 1957, and set her sights
firmly on competition in the Olympic Games.
Her Olympic victories and her example inspired
younger American women sprinters, Edith
McGuire and Wyomia Tyus, who won medals
for the United States in succeeding Olympic
Games.

BILL RUSSELL

(Basketball   46)

Born: 1934, Monroe, Louisiana

Education: McClymonds High School,
    Oakland, California; University of San
    Francisco, California

Significance: *First Negro to coach and
    play in the National Basketball
    Association*

In high school Bill Russell was an awkward
but determined basketball player. He eventually
received a scholarship to nearby University of
San Francisco, where he came into his own. In
his sophomore year, he became the most publi-
cized athlete on the West Coast. Over the next
two years, his fame spread across the nation as
he led his team to sixty consecutive victories and
two straight NCAA titles.

Russell became a member of the Boston Celtics of the National Basketball Association. His
specialties of blocking shots and rebounding
helped the Celtics become the most successful
team in the history of professional sports, winning the world championship eight years in a
row. Russell himself was named Most Valuable
Player four times. He was the first Negro to
coach and play in the National Basketball Association. He retired from basketball at the close
of the 1969 season in favor of a career in movies
and broadcasting.

JOHN B. RUSSWURM

(Journalism   1, 7)

Born: 1799, Jamaica, British West Indies

Died: 1851

Education: A.B., M.A., Bowdoin College,
    Brunswick, Maine

Significance: *Abolition movement leader*

Born of a white father and a Negro mother, Russwurm was sent to Canada by his father under an assumed name. After his father's death, his mother financed his college education and gave him the right to use his father's name. He was one of the first Negroes to graduate from an American college. He and Samuel Cornish published the Negro newspaper, *Freedom's Journal,* which played an important role in the abolition movement. In 1828, Russwurm migrated to Liberia, "the promised land," deciding that the American Colonization Society had the right solution to racial problems, with their "return to Africa" movement. In Liberia he founded the *Liberia Herald,* became superintendent of schools, governor of the colony, and finally died there.

BAYARD RUSTIN
    (Civil Rights   7)
    Born: 1910, West Chester, Pennsylvania
    Education: Studied Abroad
    Significance: *Civil Rights Leader*

Bayard Rustin joined the Young Communist League in 1936 and was sent to New York as an organizer. He left the YCL in 1941 to join the Fellowship of Reconciliation and has been an active pacifist ever since. During World War II he went to California to help protect the property of Japanese-Americans who had been interned. He refused to serve in the Army in 1943 and went to prison.

In 1947 he helped organize the first Freedom Ride, in North Carolina. He was arrested and put on a chain gang; his expose of chain-gang life was responsible for its abolition in North Carolina. He was the Race Relations Secretary for the Fellowship of Reconciliation and one of the organizers of the Congress of Racial Equality. He served Martin Luther King Jr. as a special assistant for seven years after the Montgomery bus boycott of 1955-56, and was instrumental in the founding of the Southern Christian Leadership Conference.

Rustin planned and organized the successful March on Washington in 1963 and directed the first New York City school boycott in 1964. He is the executive director of the A. Philip Randolph Institute in New York City.

PETER SALEM
    (Military   49)
    Born: Mid 1700's, Framingham,
        Massachusetts
    Died: 1816
    Significance: *Revolutionary War leader*

Peter Salem was born a slave about twenty years before the beginning of the Revolutionary War. He joined the Massachusetts volunteers as a freeman. He first fought at Concord and Lexington, and then with the forces on Breed's Hill (the Battle of Bunker Hill). Two other free Negroes fought with him. On the third assemblage of the forces, when the hillside was already strewn with dead and dying redcoats, Salem took his place at the gun slot and killed Major John Pitcairn. Neither side had won a clear victory but the courageous stand of the small contingent of Continentals raised the morale of the whole country. A picture showing the incident was sent through those colonies which had not yet declared their independence. He became the hero of the moment, second only to his commander, William Prescott. Salem was present at General Burgoyne's surrender at Saratoga. More than a half a century after Salem's death the town of Framingham erected a monument over his grave, carved with these words:

Peter Salem - Soldier of the Revolution; Died August 16, 1816 - Concord.

EDITH SAMPSON
    (Law, Government   46)
    Born: ca. 1900, Pittsburgh, Pennsylvania
    Education: John Marshall Law School,
        Chicago, Illinois; LL.M., Loyola
        University, Chicago, Illinois
    Significance: *Alternate Delegate to
        United Nations, judge*

Edith Sampson has been a member of the Illinois bar since 1927 and was admitted to practice before the Supreme Court in 1934. During the 1930's she maintained her own private practice, specializing in domestic relations and criminal law.

Appointed by President Harry S. Truman, Edith Sampson was the first Negro woman to be named to the United Nations, serving from 1950 to 1953. After her United Nations appointment, Edith Sampson traveled around the world as a lecturer under the auspices of the State Department. She was elected Associate Judge of the Municipal Court of Chicago in 1962.

JEREMIAH B. SANDERSON
    (Education   5, 27)
    Born: 1821, New Bedford, Massachusetts
    Died: 1875
    Significance: *Leader in California
        education and civil rights*

Jeremiah B. Sanderson became an indefatigable worker in organizing schools for Negro children and in gaining financial support. He had located first in Sacramento, California, and asked the Board of Education to establish a public school for Negro children. This school was built and opened in May, 1855. He taught in San Francisco and in Stockton, California. He soon earned the title, "the greatest Negro teacher in the West."

He was also a worker for the civil rights of the Negro. Most, if not all, of the proceedings of the California Colored Conventions are in his handwriting. The first of these conventions was held in Sacramento in 1855. Sanderson also undertook the task of seeking to revoke the California statutes prohibiting Negroes from offering testimony in court. In 1872 he was ordained in the African Methodist Episcopal Church and in 1875, appointed pastor of Shiloh Church in Oakland.

Sanderson was the only western Negro to be included in the book, *The Black Man,* by William Wells Brown, published during the Civil War.

AUGUSTA SAVAGE
    (Sculpture   7, 46)
    Born: 1900, Green Cove Spring, Florida
    Died: 1962

    Education: Tallahassee State Normal
        School, Florida; Cooper Union, New
        York City
    Significance: *Leading sculptor in "Negro
        Renaissance"*

Augusta Savage studied in France following her training at Cooper Union. Her studies abroad were financed by Carnegie and Rosenwald Fund fellowships.

During the 1930's she organized an art studio and workshop in Harlem. Her workshop and sculptures, notably "African Savage" and "The Tom Tom," effectively influenced young Negro artists, and reflected her interest in African art and sculpture.

She was one of several artists represented in the first all-Negro exhibition in America sponsored by the International House in New York City. Her "Lift Every Voice and Sing," a symbolic group piece, was shown at the New York World's Fair in 1939. She was the first Negro accepted to membership in the National Association of Women Painters and Sculptors.

PHILIPPA SCHUYLER
    (Music   46)
    Born: 1932, New York City
    Died: late 1960's
    Significance: *Musical prodigy*

Philippa Schuyler was a prodigy—an accomplished pianist and composer. She composed and played "Manhattan Nocturne" with the New York Philharmonic Orchestra at the age of twelve. Her scherzo, "Rumpelstilskin," written when she was thirteen, was subsequently performed by the Boston Pops, the New Haven Symphony, and the New York Philharmonic Orchestras. She made her debut at Town Hall in New York City in 1953. During the fifties she traveled widely on goodwill concert tours sponsored by the United States Department of State.

Philippa Schuyler is the author of several books including *Adventures in Black and White, Jungle Saints,* and *Who Killed the Congo?*

FRANK ALVIN SILVERA
    (Acting   1)

Born: 1914, Kingston, Jamaica
Died: 1970
Education: Northeastern University,
　　Boston, Massachusetts
Significance: *Versatile actor*

Frank Alvin Silvera became a naturalized American citizen in 1922. Early in his career he demonstrated an ability to play a wide range of parts far beyond racial stereotypes. He portrayed Mexicans, Spaniards, and Italians, as well as white and black Americans. Silvera was active on stage, screen, and television and radio, giving convincing performances of any role assigned to him. In 1934, he appeared in Paul Green's *Potter's Field,* presented at the Plymouth Theater in Boston. The following year he performed in *Stevedore.* From 1935 to 1938 Silvera appeared in plays such as the *Trial of Dr. Beck, Macbeth,* and *Emperor Jones,* all sponsored by the Federal Theater Project.

While serving in the Navy during World War II, Silvera wrote and directed radio shows at the Great Lakes Naval Training Station. In 1945 he appeared in the Broadway production of *Anna Lucasta.* Two years later this versatile actor had a role in *John Loves Mary,* sponsored by the Urban League.

(From Russell L. Adams, *Great Negroes Past and Present.* Chicago: Afro-Am Publishing Co., Inc., 1967.)

ORENTHAL JAMES (O.J.) SIMPSON
　(Football　54)
　Born: 1947, San Francisco, California
　Education: City College, San Francisco,
　　California; University of Southern
　　California, Los Angeles
　Significance: *Heisman Trophy winner,*
　　professional football player

As a child, Orenthal James (O.J.) Simpson's legs were not strong and he wore braces for many years. He loved baseball, but later turned to football and track. After graduation from high school, his grades prevented his direct entrance to a four-year college so, after some hesitation about his future, he decided to go to City College in San Francisco. There, his career

became the greatest in junior college football history.

After two years he transferred to the University of Southern California where academically he achieved better than average. At USC he was a star football player for two years, winning the Heisman Trophy in 1968. After graduation he entered professional football, also serving as a sportscaster on television.

ROBERT SMALLS
　(Military, Politics　1, 7, 46)
　Born: 1839, Beaufort, South Carolina
　Died: 1916
　Education: Self-taught
　Significance: *Military service and political*
　　career

Robert Smalls was a slave with a limited formal education—and a desire to overcome the indignity of servitude. After moving to Charleston he met and married his wife, Hannah, in 1856. At the outbreak of the Civil War, Confederate authorities pressed him into the Confederate Navy where he served in the crew of the *Planter,* a dispatch and transport steamer. In 1862 he smuggled his wife and children on board and delivered the ship to the Union Navy by sailing the *Planter* into the blockading federal squadron outside Charleston harbor. This risky plan gained his freedom—its failure would have meant his death. The ship became invaluable to the North. The *Dictionary of American Biography* states: "This daring exploit gave him national fame. He was made a pilot in the United States Navy and given a share of the prize money." Later, the *Planter* came under heavy Confederate fire, its captain panicked, and Pilot Smalls took command and sailed the vessel out of danger. He was then promoted to captain and served on the *Planter* until the end of the war.

In 1868, Smalls was a delegate to the state constitutional convention. He was elected to the South Carolina House of Representatives and the State Senate. He served in the United States House of Representatives from 1875 until 1887, longer than any other Negro during the Reconstruction period. He was an eloquent supporter of legislation to provide equal accommodations for Negroes in interstate travel. He introduced and supported the post war civil rights bills aimed at establishing the right of freedom to make contracts and hold property.

BESSIE SMITH

(Music   7, 46)
Born: 1894, Chattanooga, Tennessee
Died: 1937
Significance: *Blues singer*

Bessie Smith was thirteen when she was discovered by Ma Rainey, the first of the great blues singers. She toured with minstrel groups and gradually won recognition on the Negro vaudeville circuit. It wasn't until 1923, however, that she was heard by a Columbia Records executive, Frank Walker, and recorded "Downhearted Blues," which introduced her country blues style to the urban North. The record sold two million copies. From 1924 to 1927 she was the best-known blues singer in the United States, earning more than $2,000 a week. From that point her career declined—as the Depression progressed, people were not buying records as they had, and she was beset with personal problems. In 1933 she cut her last records in a session arranged by John Hammond to honor her faded greatness. Four years later, she was injured in a car wreck near Clarksdale, Mississippi, and bled to death after being refused admission to a white hospital. Bessie Smith was one of the greatest talents of jazz history, possibly its greatest blues singer.

JAMES McCUNE SMITH

(Medicine   7, 12)
Born: 1813, New York
Died: ca. 1865
Education: M.D., University of Glasgow, Scotland
Significance: *Humanitarian work in medicine*

James McCune Smith was the son of a slave who owed his liberty to the Emancipation Act of the State of New York. After securing his medical degree he returned to New York City where he established a successful practice. He served for twenty years on the medical staff of the Free Negro Orphan Asylum in New York. In 1839 he worked with the first calculators of mortality rates for life insurance companies. He was active in the New York Underground Railroad and a contributor to *The Emancipator.* He was a leading figure in the "colored convention" movement. In 1863 Smith accepted an appointment as professor of anthropology at Wilberforce University.

ASA T. SPAULDING

(Business   32)
Born: 1902, North Carolina
Education: National Training School, Durham, North Carolina; Howard University, Washington, D.C.; B.S., New York University; M.A., University of Michigan, Ann Arbor, Michigan
Significance: *Insurance company president*

Asa T. Spaulding went to work for the North Carolina Mutual Life Insurance Company when he was 22. He became an actuary in 1933, assistant secretary in 1935, a director in 1938, vice president and controller in 1948, and president in 1959. He retired from the presidency in 1968 but retains his directorship; he is also a director of several other companies, including W. T. Grant and the Mechanics and Farmers Bank. He has been very active in community affairs, civil rights, youth work, and education. He also maintains active participation in numerous professional organizations.

EMANUEL STANCE

(Military   16)
Significance: *Congressional Medal of Honor winner*

Sergeant Emanuel Stance, on May 20, 1870, was ordered to lead a detachment of nine troopers out of Fort McKavett on a routine patrol along an old Indian trail known locally as the Kickapoo Road. The detachment was about eighteen miles north of the fort when it spied a small band of Indians driving a herd of horses across a nearby hill. Spurring their own horses to the attack, the troopers engaged the Indians in a running skirmish until the foe escaped into heavy hillside thickets of oak.

Early the next morning a band of twenty or thirty Kickapoo Indians was spotted pursuing a herd of government horses. The herd guards, outnumbered ten to one, were fighting a losing battle. Pulling far ahead of his men, Sergeant Stance repeatedly emptied his sidearm and reloaded without breaking stride. Although no Indians were killed, the fact that a detachment of ten black troopers had driven off a band of almost thirty Kickapoos was not lost on the Indians nor on Stance's superiors.

The following day, Stance and his patrol rode back into McKavett with twenty-five horses taken during the two-day patrol. Captain Carroll commended his sergeant for conspicuous courage and devotion to duty and, unknown to Stance, recommended him for the Congressional Medal of Honor. On July 24, 1870, the crusty little Indian fighter openly wept as he received the highest military honor his country could bestow.

From Philip T. Drotning, *Black Heroes in Our Nation's History.* © 1968 by Philip T. Drotning. Reprinted by permission of Doubleday & Company, Inc.

MABEL KEATON STAUPERS
  (Health   18)
  Born: 1890, Barbados, British West
    Indies
  Education: Freedman's Hospital,
    Washington, D.C.; Henry Phipps
    Institute, Philadelphia, Pennsylvania
  Significance: *Nursing career*
Mabel Keaton Staupers, a registered nurse, came to the United States as a child in 1903, was naturalized in 1917, and married Fritz C. Staupers in 1931.

In 1920, Mrs. Staupers was superintendent of the Booker T. Washington Sanitorium in New York City. She also nursed in the Tuberculosis Clinic at Jefferson Hospital in Philadelphia. She organized the Harlem Community for the New York Tuberculosis and Health Association. She was executive secretary and then president of the National Association of Colored Graduate Nurses, which merged with the American Nursing Association in 1951.

WILLIAM GRANT STILL
  (Music   46)
  Born: 1895, Woodville, Mississippi
  Education: Wilberforce University, Ohio;
    Oberlin Conservatory of Music,
    Oberlin, Ohio
  Significance: *Prolific American Negro
    composer*
William Grant Still received his early musical training in Little Rock, Arkansas where his mother was a school teacher. He later held both Guggenheim and Rosenwald Fellowships. Still's early work was as an arranger for jazz orchestras, and when he turned to composition, he used his jazz background in the classical framework.

In 1936 Still became the first Negro to conduct a major American orchestra when he gave a program of his own composition at the Hollywood Bowl. His symphonic poem, "Darker America," was performed by the Rochester Symphony Orchestra. In 1935, his "Afro-American Symphony" was played by the New York Philharmonic Orchestra at the International Music Festival in Frankfurt, Germany. He also composed an opera, *Troubled Island* (libretto by Langston Hughes), and such successful musicals as *Running Wild* and *Dixie to Broadway.*

CARL STOKES
  (Politics   43)
  Born: 1927
  Education: West Virginia State College,
    Institute, West Virginia; LL.B.,
    Cleveland College of Western Reserve
    University, Ohio; B.S.L., University of
    Minnesota Law School, Minneapolis,
    Minnesota
  Significance: *Legal and political career,
    mayor of Cleveland, Ohio*
Carl Stokes, as a boy, worked in neighborhood stores and as a newspaper carrier. He dropped out of high school and after his eigh-

teenth birthday entered the Army. While serving with the Army of Occupation in Germany, he decided to complete his education.

During law school he supported himself by working weekends as a dining car waiter. Upon his return to Cleveland, he worked as a municipal court probation officer. He then entered the practice of law with his brother. In 1958 he was appointed an assistant city prosecutor. In 1962 he was elected to the Ohio State Legislature, its first Negro Democrat. He served for two terms and was rated one of the most effective and hard working members. He resigned upon his election as mayor of Cleveland, Ohio.

LEWIS TEMPLE
    (Invention   46)
    Born: 1800, Richmond, Virginia
    Died: 1854
    Significance: *Inventor in the whaling industry*

As a young man, Lewis Temple moved to New Bedford, Massachusetts, one of the major American whaling ports. He found work as a metalsmith. He became interested in trying to modify the design of the whaler's harpoon then in use. In the 1840's, Temple designed a new version of the harpoon which allowed lines to be securely fastened to a whale.

Temple's "toggle" harpoon so improved 19th-century whaling methods that the industry entered into a period of unprecedented prosperity. Unfortunately, Temple never patented his invention. He died in poverty in 1854.

ERA BELL THOMPSON
    (Journalism   50)
    Born: ca. 1910, Des Moines, Iowa
    Education: B.A., Morningside College, Sioux City, Iowa
    Significance: *Journalist*

Era Bell Thompson was the daughter of a mulatto cook. She moved with her family to a farm in North Dakota where they shared community life with Norwegians, Russians, Germans, Irish, and a few Indians. Most of the community had never seen a Negro. After college she moved to Chicago and worked as an interviewer with the Illinois and United States Employment Services.

Miss Thompson joined the staff of *Ebony* magazine as an associate editor and in 1951 was named co-managing editor. In 1964, she was appointed International Editor for the Johnson Publishing Company. This position brought her into contact with world leaders and enabled her to travel extensively on all five continents. She has written many articles about racial situations throughout the world, and was co-compiler of a book, *White on Black* which is material about black people written by whites. In 1965, Morningside College conferred an honorary doctorate on Miss Thompson in recognition of her distinguished contribution to the field of journalism. She is the author of *American Daughter,* her autobiography, published in 1946 and reprinted in 1967.

HOWARD THURMAN
    (Religion   32)
    Born: 1900, Daytona Beach, Florida
    Education: Florida Baptist Academy;
        Morehouse College, Atlanta, Georgia;
        B.A., Colgate-Rochester Divinity
        School, New York; Haverford College,
        Pennsylvania
    Significance: *Theologian*

Howard Thurman was ordained in the Baptist ministry in 1925 and was pastor of a church in Oberlin, Ohio, for two years before joining the Morehouse College faculty as a professor of religion in 1928. In 1932 he moved to Howard University, where for twelve years he was professor of systematic theology and dean of the chapel. He was pastor of San Francisco's Church for the Fellowship of all People from 1944 to 1953. He then moved to Boston University as professor of spiritual disciplines and resources and dean of Marsh Chapel. He retired from that position in 1965.

Dr. Thurman has always maintained an extremely busy lecture schedule, visiting hundreds of college campuses in the United States, Canada, and abroad. After retirement he was a visiting professor at Earlham College School of Religion in 1966, and at the Presbyterian Theological Seminary in Louisville, Kentucky in 1967. Dr. Thurman has written sixteen books since *The Greatest of These* was published in 1945, including *Deep River* (1946, revised 1955), *Meditations for Apostles of Sensitiveness* (1947, 1948), *The Luminous Darkness* (1965), and *The Centering Moment* (1969).

JAMES MONROE TROTTER
     (Government   1)
     Born: 1844, Gulfport, Mississippi
     Died: 1912
     Education: Harvard University,
          Cambridge, Massachusetts
     Significance: *Government service*

James Trotter grew up in Ohio where he attended school and studied music. Bright, apt and alert, he enlisted in the famous 54th Massachusetts Regiment and was soon promoted from sergeant to lieutenant. Later, living in Boston, he became interested in politics, and was appointed assistant superintendent of the registered letter department in the Boston Post Office. He left this position in 1883 due to the creeping color line which was being drawn in the office and also because he was disgruntled with the way the Republican Party had handled its victory at the Appomattox Convention.

During the Reconstruction era, one of the government posts most prized by Negroes was the federal office of Recorder of Deeds. Trotter succeeded Frederick Douglass in this office.

His nomination as Recorder of Deeds at Washington, D.C. provoked a storm over the role of the Negro in the federal government. His nomination was held up for a time on the grounds that he was not a resident of Washington, D.C. However, the Negro press and fair-minded journalists were quick to point out that this and many other offices were filled with non-residents of the District. After much debate and procrastination, Trotter's appointment was finally confirmed on March 4, 1887.

(From Russell L. Adams, *Great Negroes Past and Present.* Chicago: Afro-Am Publishing Co., Inc., 1967.)

HARRIET TUBMAN
     (Civil Rights   32, 45)

Born: 1820, Tidewater, Maryland
Died: 1913
Significance: *"Conductor" on the
     Underground Railroad*

Harriet Tubman, born a slave, married John Tubman, a free Negro, in 1844. In 1849, she was sold by her owner, but she escaped to the free state of Pennsylvania. Early in 1850, she joined the Philadelphia Vigilance Committee and became a "conductor" on the Underground Railroad, initially to help other members of her family escape. After the passage of the Fugitive Slave Act she took runaways on to Canada, making eleven trips from 1851 to 1857.

In 1860, she made her last trip to Maryland. In May, 1962, she began to work for the Union Army. She was a nurse in the Contraband Hospital in Port Royal, South Carolina. In February, 1863, she began serving as a scout for the Second Southern Carolina Volunteers, a regiment of ex-slaves. In June she helped free 750 slaves in one raid. She was respected and known by generals and governors and had passes granting her freedom of movement anywhere.

After the Civil War ended, Mrs. Tubman worked for women's suffrage and raised money for schools for former slaves.

ROBERT L. VANN
     (Journalism, Law   1)
     Born: 1887, North Carolina
     Died: 1940
     Education: University of Pittsburgh Law
          School, Pittsburgh, Pennsylvania
     Significance: *Founder of the* Pittsburgh
          Courier

Robert L. Vann's parents were tenant farmers in backwoods North Carolina. He converted a two-page news sheet started by a worker in a pickle factory into a newspaper. Its first edition was published March 10, 1910. *The Pittsburgh Courier* caught on. Utterly candid, it spoke for the Negro community in Pittsburgh. Eventually many famous Negro writers contributed to it. In 1940, it was the most widely read Negro paper, with branches in many large cities. In 1917, Vann was made city solicitor. He also served as publicity director in Calvin Coolidge's cam-

paign for the presidency. He served on a committee to revise the Pennsylvania State
Constitution. Later Vann was appointed Assistant United States Attorney General by Franklin Roosevelt.

C. J. WALKER
(Business   9)
Born: 1869, Louisiana
Died: 1919
Significance: *Millionaire cosmetic
    manufacturer for blacks*

Mrs. C. J. Walker was a widow at 20, taking
in laundry to make a living. In 1905 she developed a hot iron which straightened tight curls.
For millions of black women this was the an-
swer to problems of hair control. Because of the
demand she opened a school of cosmetology to
train her operators. She built a factory to produce her straightening comb and employed
agents to sell her products. Shortly she developed the "Walker System" of hair styling and
cosmetics. She reaped a sizeable fortune from
her factory and maintained an annual payroll of
over a quarter million dollars. She built a
$250,000 mansion at Irvington-on-the-Hudson.
Despite her display of wealth, Mrs. Walker
was deeply concerned with the poverty of others
and became a philanthropist. She donated
$100,000 toward the establishment of an
academy for girls in West Africa and contributed large sums to black institutions and
charities in America.

MAGGIE LENA WALKER
(Finance   32)
Born: 1867, Richmond, Virginia
Died: 1934
Education: High school
Significance: *Organizer and founder of St.
    Luke Penny Savings Bank*

The Independent Order of St. Luke was one
of the fraternal orders that proliferated in Negro
communities in the latter years of the 19th century. It differed from some similar organizations
in that its membership was open to both men
and women, but like many it offered important
social services to its membership. Maggie Lena
Walker became the organization's secretary at

22 after several years of teaching. She became
secretary-treasurer in 1899 and continued in
that office for 35 years. When she took over the
order had fewer than 5,000 members and almost
no assets. By 1924, largely through her efforts,
it had grown to a membership of 100,000, acquired a $100,000 headquarters building and a
contingency fund of $70,000, and established a
newspaper, the *St. Luke Herald.* The organization also controlled a thriving insurance business and a bank, the St. Luke Bank and Trust
Company, now the Consolidated Bank and
Trust Company. Mrs. Walker presented the
original plan for a penny savings bank under St.
Luke sponsorship in 1902 and served as the
resulting institution's chief executive for many
years. In addition to her successful career as a
banker, Mrs. Walker was president of the Council of Colored Women and active in the
NAACP and the Urban League.

THOMAS WALLER
(Jazz   46)
Born: 1904
Died: 1943
Significance: *Songwriter and jazz organist*

Thomas (Fats) Waller was born in New York
City where his father was a minister in the
Abyssinian Baptist Church in Harlem. As a boy
he received a sound classical music training; by
the age of fifteen he accompanied such premier
blues singers as Bessie Smith. In the 1920's he
played at theaters, night clubs, and Harlem
"rent parties." In 1932 he toured Europe and
won wide recognition. Among the popular song
hits he composed are "Ain't Misbehavin' " and
"Honeysuckle Rose." Waller was the first jazz
musician to use the organ successfully as a jazz
instrument.

BOOKER TALIAFERRO WASHINGTON
(Education   1)
Born: 1856, Hales Ford, Virginia
Died: 1915
Education: Hampton Institute, Hampton,
    Virginia
Significance: *Founder of Tuskegee
    Institute*

When the Board of Commissioners of Tuskegee Normal Institute in Georgia asked General Samuel C. Armstrong of Hampton Institute for a principal to head their institution, they wanted a white man. Instead, Booker T. Washington was selected.

On July 4, 1881, Booker T. Washington opened the doors of the school to thirty-one students from nearby farms in a rickety church and one small shanty. With a directness typical of him, Washington then led the way in felling trees, clearing the land, digging wells for water, and constructing buildings to house the new school.

A natural politician, Washington cultivated the good will of the white and Negro people in Macon County. He explained that Tuskegee was to be an industrial training school, not a liberal arts college. His gospel of self-help appealed to many people. The student body increased and by 1900 over forty buildings dotted the clearing that was Tuskegee. His industrial school was turning out graduates who were successful farmers, carpenters and bricklayers; sober, hardworking citizens who minded their own business.

In a speech in 1895 at the Atlanta Exposition, Washington apologized for the "errors" his race made in beginning "at the top instead of at the bottom," in seeking seats in state legislatures rather than developing skills in industry and real estate, in pursuing politics rather than cultivating truck gardens. He urged the southern Negro to "Cast down your bucket where you are" in agriculture, mechanics, commerce, domestic service and the like. He said that "The wisest among my race understand that the agitation of questions of social equality is the extremest folly," and he felt that "in all things that are social we can be as separate as the fingers, yet one as the hand in all things essential for mutual progress."

The nation's press heralded his speech as the greatest utterance of an American Negro. Overnight Washington was a national figure with more speaking engagements than he could possibly handle. Philanthropists pressed money upon his Institute. At this time Tuskegee had eight hundred students and a staff of fifty-five. By 1915 it had over sixty buildings and an endowment of nearly three million dollars. Both the school and the man were internationally famous.

Debate over his racial adjustment philosophy continues to this day; however, there was never any question of his role and place in the building of Tuskegee Institute. His autobiography, *Up From Slavery,* has gone through many editions.

(Based on Russell L. Adams, *Great Negroes Past and Present.* Chicago: Afro-Am Publishing Co., Inc., 1967.)

ETHEL WATERS
(Music, Acting   1, 46)
Born: 1900, Chester, Pennsylvania
Significance: *Stage, screen, television, and recording success*

Ethel Waters' career is a dramatic rags to riches saga. She was raised in poverty—often all she had to eat were the meals supplied by the convent school she attended. She married at the age of 12 and went to work as a maid in a Philadelphia hotel. A quarter of a century later she was a famed and versatile performing artist earning $2,000 a week and the owner of two apartment houses in Harlem. But her path from maid to stage and movie stardom was long and difficult.

She created her greatest role in *Cabin in the Sky* on Broadway in 1940 and repeated that triumph in a later movie version. Her several successful films included *Rufus Jones for President, Stage Door Canteen,* and *Pinky.* Ethel Waters' mature and sensitive performance in the Broadway play *Member of the Wedding,* and the later movie version, moved huge audiences to an appreciation of her artistry and won her a permanent reputation as a premier American actress. Her autobiography, *His Eye Is on the Sparrow,* was a 1951 Book-of-the-Month Club selection. The title was taken from a song she sang in *Member of the Wedding.*

ANDRE WATTS
(Music   46)
Born: Nuremberg, Germany

Education: Peabody Conservatory of
Music, Baltimore, Maryland

Significance: *Concert pianist*

Andre Watts, son of a Hungarian mother
and an American Army father, was born in Europe in 1946. He moved to Philadelphia at the
age of eight. The following year he made his first
public appearance as a soloist with the Philadelphia Orchestra Children's Concert. His debut as
a concert pianist in 1962, substituting with the
New York Philharmonic Orchestra under
Leonard Bernstein, was greeted with great critical acclaim. He received a standing ovation
from both audience and orchestra. He has appeared on national television in Bernstein's
Young People's Concert series. In 1966 he performed in London and has since appeared as the
principal soloist in the Philharmonic Stravinsky
Festival in New York City. The spectacular success of Andre Watts has opened doors previously closed to Negro instrumentalists.

ROBERT CLIFTON WEAVER

(Government, Economics   20)

Born: 1907, Washington, D.C.

Education: B.S., M.A., Ph.D., Howard
University, Washington, D.C.

Significance: *Secretary of Housing and
Urban Development in President
Johnson's Cabinet*

Robert Weaver entered government service
in Washington, D.C. as a race relations officer
in the Department of the Interior. Serving during the Roosevelt New Deal program, he was
employed as an adviser-specialist in problems of
discrimination in housing and employment. He
was appointed to the Housing Authority Administration in 1937 as a special assistant. During World War II, from 1940 to 1942, he
became chief of the minority group service division of the War Production Board.

Subsequently, the John Hay Whitney Foundation appointed him to administer its fellowship program. Actively participating in the
affairs of the Democratic Party while residing in
New York, he was appointed by Governor Har-
riman as state rent commissioner. He was vice-
chairman of the New York City Housing and
Redevelopment Board, and during the 1960
presidential campaign, he served as adviser on
civil rights to the presidential candidate, John
F. Kennedy. Later President Kennedy appointed him administrator of the Housing and
Home Finance Agency, where he served for five
years.

Weaver was appointed by President Lyndon
B. Johnson on January 13, 1966 to the newly
created cabinet post of Secretary of Housing
and Urban Development. He is the author of
The Negro Ghetto (1948) and *The Urban Complex* (1964)

IDA B. WELLS

(Journalism   18)

Born: 1862, Holly Springs, Mississippi

Died: 1931

Education: Rust College (a Freedman
School); Fisk University, Nashville,
Tennessee

Significance: *Journalist in fight for civil
rights*

Ida Wells' parents were slaves, but her father
was literate and also a skilled laborer. She lost
a teaching position due to her protest against
educational injustice. She became part owner
and editor of the *Memphis Free Speech,* an organ which fought racial inequality. She exposed
a deliberate lynching plot and urged Negro migration to Oklahoma Territory, and her presses
were destroyed and her life threatened. She received international notice for her war on lynching and was honored by the first Negro
Women's Club. A close friend of Frederick
Douglass, she remained active in politics and
civic affairs until her death. She was the author
of *Free Speech.*

PHILLIS WHEATLEY

(Literature   1)

Born: 1753, Senegal, Africa

Died: 1784

Significance: *The first recognized Negro
poetess*

Phillis Wheatley was brought from Africa as
a slave when a child and sold at the age of eight
to a wealthy man, John Wheatley of Boston. She

was a servant for Wheatley's wife and companion to his twin children. Taught in the family, she soon read the classics in English and Latin and became proficient in writing verse. Mrs. Wheatley freed her in 1772 and helped her secure passage to England. The Countess of Huntington arranged for her first book to be published in 1773. While in England, Phillis Wheatley was presented to the Lord Mayor of London. On her return to the colonies of America, she wrote a poem to George Washington, who invited her to visit him. She was said to be the first to use the phrase, "first in peace" and was quoted by Congress in a resolution on Washington's death. Her verse was influenced by Calvinism and her literary contemporaries, and was highly commended by prominent colonials of the day.

WALTER FRANCIS WHITE
  (Civil Rights   46)
  Born: 1896, Atlanta, Georgia
  Died: 1955
  Education: B.A., Atlanta University,
    Georgia
  Significance: *Writer in the field of civil
    rights*
Walter White received a Guggenheim Award in 1926 for his novel, *Flight.* In 1931 he became secretary of the NAACP and served on various government commissions. He fought tirelessly against racial discrimination and lynchings in the United States. His autobiography, *A Man Called White,* has been widely read. His other books include *Rope and Faggott* and *A Rising Wind.*

ROY WILKINS
  (Civil Rights   7, 46)
  Born: 1901, St. Louis, Missouri
  Education: B.A., University of
    Minnesota, Minneapolis, Minnesota
  Significance: *Leadership in the Negro
    rights movement*
Roy Wilkins was raised in the home of an aunt and uncle in St. Paul. He attended an integrated school and lived in a racially mixed community. While attending the University of Minnesota he joined the National Association for the Advancement of Colored People (NAACP). After graduation he was managing editor of the Negro weekly, *The Call,* in Kansas City (1923-31).

In 1931 he joined the NAACP staff as an assistant secretary and the next year disguised himself as an intinerant laborer to investigate working conditions for Negroes employed on Mississippi flood-control projects financed by the federal government. His report led to a Senate investigation and significant improvement.

Succeeding W. E. B. DuBois as editor of the NAACP's monthly *Crisis* in 1934, Wilkins became acting secretary of the organization in 1949 and executive secretary in 1955, upon the death of Walter White. He served as consultant on the training and placement of Negroes for the War Department during World War II and attended the United Nations Conference in San Francisco in 1945 as consultant to the American delegation. He chaired the National Emergency Civil Rights Mobilization, a massive lobbying effort in Washington in 1949. He was a major sponsor of the 1963 March on Washington.

DANIEL HALE WILLIAMS
  (Medicine   49, 53)
  Born: 1858, Hollidaysburg, Pennsylvania
  Died: 1931
  Education: M.D., Chicago Medical
    College (later became Northwestern
    University School of Medicine),
    Chicago, Illinois; LL.D., Wilberforce
    University, Ohio
  Significance: *Performed first recorded
    successful heart operation; called the
    "Father of Negro Hospitals"*
After the death of his father, Daniel Williams was taken as a small boy to live with relatives in Janesville, Wisconsin. He worked during his school days at many odd jobs. It was one of his employers, a barber, who took an interest in him and persuaded a local doctor to let the boy study medicine under him. Williams passed the entrance examination for the Chicago Medical College. After his graduation in 1883, he in-

terned at a Catholic hospital in Chicago. Because at this time there were no training schools for Negro nurses and few hospitals where Negro doctors could intern, Dr. Williams called a meeting of interested persons, both Negro and white. The result was the founding of Provident Hospital and Training School for Nurses in 1891.

Two years later, President Grover Cleveland made him Surgeon-General of Freedmen's Hospital, a government hospital in Washington, D.C. After five years he returned to Chicago to join the staff of the Cook County Hospital and St. Luke's Hospital where he continued for the remainder of his life. Dr. Williams became internationally famous for his successful operation on the human heart. Early in his medical career he was a member of the Illinois State Board of Health. He was one of the founders of the National Medical Association and a charter member of the American College of Surgeons. He spent much time traveling and lecturing to help build hospitals and training schools for Negroes in many cities.

PAUL REVERE WILLIAMS
    (Architecture   16, 18)
    Born: 1896, Los Angeles, California
    Education: University of Southern
        California, Los Angeles; Beaux Arts
        Institute of Design, France
    Significance: *Architect of public buildings*
Paul R. Williams was director of architecture at Howard University in Washington, D.C., and director of fine arts at Tuskegee Institute, at Tuskegee, Alabama, 1956.

He designed many important buildings in the Los Angeles area, including the Beverly-Wilshire Hotel, the 20th Century Fox Studios, the Saks Fifth Avenue Store, the Federal Customs Buildings, the Music Corporation of America office buildings in New York City and Beverly Hills, and Franz Hall and Botany Hall at the University of California in Los Angeles. He has also designed many homes for motion picture stars.

Williams was a member of the President's Advisory Commission on Housing and a member of the California Civil Rights Commission. He has received many honors, such as the Man of the Year Award from Omega Phi Psi, the Spingarn Medal from NAACP in 1953, and the Award for Creative Planning from the Los Angeles Chamber of Commerce in 1955. He is a Fellow of the American Institute of Architects. Williams is the author of *Small Homes of Tomorrow* and *New Homes for Today.*

CLEROW (FLIP) WILSON
    (Entertainment   46)
    Born: 1933, Jersey City, New Jersey
    Significance: Television personality and
        network show
Clerow (Flip) Wilson is one of the most engaging television personalities of this era. His impersonations, and especially his characterizations (notably the Reverend Leroy, Geraldine, and Queen Isabella) have brought him wealth and fame. But that fame came slowly. Wilson lived most of his early life in foster homes and schools. He falsified his age to enlist in the Air Force at sixteen and later worked as a bellboy in San Francisco. His entry into show business was via the night club circuit—initially as a fill-in in San Francisco, later in small night clubs, then at the Apollo Theater in Harlem. After appearing on Johnny Carson's "Tonight Show" in 1965 when he performed his Christopher Columbus routine his career and success were assured.

GRANVILLE T. WOODS
    (Invention   1, 46)
    Born: 1856, Columbus, Ohio
    Died: 1910
    Significance: *Inventor holding many
        patents*
Granville T. Woods left school at ten and worked in a machine shop. His basic mechanical knowledge was enhanced by working on a Missouri railroad in 1872 and in a Springfield rolling mill in 1874. In 1876 he studied mechanical engineering in an eastern college. This fertile inventive genius held more than thirty-five patents—including one for a steam boiler furnace (1884), an incubator for hatching eggs

(1900), and the automatic air brake (1902). Many of his electrical inventions were sold to the American Bell Telephone Company and the General Electric Company. His air brake patent eventually became the property of the Westinghouse Air Brake Company.

In 1887 he patented the Synchronous Multiplex Railway Telegraph. Up to that time many electrical engineers were seeking ways to prevent accidents by keeping trains informed of other trains ahead or behind on the same track. Woods' invention allowed moving trains to communicate with the stations. Although his patent was contested by the Edison and Phelps Company whose engineers were working on a similar device, the Patent Office twice upheld Woods' rights as the inventor. He marketed the product and others through his own company.

CARTER GOODWIN WOODSON
   (History   49)
   Born: 1875, New Canton, Virginia
   Died: 1950
   Education: Berea College, Kentucky;
      A.B., University of Chicago, Illinois;
      Graduate work, Sorbonne, Paris;
      Ph.D., Harvard University,
      Cambridge, Massachusetts
   Significance: *Achievement in the history*
      of the Negro people

Carter Goodwin Woodson had great difficulty getting any schooling and was twenty when he entered high school. After two years at Berea College in Kentucky he returned to Douglass High School where he had graduated with honors, this time as its principal. After several summers at Berea he became a supervisor of schools in the Philippine Islands where he stayed four years. Upon returning to the United States, he went back to college and in 1909 became a high school teacher in Washington, D.C.

From the early years of his academic career he had been reading Negro history. He found that many Negro achievements were ignored or even suppressed by writers of history textbooks. It was his greatest ambition that Negro youth should grow up with a knowledge of the contributions of the Negro to American history. His monumental record of the lost and ignored history of the American Negro became the basis for a number of books on the subject. Another outgrowth of his studies was the founding of the Association for the Study of Negro Life and History and its publication, the *Journal of Negro History.*

Dr. Woodson was Dean of the School of Liberal Arts at Howard University, then Dean of West Virginia State College. During this time he published his widely used textbook, *The Negro in Our History,* which has gone through ten editions. He also started the *Negro History Bulletin* for use in elementary and high schools. In 1926 he originated Negro History Week, celebrated each year in February at a period which covers the birthdates of both Abraham Lincoln and Frederick Douglass.

In 1926, Dr. Woodson was awarded the Spingarn Medal for "Outstanding Achievement in the Field of Research and History of the Negro."

RICHARD WRIGHT
   (Literature   12)
   Born: 1908, Natchez, Mississippi
   Died: 1960
   Education: High School
   Significance: *Novelist*

Richard Wright developed his writing technique as a W.P.A. Project writer. His first writing was based on his childhood in Mississippi. He sought to call attention to poverty, injustice, and oppression. After years of odd jobs in Memphis and Chicago he moved to Paris, where he was influenced by existentialism and settled as an expatriate. One of his books was chosen as a Book-of-the-Month Club selection. He received the Spingarn Medal and a Guggenheim Fellowship. Early in his career he was a contributor to *The Daily Worker* and *New Masses.* Wright was the author of *Native Son, Black Power, White Man Listen,* and *Black Boy.*

MALCOLM X (LITTLE)
   (Civil Rights   46)
   Born: 1925, Omaha, Nebraska

Died: 1965
Education: New York public schools
Significance: *Militant leadership for civil
   rights*

Malcolm X was a prime leader of the modern black nationalist movement in the United States. He came to wide public attention as an outspoken advocate of the doctrines of the Nation of Islam, the Black Muslims. His view that the white man is evil and that the Negro needs revenge for past inequities made him one of the most controversial figures in the black movement. He left school after finishing the eighth grade and went to Boston and New York, supporting himself for a while as a waiter at Small's Paradise in Harlem, later by selling marijuana. He was imprisoned for burglary in 1946. While in prison he was introduced to the Black Muslim sect. He was paroled in 1952, and began his career as proselytizer for the Black Muslims in Detroit. He broke with the Nation of Islam and pilgrimaged to Mecca in 1964. After his return he formed a militant group of his own, the Organization of Afro-American Unity. Malcolm X was murdered in 1965, the same year *The Autobiography of Malcolm X* (which he wrote with Alex Haley) appeared.

CHARLES YOUNG
   (Military   23, 49)
   Born: 1864, Mayslick, Kentucky
   Died: 1922
   Education: United States Military
      Academy, West Point, New York
   Significance: *Leadership in world-wide
      military ventures*

Charles Young was the ninth Negro to be admitted to West Point. He graduated in 1889 with a commission as second lieutenant in the all-Negro Tenth Cavalry. At one time he taught military science at Wilberforce University in Ohio. During the Spanish-American War, he was promoted to the rank of major, put in charge of the Ninth Ohio Regiment and sent to Cuba. The Ninth and Tenth Cavalries distinguished themselves at San Juan Hill, coming to the aid of Teddy Roosevelt and his Rough Riders. Some believed that the strength of the Negro troops turned the tide of the battle and won the Spanish fort. Later, Young served in the Philippine Islands and in Haiti. After seeing action against the Mexican guerrillas in 1915, he was made a lieutenant colonel and led further raids against Pancho Villa.

Despite his outstanding record of bravery, his rank, and his experience, Young was not assigned in World War I to European service. The reason is variously given as high blood pressure and racial prejudice. To prove that he was in top physical condition he rode a horse from Xenia, Ohio, to Washington and back again, to no avail.

Later as a military attache he was sent to Monrovia, Liberia to help reorganize the Liberian army. He was pleased at this opportunity to deepen his interest in African life and culture. At his death, he was buried in the National Cemetery at Arlington, Virginia, with full military honors. A tall marble shaft marks his resting place.

WHITNEY M. YOUNG, JR.
   (Civil Rights   7, 46)
   Born: 1921, Lincoln Ridge, Kentucky
   Died: 1971
   Education: Kentucky State College,
      Frankfort, Kentucky; Atlanta
      University, Georgia; M.A., University
      of Minnesota
   Significance: *Civil Rights leadership*

Whitney Young was executive director of the National Urban League beginning in 1961 and presided over a massive reinvigoration of the League's social welfare work among urban Negroes, putting together a staff of some 500 professionals attached to sixty-four local Urban League affiliates in industrial cities. Before his appointment to the Urban League post, Young had been Dean of the Atlanta University School of Social Work (1954-60) and instructor in social work at the University of Nebraska (1950-58). He was a member of many governmental commissions and foundation boards of directors, co-founder of the Urban Coalition (1967), and one of the sponsors of the 1963 March on Washington.

Young was the prime spokesman for the conservative position within the civil rights movement of the sixties, advocating the full use of existing legal, economic, and social machinery for the achievement of Negroes' rights. He was a frequent lecturer, the subject of a nationwide television documentary, and the author of several books, including *To Be Equal* (1966) and *Beyond Racism* (1969). He died in Lagos, Nigeria, while participating in a Ford Foundation-sponsored African-American dialogue series.

AFRO AMERICANS

BIBLIOGRAPHY OF SOURCES USED

1   Adams, Russell L. *Great Negroes Past and Present.* Chicago: Afro-Am Publishing Co., 1964.
2   *American Medical Directory.* 20th ed. Chicago: American Medical Association, 1967.
3   *American Men of Science: Physical & Biological Sciences.* Edited by Jaques Cattell Press. 11th ed. New York: R. R. Bowker Company, n.d.
4   Barbour, Floyd B. (ed.). *Black Power Revolt.* Boston: Porter Sargent, 1968.
5   Beasley, Delilah Leontium. *The Negro Trail Blazers of California.* Los Angeles: Times-Mirror, 1919.
6   Bennett, Lerone. *Before the Mayflower: A History of Black America.* 3rd ed. Chicago: Johnson Publishing Co., 1966.
7   Bergman, Peter M. *The Chronological History of the Negro in America.* New York: New American Library, Inc., 1969.
8   Boning, Richard. *Profiles of Black Americans.* Rockville, New York: Dexter & Westbrook, 1969.
9   *Calendar of Great Blacks.* Los Angeles, California: Progressive Black Associates, 1969.
10 *Collier's Yearbook.* New York: Crowell-Collier Publishing Co., 1968.
11 *Current Biography.* Yearbooks. New York: H. W. Wilson Co., 1946, 1967, 1968, 1969.
12 Davis, John P. (ed.). *American Negro Reference Book.* Englewood Cliffs, New Jersey: Prentice-Hall, Inc., 1966.
13 *Dictionary of American Biography.* Edited by the American Council of Learned Societies. New York: Charles Scribner's Sons, 1928.
14 *Directory of Medical Specialists.* Chicago: Marquis – Who's Who, Inc., 1968.
15 Dover, Cedric. *American Negro Art.* Greenwich, Connecticut: New York Graphic Society, 1960.
16 Drotning, Phillip T. *Black Heroes in Our Nation's History.* New York: Doubleday and Co., 1968.
17 _____. *A Guide to Negro History in America.* New York: Doubleday and Co., 1968.
18 Ebony. *The Negro Handbook.* Chicago: Johnson Publishing Co., 1966.
19 Emanuel, James A., and Gross, Theodore L. (eds.). *Dark Symphony: Negro Literature in America.* New York: Free Press, 1968.
20 Encyclopaedia Britannica. *The Negro in American History.* 3 volumes. Chicago: Encyclopaedia Britannica, Inc., 1969.
21 Felton, Harold W. *Edward Rose, Negro Trail Blazer.* New York: Dodd, Mead and Co., 1967.
22 Flint, Michigan, Board of Education in association with Ebony Magazine. *Today's Negro-Americans and Their Contributions to Their Country.* Flint, Michigan: Board of Education, n.d.

23 Franklin, John H. *From Slavery to Freedom: History of Negro Americans.* 3rd ed. New York: Alfred A. Knopf, 1967.

24 Frazier, E. Franklin. *The Negro in the United States.* New York: Macmillan, Co., 1969.

25 Haber, Louis. *The Role of the American Negro in the Fields of Science.* Unpublished material. Washington, D. C.: Division of Elementary and Secondary Education, Bureau of Research, Office of Education, 1966.

26 Harlan, Louis R. *The Negro in American History.* Washington: American Historical Association, 1965.

27 Hearne Brothers. *The Afro-American's Contribution to California and Other Individuals Who Have Contributed to Afro-American History.* 2 charts. Detroit: Hearne Brothers, 1969.

28 Hill, Herbert. (ed.). *Anger and Beyond: The Negro Writer in the United States.* New York: Harper & Row Publishers, 1966.

29 Hughes, Langston. *Famous Negro Heroes of America.* New York: Dodd, Mead & Co., 1958.

30 Hughes, Langston, and Bontemps, Arna. *The Poetry of the Negro, 1946–1949.* New York: Doubleday and Co., 1949.

31 Hurley, Jane, and Haynes, D. M. *Afro-Americans Then and Now.* Westchester, Illinois: Benefic Press, 1969.

32 *International Library of Negro Life and History.* Produced under the auspices of The Association for the Study of Negro Life and History. Edited by Charles H. Wesley. 2nd ed., 10 vols. New York: Publishers Co., Inc., 1968.

33 Jones, Le Roi, and Neal, Larry (eds.). *Black Fire: An Anthology of Afro-American Writing.* New York: William Morrow and Co., 1968.

34 Katz, William L. (comp.). *Eyewitness: The Negro in American History.* New York: Pitman Publishing Corp., 1967.

35 King, Coretta Scott. *My Life with Martin Luther King, Jr.* New York: Holt, Rinehart & Winston, 1969.

36 Lapp, Rudolph. "Negro Rights Activities in Gold Rush California," *California Historical Society Quarterly,* Vol. XLV, 1969.

37 Levine, Richard. "Jesse Jackson, Heir to Dr. King?", *Harper's,* March, 1969.

38 "L/J News," *Library Journal,* Vol. 95, No. 7, (April 1, 1970), p. 1265.

39 Longstreet, Stephen. *The Real Jazz Old and New.* Baton Rouge: Louisiana State University Press, 1956.

40 Malone, Mary. *Actor in Exile.* London: Crowell-Collier Publishing Co., 1967.

41 Meier, August, and Rudnick, Elliott (eds.). *The Origins of Black Americans.* New York: Atheneum Publishers, 1969.

42 Metcalf, George R. *Black Profiles.* New York: McGraw-Hill Book Co., 1968.

43 *Negro History Bulletin.* Vol. 31, No. 4. March, 1968.

44 *Negroes and Mexican-Americans in the California State Government.* A cooperative project conducted by the Office of the Governor Edmund G. Brown, selected California newspaper publishers, and the State Personnel Board. Sacramento: State of California, 1965.

45 Petry, Ann. *Harriet Tubman: Conducter of the Underground Railroad.* New York: Thomas Y. Crowell Co., 1955.

46 Ploski, Harry A., and Brown, Roscoe C., Jr., (eds.). *Negro Almanac.* New York: Bellwether Publishing Co., 1967.

47 Porter, Dorothy B. "Early American Negro Writings: A Bibliographical Study," *The Bibliographical Society of America.* Vol. 39.

48 Rollins, Charlemae. *Famous American Negro Poets.* New York: Dodd, Mead & Co., 1965.

49 _____. *They Showed the Way: Forty American Negroes.* New York: Thomas Y. Crowell Co., 1965.

50 Thompson, Era Bell. *American Daughter.* Chicago: Follett Publishing Co., 1967.

51 *Who's Who in Colored America.* An illustrated biographical directory of notable living persons of African descent in the United States. Yonkers-on-Hudson, New York: C. E. Burkel, 1950.

52 *World Book Encyclopedia.* Chicago: Field Enterprises Educational corp., 1968.

53 *World Who's Who in Science.* A biographical dictionary of notable scientists from antiquity to the present. Chicago: Marquis – Who's Who, Inc., 1968.

54 Young, A. S. (Doc). *Black Champions of the Gridiron.* New York: Harcourt, Brace and World, 1969.

AFRO AMERICANS

OTHER REFERENCES

BOOKS FOR TEACHERS

Aplin, Norita. *The Negro American, His Role, His Quest.* Cleveland, Ohio: Cleveland Public Schools, 1968.

Clemons, Lulamae. *Americans All: The American Negro.* New York: McGraw-Hill Book Co., 1965.

Cruse, Harold. *Crisis of the Negro Intellectual.* New York: William Morrow & Co., 1967.

Douglass, Frederick. *Life and Times of Frederick Douglass.* New York: Collier Books, Macmillan Co., 1966.

Du Bois, W. E. *The Souls of Black Folk.* New York: Fawcett World Library, 1964.

Durham, Philip, and Jones, Everett L. *Negro Cowboys.* New York: Dodd, Mead & Co., 1965.

Ferguson, Blanche E. *Countee Cullen and the Negro Renaissance.* New York: Dodd, Mead & Co., 1966.

Fishel, Leslie H., Jr. *The Negro American: A Documentary History.* New York: William Morrow & Co., 1967.

Franco. *Afro-American Contributors to American Life.* Westchester, Illinois: Benefic Press, 1970.

Franklin, John H. "Black Strength," *Life Magazine,* (December 6, 1968).

Heard, J. Norman. *Black Frontiersmen.* New York: John Day Co., 1969.

Hicks, John D. "California in History," *California Historical Society Quarterly,* Vol. XXIV.

Isaacs, Harold R. *New World of Negro Americans.* New York: John Day Co., 1963.

Katz, William L. *Teacher's Guide to American Negro History.* Chicago: Quadrangle Books, 1968.

Killian, Lewis, and Grigg, Charles. *Racial Crisis in America.* Englewood Cliffs, New Jersey: Prentice-Hall, 1964.

Pinkney, Alphonso. *Black Americans.* Englewood Cliffs, New Jersey: Prentice-Hall, 1969.

Rolle, Andrew F. *California, A History.* Based in part upon *A Short History of California* by Rockwell D. Hunt and Nellie Van de Grift Sanchez. New York: Thomas Y. Crowell, Co., 1963.

Salk, Erwin A. (comp. and ed.). *A Layman's Guide to Negro History.* New York: McGraw-Hill Book Co., 1967.

Spangler, E. *The Negro in America.* Minneapolis: Lerner Publishing Co., 1968.

Sterling, Dorothy. *Tear Down the Walls. A History of the American Civil Rights Movement.* New York: Doubleday & Co., 1968.

Sussman, Murray. *American Biographies.* New York: Holt, Rinehart & Winston, Inc., 1968.

Williams, Robin M. *Strangers Next Door. Ethnic relations in American Communities.* Englewood Cliffs, New Jersey: Prentice-Hall, 1964.

BOOKS FOR CHILDREN

Adoff, Arnold. (comp.). *I Am the Darker Brother. An Anthology of Modern Poems by Negro Americans.* New York: Macmillan Co., 1968.

Baum, Betty. *Patricia Crosses Town.* New York: Alfred A. Knopf, 1965.

Bontemps, Arna. (ed.). *Golden Slippers.* An Anthology of Negro Poetry. New York: Harper & Row, Publishers, 1941.

Boone-Jones, Margaret. *Martin Luther King, Jr., A Picture Story.* Chicago: Children's Press, 1968.

Campanella, Roy. *It's Good To Be Alive.* Boston: Little, Brown & Co., 1959.

Carlson, Natalie. *Empty Schoolhouse.* New York: Harper & Row, Publishers, 1965.

De Angeli, Marguerite. *Bright April.* New York: Doubleday and Co., n.d.

Felton, Harold W. *Jim Beckwourth, Negro Mountain Man.* New York: Dodd, Mead & Co., 1966.

Freeman, Don. *Corduroy.* New York: Viking Press, 1968.

Graham, Lorenz. *South Town.* Chicago: Follett Publishing Co., 1966.

————. *Whose Town?* New York: Thomas Y. Crowell Co., 1969.

Hamilton, Virginia. *House of Dies Drear.* New York: Macmillan Co., n.d.

————. *Zeely.* New York: Macmillan Co., 1967.

Hill, E. S. *Evan's Corner.* New York: Holt, Rinehart and Winston, 1966.

Humphreville, Frances T. *Harriet Tubman: Flame of Freedom.* Boston: Houghton-Mifflin Co., 1967.

Hunter, Kristin. *Soul Brothers and Sister Lou.* New York: Charles Scribner's Sons, 1968.

Keats, Ezra Jack. *John Henry, An American Legend.* New York: Pantheon Books, Inc., 1965.

————. *Snowy Day.* New York: Viking Press, 1962.

————. *Whistle for Willie.* New York: Viking Press, 1964.

Lester, Julius. *To Be A Slave.* New York: Dial Press, 1968.

McGovern, Ann. *Runaway Slave: The Story of Harriet Tubman.* Englewood Cliffs, New Jersey: Scholastic Book Services, 1965.

Meltzer, Milton. *In Their Own Words.* New York: Thomas Y. Crowell Co., 1964.

Montgomery, Elizabeth R. *William C. Handy.* Champaign, Illinois: Garrard Publishing Co., 1968.

Patterson, Lillie. *Booker T. Washington, Leader of His People.* Champaign, Illinois: Garrard Publishing Co., 1962.

Petry, Ann. *Tituba of Salem Village.* New York: Thomas Y. Crowell Co., 1964.

Rollins, Charlemae (comp.). *Christmas Gif'.* Chicago: Follett Publishing Co., 1963.

————. *They Showed the Way.* New York: Thomas Y. Crowell Co., 1964.

Scott, Ann Herbert. *Sam.* New York: McGraw-Hill Book Company, 1967.

Shotwell, Louisa R. *Roosevelt Grady.* New York: World Publishing Co., 1963.

Sterling, Dorothy. *Lift Every Voice.* New York: Doubleday and Co., 1965.

Yates, Elizabeth. *Amos Fortune, Free Man.* New York: E. P. Dutton & Co., 1958.

PART TWO

ASIAN AMERICANS

This is our dream that all men shall be free!
This is our creed we'll live in loyalty
God help us rid the land of bigotry
That we may walk in peace and dignity.

MARION GUYO TAJIRI

ASIAN AMERICANS

HISTORICAL PERSPECTIVE

THE CONTRIBUTIONS of all Asian Americans to the American scene were well summarized by an observation made by historian Bradford Smith. In writing of the first generation Japanese American, he said: "The Issei contribution to America was not in great men, but in the anonymous little men who made the desert spaces green with the labor of their hands, who kept the track even so that Americans could ride comfortably across the land, who tended the comfort of the well-to-do, and grew vegetables the poor could afford to buy, who sacrificed for the welfare of their children."

JAPANESE AMERICANS

According to Bill Hosokawa,* contemporary journalist, editor, and writer, not all Japanese Americans were anonymous little men as described by Smith. There were Japanese immigrants who left a mark in the story of America.

The Japanese did not begin immigration to the United States until the 1860's, when they began to trickle into Hawaii as plantation laborers. Immigration began because of a two-way need: the need for laborers by the host country and the need for opportunities for self-betterment by the immigrants.

This immigrant group of laborers was largely better educated than similar groups, because universal education had already been introduced in Japan. The immigrants, often second or third sons, with no hope of inheriting the family farmlands, came to the United States to earn a grubstake, fully intending to return home and purchase land or a small business with their savings.

The laborers proved industrious and were soon imported in large numbers to Hawaii. In addition to plantation work, many thrifty and hard working Japanese immigrants learned skilled trades, became businessmen, or acquired small farms of their own.

In 1900 some 12,626 Japanese arrived on the mainland, mainly in California. Many worked as farm laborers. Another 12,000 came in 1905 to meet the need for railroad workers. These first generation Japanese immigrants are called Issei (EE-say). Their children are called Nisei (Nee-say). The Nisei are American citizens by birth, as are their third generation Sansei children. But citizenship for the Issei was long in coming. Until 1952 American prejudice, reflected in the laws of the land, denied Issei the right to become citizens.

Many Japanese, who originally worked as farm laborers, railroad men, or houseboys, opened small businesses or ran their own small farms. Before 1900 they often worked in the service trades —as barbers, restauranteurs, hotel managers—in the predominantly male frontier community.

*For a fuller and beautifully written account of these men, the reader is referred to Bill Hosokawa's *Nisei: the Quiet Americans.*

Although the early immigrants did not plan to stay in America, they soon recognized the need to learn English and adopt American modes of dress.

The Gentlemen's Agreement of 1907 between Theodore Roosevelt and the Japanese government brought a change in the type of immigrants. The agreement was to stop immigration, but left loopholes which allowed such persons as picture brides to enter. When it became apparent to the majority of immigrants that they were not going to earn enough to return home, many immigrants sent for picture brides.

The Japanese were not welcome to live in most parts of a city. Ghettos began to form. Institutions were set up to bridge the gap between the native heritage and the American environment. The Japanese Association, an Issei group, was established. This group provided translators, placed people in contact with legal and other services, maintained graveyards, and policed activities in the Japanese community. It also sponsored youth groups.

World War I brought great shipbuilding and other war-related activities to the cities. The war workers needed services such as hotels, dye works, and restaurants. Farm crops were in demand and reached a peak in prices. Japanese American communities involved in these activities expanded. A new wave of immigrants came. The Japanese began to move out of the ghetto. But the Anti-Alien Land Law of 1921 and the Immigrant Act of 1924 stopped this expansion. The foreign born Japanese could no longer lease or own land. No further immigration to the United States was permitted. The ghetto communities were geared to the inflow of immigrants. This blow to the economic base of its community and to its pride created a greater gap between the Japanese and the white community. The period of establishing families ended, for no new brides could be sent for and intermarriage rarely occurred.

As the first generation saw their own opportunities become more and more limited, a great emphasis was placed on the education and rearing of the second generation.

The Japanese Americans started out as farmers and laborers, but an amazingly high percentage soon became involved in trade. This was due in large part to two customs brought from Japan. In Japan, when there were too many sons for a farm, boys were often apprenticed to tradesmen. In America the custom of Ken-Jin developed, whereby a man from a certain ken (district) would seek out a member of his ken in America. This ken member would give his countryman shelter and teach him his trade. When the newcomer was ready to set up a business, a second custom came to his aid. A tanomoshi, or money pool, would be devised to finance a new shop. Friends would gather at a dinner and contribute a certain sum which would later be paid back by "gifts" to the benefactors. The tanomoshi was a social function. No security was demanded of a member other than his good name.

Japanese Americans demonstrated amazing ability to reclaim delta and desert lands. Accustomed to intensive farming in their land-starved homeland, the Japanese Americans coaxed vegetables even from the desert. Hard-working and ambitious as a group, they were often regarded with suspicion by competitors, especially when they arrived in large numbers. During hard times when jobs were scarce and prices were low, anti-Japanese feeling ran high.

The Issei carefully reared and educated their American-born children, doubly precious because they alone had a real future in this land. Japanese American children were imbued with the old Buddhist concepts of respect and filial piety. They were urged to succeed and to bring pride to the family name. Ethics, as well as the Japanese language, was taught in Japanese language schools which were conducted after the public schools were dismissed.

The Nisei were, as a group, phenomenally successful in school, and large percentages attending the universities became professionals. However, on entering the job market they found that old prejudices had not abated and jobs on a professional level were not to be had. In the decade prior to World War II, lawyers, teachers, and architects found themselves running fruit stands or working on their parents' farms.

In the early 1920's the Japanese American Citizens League (JACL) was founded to explore ways to extend the privileges of citizenship for the Nisei. The goals of the group were cultural acceleration, liaison between the Nisei and the larger community, and greater opportunities for the Nisei.

When Japan attacked Pearl Harbor, the Nisei, American citizens of Japanese ancestry, knew they were in trouble. Their parents, denied the right to become American citizens, had maintained their Japanese citizenship to avoid the legal difficulties involved in being without a country. Issei and Nisei alike were evacuated from their homes and were placed in concentration camps. American citizens of Japanese descent experienced a complete denial of civil liberties.

Japanese American reaction to this infamous act of hysteria and prejudice varied from individual to individual. A few made legal protest, many protested verbally and in writing, others quietly acquiesced. But the vast majority, after voicing their protest, decided to remain loyal to the principles of American democracy, even though these principles were being denied them. They decided to support their country, the United States of America, actively in the war effort. Under the leadership of the JACL they petitioned to be allowed to join the armed services and eventually made outstanding contributions as servicemen, nurses, and translators, and in many other capacities.

Meanwhile, those remaining in the camps used their technical and professional skills to make these overcrowded, isolated places livable. They set up schools and hospitals and forms of self-government. Those trained as teachers, but unable to find jobs as teachers before the war, gained their first experience in the camps.

The JACL played a major role in the evacuation to the concentration camps. While lobbying against evacuation prior to the actual order to evacuate, once the order was a fact, they urged cooperation with the authorities. During the war JACL officials worked constantly for improved conditions within the camps and for termination of the evacuation as soon as possible.*

After World War II the Japanese American Citizens League worked to get the government to repay the Nisei for monetary losses due to the evacuation and they also worked for, and eventually achieved, citizenship for the Issei and a liberalization of the immigration laws.

CHINESE AMERICANS

The discovery of gold in California brought the first Chinese in numbers to Gum San, the land of the Golden Mountains. Nearly all of the early Chinese immigrants were Cantonese, since Canton was the only port for China's early foreign trade.

The defeat of China in the Opium War of 1840 was followed by pressure from the West to open the door to trade. At the same time the Manchu Dynasty was entering a period of decay and decline. Corruption and injustice were common. More and more land was concentrated in fewer and fewer hands. Famines, floods, and droughts hastened the process. Local feuds between Chinese sub-groups caused further turmoil. Peasant uprisings took place. In 1851 the T'ai-p'ing Rebellion broke out and almost toppled the Manchu Dynasty. The rebellion was ruthlessly crushed.

When news came of the discovery of gold in California and of good wages to be had, some Chinese took passage to California. With the abolition of the slave trade in the 19th century a demand arose for another form of cheap labor. The indentured or contract labor system (called the coolie system) originated. Provincial authorities of Kwangtung gave permission for foreigners

*Allen R. Bosworth, *America's Concentration Camps.* (New York: W. W. Norton and Co., 1967).

to recruit Chinese labor to serve abroad. Chinese contract laborers arrived in Hawaii in 1852. A few had arrived in California during the gold rush, but it was difficult to enforce the contracts. Therefore, most of the poorer immigrants came by the credit-ticket system. By this system the immigrant was indebted to a broker, repaying him in installments for the passage cost. This system was not the same as the coolie system. Most Chinese laborers were not coolies.

By 1852 there were 20,026 Chinese in the United States. They came to mine gold, but found themselves excluded from the gold mines by the Foreign Miner's Tax and often excluded physically by miners of other races. Immigration tapered off, but did reach 50,000 by the 1860's.

The Burlingame Treaty of 1868 facilitated the entrance of Chinese laborers into the United States. The late 1860's saw the building of the transcontinental railroad. Large areas of tule swamps were to be reclaimed for agricultural use. Labor was needed.

Besides gold mining, the Chinese engaged in mining quicksilver and coal. They worked the borax beds and salt beds. Many were engaged in fishing up and down the west coast and on the Sacramento River delta. The shrimp industry was dominated by Chinese from 1871 until its demise. They engaged in the abalone industry, shark fishing, crab fishing, and seaweed harvesting. The Chinese are generally credited with developing the fishing industry to its high position in the United States. By 1871 Chinese went to work in the salmon industry. After the Chinese Exclusion Act they were replaced by the Japanese.

In 1865 Chinese were hired by the Central Pacific Railroad Company to work on the transcontinental railroad. The Chinese role in building this railroad was a major one. After 1865 four out of every five Central Pacific workers were Chinese. Chinese railroad workers divided into gangs of twelve to twenty each. Each group had a cook who made meals and prepared hot water for their nightly sponge baths. Each gang also had a head man who handled salaries and bought provisions. The hours of work were sunrise to sunset, six days a week.

The Chinese did heroic work on this railroad. Workmen were lowered in baskets over high cliffs to drill holes and plant explosives. During the winter of 1866 the Chinese remained in the High Sierras, their shacks completely covered with snow. They tunneled through the huge drifts to work their shifts. Loss of life, due to snow slides, was heavy.

At one point, in June of 1867, some 2,000 Chinese railroad workers went on strike. They asked for $40.00 a month and a workday of only ten hours; eight hours when in the tunnels. Other laborers were never required to work more than eight hours. They also asked for freedom from whippings and the right to leave for other employment. But the strike collapsed.

On May 10, 1869 the Central Pacific and Union Pacific tracks were officially joined at Promontory Point near Ogden, Utah. One of the few to pay tribute to the Chinese workman was E. B. Crocker who said, "I wish to call to your minds that the early completion of this railroad we have built has been in large measure due to that poor, despised class of laborers called the Chinese, to the fidelity and industry they have shown."

The Chinese also worked on wagon roads, stone bridges and fences, in the cigar industry, the woolen industry, the making of slippers, shoes and boots, and in the sewing trades. Even today the garment industry is one of the few remaining manufacturing industries in San Francisco's Chinatown.

Chinese began working in the vineyards in the 1860's. After the completion of the transcontinental railroad in 1869 many Chinese engaged in agricultural work - picking cotton and fruit, harvesting hops, berries, and sugar beets. Most Chinese farms were truck farms and utilized leased land. In Los Angeles it was the Chinese who introduced the cultivation of celery. They entered the flower-growing industry around the 1890's. Today, Chinese monopolize the growing of asters in the San Francisco Bay area.

By 1869 the first Chinese restaurant was reported. This business expanded rapidly and by 1920 was second only to the laundry business. The first Chinese laundry was launched in 1859. By 1870 the majority of almost 2,000 laundries in San Francisco were Chinese. With the advent of home laundry machines, self-service laundromats and new "no-iron" fabrics, the Chinese laundry began to decline.

The principal organization of the Chinese American is the Chinese Consolidated Benevolent Association, better known as the Chinese Six Companies, founded about 1860. It is composed of members from six districts (this number varies at times) of China. It was empowered to speak and act for all California Chinese in problems and affairs that affected the majority of them. It became a board for the arbitration of disputes. It initiated and promoted programs for the general welfare of California Chinese. It acted as a spokesman for the Imperial Manchu government. It kept a Chinese census, started Chinese language schools, organized medical and hospital service for sick and indigent Chinese who, in the 1860's and 70's, were not admitted to the County Hospital in San Francisco.

An economic depression hit the nation in the mid-1870's. The Chinese became scapegoats, blamed for depriving white laborers of their jobs. Violence against the Chinese spurred some migration to the east. Many Chinese left rural areas and fled to the cities. Some left the country altogether.

The Oriental Exclusion Act of 1882 stopped immigration and the Chinese population decreased from a high of 132,000 to a low of 61,639. At first Californians had welcomed the Chinese. They were considered clean, industrious, desirable workmen and they filled a need for laborers, cooks, and servants. White miners, feeling the squeeze of competition, were soon declaring, "California for Americans" and taxing foreigners out of the mines. Repressive legislation denied the Chinese the right to testify for or against white people and to attend school with them.

In jail, queues were forcibly clipped off. California's second constitution prohibited employment of Chinese by corporations, state, municipal, or county governments. The Chinese Exclusion Act of 1888 also declared the Chinese ineligible for citizenship. Labor organizations agitated against the Chinese. Anti-immigration laws were extended time and again. The Chinese Six Companies fought anti-Chinese legislation and aided in commercial negotiations until 1919, when the Chinese Chamber of Commerce was formed.

Until World War I the first generation Chinese considered themselves sojourners in America. They came here to earn sufficient money to return to China for a life of comfort and ease. But shortly after World War I the Chinese American Citizens Alliance, composed mostly of native born, was formed. It was organized by Chinese who claimed America as their home to carry on a strong legal fight to become first-class citizens.

It was not until December, 1943, that President Franklin Delano Roosevelt repealed the Chinese Exclusion Acts. Now, at last, a Chinese could apply for citizenship. Even then, the quota of Chinese eligible to enter the United States was very low. It was only 105 per year, and any person even one-half Chinese or even of another Asian country, was charged to the Chinese quota. The McCarran-Walter Act of 1952 made all races eligible for naturalization. However, it admitted Asiatics on the principle of National Origins at about 100 a year. On October 3, 1965 this bill was amended to abolish the National Origins quota system. About 6,000 Chinese entered the United States between January and October of 1966.

FILIPINO AMERICANS

The Filipino came to America not as a foreigner, but as a national. He has been a unique immigrant for he came imbued with a sense of the right to take part in all advantages afforded by American sovereignty.

Filipinos are an Asiatic people, originally of diverse local groups speaking diverse languages, such as Tagalog, Visayan, and Ilocano. In the many years that the Philippines were subject to the Spanish crown, there was much intermarriage, and Spanish became both the official language and the common language. Catholicism was introduced and made considerable progress in some areas. When the Philippine Islands became a protectorate of the United States, English became the official language. The public schools had an Americanizing affect which indirectly encouraged immigration.

Filipinos were the last Asiatic group to immigrate to the United States in any number. As nationals until 1935, they were not subject to a quota system. Migration to the United States in volume began several years after World War I. In 1931 there were 60,000 Filipinos on the mainland and 75,000 in Hawaii. Nine-tenths of these Filipinos were young men. By custom, Filipino women were not given the freedom which would allow them to immigrate, too. Filipinos generally came as sojourners to achieve a higher education, larger earnings, and a better standard of living. They encountered the traditional prejudice against Asians and often remained disappointingly far from their original goals and unwilling to return to their homeland as failures. In 1935, the Philippines were promised independence and a formal quota of fifty immigrants to the United States was set up. This was in effect until 1945, when the Filipinos received complete independence and the immigration quota was raised to 100. By 1950 there were about 40,000 Filipino Americans, mostly under fifty-five years of age. Most Filipinos landed on the west coast and nearly all stayed there. Stockton, California, with about 4,000 permanent Filipino American residents, is considered the center of Filipino American concentration.

At first, there was no community life or social solidarity, largely due to the fact that most immigrants had to become domestics, restaurant workers, or field laborers and had little free time. Also, few young men could afford to return to the Philippines for a wife. Intermarriage occurred with Anglo and Mexican Americans, but this practice was frowned upon by the white community. Therefore, the Filipino community was devoid of the stabilizing influence of women and children. However, since World War II, this situation has improved, especially as Filipino Americans gain in social and economic status. Now the Filipino American communities band together for such activities as Philippine Relief and the celebration of national festivals.

The west coast immigrant was generally employed in some form of agricultural labor, primarily migratory. Filipinos have expanded into the service occupations in hotels and cafes and gardening and the vegetable business. During World War II about one-third of the Filipino Americans served in the armed forces. From the beginning, they have been very active in the unionization movement among farm workers. During the late 1960's and early 1970's many were prominent in the Delano grape strike and subsequent events. Today, even more Filipino Americans are moving into the mainstream of American culture.

The post-World War II period has been one of lifted restrictions and expanded horizons for the Asian American. Prejudice against Asian Americans has abated and many areas of opportunity are now open to them. But areas of restriction still exist. It is to the elimination of the remaining barriers and complete freedom of opportunity that all Americans must dedicate themselves.

ASIAN AMERICANS

BIOGRAPHICAL SUMMARIES

JAPANESE AMERICANS

KYUTARO ABIKO
  (Journalism   3*)
  Born: 1865, Niigata Prefecture, Japan
  Died: 1936
  Significance: *Assistance to Japanese immigrants*

When Kyutaro Abiko was thirty-four, he bought two Japanese language newspapers and merged them under the name Nichi Bei (Japanese-American). Through his San Francisco newspaper, he encouraged Issei to take a long view of their stay in the United States, and to buy land and settle down.

To implement his editorial position, Abiko organized the Central California Land Co., and bought unimproved tracts in the arid California Central Valley. He persuaded young immigrants to buy the land. He helped them financially with liberal terms provided by the Nichi Bei Bank, which he operated. He insisted that the settlers remain on the farms.

Profits from the newspaper and the bank were used for the land project. During the Depression, the bank failed. The newspaper continued to prosper until a labor strike caused it to go bankrupt. It was then published under a receivership.

JOHN AISO
  (Law   6)

*These numbers refer to the *Bibliography of Sources Used,* found at the end of this section.

Significance: *Superior Court Judge*

Judge John Aiso was the first Japanese American to be appointed a judge on the American mainland. He was appointed to the Los Angeles Superior Court in 1953. He is also retired from the United States Army Reserve as a colonel.

MITSUYE ENDO
  (Civil Rights   4)
  Born: Sacramento, California
  Significance: *Successful challenge of the detention law*

Mitsuye Endo was one of thousands of Japanese Americans sent to concentration camps during World War II. Mitsuye Endo challenged the constitutionality of the detention of a loyal American citizen. In July of 1942, she petitioned for a writ of habeas corpus, contending that her detention in camp was unlawful. She took her case to the Supreme Court. On December 8, 1944, the Court ruled unanimously that Mitsuye Endo should be given her liberty, saying that the War Relocation Authority (WRA) had no right to detain loyal American citizens.

Mitsuye Endo's successful suit challenging the evacuation of Japanese Americans was the first favorable court decision for the Nisei.

SAMUEL ICHIYE (S.I.) HAYAKAWA
  (Education   6, 7)
  Born: 1906, Vancouver, British Columbia

Education: B.A., University of Manitoba, Canada; M.A., Magill University, Montreal, Canada; Ph.D., University of Wisconsin, Madison, Wisconsin

Significance: *Work in the field of semantics and education*

Samuel Ichiye (S.I.) Hayakawa, famous semanticist, came to the United States in 1929 as a Fellow in English at the University of Wisconsin. From 1939 to 1955, Dr. Hayakawa served on the faculty of several large universities. He has been professor of English at San Francisco State College since 1955. Following severe student demonstrations on campus in the late 1960's, Dr. Hayakawa was appointed Acting President of the college, and in 1968 he became president.

Dr. Hayakawa's interests include psychiatry, psychology, semantics, and language. He is a member of the supervisory editorial board of Funk and Wagnalls Standard Dictionaries. He is also highly regarded as a jazz historian. His books include *Language in Thought and Action* (1949), *Language, Meaning and Maturity* (1954), and *Symbol, Status and Personality* (1963).

GORDON HIRABAYASHI

(Civil Rights   4)

Born: The United States

Education: University of Washington, Seattle

Significance: *Challenge of the government order for evacuation*

Gordon Hirabayashi, a Quaker, challenged the government's orders for evacuating Japanese Americans to concentration camps. He decided to test Public Law 503, which gave the military authority over civilians without invoking martial law. Hirabayashi contended that the curfew orders were aimed against citizens of a particular race and therefore violated the equality inherent in due process of law.

Hirabayashi was apprehended, tried, and convicted. He appealed to the Supreme Court and lost. The Court supported his conviction, upholding the army's right to order a curfew and saying that he had violated the curfew.

Gordon Hirabayashi became a professor of sociology in Canada.

JOHN KIYOSHI HIRASAKI

(Engineering   5)

Born: 1941, Beaumont, Texas

Education: Vidor High School, Vidor, Texas; B.S., Lamar State College of Technology, Beaumont, Texas

Significance: *NASA manned spacecraft scientist*

John Hirasaki is a Japanese American engineer who has been associated with NASA (National Aeronautics and Space Administration) at the Manned Spacecraft Center in Houston, Texas since 1966.

Hirasaki was the engineer in charge of the Mobile Quarantine Facility for the returning crew of the Apollo 11 moon flight. As millions of people throughout the world watched the televised splashdown of the astronauts on July 24, 1969, their retrieval from the ocean, and their safe arrival aboard the USS Enterprise, they saw Hirasaki and the quarantine crew carefully checking the Mobile Quarantine Facility in readiness below decks.

ZENRO HIROTO

(Religion   3)

Significance: *Religious leadership*

Zenro Hiroto was a pioneer Japanese minister, appointed to found a Christian Church in Fresno, California in 1893. His first congregation was made up of Japanese immigrants, some hardly more than teenagers, meeting in a house on Inyo Street in Fresno.

WILLIAM (BILL) HOSOKAWA

(Journalism   6)

Born: Seattle, Washington

Education: University of Washington, Seattle

Significance: *Career in journalism*

After graduating from the University of Washington in 1937, William (Bill) Hosokawa worked on English language newspapers in Singapore and Shanghai. He returned to the United States five weeks before the Japanese attack on

Pearl Harbor, and was evacuated. The War Relocation Authority helped to place him with the *Des Moines Register.* From there he went to the *Denver Post* in 1946, where he has served as executive news editor, Sunday editor, magazine editor and currently as associate editor. As the *Denver Post's* first foreign correspondent, he covered the Korean War.

Hosokawa is the author of an extensive history of the Japanese Americans entitled *Nisei: The Quiet Americans,* published in 1969.

MAMORU IGA
(Psychology 6)
Significance: *Psychological studies of the Japanese Americans*
Mamoru Iga is a psychologist. He is the author of *Changes in Value Orientation of Japanese Americans* written in 1966.

DANIEL KEN INOUYE
(Politics 7)
Born: 1924, Honolulu, Oahu, Hawaii
Education: B.A. University of Hawaii, Honolulu; J.D., George Washington University, Washington, D.C.
Significance: *First Japanese Congressman*
Daniel Inouye was the first person of Japanese ancestry to be elected as representative from Hawaii to Congress. In 1963, he was elected to the United States Senate. *Journey to Washington* is his autobiography of the Senator from Hawaii. It is a lively, informal record of his progress from the slums of Honolulu to a position of trust and honor. He discusses his own encounters with racial discrimination quite frankly, but his positive personal philosophy avoids overemphasis.

TOMI KANAZAWA
(Music 3)
Born: California
Significance: *Opera singer*
Tomi Kanazawa is a native Californian now living in New York. She is the first Nisei to appear in a leading role with the Metropolitan Opera Company. She is widely recognized as a concert performer, nationally, and in Europe.

SABURO KIDO
(Civil Rights 3)
Born: Hawaii
Significance: *Leadership in the cause of his people*
Saburo Kido founded the Japanese American Citizens League in 1930. He was the first wartime president of the League. For many years, the League headquarters was a corner of Kido's law office in San Francisco. Under Kido's leadership, the League early adopted many resolutions which demonstrated the importance they placed on the privileges of American citizenship.

When the Japanese attacked Pearl Harbor, Kido sent a telegram to President Franklin Roosevelt assuring him of the loyalty of the Nisei and offering full support for the war effort. He urged the United States Government to allow the Nisei to fight for their country. At the close of the war, he also urged that citizenship be granted to oriental-born men who had served in the United States Armed Forces during World War II.

Kido was one of a hand-picked group of Nisei invited to accept voluntary removal to state-supervised concentration camps. He reminded California's Governor Olson that the Nisei were citizens. He refused the governor's "invitation." Kido brought the plight of the Nisei to the attention of James Purcell, a lawyer, who eventually carried the case to the Supreme Court.

After World War II, Kido set as his goals (1) the revision of the 1924 Immigration Law and (2) indemnity from the government for monetary losses suffered by the Japanese Americans in the evacuation. Both goals have been achieved.

JIN H. KINOSHITA
(Medicine 3)
Significance: *Research in ophthalmology*
Jin H. Kinoshita was an ophthalmologist who was evacuated during World War II from California to Boston. Dr. Kinoshita pioneered research into the formation of "sugar" cata-

racts, which has paved the way for prevention and treatment of the disease.

HARRY H. L. KITANO

(Sociology 4)

Significance: *Writings about the Japanese American people*

Harry H. L. Kitano, a sociologist, is an associate professor in the Graduate School of Social Welfare at the University of California in Los Angeles. His writing has been related to his own people, the Japanese Americans. In his book, *Japanese-Americans: the Evolution of a Subculture,* Kitano describes the phenomenon of the "Enryo Syndrome." Enryo refers to restraint, deference, or diffidence. Kitano contends that the Japanese were traditionally obedient to authority, and that this is one reason why they submitted to detention during World War II.

TOMMY KONO

(Sports 3)

Born: San Jose, California

Significance: *Success in the field of sports*

Tommy Kono, a Japanese American weight lifter, won Olympic titles in 1952 and 1956. During his active career, he broke twenty-six world records in weight lifting.

FRED T. KOREMATSU

(Civil Rights 3)

Born: Oakland, California

Education: High School

Significance: *Challenge of the constitutionality of the wartime evacuation of the Japanese*

After graduating from high school, Fred Korematsu became a ship welder. When the United States removed the Japanese from their homes during World War II and sent them to detention camps, Korematsu failed to show up for evacuation. He was arrested and convicted for remaining in a military area from which persons of Japanese ancestry had been excluded. His appeal was taken to the Supreme Court where he was found guilty. The court asserted that the prohibition was not racial but simply a necessary wartime precaution. The case was sig-

nificant because it required the Supreme Court to rule on the constitutionality of the evacuation.

BEN KUROKI

(Military 6)

Born: Nebraska

Significance: *An example of loyalty to his country*

Ben Kuroki was a flier in World War II who won the Distinguished Flying Cross. His biography, *Boy from Nebraska,* is a portrayal of the joys and trials of growing up as a Japanese American. It also describes his heartbreaking efforts to be accepted into the armed forces. He finally became an Air Force gunner, completing fifty-eight combat missions in two theaters.

WILLIAM MARUTANI

(Law 6)

Significance: *Success as a Japanese American lawyer*

William Marutani is the lawyer who prepared the amicus brief on the antimiscegenation laws of seventeen states in 1967. He is also the first Japanese American lawyer to argue and win a case before the Supreme Court. He is a leader in the Japanese American Citizens League.

MIKE MASARU MASAOKA

(Civil Rights 3)

Born: 1915, Fresno, California

Education: University of Utah, Salt Lake City

Significance: *Work for the repeal of oppressive legislation*

Mike Masaru Masaoka was the first full-time employee of the Japanese American Citizens League. He resigned as speech instructor at the University of Utah in August, 1941, to take this position. Masaoka, an extroverted, outgoing man, went to California to work for and strengthen the Japanese American Citizens League just before the attack on Pearl Harbor, when it became obvious that Japanese Americans would have a difficult time. Masaoka and the JACL served as a liaison between the government and the Japanese American community. After the onset of the war they disseminated information to the community, distributed contributions to the needy, and in general served as a buffer between government officials and the Issei.

When Governor Olson of California proposed a voluntary evacuation of the Japanese Americans to state-supervised concentration camps, Masaoka began to believe that the rumors of evacuation were more than rumors. Searching for a plan to block evacuation he came up with the idea of a "suicide battalion," to be made up of Nisei volunteers for combat against the Japanese. Military officials turned down the proposal saying that segregated units, except among Negroes, were not American policy. The idea was shelved temporarily.

It was Masaoka who proposed that the JACL petition the President for reinstatement of Nisei under civil service. He argued that despite the discrimination they had suffered, Nisei should go out and fight for freedom, to assure their claim for unlimited citizenship. He argued for an all-Nisei outfit so that the contributions of the Nisei would be obvious. In time he joined the 442nd Regimental Combat unit, which later became the all-Nisei outfit.

After the war, Masaoka turned his persuasive talents to winning for the Issei the right to become naturalized citizens. He went to Washington, D.C., to lobby for the entire JACL program which included revisions of the 1924 immigration law and indemnity from the government for monetary losses suffered in the evacuation.

On July 2, 1948, President Harry Truman signed into law the Japanese American Evacuation Claims Act. The McCarran-Walter Immigration and Naturalization Act of 1952 provided for repeal of the Oriental Exclusion Act of 1924. It also eliminated race as a bar to naturalization. It was Masaoka who drummed up the vote to override presidential veto of the last mentioned act. The McCarran-Walter Act was a step forward, but it still discriminated with token quotas for non-Northern Europeans. Masaoka worked for and witnessed the new im-

migration bill signed by President Lyndon B. Johnson in 1965. This bill provides for admittance to the United States on the basis of skills and relationship to residents, not on race, creed, or nationality.

GEORGE MATSUMOTO
 (Architecture   10)
 Born: 1922, San Francisco, California
 Education: B.A., Washington University,
   St. Louis, Missouri; Cranbrook
   Academy of Art, Detroit, Michigan
 Significance: *Outstanding designer and
   architect*

George Matsumoto has been a designer and planner for several large architectural firms. He is the recipient of numerous awards in architecture. His important works include office buildings, churches, government buildings, and private residences.

Matsumoto has been a professor at the University of California in Berkeley since 1961.

SHIGEMI MATSUMOTO
 (Music   6)
 Significance: *Career in singing*

Shigemi Matsumoto is a rising Japanese American opera singer and the only Japanese member of the San Francisco Opera Company.

SPARK MASAYUKI MATSUNAGA
 (Politics   7)
 Born: 1916, Kauai, Hawaii
 Education: Ed.B., University of Hawaii,
   Honolulu; LL.B., Harvard University,
   Cambridge, Massachusetts
 Significance: *Leadership in Congress
   representing Hawaii*

Spark Matsunaga served on the famous 442nd Regimental Combat Team in World War II. He was a member of the Hawaii Statehood delegations to Congress in 1950 and 1954. In 1962, he was elected to the House of Representatives.

Congressman Matsunaga has been president of the 88th Congress Club and secretary of the House Democratic Steering Committee, as well as a member of the Rules Committee.

Harry Yaemon Minami
   (Agriculture   3)
   Born: 1880, Japan
   Education: Japan
   Significance: *Successful vegetable grower*
Harry Yaemon Minami has made important contributions to the production of garden vegetables in the Santa Maria Valley, Santa Barbara County, California. He leased 4,000 acres of farmland, and soon owned 550 acres.

Patsy Takemoto Mink
   (Politics   8)
   Born: 1927, Maui, Hawaii
   Education: B.A., University of Hawaii, Honolulu; J.D., Chicago Law School, Illinois
   Significance: *Leadership in Congress*
Mrs. Patsy Takemoto Mink was the first Japanese American woman to be elected to Congress. She has had a private law practice in Hawaii and served as the National Vice-President of the Young Democrats from 1957 to 1959, and as a state senator from Hawaii from 1962 to 1964. Mrs. Mink has received many honorary Doctor of Law degrees.

Tetsuo Scott Miyakawa
   (History   3)
   Born: 1906, Los Angeles, California
   Education: M.A., Cornell University, New York; Ph.D., Columbia University, New York
   Significance: *Work in relocating Japanese Americans after World War II*
Dr. T. Scott Miyakawa has been active in the Japanese American Citizens League. During World War II, the League worked quietly and with unusual effectiveness in helping relocatees find jobs, housing, and in adjusting to life outside the camps. Miyakawa was in charge of the regional office in New York, supplementing the work of the War Relocation Authority and volunteer organizations. He and others appeared before service clubs, church groups, schools, and labor union meetings to tell the story of the evacuation and to urge tolerance and understanding. Miyakawa took leave from Boston University in 1962 to become director of the Japanese History Project at the University of California at Los Angeles.

Shotaro Frank Miyamoto
   (Sociology   3)
   Born: 1912, Seattle, Washington
   Education: B.A., M.A., University of Washington, Seattle; Ph.D., University of Chicago, Illinois
   Significance: *Studies of the Japanese Americans*
Professor Miyamoto was a sociologist at the University of Washington. His pamphlet, *Social Solidarity Among the Japanese in Seattle,* is a detailed and thorough analysis of a Japanese American community, covering the periods from early immigration to 1939. It is used by sociologists and historians as a major source of reference on Japanese Americans.

Sadao Munemori
   (Military   6)
   Born: Los Angeles, California
   Significance: *Patriotism and valor*
Private First Class Sadao Munemori was a member of the 442nd Infantry Battalion during World War II. He was presented with the Congressional Medal of Honor for outstanding heroism.

Setsuko Nishi
   (Community Service   3)
   Significance: *Leadership through social work*
Setsuko Nishi lived in Chicago, Illinois. Active in civic affairs, Mrs. Nishi served on the Chicago Resettlers Committee, the Welfare Council of Greater Chicago and the Community Fund. She was a director of Parkway Interracial Community House, organizational secretary of the Chicago Council Against Religious and Racial Discrimination, and "Chicago Mother of the Year" in the field of community service. Mrs. Nishi's efforts helped set the stage for the acceptance of all persons of Japanese ancestry.

ISAMU NOGUCHI

(Sculpture   7, 11)
Born: 1904, Los Angeles, California
Education: Pre-Med., Columbia
    University, New York City; Leonardo
    da Vinci Art School
Significance: *Outstanding sculptor*

Isamu Noguchi spent two years as a student of the famous sculptor, Gutzon Borglum. He studied in Paris on a Guggenheim Fellowship. He has also studied in London, Peking, and Mexico. During the 1940's Noguchi developed an original style in sculpture, combining simplified organic forms with abstract shape. In later years, he returned to the inspiration of Japanese archaic sculpture and pottery. Noguchi's exhibits are worldwide. His work includes a 65-foot relief in the Mercado Rodriguez in Mexico City and the design for the tomb of John F. Kennedy in Arlington Cemetery. In 1963, Noguchi was awarded the Fine Arts Medal by the American Institute of Architects.

THOMAS T. OMORI

(Engineering   3)
Significance: *Scientific work in the field of missiles*

Thomas T. Omori received the Japanese American Citizens League Award in 1964 while he was Far Eastern Manager of International Operations, Aerojet General Corporation. The award states, "The first United States rocket to the moon will bear the personal imprint of his long years of dedicated service in the field of missiles and high energy propellants."

Formerly European manager of Aerojet, Omori is considered one of the nation's top men in the field of lunar probes, rocket propulsion, nuclear energy, and ballistic missiles.

KAJIRO OYAMA

(Civil Rights   4)
Significance: *Battles for citizenship and property rights*

In 1934, Kajiro Oyama, an Issei, bought six acres of farmland near San Diego in the name of his six-year-old son, Fred Oyama. He paid $4,000 and recorded the deed in Fred's name.

He then successfully petitioned a Superior Court to be appointed Fred's guardian. When Fred was nine, his father bought two adjoining acres. The Oyama family was evacuated in 1942. In 1944, when Fred was sixteen, the Attorney General of California filed escheat action, contending that the land was purchased with the intention of violating and evading the alien land law. (Escheat means the reversion of property to the State in the United States by failure of persons legally entitled to hold the property.)

The case was appealed to the United States Supreme Court which ruled that the escheat action was unconstitutional in that it denied the defendants equal protection. California's Alien Land Law then underwent scrutiny. The United States Supreme Court supported Oyama's citizenship rights and reversed the California Court's decision against him.

KOSAKU SAWADA

(Agriculture   3)
Born: Osaka, Japan
Died: 1968
Significance: *Work in horticulture*

Kosaku Sawada was a grower and hybridizer of camellias. Working in Mobile, Alabama, he had developed thousands of new varieties.

GEORGE SHIMA (Shortened from Ushijima)

(Agriculture   3)
Born: 1863, Fukuoka Prefecture, Japan
Died: 1926
Significance: *Work in reclaiming delta land in California*

George Shima came to California in 1889. In his lifetime, he reclaimed 28,000 acres of Sacramento delta land. He built dikes around islands, drained excess waters, lowered the water table, and planted potatoes and onions. When he died in 1926, he left an estate of fifteen million dollars and a legacy of reclamation of formerly unusable lands.

TOM SHIMASAKI

(Ranching   3)
Significance: *Community service*

Tom Shimasaki is a rancher in Lindsay, California. He is the recipient of the Lindsay Community Citizen Award, president of the Y's Men's Club, officer in the Lindsay Chamber of Commerce and the Lindsay Farm Bureau, president of Kiwanis, moderator of the First Baptist Church of Lindsay, and district commissioner of the Boy Scouts. Shimasaki is credited with being the one person most responsible for the high status and acceptance of Japanese Americans in Tulare County, California.

KOTARO SUTO
  (Agriculture   3)
  Significance: *Beautification of public lands*
The Japanese American landscaper, Kotaro Suto, landscaped much of the public lands of Miami Beach, Florida.

PAT SUZUKI
  (Music   1)
  Born: 1931, Cressy, California
  Significance: *Success as an actress and singer*
Pat Suzuki is a recording star and an actress. One of her outstanding roles was the lead in the Broadway production of *Flower Drum Song.*

LARRY TAJIRI
  (Journalism   3)
  Born: ca. 1910
  Died: 1965
  Significance: *Morale-building work for the welfare of the Nisei during the evacuation and relocation period*
Larry Tajiri was a knowledgeable reporter of the Nisei scene. At the time of Pearl Harbor, he was working in the Manhattan office of the Asahi newspapers of Japan. He lost his job when the New York bureau closed. He returned to San Francisco, saw the need for a new Nisei organ, and volunteered to take over the *Pacific Citizen,* the national organ of the Japanese American Citizens League. Tajiri and his wife, Marion Guyo Tajiri, published a lively paper, writing with vigor and skill.

In later years, Tajiri joined the staff of the *Denver Post* and distinguished himself as its drama editor. After his death, his associates established an annual Larry Tajiri Memorial Award to honor persons who have made exceptional contributions to the theater.

SHINKICHI G. TAJIRI
  (Sculpture   9)
  Born: 1923, Los Angeles, California
  Education: Art Institute, Chicago, Illinois; Academie Grande Chaumiere, Paris, France
  Significance: *World famous sculptor*
Shinkichi G. Tajiri, famous as a sculptor in bronze and brass, studied art under Donald Hord of San Diego. Tajiri has received many honors and awards, including the William and Norma Copley Award for sculpture in 1959, and the Mainichi Shimbun Prize at the Tokyo Biennale in 1963. His work was exhibited at the Seattle Exposition Fine Arts Show. His sculptures are to be found in the permanent collections of art museums in Holland, Sweden, and St. Paul, Minnesota.

TOGO WILLIAM TANAKA
  (Journalism   10)
  Born: 1916, Portland, Oregon
  Education: B.A., University of California at Los Angeles
  Significance: *Editor of professional publications*
Togo William Tanaka graduated from college with high honor. He served as editor of the Los Angeles *Japanese Daily News* from 1936 to 1941. In 1942, he served as documentary historian for the War Relocation Authority. His other activities included service as a staff member of the Chicago American Friends Service Committee, editor for the director of the Publications Division of the American Technology Society, editor-in-chief of the Chicago Publishing Corporation, editor of the *American School News* since 1952, and editor-in-chief of the School-Industrial Press, Inc. of Los Angeles since 1956. He is also president of Gramercy Enterprises, Inc. of Los Angeles. Tanaka has

received several honors and awards in the field of journalism.

DONALD K. TORIUMI

(Religion   3)

Significance: *Service in the ministry*

Reverend Donald K. Toriumi is moderator of the Los Angeles Presbytery with a membership of 200 churches and 150,000 communicants in southern California. He is also vice-president of the Pasadena Council of Churches, chairman of the committee on Christian Education of the Los Angeles Presbytery and a member of the National Committee of the Presbyterian General Assembly on Segregated Presbyteries and Synods.

WILFRED TSUKIYAMA

(Law   6)

Born: Hawaii

Significance: *Judiciary service*

Wilfred Tsukiyama became an attorney in the 1920's. He later served as city and county attorney of Honolulu, and then chief justice of the Supreme Court of Hawaii.

MINORU TSUTSUI

(Physical Science   7)

Born: 1918, Wakayama City, Japan

Education: M.S., Tokyo University, Japan; M.S., Ph.D., Yale University, New Haven, Connecticut

Significance: *Field research in organometallic chemistry*

Minoru Tsutsui became a naturalized citizen in 1960. He is an associate professor in the Chemistry Department of New York University.

YOSHIKO UCHIDA

(Literature   2)

Born: 1921, Alameda, California

Education: B.A., University of California at Berkeley; Smith College, Northhampton, Massachusetts

Significance: *Bringing the folklore of Japan to American children*

Yoshiko Uchida grew up in Berkeley, California. She graduated *cum laude* from the university there, and attended Smith College on a fellowship. With others of Japanese descent, Yoshiko Uchida was evacuated to Utah in 1942. She taught second grade at the relocation center. She served as membership secretary for the Institute of Pacific Relations from 1946 to 1947. In 1953, she went to Japan on a Ford Foundation Research Fellowship.

Yoshiko Uchida began recording Japanese folktales in 1946 and has been a full-time writer for many years. She is the author of more than twelve books, illustrating several herself. She received the 1955 New York Herald Tribune Children's Spring Book Festival Honor Award for her *Magic Listening Cap.* Some of her books have been translated into German and Dutch. Another of her books is *Makoto, the Smallest Boy,* a story of Japan. She has a special interest in fine arts and folk craft.

CAESAR UYESAKA

(Community Service   3)

Born: 1916, Santa Barbara, California

Significance: *Leadership in civic affairs*

Caesar Uyesaka is a businessman in Santa Barbara, California. He was president of the nonprofit organization that operated the Santa Barbara Rancheros, a professional baseball farm team of the New York Mets. Uyesaka was selected Santa Barbara's "Father of the Year" in 1959. Mr. Uyesaka has also been a commissioner of city recreation and is now a Boy Scout commissioner.

YORI WADA

(Community Service   6)

Significance: *Service to Japanese American youth*

Yori Wada is the president of the San Francisco Civil Service Commission and executive director of the San Francisco Buchanan Young Men's Christian Association.

NEWTON (UYESUGI) WESLEY

(Medicine   6)

Significance: *Ingenious experimentation in optometry*

Newton (Uyesugi) Wesley was a young optometrist who was evacuated to the midwest from Portland, Oregon. He discovered that he was going blind from keratoconus, a mysterious condition in which the cornea grows out like a cone. Ordinary glasses could not help. He reasoned that a contact lens resting over the cornea and exerting a gentle pressure on it might arrest the condition and restore normal sight. Contact lenses in 1943 were large, crude and too uncomfortable to wear for more than a few hours at a time. Dr. Wesley and his partner, Dr. George Jessen, eventually learned to make a small plastic lens which could be worn comfortably. It not only stopped the deterioration of Dr. Wesley's sight, but the techniques in manufacturing the lens were applied to making lenses for patients with more common eye troubles.

Dr. Wesley's work played a large part in perfecting plastic contact lenses and in popularizing their use. Today, these lenses are worn by people all over the world. Much of the profits has been plowed back into the non-profit Eye Research Foundation. Dr. Wesley legally changed his name from the original Uyesugi when his patients complained that they couldn't find him in the directory.

MINORU YAMASAKI
　(Architecture　7)
　Born: 1912, Seattle, Washington
　Education: University of Washington, Seattle
　Significance: *Designing public buildings*

Minoru Yamasaki's many architectural designs include the Japanese Cultural Center in San Francisco, the St. Louis Airport, the Consulate General's office in Kobe, Japan, the Oberlin College of Music Conservatory in Ohio, the Exposition of Science Pavilion at the Seattle Fair in 1962, and the Reynolds Metal Company building in Detroit, Michigan.

MASUO YASUI
　(Business　3)
　Born: 1890, Japan

Significance: *Early Oregon farm developer and businessman*

Masuo Yasui came from Japan to the United States in 1906, at the age of sixteen. After working as a railroad hand and doing housework while attending school, he went to Hood River, Oregon. In Hood River, he worked with crews of Japanese to clear the hillsides of pine and fir and replace them with pear and apple seedlings. He soon opened a small shop which was frequented by other Issei. He urged the Issei to buy land to settle, and he loaned them money. In time, he had an interest in one of every ten boxes of apples and pears shipped out of Hood River.

Yasui reared seven children. Two sons became doctors, one became an attorney, one is a member of the Oregon State Board of Education, and another, Minoru Yasui, is director of Denver's Commission on Community Relations. Among them, his children have completed fifty-six years of education beyond high school.

MINORU YASUI
　(Civil Rights　3)
　Born: ca. 1915, Hood River, Oregon
　Education: LL.D., University of Oregon, Eugene, Oregon
　Significance: *Leadership in establishing the civil rights of Nisei*

Minoru Yasui, a son of Masuo Yasui, was commissioned an infantry lieutenant in the United States Army Reserve upon graduation from law school in 1939. He received orders to report to active duty at Fort Vancouver, Washington, a month after the attack on Pearl Harbor. On arrival, he was put in charge of a platoon of troops. Twenty-four hours later before he could be formally inducted, he was dismissed from the Army.

A wartime measure severely restricted enemy aliens which included "all other persons of Japanese ancestry." Yasui deliberately challenged this curfew law. He was arrested, charged, and released on bond. During his trial, the United States District Court in Portland ruled that since he had been employed by the Japanese Consular service handling English correspondence to earn money prior to passing his bar examination, Yasui had lost his citizenship. The District Court also ruled that the curfew was illegal. Yasui won that point, but lost his citizenship rights. Yasui's appeal to the Circuit Court of Appeals in San Francisco was referred to the Supreme Court. Meanwhile, he was confined in the Multnomah County jail in Portland, where, for nine months, he was denied a haircut, a razor, fingernail clippers, and even a typewriter.

The Supreme Court reversed both of Yasui's convictions. The court ruled that Yasui had not lost his citizenship, but that the Army did have the right to establish a curfew, even in the absence of martial law. His fine of $5,000 was suspended on the grounds that he had served nine months in prison while awaiting trial. Yasui estimates that it cost his family $10,000 to take his case through the courts. In 1945 Yasui took the Colorado Bar examination. He scored the highest marks of any candidate, but he was denied a license on the basis of his criminal record. After an appeal to the State Supreme Court, his license was issued.

Yasui has served as regional director of the Japanese American Citizens League. In 1952 he was elected Nisei of the Biennium for his sacrifice in challenging the evacuation orders. He is now director of Denver's Commission on Community Relations.

CHINESE AMERICANS

SHAU WING CHAN
(Language   20)
Born: 1907, Canton, China
Education: B.A., Lingman University, China; M.A., Ph.D., Stanford University, California
Significance: *Research in Chinese studies*
Professor Shau Wing Chan has been on the faculty of Stanford University since 1938. He is executive head of the Department of Asian Languages and director of the Chinese-Japanese Language and Area Center.

WING-TSIT CHAN
(Philosophy   21)
Born: 1901, Kwangtung, China
Education: Ph.D., Harvard University
Significance: *Research in the field of Chinese philosophy*
Wing-Tsit Chan is noted for his many publications in the field of Chinese philosophy and religion. He is the author of the following publications: *Religious Trends in Modern China, An Outline and Annotated Bibliography of Chinese Philosophy, Source Book in Chinese Philosophy and Instruction for Practical Living* and *Other Neo-Confucian Writings by Wang Yang-ming.*

CATHERINE SHUIHUA HSIA CHEN
(Physical Science   25)
Born: Chungking, China
Education: B.A., Barnard College, New York; M.A., Columbia University, New York; Ph.D., Polytechnic Institute, Brooklyn, New York
Significance: *Discoveries in the field of chemistry*
Dr. Catherine Chen is a member of the American Chemistry Society of the American Association for the Advancement of Science. She has done research in the Polymer Institute in Brooklyn, and has been as associate professor of Chemistry at Columbia University. From 1956 to 1961 she has worked in the chemical research department of the American Cyanamid Company at Stamford, Connecticut. Dr. Chen is a research chemist for the Celanese Corporation.

DI CHEN
(Physical Science   26)
Born: 1929, Chekiang, China
Education: B.S., National Taiwan University; M.S., University of Minnesota, Minneapolis, Minnesota; Ph.D., Stanford University, California
Significance: *Research in physics*
Di Chen is a research scientist in the area of physics. Among Dr. Chen's accomplishments is

his invention of the absorption type laser modulator.

KAS KARL CHEN
(Engineering 23)
Born: 1919, Shanghai, China
Education: B.S., Chiao-Jung University;
   M.A., Harvard University, Cambridge,
   Massachusetts
Significance: *Research in the field of
   electrical engineering*
Kas Karl Chen has developed patents in power and lighting apparatus.

KENNETH KUAN-SHEN CH'EN
(Education 21)
Born: 1907, Honolulu, Oahu, Hawaii
Education: Ph.D., Harvard University,
   Cambridge, Massachusetts
Significance: *Research in the field of
   oriental history*
Dr. Kenneth Kuan-Shen Ch'en is professor of Buddhism at Princeton University. He is a member of the American Oriental Society, the Association of Asian Studies and the American Society for the Study of Religions. Dr. Ch'en is the author of *Buddhism in China, a Historical Survey.*

KO KUIL CHEN
(Medicine 21)
Born: 1898, Shanghai, China
Education: B.S., University of Wisconsin,
   Madison; M.D., Ph.D., Johns Hopkins
   University, Baltimore, Maryland
Significance: *Research in pharmacology*
Ko Kuil Chen is a naturalized citizen living in Indianapolis, Indiana. His research in the field of drugs has brought him many honors, including the Remington Honor Medal and the J. W. Shurman Award in pharmacy and science.

REIGNSON CHANGTUNG CHEN
(Finance 21)
Born: 1896, Foo Chow, China
Education: B.A., Colorado College,
   Colorado Springs; M.A., New York

University, New York City
Significance: *Achievements in
   international banking*
Reignson Changtung Chen is an internationally known banker living in Washington, D.C. He is the recipient of the United States Medal of Freedom for his work in the reconstruction and development of the World Bank.

CHI CHENG
(Sports 18)
Born: 1944, Taiwan
Education: California State Polytechnic
   College, San Luis Obispo
Significance: *Outstanding woman athlete*
Chi Cheng is a fast-rising star in the American track and field scene. Born in Taiwan, she came to the United States at the urging of the American coach of the Nationalist team for the Asian games.

Chi Cheng learned to speak English after she arrived in this country. She entered California State Polytechnic College and began to train for worldwide competition. Her specialities are pentathlon, long jump, sprints, and hurdles. She holds eleven Asian, six American, and two world records.

SIN-I CHENG
(Engineering 21)
Born: 1921, Changchow, China
Education: B.S., Chiaotung University;
   M.S., University of Michigan, Ann
   Arbor; M.A., Ph.D., Princeton
   University, New Jersey
Significance: *Aerospace research*
Sin-I Cheng began his teaching career at Princeton University in 1952 and has taught there continuously. Dr. Cheng is a member of both the American Institute of Aeronautics and Astronautics and the Combustion Institute, a fellow in the Institute of Aerospace Science, and a member of the Rocket Society. Dr. Cheng's research is in gas dynamics, fluid mechanics and propulsion, and applied mathematics.

THOMAS W. CHINN
(History 17)

Born: Coos Bay, Oregon
Education: Public schools, Oregon and
California; University of California
Extension
Significance: *Research and writing about the history of the Chinese in America*

Thomas W. Chinn is a typographer. Early in his career, he was editor and co-publisher of the *Chinese Digest,* a weekly Chinese news magazine in English. In 1942, he became editor and publisher of the *Chinese News.* His major interest has been the history of the Chinese in America. He founded the Chinese Historical Society in 1963 and was its first president. In 1967, he became executive director of the Society and editor of its monthly bulletin. He serves voluntarily.

Deeply interested in boys, Chinn is an executive board member of the San Francisco Bay Area Council of the Boy Scouts of America, and a national representative. He was elected Most Distinguished Alumnus in Troop Three's fifty-year history in 1964. He was also awarded Silver Beaver for Distinguished Service to Boyhood by the San Francisco Area Council in 1964. Chinn is a governing member of the San Francisco Y.M.C.A., a member of the Society of California Pioneers, and a charter member of the San Francisco Corral of The Westerners. His honors also include an invitation to present a paper on *Genealogical Sources for the Chinese Immigrants to the United States* at the World Conference on Records and Genealogy Seminar held in Salt Lake City in 1969. On January 15, 1970, Chinn was awarded the California Historical Society's "Award of Merit" for work on Chinese history in America, especially California. He is also the editor of a syllabus entitled *A History of the Chinese in California* which is used widely by schools and colleges as a reference for new ethnic courses.

DAVID TA WEI CHOW
(Business   22)
Born: 1919, Chefoo, North China
Education: M.A., University of Colorado, Boulder, Colorado

Significance: *Language teacher and businessman*

David Ta Wei Chow is a naturalized citizen who became an instructor in the Chinese Language School of the University of Chicago. Later, he served as an instructor in Chinese at the Army Training School at the Presidio in Monterey, California. He is now the manager of David Chow & Company.

HIRAM FONG
(Politics   19)
Born: 1907, Honolulu, Oahu, Hawaii
Education: University of Hawaii, Honolulu; Harvard Law School, Cambridge, Massachusetts
Significance: *First Chinese-American Congressman*

Hiram Fong became a lawyer, founding the multi-racial partnership firm of Fong, Miko, Choy and Robinson. This set a social precedent in Hawaii. Upon election to Congress in 1959, Fong was the first person of Chinese origin to become a United States Congressman.

MARCH (KONG) FONG
(Education, Politics   17)
Born: Oakdale, California
Education: B.S., University of California at Berkeley, California; M.E., Mills College, Oakland, California; Ed.D., Stanford University, Palo Alto, California
Significance: *Active participation in education and leadership in the California legislature*

Assemblywoman March K. Fong has had an outstanding career associated with education prior to her election to the California Legislature in 1967.

One of her major interests is in health. Early in her career, she was a dental hygienist in the Oakland Public Schools, then Supervisor of Dental Health Education for the Alameda County Schools, and Lecturer in Health Education at Mills College in Oakland.

Mrs. Fong was a member of the Alameda County Board of Education from 1956 to 1966, and president of the Board in the school year 1961 to 1962. She has also been president of the Alameda County School Boards Association. Her knowledge of educational needs and legislative procedures led her to her work as Legislative Advocate for the Alameda County Board of Education and consultancy for various school districts in the San Francisco Bay Area. She has served with distinction on civic and governmental committees. She has been politically active in California since 1963, working in responsible positions within the Democratic Party. Her memberships in many professional organizations reflect her wide interests in educational and civic affairs.

She is the recipient of the Phoebe Apperson Hearst Distinguished Bay Area Woman of the Year Award.

Mrs. Fong actively represents her constituents in the 15th Assembly District. Legislation sponsored by Assemblywoman Fong has been concerned with conservation, natural resources, litter and air pollution, school libraries, health, and social welfare.

CHARLES GEE
(Finance   15)
Significance: *Leadership in establishing banking services for the Chinese*
Charles Gee was a San Francisco merchant who owned a small chain of shoe stores. After the San Francisco fire of 1906 he convinced the First National Bank of Oakland to hire Chinese employees. He became the first manager of the Chinese Department of the bank, receiving deposits and making loans to help put Chinese businessmen back on their feet. When San Francisco's Chinatown was rebuilt, Gee became the manager of the first bank in America with a branch in a Chinese community. Today, this bank is a unit of the Bank of America.

DOROTHY GEE
(Finance   20)
Significance: *Bank manager*
Dorothy Gee, manager of the Chinatown Branch of the Bank of America, is the only woman among some 700 branch managers of the world's largest banking organization. Dorothy Gee, the daughter of Charles Gee, has managed the bank for over thirty years.

FUNG JOE GUEY
(Invention   13)
Significance: *Aviation pioneer*
Fung Joe Guey was an inventor and an aviator. On September 20, 1909, he circled through the air for twenty minutes in a bi-plane of his own manufacture. He was the first aviator on the Pacific Coast.

ELIZABETH LING-SO HALL
(Education   20)
Significance: *Teacher and school administrator*
Elizabeth Ling-So Hall, a teacher since 1941, is the first Chinese American to hold an administrative position in the San Francisco public school system. In 1953, she was appointed assistant principal of two elementary schools, Hancock and Sarah B. Cooper. Four years later, Miss Hall became principal of these schools.

CHINN HO
(Business   23)
Born: 1904, Honolulu, Oahu, Hawaii
Education: University of Hawaii, Honolulu
Significance: *Financier and land developer*
Chinn Ho is an entrepreneur who organizes, manages and assumes the risks involved in his business of dealing in real estate and developing agricultural lands and buildings, particularly in Hawaii. He is also a financier, dealing in investments and securities.

JAMES WONG HOWE
(Cinematography   15, 21)
Born: 1899, Kwangtung, China
Education: High school, Pasco, Washington
Significance: *Artistic success as a cinematographer*
James Wong Howe, photographer for such successful films as *Picnic, Hud, Old Man of the*

Sea and *Come Back Little Sheba,* became an assistant cameraman at the Lasky Studios in Hollywood in 1917. In 1922, he became director of photography. His films have won him two Academy Awards, two *Look* Awards, and sixteen Oscar nominations.

LEONARD SHIH LIEN HSU
(Business 15)
Significance: *Achievement in international business development*
Dr. Leonard Shih Lien Hsu served as coordinator of Foreign Operations for the Reynolds Metals Company. He later became president of a prospecting and mining corporation.

NAI LI HUANG-LIU
(Physical Science 12)
Born: Taiwan
Education: B.A., Taiwan University; Ph.D., University of California, Los Angeles; Post-doctoral work, Harvard University, Cambridge, Massachusetts
Significance: *Physicist*
Dr. Nai Li Huang-Liu, a physicist at the University of California at Riverside, left her birthplace in Taiwan to come to the United States in 1960. Her major contributions have been in the research of magnetism.

DONG KINGMAN
(Painting 15)
Born: 1911, Oakland, California
Education: Ling Nom Academy, Hong Kong, China
Significance: *Nationally known artist and teacher*
Dong Kingman is famous for his watercolor paintings of familiar San Francisco scenes, such as the cable cars, flower stalls, the Golden Gate Bridge, and Chinatown. He also did the title paintings for the motion picture, *The Flower Drum Song.* He has illustrated several books for children, including *The Bamboo Gate* by Vanya Oakes and *Johnny Hong of Chinatown* by Clyde Robert Bulla. Mr. Kingman teaches at Columbia University and at the Famous Artists Schools in Westport, Connecticut.

AGNES KWAI YING LEE
(Medicine 25)
Born: 1922, Honolulu, Oahu, Hawaii
Education: B.A., Sacred Heart Academy of Music; United States Hospital Radiology Technical School, Baltimore, Maryland
Significance: *Work in radiology*
Agnes Kwai Ying Lee is one of the few women who are registered radiologists and technologists. This exact and important science was formerly open only to men. Agnes Lee is the chief radiologist and technologist at Kauikeolani Children's Hospital in Honolulu.

CHIN YANG LEE
(Literature 15)
Born: 1917, Hunan, China
Education: B.A., National South-West Associated University, Kunming, China; M.F.A., Yale University, New Haven, Connecticut
Significance: *Popular novelist*
Chin Yang Lee lives and writes in San Francisco, where he first worked on two Chinese language papers in the heart of Chinatown. He is particularly famous as the author of the book, *Flower Drum Song.* Since this book was published, Mr. Lee has written a novel a year, including *Lover's Point, The Sawbwa and His Secretary, Madam Goldenflower,* and *Cripple Mah and the New Society.*

CHIN-YUAN LEE
(Engineering 23)
Born: 1926, Shanghai, China
Education: M.S., Cornell University, Ithaca, New York; Ph.D., University of Washington, Seattle
Significance: *Technical telephone system development*
Chin-Yuan Lee helped to develop technical telephone systems in the Bell Telephone Laboratory.

CHINGWAH LEE
(Art 20)

Significance: *Eastern art collector and publisher*

Chingwah Lee was co-publisher of the *Chinese Digest,* the first Chinese newspaper in English. Mr. Lee, a connoisseur of Far Eastern oriental art, is also a private collector. He is a technical consultant to the film industry in Hollywood and also an actor. He has lectured on art and exhibited his private art collection since 1933, and has long been an advocate of Far Eastern fashions and furnishings for occidental homes. Lee is one of the founders of the Chinese Historical Society.

DAI-KEONG LEE
    (Music 21)
    Born: 1915, Honolulu, Oahu, Hawaii
    Education: Juilliard School of Music,
        New York; M.A., Columbia
        University, New York
    Significance: *Composer*

Dai-Keong Lee worked under Aaron Copland as a Juilliard Fellowship student. He is a composer of orchestral, symphonic, and chamber music. In 1954, Lee wrote the score for *The Tea House of the August Moon.* He has also composed "Mele Ololi" for chorus, solo, and orchestra; "The Golden Lotus;" and "The Gold of Their Bodies."

J. CHONG LEE
    (Engineering 20)
    Significance: *Space Program engineering
        and research*

Dr. J. Chong Lee, head of the Missiles and Space Division of Lockheed Aircraft Corporation in Sunnyvale, California, directs and coordinates all departmental activities for the Satellite Systems program. He is also in the Theoretical Nuclear Physics, Nuclear Physics, and Spacecraft and Missiles Research programs.

TSUNG-DAO LEE
    (Physical Science 15, 21)
    Born: 1926, Shanghai, China
    Education: Ph.D., University of Chicago,
        Illinois
    Significance: *Nobel Prize physicist*

Tsung-Dao Lee has been a professor at Columbia University. Dr. Lee was awarded the 1957 Nobel Prize in Physics for his theoretical work in that field.

YUEN CHUEN LEE
    (Engineering 14)
    Born: 1913, Chengtu, China
    Education: B.S., California Institute of
        Technology, Pasadena
    Significance: *Research in the field of
        aerospace*

Yuen Chuen Lee came to the United States in 1935, becoming a naturalized citizen in 1950. He was a research associate at the University of Southern California for two years, director of Corporate Research for the Aerojet General Corporation for eleven years, and president of Astropower, Incorporated, for two years. He has been manager of Power Systems, Lockheed Missile and Space Company, Sunnyvale, California, since 1962. Lee has been a member of the NASA Electrical Energy Commission and a consultant to the United States Air Force Science Advisory Board. He is a Fellow of the American Institute of Aeronautics and Astronautics.

FAITH LEONG
    (Medicine 20)
    Education: Physicians and Surgeons
        College
    Significance: *Early woman dentist*

Faith Leong was the first woman dentist in Chinatown, San Francisco. Dr. Leong graduated from Physicians and Surgeons College in 1905, and then established her practice in Chinatown.

CHOH HAO LI
    (Life Science 21)
    Born: 1913, Canton, China
    Education: B.S., University of Nanking;
        Ph.D., University of California at
        Berkeley
    Significance: *Steroid hormone research*

Choh Hao Li came to the United States in 1935 and became an American citizen in 1955.

After receiving his doctorate, he remained at the University of California at Berkeley as a research associate, moving upward in experimental biology, biochemistry, and experimental endocrinology. Dr. Li has been director of the Hormone Research Laboratory in Berkeley and San Francisco since 1950. He has received many honors in his field, including the Ciba Award in endocrinology, a Guggenheim fellowship, the Albert Lasker Award for basic medical research, and an honorary medical degree from the Catholic University of Chile.

TUNG YEN LIN
(Engineering 20)
Significance: *Construction design authority*

Tung Yen Lin, professor of civil engineering and a research engineer at the University of California, was a Fulbright Award scholar. He is an internationally known authority on bridge construction. He is also one of the world's leading experts on pre-stressed concrete, the high-strength building material which is already recognized as one of the greatest advances in construction of the 20th century.

GIM GONG LUE
(Agriculture 13)
Born: China
Died: 1926
Significance: *Outstanding horticulturist*

Gim Gong Lue was an outstanding horticulturist. Specializing in fruit culture (pomology), he developed the Gong orange. A commercial variety, this orange can be marketed in prime condition for greater periods of time than any other variety. The trees bear uniformly large crops of high quality fruit. The Gong orange has given great impetus to the California and Florida citrus industry.

Gim Gong Lue was awarded the Wilder medal for his orange by the United States Department of Agriculture.

EMMA PING LUM
(Law 20)
Education: Hastings College, Nebraska

Significance: *First woman of Chinese ancestry admitted to the Federal bar*

Emma Ping Lum is the first Chinese woman lawyer in California and the first to practice in the United States. In 1947, she was the first woman of Chinese ancestry admitted to practice before the Federal bar. In 1958 she also practiced before the United States Supreme Court.

CHUCK MAU
(Law 17)
Born: 1907, Honolulu, Oahu, Hawaii
Education: A.B., LL.B., University of Colorado, Boulder
Significance: *Judiciary and community service*

Judge Chuck Mau received his college education in the United States and then returned to Hawaii to practice law, where he was admitted to the Territory of Hawaii bar in 1935. He has been law secretary to the justices of the Supreme Court of Hawaii, judge of the Tax Appeal Court of Hawaii, a bar examiner and a Circuit Court judge. He has had his private practice in law since 1940 and presently is with the firm of Mau and Ho, Attorneys at Law. He is a member of both the American and Hawaiian Bar Associations. Judge Mau's appointment to an American bench opened the way for other qualified oriental Americans.

Judge Mau is also president of the First Hawaiian Title Company, Incorporated, and Hawaii Recreation Properties Corporation. He is director and secretary of the Hawaii National Bank; the World-Wide Factors, Incorporated; the Chun-Hoon Pharmacy, Limited; WADCO, Limited; Town Properties, Limited; Town Investment, Limited; and the Chun-Hoon Drive-In, Incorporated. He is a member of the Board of Directors of the Kokokahi Trust Company, Kapiolani Maternity and Gynecological Hospital, Leahi Hospital, Honolulu Community Theater, the Child and Family Service of Honolulu, and a member of the board of managers of the Honolulu YMCA. Active in civic affairs, Judge Mau was president of the Oahu Society for Crippled Children and Adults from 1955 to 1957, and president of the Hawaii State Chapter of the Society for Crippled Children and Adults from 1960 to 1964. From 1940 to 1946 and from 1948 to 1950, he was a member of the Honolulu board of supervisors of the city and county of Honolulu.

STANLEY MOY

(Engineering   15)

Education: M.A., Stanford University, Palo Alto, California

Significance: *Aeronautics maintenance*

Stanley Moy heads the maintenance shop for the Pacific-Alaska Division of Pan-American World Airways.

IEOH MING PEI

(Architecture   21)

Born: 1917, Canton, China

Education: B.A., Massachusetts Institute of Technology, Cambridge, Massachusetts; M.A., Harvard University, Cambridge, Massachusetts

Significance: *Architectural design*

Ieoh Ming Pei became an American citizen in 1954. He served for several years as director of the architectural division of a large real estate firm. He then formed his own company of I. M. Pei and Associates. His firm has designed Denver's Mile-High Center, Long Island's Roosevelt Field Shopping Center, the Kips Bay Apartments in New York, the John F. Kennedy Memorial Library at Harvard University, and scores of other major construction projects.

JOE SHOONG

(Business   20)

Significance: *Philanthropist and financier*

Joe Shoong, pioneer manufacturer, merchandiser, and financier, has built a chain of department stores in the west and in the Hawaiian Islands. Known for his many philanthropies, he founded the Joe Shoong Foundation which annually dispenses large sums of money to charitable enterprises.

TSUNG WEI SZE

(Engineering   21)

Born: 1922, Shanghai, China

Education: B.S, University of Missouri, Columbia, Missouri; M.S., Purdue University, Lafayette, Indiana; Ph.D., Northwestern University, Evanston, Illinois

Significance: *Research and design in electrical engineering*

An electrical engineer, Tsung Wei Sze has done research in logical design and digital computing systems. His publications include "Switching Circuit Foundations" and many other technical papers. Dr. Sze became a naturalized citizen in 1962.

THOMAS TANG

(Law   24)

Born: 1922, Phoenix, Arizona

Education: B.S., University of Santa Clara, Santa Clara, California; LL.B., University of Arizona, Tucson

Significance: *Judicial service*

Judge Thomas Tang was admitted to the Arizona bar in 1950, and the California bar in 1951. He has been a practicing attorney, a deputy attorney in Maricopa County, Arizona, and an assistant attorney general for the State of Arizona. He was appointed a judge of the Arizona Superior Court in 1963, and a judge of the Maricopa County Juvenile Court in 1966.

JADE SNOW WONG

(Art   17)

Born: San Francisco, California

Education: B.A., Mills College, Oakland, California

Significance: *Original work in ceramics and successful author*

Jade Snow Wong is a well-known ceramist, working and living in San Francisco. Her autobiography, *Fifth Chinese Daughter,* written in 1950, tells of growing up in San Francisco's Chinatown and her high school years, and then earning her way through college at Mills, across San Francisco Bay. There she found such satisfaction in working with clay that she decided to make it her life's work. After graduation, she set up her potter's wheel in the window of a store in Chinatown, to the horror of her Chinese parents. Her book has been translated into nine foreign languages.

Miss Wong's original works in ceramics and in copperware fused with enamels are represented in the New York Museum of Modern Art. Her one-woman show, sponsored by the Chicago Art Institute in 1952, was also invited to Detroit, Kansas City, Omaha, St. Louis, and Portland.

Miss Wong's autobiography and her government sponsored lecture tours in 1953 demonstrated that it is possible for cultures to fuse in the United States.

Miss Wong has been honored in many ways. Her name and work have been featured in many publications. As a craftswoman, she received the 1948 *Mademoiselle* Merit Award given to the ten most outstanding young women of the United States in different professions. In 1953, she was named by Collier's magazine as one of the ten most glamorous women in San Francisco. In 1957, she was selected Woman of Distinction in the field of the arts by the Professional and Business Women's Club of San Francisco.

WORLEY K. WONG
(Architecture 20)
Born: 1912, Oakland, California
Education: B.A., University of California, Berkeley
Significance: *Architectural design*
Worley K. Wong is an internationally known architect. His work has appeared in many national and international publications. His honors include a Meritorious Service Award from the United States State Department for his work at the Brussels Universal and International Exhibition. He served on the Board of Directors of the San Francisco Planning and Urban Renewal Commission and is a member of the State Board of Architectural Examiners.

CHEN-NING YANG
(Physical Science 21)
Born: 1922, Hofei, Anhwei, China
Education: Ph.D., University of Chicago, Illinois
Significance: *Research in physics*
Chen-Ning Yang, an outstanding physicist, was born in China and educated in the United States. Dr. Yang was a professor at the Institute for Advanced Study at Princeton, New Jersey. In 1957, when he was only thirty-four years old, he was awarded the Nobel Prize for Physics.

LIEN SHENG YANG
(Education, History 21)
Born: 1914, Paoting, China
Education: Ph.D., Harvard University, Cambridge, Massachusetts
Significance: *Research in Chinese history*
Lien Sheng Yang is a professor of Chinese history at Harvard University. He is a naturalized citizen.

ALICE FONG YU
(Education 20)
Significance: *Work in special education*
Mrs. Alice Fong Yu, in 1926, became the first San Francisco teacher of Chinese descent. She was assigned for many years to the Commodore Stockton Elementary School. Deeply interested in the problems of cerebral palsied children, she holds the position of speech correction teacher-at-large, assigned to the Child Welfare Division.

FILIPINO AMERICANS

JOSE ARUEGO
(Literature 27)
Born: Manila, Philippine Islands
Education: B.A., University of the Philippines; LL.D., University of the Philippines
Significance: *Children's literature and artist*
Jose Aruego, a Filipino American, is a member of the Philippine Bar Association. Becoming interested in art, he came to New York City where he studied at the Parsons School of Design. In addition to his talent as a cartoonist, he executed one of the murals at International House in New York City. His first book, *The*

King and His Friends, was published in 1969. This was followed in 1970 by a very different kind of book for young children entitled *Symbiosis, A Book of Unusual Friendships.* His third book is *Juan and the Asuangs,* a tale of Philippine ghosts and spirits.

LARRY ITLIONG

(Civil Rights   29)
Born: 1913, Pengasinnan, Philippine
   Islands
Education: in the Philippines
Significance: *Work in behalf of laborers
   and farm workers*

Larry Itliong came to the United States in 1929. He worked in the fields of California as a laborer and then in the fish canneries. He became actively involved in unionization as a means of obtaining better working conditions. In 1936, he organized the Simon Canneries Union in Seattle and the Sardine Cannery Workers Union in San Pedro, California.

Itliong has long been active in working toward a better life for California farm workers, both migrant and local. He has worked side by side with César Chávez in negotiating a union contract with the grape growers in the San Joaquin Valley. He is the assistant director of the United Farm Workers Organizing Committee (UFWOC).

At various times, Itliong has been president of the Philippine Community organizations in Seattle, Washington and in Stockton and San Pedro, California. He is president of the Filipino American Political Association in California. He is also a member of the Board of Directors of the California Rural Legal Assistance organization (CRLA) and of the Citizen's Crusade Against Poverty in Washington, D.C. Itliong is also advisor to the Ethnic Group Studies of the University of California at Berkeley.

JULITA (TAMONDONG) MCLEOD

(Education   30)
Born: Manila, Philippine Islands
Significance: *Teacher and school
   administrator*

Julita Tamondong McLeod was married to a guerilla fighter during the Japanese occupation of her homeland. When her husband left the Air Force in 1957 he brought his wife and three children to San Francisco.

Mrs. McLeod has made her voice heard in the education of Filipino and other ethnic-group children by bringing their cause to the attention of the San Francisco Board of Education. She has been a language arts specialist and compensatory education teacher. She is now the principal of the Washington Irving Elementary School in San Francisco.

Mrs. McLeod was named one of the Ten Most Distinguished Women of 1969 during the 11th annual Phoebe Apperson Hearst Gold Medallion Award ceremonies.

BERTHA SANCHEZ

(Health   30)
Born: 1937, Philippine Islands
Education: M.S., University of California
   Medical Center, San Francisco
Significance: *Nursing director of hospital
   in South Vietnam*

Bertha Sanchez, born in the Philippines, was seven when her family returned to California. She grew up in San Mateo, where she was active in the Girl Scouts. Miss Sanchez became a nurse, and in the summers during her nurse's training she was a Project Concern Tijuana Clinic volunteer. She served as school nurse at Jefferson High School in Daly City, California, and then took a year off to earn her Master's degree.

She is nursing director of the Project Concern team with two hospitals for South Vietnamese in the remote Central Highlands northeast of Saigon. The isolated Dampoo Medical Center treats everything from snake bite to sniper wound. Her international staff serves 5000 Koho tribespeople eighty miles from the Cambodian border. Medical care, training villagers in the basics of medical assistance, and supervising the building of a second hospital are all a part of Miss Sanchez' day.

Miss Sanchez was named one of the Ten Most Distinguished Women of 1969 by the San

Francisco Examiner during the 11th Annual Phoebe Apperson Hearst Gold Medallion Award ceremonies.

PHILLIP VERACRUZ
   (Civil Rights   28)
   Born: Ilocos Sur, Philippine Islands
   Education: Gonzaga University, Spokane,
      Washington
   Significance: *Leadership in behalf of the California farm laborers*

Phillip Veracruz came to the United States as a student in 1926. After attending college he served in the Armed Forces until 1943. He then worked as a farm laborer, later becoming a prominent organizer of the Delano Grape Strike in California. He is vice-president of the United Farm Workers Organizing Committee (UFWOC). Veracruz is also a major contributor to *El Malcriado* (The Voice of the Farm Worker), a newspaper published in Delano, California.

Bibliography of Sources Used

JAPANESE AMERICAN

1 *Celebrity Register.* New York: Harper and Row, Publishers, 1963.
2 *Contemporary Authors.* Vol. 13-14. Detroit: Gale Research Co., 1965.
3 Hosokawa, Bill. *Nisei: The Quiet Americans.* New York: William Morrow & Co., 1969.
4 Kitano, Harry. *Japanese Americans.* New York: Prentice-Hall, Inc., 1969.
5 Personal Statement.
6 San Mateo City School District. Intergroup Education Department, *Japanese American Curriculum Project Bulletin.* San Mateo, California: San Mateo School District, 1969.
7 *Who's Who in America.* Vol. 35. Chicago: Marquis–Who's Who, Inc. 1969.
8 *Who's Who in American Politics.* New York: R. R. Bowker Co., 1967.
9 *Who's Who in Art.* 14th edition. Havant, Hampshire, England: Art Trade Press, Ltd., 1968.
10 *Who's Who in the West.* United States of America and Canada. 11th edition. Chicago: Marquis–Who's Who, Inc., 1969.
11 *World Book Encyclopedia.* Chicago: Field Enterprises Educational Corporation, 1970.

CHINESE AMERICAN

12 California, University of, University Relations, Berkeley. *Clip Sheet.* Volume 45. (January 6, 1970)
13 Chinn, Thomas W. (ed.). *A History of the Chinese in California* A syllabus. San Francisco: Chinese Historical Society of America, 1969.
14 *Leaders in American Science.* 8th edition. Hattiesburg, Mississippi: Who's Who in American Education, 1968-69.
15 Maisel, Albert Q. "The Chinese Among Us," *Reader's Digest,* Vol. 74, No. 442 (February, 1959), pp. 203-212.
16 *National Observer,* October, 1969.
17 Personal summary.
18 "Records are Falling to a China Doll," *Life Magazine,* Vol. 69, No. 2 (July 10, 1970), pp. 34-35.
19 Ritter, E., Ritter, H., and Spector, S. *Our Oriental Americans.* St. Louis, Missouri: Webster Division, McGraw-Hill Book Co., 1965.
20 *San Francisco Chinatown on Parade in Picture and Story.* Edited by K. K. Wong. San Francisco: Chinese Chamber of Commerce, 1961.
21 *Who's Who in America.* Vol. 35. Chicago: Marquis–Who's Who, Inc., 1969.

22   *Who's Who in California.* Edited by Alice Catt Armstrong. Los Angeles: Who's Who Historical Society, 1961.
23   *Who's Who in Commerce and Industry.* Chicago: Marquis—Who's Who, Inc., 1966-67.
24   *Who's Who in the West.* United States of America and Canada. 11th edition. Chicago: Marquis—Who's Who, Inc., 1968.
25   *Who's Who of American Women.* 6th edition. Chicago: A. N. Marquis Co., 1970-71.
26   *World Who's Who in Science: From Antiquity to the Present.* Chicago: Marquis—Who's Who, Inc., 1968.

FILIPINO AMERICAN

27   Aruego, Jose. *The King and His Friends.* New York: Charles Scribner's Sons, 1969. (Information from book jacket)
28   *El Malcriado.* The Voice of the Farm Worker (Delano, California), April, 1970.
29   Personal summary.
30   *Philippine News* (San Francisco), January 15-21, 1970.

ASIAN AMERICANS

OTHER REFERENCES

BOOKS FOR TEACHERS

Bosworth, Allan R. *America's Concentration Camps.* New York: W. W. Norton and Co., 1967.

Burma, John H. *Spanish-Speaking Groups in the United States.* Durham, North Carolina: Duke University Press, 1954.

Chinese Historical Society of America. *Bulletin.* Thomas W. Chinn, editor (San Francisco).

Chu, Daniel, and Chu, Samuel. *Passage to the Golden Gate. A History of the Chinese in America.* New York: Doubleday and Co., 1967.

Edmiston, James. *Home Again.* New York: Doubleday and Co., 1955. (Fiction)

Inouye, Daniel K. *Journey to Washington.* Englewood Cliffs, New Jersey: Prentice-Hall, 1967.

Leathers, Noel L. *Japanese in America.* Minneapolis: Lerner Publishing Co., 1967.

Miyamoto, Kazuo. *Hawaii: End of the Rainbow.* Rutland, Vermont: Charles E. Tuttle Co., 1964. (Fiction)

Okubo, Mine. *Citizen 13660.* New York: Columbia University Press, 1946.

Smith, Bradford. *Americans from Japan.* Philadelphia: J. B. Lippincott Co., 1948.

Sone, Monica. *Nisei Daughter.* New York: Little, Brown and Co., 1953.

ten Broek, Jacobus. *Prejudice, War and the Constitution: Japanese American Evacuation and Resettlement.* Berkeley, California: University of California Press, 1968.

BOOKS FOR CHILDREN

Behrens, June. *Soo Ling Finds a Way.* San Carlos, California: Golden Gate Junior Books, 1965. (Chinese American)

Bonham, Frank. *Mystery in Little Tokyo.* New York: E. P. Dutton & Co., 1966. (Japanese American)

Bulla, Clyde Robert. *Johnny Hong of Chinatown.* New York: Thomas Y. Crowell Co., 1952. (Chinese American)

————. *Sugar Pear Tree.* New York: Thomas Y. Crowell Co., 1960. (Japanese American)

Cavanna, Betty. *Jenny Kimura.* New York: William Morrow & Company, 1964. (Japanese American)

Lenski, Lois. *San Francisco Boy.* Philadelphia: J. B. Lippincott Co., 1955. (Chinese American)

Martin, Patricia Miles. *Rice Bowl Pet.* New York: Thomas Y. Crowell Co., 1962. (Chinese American)

Miles, Miska. *Pieces of Home.* Boston: Little, Brown & Company, 1967. (Chinese American)

Newman, Shirlee Petkin. *Yellow Silk for May Lee.* Indianapolis: Bobbs-Merrill Co., 1961. (Chinese American)

Politi, Leo. *Mieko.* San Carlos, California: Golden Gate Junior Books, 1969. (Japanese American)

_____. *Moy Moy.* New York: Charles Scribner's Sons, 1960. (Chinese American)

Shannon, Terry, *Red is for Luck.* San Carlos, California: Golden Gate Junior Books, 1963. (Chinese American)

Uchida, Yoshiko. *Mik and the Prowler.* New York: Harcourt, Brace & Co., 1960. (Japanese American)

Yashima, Taro. *Momo's Kitten.* New York: Viking Press, 1961. (Japanese American)

_____. *Umbrella.* New York: Viking Press, 1958. (Japanese American)

PART THREE

INDIAN AMERICANS

I see unhappy years ahead for the Sioux.
The white men will show anger
for years to come. We must pray to
the Holy Mystery and ask that some day
the white man will better understand us;
that the seeds of their conscience
will awake and grow.

D. CHIEF EAGLE

INDIAN AMERICANS

HISTORICAL PERSPECTIVE

A primitive people is not a backward or retarded people; indeed it may possess a genius or action that leaves the achievements of civilized peoples far behind.

CLAUDE LEVI-STRAUSS

"We think kind thoughts of you" is a Navajo saying. Considering the treatment that American Indians have received, it is difficult to imagine any Indian thinking kind thoughts of anyone but another Indian. This history of the American Indian is one of demoralization, sadness, reproach, tragedy, and shame.

When the Europeans first made contact with the Indians, it was generally on a friendly basis and as equals. The Indians were willing to share their land and all things in it with their white brothers since they felt that the Great Spirit meant the land for everyone's use. Trouble developed because of the differing ideologies regarding land use. The white man put up fences. The Indians could not roam at will to hunt and fish. Even with the coming of more white people and more fences, the Indians were still willing to negotiate peacefully. But the Indians became victims not only of color and cultural barriers, but also of land barriers.

Indian history has been distorted since the first error committed by Columbus when he termed native inhabitants Los Indios, falsely believing them to be people of islands off the coast of Asia. The Indian was also termed a savage and a barbarian, and often only because he was different from and strange to the white man. James Fenimore Cooper's version of the Noble Red Man helped gain sympathy among the settlers and Europeans for the Indian, yet the sentiment persisted that "the only good Indian is a dead Indian." This image was succeeded by the term "Whiskey Indian." People failed to recognize the causes of the degradation of Indians. Motion pictures and other mass media continue to perpetuate the stereotype of a sour-faced and warlike Indian.

Indians from Alaska to Cape Horn differ in both language and customs. Even the term "redskin" is a misnomer, for the Indian skin ranges from a coppery brown to a yellowish brown. Indians are believed to have originated in Asia, spreading out to the Western Hemisphere and becoming different as they adapted to the various environments of plains, woodlands, coasts, deserts, canyons, and mountains. Thus the concept of "Indianness" becomes difficult, reflecting as it does such a variety of peoples.

Common to almost all Indian societies were faith in supernatural forces; individuals with supernatural powers; rituals with dancing, drumming, and singing; reverence for nature; and the concept of communal land ownership. Associated with almost all of their cultures were implements such as spears and bows and arrows.

Some of the forces which have brought various tribes into greater contact with each other are

125

relocation, education, government programs, social gatherings, and political strivings. These forces have encouraged sameness among the differing tribes. Differing tribes, however, rarely unified. The great League of the Iroquois was made up of related tribes. The Hurons and Algonquians remained enemies and had to move westward by sheer force of the League's might. Confederacies were formed under such great leaders as Tecumseh, Black Hawk, Osceola, Pontiac, Little Turtle, Quanah Parker, Sitting Bull and others, only eventually to crumble under the force of the white man's relentless move westward. Recently Indian leaders have said that if the tribes had been united, the white man would not have been successful in the settlement of America.

Other forces in recent years helped to develop a unifying spirit among Indian tribes throughout the country transcending tribal affiliations and traditions. Such forces include the Indians' own need to identify as a race, resulting in the National Congress of the American Indian, founded in 1944. The unifying spirit has also been advanced by the ideals of the United Nations, the "war" on poverty and the Negroes' civil rights struggle in the United States. The latter force has provided momentum to the Indians' struggle for equal rights with their occupation of Alcatraz Island and "sit-ins" at Mount Lassen in northern California.

The innate dignity of the American Indian, his disinclination for confrontation, his allegiance to about 300 tribes, and his dependence upon the white man for land and livelihood have kept the Indian from claiming his rightful place as a first-class citizen in his own homeland. Although there are countless incidents through history where Indians have claimed treaty rights and received retroactive payment for their land, the Indian American remains for the most part a disadvantaged person. Indians cite the Bureau of Indian Affairs, the countless broken treaties, land thefts, and the attempts of re-culturation as reasons for past apathy and bitterness. The new militants reject such resignation and are determined to be heard. In explaining that each man must respect his brother's dream, his brother's vision, one Indian said, "The question is not how you can Americanize us, but how we can Americanize you."

Few people appreciate the white man's debt to the Indian. Without Indian environmental and land-use knowledge and without Indian crops, the first white settlers of this country surely would have perished. The shamans, or medicine men, taught the settlers to use natural medicines to cure disease. Many aspects of modern arts and crafts reflect the Indian influence. Indian political traits and institutions also had an impact on the white man. Benjamin Franklin urged emulation of the League of the Iroquois when he made proposals for a union of the colonies in 1754. The League had flourished under the rule of law long before the advent of white men and the development of the government of the United States as it was constituted in 1789. Montaigne and Rousseau were but two of the serious philosophers who were impressed by the Indian way of life, comparing the Indian's freedom to the European's state of living.

Indian population numbers have changed greatly since the white man's conquest of the New World. Estimates of the population of America in 1492 range from eight to seventy-five million. It is certain that many tribes of Indians were exterminated and that many approached extinction but survived. By 1910, only some 220,000 Indians remained in the United States. Such was the decline of the "vanishing American." The Indian net birth rate subsequently increased until, according to the 1960 report of the United States Bureau of Census, there were about 550,000 Indians, Aleuts, and Eskimos in the United States.

The population story affords a ray of hope to each great Indian family line which suffered economic or military defeat and confinement upon reservations. Most tribes have survived these disasters and are increasing in numbers as they develop greater independence through self-determination, education, economic improvement, and pride in their cultural heritage. The vast majority of tribes have kept their languages alive. Bilingualism has been a trend among most tribes and trilingualism in the southwest because of the earlier Spanish influence.

Indians have been classified according to tribe, ways of making a living, and geographical location. Differences blended together with proximity, so that neighboring tribes tended to resemble each other in housing, dress, food, crafts, and habits. For the purpose of this writing the Indian tribes of the United States are classified according to geographic location. The tribes listed under each geographic category entered below are not all-inclusive.

Eastern Woodland Area
Algonquian, Delaware, Iroquois, Massachuset, Mohawk, Mohegan, Narraganset, Onandaga, Penabscot, Powhatan, Tuscarora, Passamaquoddy, Pawtuxet, Tippecanoe, Wampanoag, Wyandot

Great Lakes Woodland Area
Chippewa/Ojibwa, Huron, Illinois, Kickapoo, Miami, Oneida, Ottawa, Potawatomi, Sauk and Fox, Seneca, Shawnee, Winnebago

Southeastern Area
Catawba, Cherokee, Creek, Lumbi, Natchez, Seminole, Yuchi

North Central Plains Area
Arapaho, Arikara, Assiniboine, Blackfeet, Cheyenne, Cree, Crow, Gros Ventre, Mandan, Pawnee, Shoshone, Sioux/Dakota

South Central Plains Area
Caddo, Chickasaw, Choctaw, Comanche, Iowa, Kaw/Kansa, Kiowa, Omaha, Osage, Ponca, Quapaw

Southwest Area
Apache, Hopi, Maricopa, Navajo, Papago, Pima, Pueblo, Zuñi

California Area
Chumash, Hoopa, Maidu, Mission, Modoc, Mohave, Mono, Pit River, Pomo, Tule River, Wailaki, Yahi, Yokuts, Yuma, Yurok

Northwestern Plateau Area
Bannock, Cayuse, Coeur D'Alene, Colville, Flathead, Kalispel, Klamath, Kootenai, Nez Percé, Paiute, Puyallup, Spokane, Ute, Wallawalla, Wasco, Washoe, Yakima, Nisqually

Northwest Pacific Coast Area
Aleuts, Eskimo, Haida, Lummi, Makah, Muckleshoot, Nootka, Quinault, Salish, Shoalwater, Snohomish, Suquamish, Tlingit

The usefulness of this classification is that, within each area, the basic modes of life are similar. Differences dictated by geographical regions may be seen in the following example of agricultural customs: while the Northwest Coast Indians developed fishing as their main food supply, the Navajos of the southwest area dry-farmed corn, beans, and squash, and raised sheep and goats.

Horses were one of three gifts from the white man to the Indian. The other two were guns and liquor. Horses and guns prolonged the Indian wars. The liquor trade is an ugly page in United States history. From the early days when Henry Hudson introduced liquor to the Manhatten Indians, alcohol was used as an escape from boredom and oppression.

The story of the bloody wars between the white settlers and Indians during the 1700's and 1800's is familiar to most Americans. These accounts tell of sudden Indian raids, scalping, and other savage practices. It should be noted that the practice of cutting off ears as punishment for debts was not unknown to the Europeans, and the practice of scalping was introduced by the English during the early French and Indian Wars. The Indian was exploited, degraded, and demoralized in defeat. A prime example was the "Long Walk" to Bosque Redondo, east of the Rio Grande, suffered by the Navajos after their land in Arizona was taken from them. Enroute many of them died of starvation or exposure to the elements. Others were killed or kidnapped by Mexican raiders to be sold as slaves.

Tens of thousands of Indians had suffered incredible hardships in the 1830's after the passage of the Removal Bill. This bill gave President Jackson power to exchange land west of the Mississippi River for territory still held by Indian tribes in the southeast. The helpless Choctaws, Creeks, and Chickasaws of the five civilized tribes were driven west, along with the Cherokees from Georgia. The latter experienced a particularly bitter trek with the result that nearly one-fourth of the tribe died of starvation, disease, and hardship. This torturous trip west to Oklahoma in 1838 and 1839 is referred to as the "Trail of Tears."

In December of 1890 at Wounded Knee, South Dakota, the anguished rebellion of the Indian American against intolerable conditions ended. This rebellion had come to a seeming end with the campaign following Custer's defeat in the Battle of the Little Big Horn of 1876. It had been rekindled by the great Messiah Movement of 1888–90 and its accompanying Ghost Dance. Two hundred members of the Sioux band of the great chief, Sitting Bull, were killed at Wounded Knee. Sitting Bull himself had died two weeks earlier while resisting arrest. This episode marked the completion of the white man's conquest of the Indian in the United States.

After their military defeat, tribes were placed on reservations administered by the United States Department of Interior, Bureau of Indian Affairs, and sometimes policed by the Army. Congress appropriated funds to feed the Indians and meet treaty obligations. Unfortunately, the commissioners and agents responsible for this program sometimes were not completely sympathetic nor understanding and caused further confusion and defeatism among the tribes. Most tribes have been afforded little opportunity to manage their own affairs. Efforts over the years have been made to end tribal cultures, with no satisfactory substitute offered.

Statistics show that there are a significant number of Indians who have left reservations and joined the mainstream of American life, most of whom have settled in large urban centers. Many have made the adjustment, but too many are often lost and frustrated in the dominant culture.

Although the Cherokee have enjoyed full citizenship since 1901 when the Territory of Oklahoma was being considered for statehood, all other tribes were not granted this status until 1924. In 1934, the Indian Reorganization Act offered some hope through advancement in economy and self-government. The General Allotment Act of 1887 (Dawes Act) had been tailored to hasten assimilation. Instead, it resulted in the suppression of the Indian's only remaining shred of self-esteem, his culture. The 1935 Indian Arts and Crafts Act counteracted the old General Allotment Act (Dawes Act) by encouraging cultural development and a market for Indian crafts through government financial assistance.

In 1953, the so-called "termination" policy was adopted. This meant that the intention of Congress was to terminate federal relations with the tribes at the earliest opportunity. The goal again was to speed assimilation. Misleading appeals such as "free the Indians from the reservations" brought new confusion to the Indians. For, as restrictive as they may appear, the reservations are not concentration camps and the Indians are not prisoners on them. Despite the tribes' almost unanimous opposition to immediate termination, it may be inevitable. The reason is that Indians who have left the reservations, assimilating into white society, no longer have an interest in the reservations. They feel that the better course is to liquidate and divide tribal resources among the people. The Indians remaining on reservations in notable instances are moving toward economic independence, self-determination, and pride in cultural heritage and want termination on a gradual basis.

Despite attempts at assimilation, the Indian way of life persists, especially in the larger centers of Indian population. The Hopi, the Pueblo, and other tribes of the southwest retain their religious, social, and political organizations and customs with remarkably little change. Many Indian leaders are encouraging the youth to have a foot in each culture, so to speak. They urge education and training in order to be comfortable in both cultures, on or off the reservation. Whatever their future, a low self-image and lack of proper identity are plaguing elements. Indian students have higher dropout rates than others. The suicide rate is in excess of the national average, as is alcoholism. Lack of motivation may be traced to feelings of disgust, humiliation and anomie - a term meaning stripped of one's culture.

There is a great need for written material which properly portrays the Indians' role in American history. An accurate, fair, and balanced picture needs to be drawn. The rich cultural Indian heritage that includes harmony with nature and all living things of the earth and sky as well as the innate worth of the individual needs to be stressed.

The history of the Indian is so intimately interwoven with the history of the United States that no school child can understand his country without an appreciation of the long travail of the Indian and the contributions he has made to the total culture. Indianness is truly a part of our American heritage. One needs only to study a map to see the myriad of place names of Indian origin, or to study present-day advertising to find the names of famous tribes or great Indian chiefs used to signify some admirable quality or strength. Expressions, too, have become such a part of our language that we accept them without thought of origin. The contributions of individual Indians through the long course of history certainly enhance and enrich our heritage. It is the purpose here to document such contributions which reveal the dignity and cultural attributes of the Indian. The following section presents only a sampling of the Indians who have made outstanding contributions to the larger society in every field of human endeavor. Many, many have not been included here. It is hoped that all children will benefit from the knowledge of the great variety of worthy contributions which are briefly narrated here.

INDIAN AMERICANS

BIOGRAPHICAL SUMMARIES

DIEGO ABEITA, Isleta Pueblo
(Civil Rights   40*)
Born: 1920, Isleta Pueblo, New Mexico
Education: Reservation school
Significance: *Developing Indian land and water rights*

Diego Abeita has been the chairman of The Six Middle Rio Grande Pueblos Irrigation Committee since 1950. He has served for ten years on the official board of Bernalillo County Indian Hospital. He is also a member of the Finance and Legislation Committee of the Albuquerque Technical Vocational Institute. He is a leader in the promotion of the development of Pueblo Indian irrigated lands and is an avid proponent of Indian water rights. Presently Abeita is serving as adviser to attorneys in defense of Indian water rights. He operates a range-livestock unit at Isleta Pueblo.

NARCISO ABEYTO, Navajo
(Government   16)
Born: 1918, Canyoncito, New Mexico
Education: Santa Fe Indian School; B.A., University of New Mexico, Albuquerque
Significance: *Working at the state level in behalf of his people*

Narciso Abeyto has been an interviewer-interpreter for the New Mexico State Employment Commission since 1952. He served in the United States Army from 1941 to 1945. He has

*These numbers refer to the *Bibliography of Sources Used,* found at the end of this section.

been a member of the American Legion and the International Association of Personnel in Employment Security since 1953. Abeyto won second prize for an advertising poster submitted at the San Francisco Exposition in 1939. He is also the illustrator of *Aychee, Son of the Desert,* published in 1935.

SAM AHKEAH, Navajo
(Tribal Leadership   13)
Born: 1896, near Shiprock, Arizona
Died: 1967
Education: Elementary school, Fort Lewis, Colorado; San Juan Boarding School, Shiprock, Arizona
Significance: *Lifetime of leadership to his people*

Sam Ahkeah is best known for the leadership given his people through the Navajo Tribal Council, of which he was chairman from 1946 to 1954.

As a developing adolescent, Ahkeah triumphed over tuberculosis. He had only an eighth grade education himself, and the one main theme of his life was to encourage Navajo children to continue their education as far as possible. He established the Navajo Tribal Scholarship Fund. During Ahkeah's term of office the Navajos gained in health facilities, housing and land management. Ahkeah was greatly admired by his people. A tribute written by Will Rogers, Jr. states:

The death of Sam Ahkeah brought a great sadness to me. He was chairman of the

130

Navajo Tribe when I was a member of Congress. It was a time when the Navajo people were not doing so well, but I remember his confidence in their future, his dignity, his bearing, and his leadership. The Navajo Tribe has been very fortunate in the calibre of its leadership. It has lost one of the very great in Sam Ahkeah.

DOLLY SMITH AKERS, Assiniboine
(Politics   11)
Born: Early 1900's, Montana
Education: Public Schools, Montana;
    Sherman Institute, California
Significance: *Promotion of health,
    economic welfare, and education of
    her people through politics*
Dolly Smith Akers is perhaps the only Indian woman actively engaged in politics. She was the only elected woman member of her tribal council of which she was also chairman, one of few Indian women to hold such office. In 1932 she was elected to the Montana Legislature, the only woman legislator and the first Indian woman to be so elected. She was chairman of the Federal Relations Committee and was a special representative from the Governor to the Secretary of Interior. Mrs. Akers entered politics as a means of promoting better things for her people. At the same time she was caring for a semi-invalid husband and running a 2,000-acre ranch.

ARTHUR DOUGLAS AMIOTTE, Oglala-Teton
    Sioux
(Art, Education   24, 36)
Born: 1942, Pine Ridge, South Dakota
Education: B.S. in Art Education,
    Northern State College, South Dakota;
    M.S., Pennsylvania State University,
    Philadelphia
Significance: *Promoting the culture of his
    people through his art*
Arthur Douglas Amiotte has been an artist-teacher since 1964, having taught art education at Northern State College, Aberdeen, South Dakota. He is presently teaching in the Porcupine Day School on the Pine Ridge Reservation in South Dakota. He is on a community speaker's panel for the promotion of awareness of minority and ethnic groups. He also lectures on American Indians.

Amiotte is a member of many art and educational associations and has received many honors for his paintings, his lecturing and his contributions to art education. In 1966, Amiotte was nominated as Outstanding Teacher of the Year in Sioux City, Iowa, where he taught art at the Woodrow Wilson Junior High School. His art is exhibited widely in group shows and one-man exhibitions in South Dakota and throughout the United States.

JOHN HOBART ARTICHOKER, Sioux
(Government, Education   11)
Born: 1930, Pine Ridge, South Dakota
Education: B.S., M.A., University of
    South Dakota, Vermillion
Significance: *Promoting Indian education*
John Hobart Artichoker is an agency superintendent for the Bureau of Indian Affairs. He was the director of Indian Education for the State of South Dakota from 1951 to 1961. In 1965, he was awarded the Ten Outstanding Young Men Award by the United States Junior Chamber of Commerce. He also received the Indian Achievement Award in 1965. He is the author of *Indians of South Dakota,* published in 1965, and *The Sioux Indian Goes to College,* written with Neil Palmer as a master's thesis for the Institute of Indian Studies at the University of South Dakota, South Dakota.

LOUIS WAYNE BALLARD,
    Quapaw-Cherokee
(Education, Music   16)
Born: 1931, Miami, Oklahoma
Education: A.A., Northeast Oklahoma
    Agricultural and Mechanical College,
    Stillwater; B.A., B. Mus., M. Mus.,
    Tulsa University, Oklahoma
Significance: *Promoting the culture of his
    people through music*
Louis Wayne Ballard is president of the Santa Fe Symphony. He is a member of the National Music Educators Association, a mem-

ber of the New Mexico Music Teachers Association, and head of the music and drama department at the Institute of American Indian Arts, Santa Fe, New Mexico. In 1961, he was the recipient of the F. B. Parriott Graduate Fellowship Award. His composition, "Koshare, An American Indian Ballet," was published in 1966.

ROBERT R. BARAY, Blackfeet-Sioux
  (Military, Engineering   27)
  Born: 1900, Pine Ridge Reservation,
    Clearwater, South Dakota
  Education: Carlisle Institute,
    Pennsylvania; B.S.C.E., Cornell
    University, Ithaca, New York; U.S.
    Military Academy, West Point, New
    York; M.S.C.E., Blackpool Institute of
    Technology
  Significance: *Serving his country in both
    war and peace times*

Colonel Robert R. Baray was the first American Indian to attend West Point. Now retired, he has had a long and brilliant career with the United States Army Corps of Engineers beginning with World War I. In World War II, he served with the 3rd Battalion Engineers in Hawaii, followed by an assignment to the Los Angeles Corps of Engineers as executive director. He was in the European Theater of Operations, intermittently serving on General Eisenhower's staff until the close of the war in 1945. Colonel Baray was awarded the Distinguished Service Cross, the Silver Star with two oak leaf clusters, the Legion of Honor Militaire and the Croix de Guerre.

After World War II Colonel Baray served as senior instructor of engineering for NATO military forces and chief consulting engineer for the Commanding General of the United States Army Air Forces in Europe. From 1957 to 1969 he was General Staff Engineer for planning and developing the Vandenberg Air Force Base near Lompoc, California, where he still lives. He is affiliated with several local and national professional groups for engineers, and takes an active part in the civic affairs of his community.

BARBONCITO, Navajo
  (Tribal Leadership   13)
  Born: ca. 1810, Arizona
  Died: 1871
  Education: Tribal
  Significance: *Negotiating peace for his
    people*

Barboncito, known as Hastin Dagha (Man With The Whiskers) among his people, spoke for the Navajos during many important councils with General Sherman. In 1868, he traveled to Washington, D.C., accompanied by the trusted interpreter, Jesus Arviso, to lay before President Andrew Johnson the terrible plight of his people on the Bosque Redondo Reservation. This was located near Fort Sumner, east of the Rio Grande far from their traditional homeland. As a result, President Johnson appointed the now historic United States Peace Commission which met several months later with all of the Navajo chiefs on the Bosque Redondo.

It was at this conference that Barboncito, the official spokesman for the Navajos, and Jesus Arviso, his brilliant interpreter, negotiated for the return of the Navajos to their homeland and a fair return of the land which had been taken from them. He was able to get back only one-tenth of the original land, however. He tried to honor the Treaty of 1868, which he had signed along with the other Navajo chiefs, by preventing Navajo raids on Mexican and American farms and ranches enroute home. This was most difficult, because his people were starving. Barboncito had led his people on the long walk to Fort Sumner and encouraged them during their trying times at Bosque Redondo.

HARRISON BEGAY, Navajo
  (Art   28)
  Born: ca. 1920, Navajo country - Arizona
  Education: Fort Wingate and Santa Fe
    Indian Schools
  Significance: *Building a bridge of
    understanding to the way of life of his
    people through his sensitive, stylized
    earth paintings*

Harrison Begay is one of the outstanding and best known **Navajo** artists. He is also chief artist for a silk screen business which he helped to organize and which reproduces the paintings of a number of Indian artists. Softened earth colors and delicate lines are his distinguishing mark.

After two years of college, Begay entered military service in World War II in the Army Signal Corps. He was stationed in Iceland and Europe and participated in the Normandy Campaign.

JOHN BELINDO, Kiowa-Navajo
   (Literature   40)
   Born: Early 1900's, Navajo Indian
     Reservation, Arizona
   Education: Indian schools
   Significance: *Arousing interest in Indian*
     Americans through his daily
     newspaper column
John Belindo was executive director of the National Congress of American Indians. From 1965 to 1966 he wrote a daily column, "Changing Profile," for the *Oklahoma Journal,* devoted to the history and problems of Indian Americans. He served as staff announcer for two radio stations in Oklahoma City where he programmed a jazz show.

HARRY J. W. BELVIN, Choctaw
   (Education, Politics   11)
   Born: ca. 1900, Choctaw County,
     Oklahoma
   Education: B.S., Southeastern State
     College, Oklahoma; M.Ed., University
     of Oklahoma, Norman
   Significance: *Promoting the education of*
     his people
Harry J. W. Belvin was a classroom teacher with the Bryan and Choctaw County Schools in Oklahoma from 1923 to 1939, and served as superintendent of public instruction in the same counties from 1941 to 1952. He served as principal chief of the Choctaw Nation from 1948 to 1965, and was the representative from Bryan County to the Oklahoma Legislature from 1954 to 1960. From 1960 to 1964, he represented Bryan and Choctaw Counties as state senator. He was named Outstanding Indian of Oklahoma by the Tulsa Indian Democratic Club in 1957 and Outstanding American Indian at the Anadarko Indian Exposition in 1959.

Harry Belvin's father, B. Frank Belvin, was the first full-blooded Indian to qualify for the practice of law before the Supreme Court of the United States. The father also gave much help to the settlers migrating into Oklahoma. He gave the land for a school and sacrificed much in order to educate his boys.

ROBERT L. BENNETT, Oneida
   (Government   16)
   Born: 1912, Wisconsin
   Education: Haskell Institute, Lawrence,
     Kansas; L.L.B., Southeastern
     University, Oklahoma
   Significance: *Encouraging Indians to*
     improve their situations and assume
     more responsibility for the
     management of their affairs
Robert Bennett was appointed by President Johnson in 1966 as head of the Bureau of Indian Affairs. He was the first Indian in this century to hold this position. A career BIA man, he is admired by most moderate Indian leaders. In July of 1968, Bennett resigned in dismay, charging that "the new Administration has completely ignored Indians."

Bennett's first major appointment by the United States Bureau of Indian Affairs came after his graduation. He was then named superintendent of the Navajo Agency. This work was interrupted, however, by World War II duty with the Marines. After the war Bennett returned to the agency and became the charter commander of the Navajo American Legion Post which he organized. He has done much to develop training programs for Indian youth and veterans. He is an active member of the National Congress of American Indians; of Arrows, Inc., and of the Lions Club Committee for the Blind. In 1962, he won the Indian Achievement Award granted by the Indian Council Fire.

TED BERRIGAN, Choctaw
   (Literature   16)
   Born: 1934, Providence, Rhode Island

Education: La Salle Academy; B.A.,
M.A., University of Tulsa, Oklahoma
Significance: *Promoting an understanding
of Indians through his journalism and
poetry*

Ted Berrigan is a poet as well as an editor. He has been editor of *"C" - A Journal of Poetry* since 1963, the New York editor of *Long Hair,* a magazine published in London, and editorial assistant of *Art News* magazine. He served from 1954 to 1957 with the United States Army during which time he was awarded the United Nations Service Medal and the Korean Service Medal. His book of poetry, *The Sonnets,* was published in 1964.

ED BEYUKA, Zuñi
(Handicrafts   40)
Born: ca. 1920, New Mexico
Education: Reservation school
Significance: *Expressing his culture
through his art*

Ed Beyuka was with the New Mexico Anti-Aircraft Battalion on Bataan. He was captured by the Japanese and held prisoner-of-war for three years. He participated in the historic Bataan Death March. Today Beyuka works as a silversmith. His work is prized for its uniqueness of design.

WILSIE H. BITSIE, Navajo
(Military   38)
Born: ca. 1920, New Mexico
Education: Federal Indian schools
Significance: *Unique wartime service to
his country*

PFC Wilsie H. Bitsie was an instructor in the Navajo School for "Code Talkers" at Camp Elliott during World War II. He helped work out the addition of needed military terms to the Navajo language. He then joined the Marine Raiders and at New Georgia his ability as a code talker helped the Raiders maintain contact with the army command at Munda.

It soon became apparent that the Navajo code talkers could effectively transmit vital information by direct communication since their language-code defied decoding even to the lin-

guistically keen ear. The Navajo language is a strange tongue, one of the most select in the world. The voice shows a trace of Asiatic origin. The language was embellished by the code talkers with improvised words and phrases for military use. Since transmitting messages which the enemy cannot decode is a vital military factor, the number of Navajos serving with the Marines in all theaters of operations rose from thirty to 420.

BLACK ELK, Oglala Sioux
(Religion   25)
Born: 1863, Little Powder River,
Wyoming
Died: ca. 1940
Education: Tribal
Significance: *Contributing another
dimension to significant historical
events*

Black Elk, a Sioux holy man, told his life story in 1931 to John G. Neihardt, poet laureate of Nebraska. In recording the spoken words of Black Elk, Neihardt puts on record the events that led up to the historic Battle of the Little Big Horn of 1876, also known as Custer's Last Stand. Experiences related to the battle itself and the devastating aftermath as it affected the lives of a once proud, free people who were "one with all living things of the earth and with the Great Spirit" were recorded also. The biography includes an account of the rise of the Messiah or Ghost Dance Movement, which spread like wildfire during the last two decades of the 1800's, particularly among Indians of the north central plains. The Massacre of Wounded Knee, South Dakota, was directly related to this movement.

BEN BLACK ELK, Oglala Sioux
(History, Education   40)
Born: Early 1900's, South Dakota
Education: Reservation schools; Carlisle
Institute, Pennsylvania
Significance: *Authority on Indian history,
lore, and culture*

Ben Black Elk, son of Black Elk, the holy man, teaches a high school class on Indian history and has been a guest lecturer at the University of South Dakota and the University of Chicago. He is chairman of the Manderson Planning Commission, has served for ten years as a member of the Oglala Sioux Tribal Council and is an honorary member of the Black Hills, Badlands and Lakes Association.

Ben Black Elk is probably the most photographed Indian in America. Since 1947 he has spent his summers at Mt. Rushmore in the Black Hills of South Dakota where, in Indian costume, he has been seen and photographed by tourists from all parts of the world. He has appeared in many movies and documentaries, among them *How the West Was Won.* He narrated "Legends of the Sioux" and "Tahtonka" and collaborated on his father's biography, *Black Elk Speaks,* on *The Sacred Pipe,* and on *When the Tree Flowers.* He has been on television many times and has the singular honor of having been the first person whose image was transmitted via Telstar.

BLACK HAWK, Sauk
   (Tribal Leadership   22)
   Born: 1767, what is now Illinois
   Died: 1838
   Education: Tribal
   Significance: *Struggling to preserve Sauk lands and rights*
Black Hawk, known as Makataimeshekiakiah among his people, was the great Sauk chief and warrior who tried to form an Indian confederacy strong enough to withstand the encroachment of white settlers. For centuries the Sauk and Fox tribes had hunted and fished in the rich prairie valleys of the Mississippi. In the Treaty of 1804 the Sauks and Foxes were to give up their homeland east of the Mississippi when the white settlements extended that far. In the 1820's, immigrants began appropriating Indian cornfields and plowing among their groves. Black Hawk reasoned, "The Great Spirit gave the land to his children to live upon. So long as they occupy and cultivate it they have a right to the soil. Nothing can be sold but such things as can be carried away," but to no avail.

In 1831 the Black Hawk War began in earnest. The Sauks and Foxes eluded the army and terrorized the Illinois frontier. The Indians were finally evicted, however. In 1832 Black Hawk visited Washington, D.C., and talked to President Jackson, saying, "We did not expect to conquer the whites. . . . I took up the hatchet to revenge injuries which my people could no longer endure." He returned to his people a hero with gifts from President Jackson. His portrait hangs in the Smithsonian Institution.

BLACK KETTLE, Cheyenne
   (Tribal Leadership   3)
   Born: Early 1800's, Colorado-Wyoming
   Died: Late 1800's
   Education: Tribal
   Significance: *Efforts to keep the peace*
Chief Black Kettle, with his band joined with other Cheyenne and Arapaho bands in 1864 to talk peace in Denver with the Governor of Colorado. The southern Cheyennes had lived in peace during the early days of the settlement of Denver. In fact, both the southern Cheyennes and Arapahoes were at home in the heart of Denver. By 1861, conditions became strained when a railroad was being planned across Indian lands.

Instead of peace talks, an entire Cheyenne village was massacred at Sand Creek, including more than 110 men and 200 women and children. Chief Black Kettle ran up both the American flag and a white flag, to no avail. Black Kettle's wife was shot down and passing soldiers fired seven more bullets into her body. She had nine wounds, but lived. Black Kettle managed to escape. The Cheyenne plains went up in flames during the next three years.

BERYL BLUE SPRUCE, San Juan-Laguna
   Pueblo
   (Medicine   16)
   Born: 1934, Santa Fe, New Mexico
   Education: B.S., Stanford University,
      Palo Alto, California; M.D.,
      University of Southern California, Los
      Angeles

Significance: *Activity in support of Indian rights*

Dr. Beryl Blue Spruce is an obstetrician. He works actively with the Indian Rights Association and the National Indian Youth Council. He is a member of the American College of Obstetrics and Gynecology as Junior Fellow. In 1961 and 1962, he was awarded the John Hay Whitney Fellowship which helped him through his medical studies.

GEORGE BLUE SPRUCE, San Juan Pueblo
(Medicine   11)
    Born: ca. 1930, San Juan Pueblo, New Mexico
    Education: Parochial school; D.D.S., Creighton University, Omaha, Nebraska
    Significance: *Promoting health interests of his people*

George Blue Spruce is the first Pueblo Indian dentist and the only Indian dentist in the Commissioned Corps of the United States Public Health Service. He is stationed on the Fort Belknap Reservation. His interest in dentistry began while he was still in high school. When he was the winner of a contest held for outstanding high school graduates on a statewide basis, his training was launched. The various lodges of the New Mexico B.P.O.E. (Benevolent and Protective Order of Elks) pledged the money for his professional training. After receiving his degree, Blue Spruce served in the Dental Corps of the United States Navy.

CHER BONO, Cherokee
(Music   37)
    Born: 1946, El Centro, California
    Education: Public schools
    Significance: *Recording and singing star of the mid 1960's*

Cher Bono of Sonny and Cher appeared on the American scene of pop music and op fashion when one-half the population of the United States was under twenty-one. She grew up in Fresno, California, as Cheryl La Piere. She met Sonny Salvatore Bono in 1964 in Los Angeles where she was studying drama and dancing, and

married him a year later. They became instant teenage idols, and have been recording since 1965.

Their first record, "Just You," was a hit on the west coast. Their second record, "I Got You Babe," sold four million copies. Their first album, "Look At Us," sold a million copies. Their concerts sold out, they appeared on TV, and made a movie called *Good Times.* They performed at the White House and at the WAIF Ball in London at the request of Princess Margaret. They have also had a Papal audience. Their own musical variety show on television was one of the big hits of the 1971-72 season.

JOSEPH BRANT, Mohawk
(Tribal Leadership   35)
    Born: 1742, in what is now New York
    Died: 1807
    Education: Moor's Indian Charity School, Lebanon, Connecticut, which later became part of Dartmouth College
    Significance: *Translation of the Prayer Book and St. Mark's Gospel into the Mohawk language in 1787*

Joseph Brant, known as Thayendanegea among his people, was the Mohawk warrior chief of the powerful Iroquois League of Indian Nations. Prior to the Revolutionary War he was the most influential friend the white settlers had. He became the protégé of Sir William Johnson, superintendent of Indian Affairs, and was educated and converted to the Church of England. In 1774 Joseph Brant acted as secretary to Guy Johnson, nephew of Sir William Johnson, when Guy succeeded his uncle as head of Indian Affairs.

Joseph Brant had fought with the British in the French and Indian War, and later with the white settlers against Pontiac. As a colonel in the British Army, he and his warriors fought against the colonial rebels in the American Revolutionary War. He led devastating raids against colonial villages in the Mohawk Valley and northern Pennsylvania.

After the Revolutionary War Brant sought, without success, to procure a settlement from the United States for the Iroquois. He then secured land for them in Canada. He spent the rest of his life in Christian missionary work among his people. With funds collected during a visit to England in 1786, he established an Episcopal Church in Upper Canada.

GODFREY BROKEN ROPE, Brule Sioux
(Painting, Religion   36)
Born: 1908, Okreek, South Dakota
Education: Rapid City Indian School, South Dakota; Flandreau Indian School, South Dakota
Significance: *Reflecting 20th century life and culture of his people through his paintings*

Godfrey Broken Rope produces landscapes with seldom even a suggestion of a human figure. He works in muted neutral tones using simple house paints capturing the vast, silent beauty of the South Dakota plains. Since 1950 he has traveled extensively throughout the United States as a self-appointed minister of the gospel. He also presents public demonstrations of his self-taught style of painting.

RUTH MUSKRAT BRONSON, Cherokee
(Tribal Affairs   11)
Born: Early 1900's, Oklahoma
Education: A.B., Mount Holyoke College, Massachusetts; George Washington University, Washington, D.C.
Significance: *Service in the best interests of all Indians*

Ruth Muskrat Bronson became a playground instructor to Apache children through the YWCA. In 1933, she was sent by the Student Christian Federation to represent Indians at a conference held in Peiping, China. On her return she was awarded a college scholarship and immediately after her graduation she entered the Indian Service of the United States Government Bureau of Indian Affairs as a teacher. Within the year she received a gift of one thousand dollars from Henry Morgenthau for having accomplished the most among the seniors in the first year after graduation.

Mrs. Bronson became Assistant Guidance and Placement Officer in the Bureau of Indian Affairs. She was in charge of government loans and scholarships and general adviser to Indian students in college. From 1946 to 1947 and from 1948 to 1949, Mrs. Bronson served as executive secretary of the National Congress of American Indians. In this capacity she made an extensive survey of Indian conditions in Alaska.

Mrs. Bronson is the author of *Indians Are People Too,* published in 1947. She is an active member of Arrow, Inc., having served as its vice-president and as chairman of its scholarship committee.

JOSEPH F. BROWN, Blackfeet
(Religion   11)
Born: ca. 1910, Montana
Education: A.B., West Baden College; Ph.L., Loyola University, Chicago; S.T.L., Alma College, Alma, Michigan
Significance: *Promoting the welfare of Indian children*

Joseph F. Brown is probably the only Indian Catholic priest in the United States. Two others are now deceased. Father Brown believes that the present and future of the Indian people are far more important than the past. He was ordained in 1948 and is now pastor of the St. Charles Mission and the Church of Our Lady of Loretto in Montana. He has served among the Coeur D'Alene and Colville Indians in Idaho. While in Idaho he was Child Consultant for the State Welfare Department.

LOUIS R. BRUCE, JR., Mohawk-Oglala Sioux
(Government, Ranching   11, 28)
Born: ca. 1915, New York State
Education: A.B., University of Syracuse, New York
Significance: *Working at state and national levels to further understanding of the Indians as people*

Louis R. Bruce, Jr., was appointed commissioner of the Bureau of Indian Affairs in 1968 by President Nixon. He grew up on an Indian Reservation and worked his way through school. Shortly after his graduation he entered the business world. In 1935, he was appointed New York State Director of Indians under the National Youth Administration and continued in this capacity until 1941. In 1939, Bruce was invited to participate in the North American Indian Conference held at the University of Toronto. In 1940, 1950, and 1960 he was a delegate to the White House Conference on Children and Youth.

In 1949, his article, "What America Means To Me," was published in the *American Magazine* and reprinted in the *Reader's Digest* in sixteen different languages for distribution throughout the world. In this same year, Bruce received the Freedoms Foundation Award for "Outstanding Contribution in Promotion of the American Way of Life" and in 1953, he received the Indian Achievement Award for his efforts in behalf of his people. He has a long list of affiliations with organizations and civic activities.

Bruce is the owner and operator of a 480-acre dairy farm and has stimulated interest in the need for programs for rural youth.

His father, Louis R. Bruce, Sr., is noted for a lifetime of personal, humanitarian achievements. His father was the first of his race to become a dentist. However, he felt that only through Christianity could Indian Americans find the resources to become respected citizens in modern America. He became a minister and was appointed pastor of the church on his own reservation. One of the happiest moments of his life was when he cast his first vote after the enactment of the Indian Citizens Bill in 1924.

BUFFALO HORN, Bannock
   (Tribal Leadership   15)
   Born: Early 1800's, southern Idaho
   Died: Late 1800's
   Education: Tribal
   Significance: *Fighting for what he
      believed was right*
Chief Buffalo Horn tried to lead his people in their independent way of life. Under the treaty of 1855, the Bannock Indians had been assigned to the Fort Hall Reservation. The tribe, however, continued to wander over southern Idaho fighting for their fields of camas. When the Nez

Percé Indians were defeated, the Bannock Indians rose in rebellion. A series of murders and raids throughout the white settlements ended in the death of Buffalo Horn.

Although they had fought bitterly for their traditional homes, by 1880 the Bannocks, completely disorganized by the death of their chief, were returned to the Fort Hall Reservation. Their resistance to the dominant society was at an end. The same fate befell most of the surviving Indians of Idaho, Oregon, and Washington.

ANGELA P. BUTTERFIELD,
   Shoshone-Bannock
   (Tribal Leadership   37)
   Born: Early 1900's, Idaho
   Education: High school, American Falls,
      Idaho
   Significance: *Encouragement of young
      Indians to become educated*
Mrs. Angela P. Butterfield is an active and outspoken delegate at most Indian conventions as well as a leader in the development of her tribe. She served two terms on the Shoshone-Bannock Tribal Council and was vice-chairman of the council. She was executive director of the Affiliated Tribes of Northwest Indians, secretary of the Idaho Governor's Indian Advisory Council and a member of the Governor's Comprehensive Health Planning Council.

Her primary interests in local tribal affairs continue to be protecting tribal lands and water rights, assisting and encouraging Indian children to achieve higher educational levels and aiding adult Indians to train for better jobs and permanent employment. Mrs. Butterfield is an accomplished musician. While in high school she won scholastic honors.

CAPTAIN JACK, Modoc
   (Tribal Leadership   30)
   Born: ca. 1834, northeastern California
   Died: 1873
   Education: Tribal
   Significance: *Fighting for the right of his
      people to live in peace*
Captain Jack, known to his people as Kintpuash, was the chief of a small obscure moun-

tain tribe. In defense of their homeland, they became the terror of the white settlers of northeastern California and a constant frustration to the United States Army during the four-month Modoc War of 1872–1873. In the beginning the Modoc Indians were friendly and even cooperated with the government officials in the Treaty of 1868, which called for their removal to the Klamath Reservation in Oregon. Captain Jack and his tribe of 300 merely wanted a place to fish and hunt in peace and quiet. The Modoc Indians, however, soon found themselves in the minority among the Klamath Indians on the Oregon reservation, so they quietly returned to their homeland in the Lost River-Tule Lake country of California.

Negotiations were opened in which the Modocs asked for 2,000 acres on the Lost River. Captain Jack's many astutely honest yet embarrassing questions went unanswered, and the negotiations broke down. In tragic circumstances, Captain Jack and his people were forced to hide in the lava beds north of Mt. Lassen—"fifty thousand acres of hell." Here Captain Jack and fifty warriors undertook a David and Goliath struggle with the Army. Captain Jack's ultimate defeat and capture cost the United States Government $500,000—against the estimated $20,000 that the Lost River reservation might have cost. It was this episode that gave currency to the motto, "The only good Indian is a dead Indian." Captain Jack and several of his lieutenants were hanged.

PADDY CARR, Creek
   (Military   22)
   Born: Late 1700's, near Fort Mitchell,
      Alabama
   Died: Mid 1800's
   Education: Tribal
   Significance: *Example to his people by
      freeing his slaves*
Paddy Carr, the son of an Irish father and Creek mother, was reared in the home of Colonel Crowell, an Indian Agent. Here he learned to speak English with considerable fluency while retaining great facility with the language of his mother's people. His intelligence, his

quick perception of human character, and his wit and humor enabled him to become an excellent interpreter. His accurate and spirited translations made him admired by Indians and white settlers alike.

Following President Washington's advice to the Indians of the Five Civilized Tribes, Carr took up farming and became wealthy. He owned many horses and also many slaves which had been kidnapped from other Indian tribes. He served as guide in 1836 during the revolt of a portion of the Creek Nation. After the Creek revolt was over, Carr marched to Florida in command of 500 Creek warriors who volunteered service to the United States government. He was known for his courage and admired for his hospitality, his fairness, and his generosity.

CHARLES DAVID CARTER, Choctaw
   (Politics)
   Born: 1868, near Boggy Depot, Choctaw
      Nation, Indian Territory
   Died: 1929
   Education: Indian day schools,
      Chickasaw Manual Training Academy,
      Tishamingo
   Significance: *Political service to state and
      country*
Charles David Carter became auditor of public accounts for the Chickasaw Nation in 1892, member of the Chickasaw Council in 1895, and Superintendent of Schools of the Chickasaw Nation in 1897. He was a member of the first Oklahoma Congressional delegation, serving in Congress from 1907 to 1927.

JOHNNY CASH, Cherokee
   (Music   8)
   Born: 1932, Kingsland, Arkansas
   Education: High school
   Significance: *Popularization of country
      music*
Johnny Cash grew up on a marginal cotton farm of twenty acres. He worked as a waterboy for work gangs when he was fourteen. From 1950 to 1954, he served in the United States Air Force in Germany. When discharged, he took a job as door-to-door appliance salesman. He be-

gan performing with Luther Perkins and Marshal Grant as Johnny Cash and the Tennessee Two. His first record, released in 1955, included "Hey Porter" and "Cry, Cry, Cry." It was successful and led to a contract with Sun Records. His 1968 income was reported to be about $2,000,000. He starred in his own television program and in 1970 was named the outstanding folk singer and composer of folk music.

PHILIP CASSADORE, Apache
    (Music, History   29)
    Born: 1933, San Carlos Apache
        Reservation, Peridot, Arizona
    Education: San Carlos Apache
        Reservation School; Public high
        school; Phoenix College; Brigham
        Young University, Provo, Utah
    Significance: *Promoting appreciation for
        Apache culture*
Philip Cassadore and his sister Patsy are known as the singing Cassadores, having inherited their gift of song through their father, Broken Arrow, a tribal chief and medicine man, and through their famed grandfather, Chief Cassadore. They began recording songs for Canyon Records in 1966 with "Apache" as the first release, followed in the same year by "Apache Songs." "Philip Cassadore Sings Apache Songs" followed in 1968. He and his sister, Patsy, have sung at the Burbank Starlight Bowl in California, at the All Indian Days in Sheridan, Wyoming, and at the Heard Museum Fair in Phoenix, Arizona.

In his daily occupation on radio and T.V., Cassadore promotes an understanding of his people. He is much in demand as a speaker. Since 1967, he has been cooperating with the University of Arizona's Anthropology Department in writing a history of the Apaches.

His grandfather, Chief Cassadore, is noted for his efforts in the peace negotiations in 1874 between his people and the United States government. The resulting treaty averted the annihilation of the Apache.

D. CHIEF EAGLE, Rosebud Sioux
    (Literature, Music   6)
    Born: 1925, Rosebud Sioux Indian
        Reservation, South Dakota
    Education: Jesuit Missionary School,
        Rosebud Reservation; Oklahoma
        Agricultural and Mechanical College,
        Stillwater
    Significance: *Dedication to the education
        of his people*
D. Chief Eagle was born in an Indian tent, orphaned and raised by the elders of his tribe who grounded him in Sioux culture and the history of his people. He is a Marine veteran of World War II and an author, composer and painter of Indian life. All the proceeds from his writings, musical plays, albums and sheet music go to the Winter Count Foundation to fulfill his vow to help his people. He is the composer of the "Winter Count Indian Opera" and the author of the book *Winter Count* published in 1967.

ERNEST CHILDERS, Creek
    (Military   11)
    Born: ca. 1920, Broken Arrow,
        Oklahoma
    Education: Federal Indian schools
    Significance: *Service to his country in
        war and in peace*
Lieutenant Ernest Childers entered military service during World War II at Tulsa, Oklahoma and was assigned to the 45th Infantry Division of Oklahoma. He was awarded the Distinguished Service Cross, the first medal of its kind to be presented to anyone in the State of Oklahoma. He was also awarded the Congressional Medal of Honor, the nation's highest decoration, for his leadership and courage on the battlefield. His citation reads:

For conspicuous gallantry and intrepidity at risk of life above and beyond the call of duty in action of 22 September 1943, at Oliveto, Italy ... The exceptional leadership, initiative, calmness under fire, and conspicuous gallantry displayed by Lieutenant Childers were an inspiration to his men.

Childers is a training officer with the Department of Interior Job Corps in Washington, D.C.

GOINGBACK CHILTOSKEY, Cherokee
(Handicrafts 16)
Born: 1907, Cherokee, North Carolina
Education: Oklahoma Agricultural and
Mechanical College, Stillwater; Purdue
University, Purdue, Indiana; Chicago
Art Institute, Illinois
Significance: *Talent in wood carving*

Goingback Chiltoskey is one of the foremost woodcarvers of the country. He started to whittle long before he learned to speak English. His carvings, mostly of animals, have won numerous blue ribbons and are widely sought by collectors. A carving of St. Francis, exhibited at the Smithsonian Institution, has been ordered in large dimension as a statue for a church in Washington, D.C.

Chiltoskey has been an instructor with the Cherokee Indian School, Cherokee, North Carolina. Later he worked at the United States Army Engineer Research and Development Laboratories at Fort Belvoir in Virginia, where he applied his artistic skills in developing training aids, displays, and dioramas. Much of his work there was of "top secret" or restricted nature. Some of it was used to iron out kinks before expensive and actual construction was undertaken. He is the author of *To Make My Bread,* a book about Cherokee cooking, published in 1951.

JESSE CHISHOLM, Cherokee
(Scouting 40)
Born: Late 1800's, Oklahoma
Died: Mid 1900's
Education: Reservation schools
Significance: *Opening of the West*

Jesse Chisholm supposedly blazed the trail from Texas across Oklahoma to railroad shipping points in Kansas. Known in history as the Chisholm Trail, it is now U.S. Highway 81.

LOUISE ABEITA CHIWIWI, Isleta Pueblo
(Education 40)
Born: ca. 1926, New Mexico
Education: University of New Mexico,
Albuquerque

Significance: *Leadership in the education of her people*

Louise Abeita Chiwiwi graduated from the University of New Mexico with a degree in sociology. She taught in the Bureau of Indian Affairs schools for eleven years at Alamo, Acoma, and Laguna in New Mexico. In 1965 she began the Head Start program at the Isleta Pueblo. At the age of eleven Louise Chiwiwi wrote *I Am A Pueblo Indian Girl,* published in 1937.

JOSEPH J. (JOCKO) CLARK, Cherokee
(Military 41)
Born: 1893, Pryor, Oklahoma
Education: Willie Halsell College, Vinita,
Oklahoma; Oklahoma Agricultural
and Mechanical College, Stillwater;
United States Naval Academy,
Annapolis, Maryland
Significance: *Distinguished naval service to his country*

Admiral Joseph Clark served on several ships during World War I, commanding the *Brooks* and as executive officer of the *Bulmer.* He was an instructor at the Naval Academy from 1923 to 1924 and served with the Naval Air Force from 1925 to 1941. He was aboard the *Yorktown* when the United States entered World War II.

His many decorations include the Navy Cross, the Distinguished Service Medal, the United Nations Service Medal and the National Defense Service Medal. He also received the Presidential Unit Citations awarded to the *USS Swannee,* the *USS Yorktown,* and the *USS Hornet.* After his retirement Admiral Clark became a business executive in New York.

ALBERT COBE, Chippewa
(Golf, Business 7)
Born: ca. Early 1900, Lac du Flambeau
Reservation, Wisconsin
Education: Lac du Flambeau Reservation
School; Mount Pleasant Indian School,
Michigan; Haskell Institute, Lawrence,
Kansas

Significance: *Promotion of economic independence for his people*

Albert Cobe, in his autobiography *Great Spirit,* describes his childhood and youth as a rebellion against white man's domination. He tells of the positive, understanding influence of his father who insisted that he pursue his education. He relates the circumstances that sustained his determination to prove himself as a man in an alien society yet always retaining the pride and dignity of his own heritage.

Cobe's achievement as an eminent golf instructor is a credit to his determination to compete as an equal in the white man's world. His success as a businessman and organizer is evidenced in his leadership among his own people in developing and managing the hunting and fishing guide service to which he applies himself every summer.

COCHISE, Apache
(Tribal Leadership   21)
Born: ca. 1825, Arizona Territory
Died: 1874
Education: Tribal
Significance: *Defending tribal lands and rights*

Cochise was the famed Apache chief of the Chiricahua band. These Apache were constantly battling their traditional enemy, the Mexicans, but were not unfriendly to the early settlers of the 1850's in the Arizona Territory. In fact, members of the band worked as woodcutters at the stagecoach station in Apache Pass. Through unfortunate misunderstandings, however, the Apaches' peaceful attitude came to a sudden end in 1861.

Cochise began a campaign of guerrilla attacks up and down the territory to avenge his tribesmen who had been taken prisoners and killed under a flag of truce. His attacks continued over a period of ten years, holding the United States Army at bay with no more than 200 tough, skillful warriors. In 1871 General George Crook, who recognized the just claims of the Apache, and respected their ability as warriors, dealt honorably with them. He began to restore peace and law in the Arizona Terri-

tory. In 1872 Cochise and his band surrendered and lived peacefully on the Chiricahua Reservation in Arizona.

GEORGE McKEE COCHRAN, Cherokee
(Art, Business   16)
Born: 1908, Stillwell, Oklahoma
Education: Haskell Institute, Lawrence, Kansas; Chilocco Indian School, Oklahoma
Significance: *Changing the law to benefit Oregon Indians*

George McKee Cochran from an early age showed unusual ability in art. He became a barber, however, through an odd circumstance. When his father entered him in school, they stopped on the way to get haircuts. The principal liked the style so much he wanted the other boys to look the same, and young Cochran was taught to cut hair.

During World War II Cochran served as a GI barber. In Oregon, at the end of the war, he was unable to secure a barber's license because he was an Indian. Undaunted, he succeeded in bringing about a change in the law. In the meantime, Cochran did odd jobs and developed his artistic talent. He sold his sketches for money, food, lodging or fuel. Today they command high prices.

Cochran is the author and illustrator of *Indian Portraits of the Pacific Northwest,* published in 1959. He is active in the Kiwanis Club, the National Congress of American Indians, and the Oregon Archaeological Society. Cochran owns his own barber shop and devotes much of his time to artistic pursuit and efforts in behalf of Indian people.

CORNPLANTER, Seneca
(Tribal Leadership   22)
Born: ca. 1736, Conewaugus, New York
Died: 1836
Education: Tribal
Significance: *Negotiation and maintenance of peace*

Chief Cornplanter was the son of a trader named John O'Bail, or O'Beel, and a full-blooded Seneca Indian mother. He was known as Garganwahgah, "By what one plants," to the Iroquois and John O'Bail to white people. He fought the rebellious colonists during the American Revolutionary War. At the conclusion of the peace negotiations, however, he became a firm friend of the young Republic. He used every means to cement goodwill between his people and the United States. In 1784 he participated in the treaty negotiations at Fort Stanwix near Rome, New York, when the Iroquois ceded much Indian land. Because of his close friendship toward the white settlers, he became exceedingly unpopular with his tribe.

In 1790 Cornplanter visited George Washington in Philadelphia to present the grievances of his people. Once peace was permanently established between the Iroquois and the United States, Cornplanter retired from public life to a large tract on the Allegheny River granted to him by Pennsylvania "for his many valuable services to the whites." There, in Warren County, he lived to the age of about one hundred.

CRAZY HORSE, Oglala Sioux
(Tribal Leadership   35)
Born: 1842, eastern Wyoming
Died: 1877
Education: Tribal
Significance: *Defensive action in the historic Battle of the Little Big Horn*

Crazy Horse, one of the greatest war chiefs of the north-central plains Indians, fiercely opposed the white settlers. At Fort Laramie he saw the demoralizing influence and high-handedness of the white settlers who sold liquor to his people and took advantage of them in many ways. His father was disturbed over Indian weaknesses and his counsel had a strong effect on the son. After seeing the destruction of his people's camp on the Blue Water, he was filled with a hatred for the white settlers that lasted to his death. He fought for liberty as he knew and saw it.

The United States Army met Crazy Horse in numerous engagements over the period of white settlement. The most famous encounter was the Battle of the Little Big Horn in 1876, in which

Crazy Horse led his warriors in a swift and decisive annihilation of Custer and his command group. In the following months, as band after band surrendered, Crazy Horse and his followers held out. Finally, in 1877, this great Indian chief, still only thirty-five, saw the futility of fighting the white intruders alone and brought his people to the Red Cloud Agency where General Crook took their guns and horses. Constantly in fear of Crazy Horse as a leader, the military authorities at the agency lured him into a guard room where he was murdered by a sentry.

Today Crazy Horse is being immortalized in an immense equestrian statue being carved in a mountain of solid granite, Thunderhead Mountain, in the Black Hills of South Dakota by the famous sculptor Korczah Ziolkowski.

AMANDA CROWE, Cherokee
(Handicrafts   11)
Born: ca. 1940, South Carolina
Education: B.A., DePaul University, Chicago, Illinois; M.A., Chicago Art Institute, Illinois
Significance: *Helping her people toward economic independence*

Amanda Crowe is a woodcarver of rare ability. While still in school, she received recognition for her lifelike creations of the creatures of the North Carolina woods. With this skill and by teaching art during the summer months, she earned her way through college. Done in the beautiful native hardwoods, cherry, holly, and walnut, her pieces are in great demand. She also works in ceramics and metal. She teaches on her home reservation. Her pupils often take prizes in exhibitions.

The woodcarving and other crafts which are being developed on the reservation through the efforts of Amanda Crowe are an increasing source of revenue to the Indian artisans. She serves on the Board of Directors of the Qualla Arts and Crafts Mutual, an Indian craftsmen's cooperative in Cherokee, North Carolina. She received the John Quincy Adams Competitive Fellowship to study sculpture in Mexico.

WOODROW CRUMBO, Potawatomie
(Art 11)
Born: ca. 1915, Oklahoma
Education: Chilocco Indian School,
Oklahoma; University of Oklahoma,
Norman; Institute of American Indian
Art, Santa Fe, New Mexico;
University of Wichita, Kansas
Significance: *Stimulation of creative
production among Indians of all tribes*

Woodrow Crumbo is one of the top Indian artists of today, equally at home at an easel or in a tribal dance. He became a ceremonial dancer while still a small boy and received thorough training in his ancient culture under the guidance of older Indian people. While still in college during the depression years of the 1930's, he organized and trained a student dance group which became popular entertainment.

After graduation Crumbo continued to dance in Indian ceremonials and did interpretative dancing with the Thurlow Lieurance Symphony Orchestra. He organized and taught the first jewelry-making classes at Oklahoma State University and became art director at Bacone College in Oklahoma. While at Bacone he designed and made a stained glass window which has received much favorable comment. Six of his murals hang in the Department of Interior Building in Washington D.C. and his paintings are in many permanent museum collections. In World War II, Crumbo was a foreman in the Douglas Aircraft foundry. Since then he has spent much time discovering and promoting Indian talents and in educating the public on Indian art.

Recently, he became interested in mineralogy and stumbled on a deposit of beryllium of incalculable potential value. With the proceeds from this prospecting venture he established a silk screen industry for the benefit of Indian art and artists.

CHARLES CURTIS, Kaw-Osage
(Government 40)
Born: 1860, North Topeka, Kansas
Died: 1936
Education: Public schools, Topeka,
Kansas
Significance: *Service to his country
through politics*

Charles Curtis was elected Vice-President of the United States with President Herbert Hoover. He had served in the House of Representatives from 1892 to 1907, and then in the United States Senate from 1907 to 1913 and from 1915 to 1929. As Senator he became an expert parliamentarian and a member of the Senate Rules Committee. During President Calvin Coolidge's administration, he became majority leader of the Senate and gained fame for his ability to move the Senate to complete its work without extra sessions.

As a boy, Curtis worked as a jockey. While still in high school, his interests turned to law. He began his law career in 1879 at the age of nineteen. He was admitted to the bar in 1881. He practiced law successfully and became Shawnee County attorney.

RUSSELL G. DAVIS, Naragansett
(Literature 16)
Born: 1922, Boston, Massachusetts
Education: B.A., Holy Cross College,
Washington, D.C.; Ed.M., M.A.,
Ed.D., Harvard University,
Cambridge, Massachusetts
Significance: *Literary works*

Dr. Russell G. Davis is a prolific writer and has received many honors for his literary work. He has lived and worked in Africa, Latin America, and the Far East. He served in the United States Marine Corps during World War II. His published works include: *The Lion's Whiskers* (1959), *Point Four Assignment,* (1959), *Ten Thousand Desert Swords* (1960), *The Choctaw Code,* (1961), *Chief Joseph,* (1962), *West Africa: Land in the Sun,* (1963), *Strangers in Africa* (1963) and thirty articles in various journals. Dr. Davis is a member of the American Association for the Advancement of Science, the American Academy of Political and Social Science, the Society of International Development, and the Linguistic Society of America.

DEGANAWIDAH, Huron
  (Tribal Affairs   30)
  Born: Mid 1500's, area of New York
  Died: Mid 1600's
  Education: Tribal
  Significance: *Inspiring the tribes of the*
    Iroquois to unite in peace under the
    rule of law

Deganawidah was a Huron refugee and prophet. In 1570, with Hiawatha, an Iroquoian medicine man, he founded the League of the Iroquois. This was a unique, democratically organized form of government located in a setting completely isolated from the European influence toward democratic thought and action. This League of Five Nations included the Mohawks, Oneidas, Onondagas, Cayugas, and the Senecas. In 1712 it was expanded to Six Nations with the addition of the Tuscaroras. The member tribes bound themselves to establish a universal peace based on harmony, justice, and a government of law. The tribes kept this "Great Peace" for over 200 years and still govern themselves today by the precepts established long before the influence of the white man.

Once established, the League dominated the whole area of New York State and lower Canada, dealing as equals with their allies, the English. They did not necessarily act in consort, however, in the Indian and colonial wars. They helped to defeat the French in the French and Indian Wars. The American Revolution, however, split the League. The Tuscaroras and Oneidas supported the rebellious colonists while the other tribes aided the English. In 1779 the power of the Iroquois was destroyed with the burning of their villages and fields. The Iroquois numbered about 40,000 people at one time. Today, the Iroquois number about 23,000.

When our founding fathers were drafting the Constitution, the organization of the League of the Iroquois was studied.

VINE DELORIA, SR., Standing Rock Sioux
  (Religion   11, 16)
  Born: ca. 1915, Standing Rock, South
    Dakota

Education: Kearney Military Academy,
  Nebraska; B.A., Bard College, New
  York; B.D., General Episcopal
  Theological Seminary
Significance: *Promoting Indian education*
  and welfare

Vine Deloria, Sr., a member of the distinguished Deloria family, attended a military academy where he rose to the highest post of Cadet Colonel. After graduation he worked in the Colorado mines until he volunteered for the Episcopal ministry, completing the theological course in three years. He was ordained in his father's church where he had been both baptized and confirmed.

Until 1951, Deloria served as missionary on the Pine Ridge Reservation, an area the size of the State of Connecticut, with eleven chapels and mission stations. He then was rector of the Trinity Church in Denison, Iowa. In 1954 he was appointed to the staff of the National Council of the Episcopal Church as assistant secretary to the Division of Domestic Missions in charge of Indian mission work. This was the first time in history that the Episcopal church had named an Indian to a national executive post. For reasons of health he resigned in 1958, but later became vicar of the St. Paul's Parish in Durant, Iowa. He received an honorary Doctor of Divinity degree from Bard College in 1954 and the Indian Achievement Award from the Indian Council Fire in the same year.

His sister, Ella, a graduate of Columbia University, is famous as a linguist and an anthropologist with the Department of Anthropology, Columbia University. She is the author of *Speaking of Indians,* published in 1944 and the co-author of works on Dakota/Sioux linguistics. In 1943, she received the Indian Achievement Award from the Indian Council Fire.

His son, Vine Deloria, Jr., continuing in the tradition of his illustrious family, is the author of *Custer Died for Your Sins,* published in 1969 and *We Talk, You Listen,* published in 1970. At the age of thirty-five he was the executive director of the National Congress of American Indians.

DAVID P. DELORME, Chippewa
  (Economics, Education   11)
  Born: ca. 1925, North Dakota
  Education: Flandreau Indian School,
    North Dakota; Cameron Junior
    College, Oklahoma; B.S., M.S.,
    Oklahoma State University, Stillwater;
    Ph.D., University of Texas, Austin
  Significance: *Teacher of economics*

David P. Delorme is one of the very few of his tribe to have completed college and possibly the only one to have completed his doctorate. He believes the social and economic uplifting of the Indian rests in education and self-determination. He worked his way through college with two loans from the Bureau of Indian Affairs. During World War II he was stationed in the Caribbean with the Navy as Chief Petty Officer. GI educational assistance and fellowships enabled him to complete his graduate studies. A specialist in economics, Delorme has taught in several universities and colleges. He has been visiting professor of economics at the University of Oklahoma and director of the Oklahoma Council on Economic Education. He is co-author of *Money and Banking,* published in 1957. He is active in civic affairs and with the National Congress of American Indians.

WILLIAM DIETZ, Oglala Sioux
  (Football   40)
  Born: ca. 1890, South Dakota
  Education: Carlisle Institute,
    Pennsylvania
  Significance: *Outstanding ability as a
    football coach*

William Dietz played football on the famous teams of 1909 to 1911 at Carlisle Institute in Pennsylvania. He was art instructor at Carlisle and assistant football coach under the famous Glenn S. "Pop" Warner. He coached at prominent colleges and universities including Washington State College and Purdue University. He took two teams to the Rose Bowl in his impressive coaching career. He also coached in the National Football League.

FREDERICK J. DOCKSTADER, Navajo
  (Anthropology   40)
  Born: 1919, Los Angeles, California
  Education: B.A., Arizona State College,
    Flagstaff; M.A., Ph.D., Case Western
    Reserve University, Cleveland, Ohio
  Significance: *Outstanding anthropologist,
    artist, and craftsman*

Dr. Frederick J. Dockstader is an anthropologist, author, silversmith, artist, and educator. He is director of the Heye Foundation Museum of the American Indian in New York and chairman of the Indian Arts and Crafts Board, United States Department of the Interior. He is a member of the American Anthropological Association and the American Association for the Advancement of Science. Dr. Dockstader was faculty member and curator of anthropology at Dartmouth College from 1952 to 1955. He has been an advisory editor for the Encyclopedia Americana since 1957.

HENRY CHEE DODGE, Navajo
  (Tribal Leadership   13)
  Born: 1860, Navajo Reservation, Arizona
  Died: 1947
  Education: Presbyterian Mission School,
    Fort Sumner, Arizona; Fort Defiance
    Indian School, Arizona
  Significance: *Leadership in
    self-government and self-determination*

Henry Chee Dodge is known as the last chief of the Navajos. He was appointed to this position in 1884, at the age of twenty-four, by the Navajo Reservation Agent with the approval of the United States Secretary of the Interior and the Commissioner of Indian Affairs. In 1923, at the age of sixty-three, Dodge became chairman of the first Navajo Tribal Council, which was the first official Navajo organ of self-government. No man had been so honored by his people.

Dodge served his people well. During his eighty-seven years there had been exciting times. In 1868, as a boy, he walked with his people from the Bosque Redondo Reservation in New Mexico back to his homeland into a future none had dreamed of. From an early age he taught his people how to master their destiny and encouraged education, although he himself had very little formal education. Dodge was born in the Ma'ii'deshgizhnii Clan, Coyote Pass People, at a time when many bands of the Navajo people were eluding Kit Carson's soldiers in the remote twisting canyon areas of Arizona. His father, a fine silversmith, had named him Henry Dodge after the trader for whom he worked, although his Navajo name, Kiilchii, was used by his aunts and mother after his father's early death. His young childhood was spent with family after family, always running, hiding, starving, and on the verge of desperation. During this time he became separated from his mother and his aunts. Finally, in his utter loneliness and only four years old, he was befriended by a little girl eight years old and her aged grandfather. With them he walked to Fort Defiance where the three received rations of food and several sheep.

His adopted grandfather encouraged Dodge to become educated. At Fort Defiance he learned English and became the official interpreter for his people. In this capacity he made several trips to Washington, D.C. with the elders of his tribe in their negotiations. He also became interested in collecting and translating Navajo legends and chants. He was successful as a storekeeper and as a rancher, setting an example of self-determination and self-direction, encompassing the needs of his people as his own and giving counsel and assistance to all.

BRUMMETT ECHOHAWK, Pawnee
(Art   11)
Born: ca. 1922, Oklahoma
Education: Reservation and public
    schools
Significance: *Promoting understanding of
    his people*
Brummett Echohawk, grandson of a famous Pawnee warrior, is on the staff of the Sooner State Studios, a film animation concern in Tulsa, Oklahoma. He is an artist, cartoonist, and illustrator who has contributed to *Blue Book, Popular Mechanics* and other magazines. He has created his own line of Indian Christmas cards and has published a number of articles on the Pawnee people and their history. He is now recording Pawnee songs and ceremonies.

Echohawk was called into military service during World War II while still in high school. He served in some of the heaviest combat fighting in North Africa, Sicily, and Italy. While in the army, he made sketches for the N.E.A. newspaper syndicate and for *Yank*. He won the European Theater Ribbon with three battle stars and the Purple Heart with oak leaf cluster.

Echohawk is active in civic organizations and in the National Congress of American Indians. He believes that education is the most important need for Indians.

DARRELL FLEMING, Cherokee
(Government   16)
Born: 1911, Bernice, Oklahoma
Education: Haskell Institute, Lawrence,
    Kansas
Significance: *Improving government
    management*
Darrell Fleming served in the United States Navy from 1944 to 1946. As assistant area director for the Bureau of Indian Affairs, Minneapolis, Minnesota, he was honored with a Presidential citation awarded in 1964 in recognition of his "outstanding contributions to greater economy and improvement in government operations."

ALICE FLORENDO, Confederated Tribes in
Oregon
(Business   37)
Born: ca. 1925, Warm Springs, Oregon
Education: Reservation School
Significance: *Personal business
    achievement*
Mrs. Alice Florendo owns and operates a cafe in Warm Springs, Oregon, and is an active member of the Confederated Tribes of the Warm Springs Reservation. Early in her life, Mrs. Florendo came to the conclusion that prejudice was simply "me, uneducated and inexperienced." She worked to improve herself and capitalized on her experiences. Her early upbringing provided her with a solid foundation

upon which to grow, and pride in her Indian heritage has carried her to success.

FOKE LUSTE HAJO, Seminole
(Diplomacy 22)
Born: Late 1700's, Florida
Died: 1839
Education: Tribal
Significance: *Influencing his people toward peace*

Foke Luste Hajo, a courageous and high-minded man, was the principal war chief of the Seminoles, but since he was friendly to the United States, he was superseded by Holato Mico or Blue King. Foke Luste Hajo was one of the chiefs who assisted at the Council of Payne's Landing in 1833, near Fort Gibson, Florida. He was also one of seven appointed to inspect the country west of the Mississippi River, offered to his people as their future home. The seven returned in high praise of the country, but the general council of the Seminoles condemned the treaty because of several conditions which did not permit the Negroes among the Seminoles to move with them. This meant that families would have been broken up, since the Negroes, runaway slaves who had found refuge among the Seminoles, had often inter-married. Foke Luste Hajo continued to speak boldly and eloquently in favor of the move during councils held in 1835. The majority of the Seminoles under Osceola refused to sign the treaty and resolved to retain possession of their country in what is now Florida at any cost. Thus began the historic Seminole Wars. Foke Luste Hajo and about 450 of his followers were forced to take refuge at Fort Brook.

ERIM FORREST, Modoc-Pit River
(Ranching 16)
Born: 1920, Alturas, California
Education: Riverside Junior College, California
Significance: *State level interest in behalf of Indians*

Erim Forrest is a cattle rancher with active interest in wildlife. He is manager of the Pit River Home and Agricultural Cooperative As-sociation, president of the Northeastern California Sportsman Council and active in the Northern Counties Wildlife Conservation Association of California. He serves on the California Advisory Committee on Indian Affairs and on the Governor's Interstate Indian Council. Recently he was honored at the American Indian Conference in Chicago with the Outstanding Indian of the West Award. With D'Arcy McNickle, he wrote the *Declaration of Indian Purpose.*

GEORGE FRAZIER, Santee Sioux
(Medicine 11)
Born: 1891, Nebraska
Education: Reservation schools; Hampton Institute, Virginia; M.D., Denver Homeopathic Medical College, Colorado
Significance: *Medical service to his people*

Dr. Frazier graduated from an Indian school at the age of 13, the youngest in his class. He entered a preparatory school for Dartmouth College, but family illness and a shortage of money made it impossible for him to continue his schooling. He saved enough money to enter medical college by working at any job available. One of his jobs was to keep fifty kerosene lamps cleaned and trimmed.

Dr. Frazier first practiced in a rural area of western Nebraska where many people still lived in sod houses. After ten years of practice, he entered the Indian Service as a physician. He was stationed on the Santee, the Lower Brule, the Crow Creek, and the Rosebud Reservations. He remained as a physician at the Rosebud Reservation Hospital until his retirement in 1951. It was here that he worked intensively with the treatment of trachoma, a serious eye condition common to Indians.

OSWALD WHITE BEAR FREDERICKS, Hopi
(Anthropology 2)
Born: 1905, Hopi Reservation, Old Oraibi, Arizona
Education: Haskell Institute, Lawrence, Kansas; B.S., Bacone College, Muskogee, Oklahoma

Significance: *Preserving the culture of his people*

Oswald White Bear Fredericks tape recorded interviews with the elders of his tribe, furnishing a key to the history and religion of his people. The tapes were compiled into a written record in collaboration with Frank Waters in the *Book of the Hopi,* published in 1963. Fredericks is an art instructor at the Boys' Club of America in Phoenix, Arizona. He has received awards in golf and other sports, and he is interested in travel, teaching, lecturing, working in vocational education for young people, as well as the history of the Hopi people.

ROBERT LEE FREEMAN, Yankton Sioux-San Louisano
  (Painting   16, 36)
  Born: 1939, Rincon Indian Reservation, Valley Center, California
  Education: Public schools, Escondido, California; Mira Costa Junior College, Oceanside, California
  Significance: *Interpretations of contemporary Indian Life through art*

Robert Lee Freeman served in the Army from 1957 to 1960. He began his art career in 1961. An excellent draftsman, he produces powerful images in both oil paintings and pen and ink sketches. He also does wood carving and welded metal sculptures. He has won many honors and awards in the several media in which he works. His work is exhibited widely throughout the United States. He now lives in San Marcos, California.

GANADO MUCHO, Navajo
  (Tribal Leadership   13)
  Born: 1809, Arizona
  Died: Late 1800's
  Education: Tribal
  Significance: *Peace leader of his people*

Ganado Mucho became a leader of his people in young manhood. He did not stray from the peaceful ways his father taught him, except for a few wild retaliatory raids against the Oraibi Indians. He refused to join the war parties of other Navajo bands and staunchly held his own band from attack. He encouraged his people during the difficult times when they were driven east to the Bosque Redondo Reservation near Fort Sumner in New Mexico. He and eleven other major Navajo chiefs negotiated with the United States Peace Commission at Fort Sumner in 1868. A treaty providing for their return to their homeland was signed, and the Navajos began their long walk west.

During the rest of his lifetime, Ganado Mucho tried very hard to work with the agents of the United States Government for the betterment of his people.

DAVID GARCIA, Zuñi
  (Law, Business   11)
  Born: 1920, New Mexico
  Education: B.S., LL.B., University of North Dakota, Grand Forks
  Significance: *Work in behalf of the Indian people*

David Garcia is a public accountant and state's attorney for Ramsay County, North Dakota. He is secretary-treasurer of two finance and investment concerns which he helped to promote and organize and which he now manages. One is capitalized at $25,000 and the other at $1,500,000. Both corporations are becoming increasingly important in the economy of the state. Through one, Garcia hopes to establish a needed industry on the Devil's Lake Reservation in North Dakota.

Before Garcia entered college, where he was a Noyes Scholarship student, he was a pharmacist's mate in the Navy on duty in the South Pacific during World War II and won a Presidential Citation. In 1957 the United States Chamber of Commerce honored him with the Distinguished Service Award as "outstanding young man of the year from North Dakota." He is an active participant in the civic life of his community, giving time and energy to the County Red Cross Chapter, the Home Service Committee, the Community Chest and the Junior Chamber of Commerce on both local and state levels.

He donates free legal advice to the reservation tribal council and indigent individual Indians. Garcia is a member of the American Bar Assocation and has been president of the Ramsay County Bar Association.

BEATRICE MEDICINE GARNER, Hunkpapa
  Sioux
  (Anthropology   11)
  Born: ca. 1935, Standing Rock
    Reservation, South Dakota
  Education: Reservation and public
    schools; B.S., South Dakota State
    College; M.A., University of
    Washington, Seattle, Washington
  Significance: *Anthropological interest in
    Indian history*

Beatrice Medicine Garner learned to take pride in her tribal history in her home. When applying for a student loan, she was advised to major in something "practical," so she studied home economics. Later, she became interested in anthropology and was supported in this study by scholarships. Her work as director of the American Indian Research Project of the University of South Dakota at Vermillion is financed by the Doris Duke Ten Percent Fund. This project involves the gathering of oral history as the Indians lived and remember it.

GERONIMO, Apache
  (Tribal Leadership   35)
  Born: 1831, Arizona Territory
  Died: 1909
  Education: Tribal
  Significance: *Fought for what he believed
    was right*

Geronimo's adopted tribe, the Chiricahua, was among the last of the Apache to capitulate to the American Army. Geronimo rose to the leadership of his rebellious tribesmen when they refused to become farmers on the San Carlos Reservation. For many years, these Indians ranged through Mexico and southern Arizona, plundering, burning and killing. Finally, Lieutenant Charles B. Gatewood, an American army officer, succeeded in gaining access to Geronimo's camp and persuaded him to surrender. There were less than two dozen warriors and their families with the great chief. Nearly

all the Chiricahuas had been imprisoned originally in Florida, then removed to a reservation in Alabama, and finally sent to Oklahoma.

Geronimo resigned himself to the inevitable and lived in peace on the reservation for the remainder of his life. He rode in President Theodore Roosevelt's inaugural parade, became a Christian, and wore the dress of his captors.

R. C. GORMAN, Navajo
  (Art   28)
  Born: 1934, Chinle, Arizona
  Education: Arizona State College,
    Tempe, Arizona; Mexico City College;
    San Francisco State College, California
  Significance: *Portrayal of the Navajo way
    of life through art*

R. C. Gorman is a descendant of sand painters, silversmiths, chanters, and weavers. As a boy, he lived in an earth-floored hogan and herded the family sheep. His talent was evident at an early age. Now he is one of the outstanding Navajo painters and works sensitively in ink, oil, pastel, water color, and acrylic. His work has won him many honors and appears in public and private collections.

Gorman is a member of the American Indian Artists Guild of San Francisco and served as its chairman in 1966. His father, Carl Nelson Gorman, also an artist of renown is manager of the Navajo Arts and Crafts Guild in Window Rock, Arizona.

LADONNA HARRIS, Comanche
  (Community Service   19, 37)
  Born: 1935, Oklahoma
  Education: Public schools
  Significance: *Promotion of equal
    opportunities for her people*

LaDonna Harris, in her attempt to bring new dignity to her people, founded the Oklahomans for Indian Opportunity in 1965. This organization helps reservation Indians fight federal red tape, gathers evidence of discrimination, trains young Indians for jobs and leadership, and forms buying clubs to combat high grocery prices. She is active as a member of the board of directors of the Oklahoma State Mental

Health and Welfare Association and of the University of Oklahoma Southwest Human Relations Center.

On the national level, Mrs. Harris is a member of the National Indian Opportunities Council established by President Johnson on March 6, 1968. As an outgrowth of her leadership on this council the organization, Americans for Indian Opportunity, is being formed. In addition to this work she is chairman of the Women's Advisory Committee on Poverty, a member of Task Force VI of the Joint Commission on Mental Health of Children and a member of the Special Committee on Minority Children.

Mrs. Harris is the wife of United States Senator Fred R. Harris of Oklahoma, immediate past chairman of the Democratic National Committee.

WILLIAM W. HASTINGS, Cherokee
   (Politics   40)
   Born: 1866, Indian Territory, now
      Oklahoma
   Died: 1938
   Education: Tribal neighborhood school;
      B.S., Tribal Cherokee Male Seminary,
      Oklahoma; LL.B., Vanderbilt
      University, Nashville, Tennessee
   Significance: *Leadership in Indian*
      legislation and education

William W. Hastings, one of the ablest men who ever represented Oklahoma in Congress, began his career as a member of the United States House of Representatives in 1915. Except for his one defeat in the Republican landslide of 1920, he served his state continuously until he retired in 1935. As a former tribal citizen who had attained distinction in a white society, he believed in federal protection of Indian lands and rights.

Hastings grew up on a farm near the prosperous Cherokee settlement of Beattie's Prairie. He attended tribal schools, including the Cherokee Male Seminary, the first school of higher education west of the Mississippi River, established by the Cherokee Nation. He taught briefly in the tribal schools and was tribal superintendent of education from 1890 to 1891. He served as at-

torney general for the Cherokee Nation for four years from 1891 to 1895 and was appointed several times to represent the Cherokee Nation in Washington, D.C.

When the courts in the Indian Territory were abolished in 1898, Hastings continued his law practice, representing Indian interests and prosecuting Indian claims before federal agencies and courts. In 1901, the Oklahoma Indians were made United States citizens in preparation for eventual statehood. The original Indian Territory was divided, and the western part, opened to white settlement, was named Oklahoma Territory. The Indians wanted the Indian Territory to become a separate state, to be known as the State of Sequoyah. Hastings served on the committee that drew up the constitution for the proposed state. Although Congress refused the plan and provided for the union of the two territories, many of the principles of that document were embodied in the constitution adopted by Oklahoma at statehood in 1907.

NED A. HATATHLI, Navajo
   (Education   31, 40, 42)
   Born: 1923, Coal Mine Canyon, Arizona
   Education: Tuba City Boarding School,
      Arizona; Haskell Institute, Lawrence,
      Kansas; B.S., Northern Arizona
      University, Flagstaff, Arizona
   Significance: *Promotion of*
      self-determination through education

Ned A. Hatathli is the first Indian president of the Navajo Community College at Many Farms, Arizona. This college is the first Indian-established institution of higher education in modern times. The Cherokee Male Seminary, established by the Cherokee Nation in the 19th century, was the first school of higher education of any kind west of the Mississippi River. The Navajo Community College was dedicated in 1968 by the Navajo Tribe, with Robert Roessel as president, Ned Hatathli as vice-president, and an all-Navajo Board of Regents. It presently shares the plant of the new Bureau of Indian Affairs Boarding High School. Plans are to construct the college campus on the 1,200 acres reserved by the tribe on Lake Tsaile in the

Lukachukai Mountains of Arizona. Navajo Community College is planned to retain the unique heritage of the Navajo and at the same time give its students the necessary tools to function in the white culture. The college opened for classes in January 1969.

ALBERT HAWLEY, Gros Ventre-Assiniboine Sioux
   (Education   11)
   Born: Early 1900's, Montana
   Education: Haskell Institute, Lawrence, Kansas; A.B., Davis and Elkins College, Elkins, West Virginia; M.A., Stanford University, Palo Alto, California
   Significance: *Leadership in Indian education*

Albert Hawley was principal of the Stewart Indian School, Stewart, Nevada, where he inaugurated innovations in Indian education. He also made possible the transition to the new Navajo program. This school is one of ten throughout the United States under the Bureau of Indian Affairs concerned with the education of Navajo youth. Later Hawley was given a position of greater responsibility as superintendent of the Fort Apache Agency.

During World War II, Hawley was commanding officer of the Lend Lease Battalion at Cabiness Field (USN). He was named to the Indian Athletic Gallery of the National Hall of Fame for Famous American Indians located in Anadarko, Oklahoma. Now retired, Hawley was honored with the Distinguished Service Award given by the Indian Council Fire for a lifetime of work dedicated to the improvement of education for Indians. He believes that management and development of human and natural resources is a business undertaking of the highest order and that education is the key to Indian self-determination.

IRA HAYES, Pima
   (Military   38)
   Born: 1920, Bapchule, Arizona
   Died: 1955
   Education: Reservation schools
   Significance: *Distinguished service to his country*

Pfc. Ira Hayes was one of six marines who raised the United States flag on the summit of Mount Suribachi, Iwo Jima, under heavy fire during World War II. He served on Iwo Jima for thirty-six days and was fortunate to remain unwounded. Previously, he had fought at Vella La Vella and Bougainville.

Because of the nationwide attention won by Rosenthal's dramatic photograph of the flag raising, an expression of the invincible American spirit, Hayes and two comrades were brought back to this country to travel extensively in support of the Seventh War Loan. More than 1,000 Indians of the Pima tribe gathered at Bapchule to pay him honor and to celebrate his safe return home. The National Congress of American Indians honored him, and Hayes was made first commander of the American Indian Veterans' Association.

His now historic and heroic flag-raising on Mount Suribachi has been immortalized in song and story. Reg Begay commemorates Hayes in his song, "The Old Glory Raising on Iwo Jima." The event was also depicted on a United States postage stamp based on Rosenthal's photograph.

BERTRAM HAYMAN, Modoc
   (Engineering   16)
   Born: 1899, Ottawa County, Oklahoma
   Education: B.S., Oklahoma Agricultural & Mechanical College, Stillwater, Oklahoma
   Significance: *Service to his country in war and peace*

Bertram Hayman was a hydraulic engineer for the Tulsa Fire Department, after which he worked as fire prevention engineer for the United States Corps of Engineers at Fort Crowder, Missouri. He was the Oklahoma representative to the first Fire Prevention Conference, called by President Truman in 1948. He served in the United States Marines during World War I from 1917 to 1919, winning the French Croix de Guerre and the Battalion Decoration. Hayman served in the Junior Chamber of Commerce in Tulsa, Oklahoma, and was an active member of the International Association of Fire Fighters from 1941 to 1950. He also played professional baseball in the minor leagues in 1921.

WILLIAM J. HENSLEY, Eskimo
(Politics   40)
Born: ca. 1935, Alaska
Education: B.A., University of Alaska, College, Alaska
Significance: *Work in behalf of native Alaska*

William J. Hensey has served in the State Legislature of Alaska since 1966. He is chairman of the governor's Native Land Claims Task Force and a member of the National Council on Indian opportunity. Hensley assisted in the organization of the Northwest Alaska Native Association and was its first executive director. He is president of the Alaska Village Electric Cooperative. Through the Experiment in International Living Program, he was awarded the second John F. Kennedy Memorial Scholarship to pursue his education.

JOE H. HERRERA, Cochiti Pueblo
(Painting, Education   11)
Born: ca. 1920, Cochiti Pueblo, New Mexico
Education: Santa Fe Indian School; B.A., University of New Mexico, Albuquerque
Significance: *Contribution as an Indian artist of talent*

Joe H. Herrera is the son of Tonita Pena, the first Indian woman to receive acclaim as a modern painter. While still in the eighth grade, Herrera painted the murals for the walls of a large store in Albuquerque, New Mexico. He served as a radar operator with the Aircraft Warning Service (AAF) during World War II. Although he was stationed in many parts of the world, he spent most of his time in the Caribbean. He continued to paint and instructed other servicemen in painting.

After his discharge, Herrera worked for the Laboratory of Anthropology in Santa Fe, New

Mexico where he learned the basic forms and designs of early Indian art. Practically all of his work depicts the great dances of his people, although he does landscapes, portraits, and symbolic painting. His first one-man show was held in the Santa Fe Art Museum where all eighteen of his paintings were sold. He has had many exhibits since, including a traveling exhibit in 1958 which was shown in Italy, Spain, Germany, and France. He has won many major art awards and honors including the Palmes Academiques in 1954, the highest art award of the French government.

In 1957, Herrera was named guidance and placement officer on the staff of the New Mexico State Department of Education. He is responsible for the development of recreation programs for Pueblo, Apache, and Navajo children and adults. He is also the executive secretary for the All Pueblo Council, the official body of nineteen pueblos, representing approximately 25,000 New Mexico Indians. At one time he addressed the Joint Congressional Subcommittee on Indian Affairs in behalf of his people.

VELINO HERRERA, Zia Pueblo
(Painting   11)
Born: ca. 1905, New Mexico
Education: Santa Fe Indian School, New Mexico
Significance: *Contribution to the development of Indian art*

Velino Herrera, known as Ma-Pe-Wi among his people, is one of the pioneer painters of the Rio Grande Valley. He began to paint in 1917 and is justly proud of the fact that he is self-taught. He has mastered water color, tempera, and oils and has painted murals in homes and prominent buildings. His subjects vary from pueblo life to modern portraits. Action is provided through rhythmic flowing lines and rich color.

From the time he won his first prize, Herrera's work has been included in important galleries. When he opened his own studio in Santa Fe in 1932, he had earned a wide reputation and received honorable mention in the art section of the New York Times. For a brief time, he taught Indian art at the Albuquerque Indian School. He has illustrated a number of books on Indian topics, including Ann Nolan Clark's *In My Mother's House,* published in 1941, which has reached a twelfth printing.

HIAWATHA, Mohawk
  (Religion, Government   30)
  Born: Early 1500's, Pennsylvania-New
    York
  Died: Early 1600's
  Education: Tribal
  Significance: *Founding of a government
    under the rule of law*

Hiawatha, a medicine man of vision, wisdom and genius, was the co-founder with Deganawidah in 1570 of the League of Iroquois, the strongest governing force in Indian America north of Mexico. The Five Nations, as the League was sometimes called, included the Mohawks, Oneidas, Onandagas, Cayugas and Senecas. In 1712 the League was joined by the Tuscaroras. Hiawatha is not to be confused with the hero of Henry Wadsworth Longfellow's poem, "The Song of Hiawatha," who was an Algonquian.

The Mohawk Hiawatha grew up at a time when the Iroquois were locked in bitter and desperate inter-tribal warfare. Hiawatha moved among his people teaching peace, reform, and the organization of a confederacy "where no man's hand would be turned against his brother." His progress seemed slow until the prophet Deganawidah appeared. One by one, the powerful tribes joined the crusade for peace, and the remarkable Confederacy of the Iroquois was born. This early, self-governing league may have influenced the colonial Constitutional Congress. As early as 1754 Benjamin Franklin at the Albany Convention had said in pleading the cause of union:

It would be a strange thing if Six Nations of ignorant savages should be capable of forming a scheme for such a union and be able to execute it in such a manner as that it has subsisted ages and appears indissoluble; and yet that a like union should be impracticable

for ten or a dozen English colonies, to whom it is more necessary and must be more advantageous . . .

THOMASINE RUTH HILL, Crow-Pawnee
  (Community Service   37)
  Born: 1948, Crow Agency, Montana
  Education: Mackinac College, Mackinac
    Island, Michigan
  Significance: *Ambassador of goodwill for
    Indian people*

Thomasine Ruth Hill, the 21-year-old Miss Indian America of 1969 from the Crow Agency in Montana, is a descendant of a chief of the Crow's Black-lodge band and of a Pawnee chief of the Skidee band. Miss Hill's activities and honors include being Crow Tribal Princess, vice-president of her high school senior class, Pep Club president, prom queen, and work with the Crow Indian Youth Advisory Committee. She has had two years' training and experience with Up With People, a project of Moral Rearmament, and has traveled extensively, particularly in South America. She is majoring in political science.

As Miss Indian America XV, Miss Hill followed a fast-paced schedule of travel from one end of the country to the other. In January, 1969, she flew to Washington, D.C., to take part in the inauguration activities which included the parade and attendance at one of the balls. Miss Indian America ended the month by taking part in the meeting of the National Indian Education Advisory Committee also held in the nation's capital.

HOOWANNEKA, Winnebago
  (Tribal Leadership   22)
  Born: Late 1700's, western Great Lakes
    area
  Died: Mid 1800's
  Education: Tribal
  Significance: *Promotion of peace*

Hoowanneka, also known as Little Elk, was the orator chief of the Winnebago Nation and a descendant of the distinguished Winnebago Caramanie family. He fought with the British in the Revolutionary War, but toward the close of the war, he became convinced that his nation had been seduced into an "unnatural" war. He therefore exerted great influence over his fierce tribe to unite in friendship with the settlers and the American government. He convinced his people that only through friendship with the Americans could the Indian people survive. In 1824, he presented himself to President James Monroe when he visited in Washington, D.C., as a delegate from his nation. He addressed the President and his cabinet eloquently in one of the drawing rooms of the White House.

ALLAN HOUSER, Apache
    (Art, Education   11, 40)
    Born: 1914, Arizona
    Education: Chilocco Indian School, Oklahoma; Haskell Institute, Lawrence, Kansas; Utah State University, Logan
    Significance: *Preservation of his culture through his art*

Allan Houser, the great-grandson of Geronimo, is a noted artist and sculptor who first began to paint in 1934. As a boy, he worked on his father's farm hoping to make a career in professional athletics. An illness during high school diverted his interest to drawing. After graduation, he opened his own studio in Santa Fe, New Mexico. He painted some of the murals in the Department of Interior building in Washington, D.C., and in 1948, completed a marble memorial statue to Haskell Institute Indians who lost their lives in World War II.

Houser paints in the typical Indian two-dimensional style with broad, flat definite brush strokes, showing splendid action, vitality, and vigor in simple lines. He has won many awards and honors including the Palmes Academiques, the highest art award of the French government. At one time, he was asked to demonstrate his technique to art students in China. He taught arts and crafts at Intermountain Indian School, Brigham City, Utah. He is a popular illustrator of Indian books, having completed eight. He hopes to write and illustrate a book about his famous ancestor, Geronimo.

OSCAR HOWE, Yankton Sioux
    (Art, Education   11, 36)
    Born: 1915, Joe Creek, South Dakota
    Education: Pierre Indian School, Pierre, South Dakota; Santa Fe Indian School, Santa Fe, New Mexico: B.A., Dakota Wesleyan University, Mitchell, South Dakota; M.F.A., University of Oklahoma, Norman, Oklahoma
    Significance: *Outstanding work in art education*

Oscar Howe has been professor of creative arts at the University of South Dakota in Vermillion since 1957. He is also artist-in-residence and assistant director of the University Museum. He is one of the most respected art educators today. Through the example of his own achievement as a creative artist and by his activities as a professional educator, Howe has encouraged and directed the development of a number of important contemporary Sioux artists. He spent three and one-half years in the Army in combat battalions in North Africa, Italy, and Germany during World War II.

Howe became a successful artist while still in high school. Before he graduated, his paintings had been on exhibit across the nation as well as in London and Paris. He has been winning awards and honors consistently since 1947. In 1952 he was commissioned to illustrate the two-volume book, *North American Indian Costumes,* published in France. He has been the yearly designer of the larger-than-life scenes made with corn in its natural colors for the famous Corn Palace in Mitchell, South Dakota.

HOWLING WOLF, Cheyenne Sioux
    (Art   33)
    Born: Mid 1800's, what is now Wyoming
    Died: Early 1900's
    Education: Tribal
    Significance: *Graphic presentations of significant events in the life of his people*

Howling Wolf was an artist of considerable note among his own people. He was the recorder of events. Some of his work is in the Rare Book and Manuscript Library of Yale

University. His work appears in *Cheyenne Memories,* by John Stands In Timber and Margot Liberty, published in 1967.

ISHI, Yahi
  (Anthropology 17)
  Born: 1861, California
  Died: 1916
  Education: Tribal
  Significance: *Assistance with research on the Yahi Indians*

Ishi was born at a time when the Indians of north central California were being systematically exterminated. His life was one of constant hiding. Members of his tribe were gradually reduced one way or another until he was the sole remaining person. In 1911, after years of living alone in mountainous country, he decided to sneak into Oroville for food. He went to the slaughter yard where dogs held him at bay.

To protect his life, the sheriff put him in jail. Much publicity was given to the fact that a "wild man" had appeared and was being held in jail. Dr. Alfred Kroeber, Professor of Anthropology at the University of California at Berkeley, investigated the situation and found the "wild man" to be one of the Yahi tribe believed to be extinct. Through permission of the United States Bureau of Indian Affairs, Ishi was taken to live in the University's Museum of Anthropology and Ethnology in San Francisco where he won the respect and esteem of all with whom he came in contact. Ishi was given an apartment at the museum and worked with the anthropologists there during the remaining four years of his life.

Ishi was of much help to the anthropologists in unraveling the way of life and language of his people. He demonstrated Indian crafts at the museum and led the anthropologists to his people's country to explore the Yahi culture in its setting and to learn how he was able to elude the white man's slaughter for so long. The remarkable thing about Ishi was that he was able to make the transition from a primitive way of life to a 20th century technological age with seemingly little effort while maintaining the naturalness and simplicity of an engaging, whole-some personality. He gave much in his short life in the white man's world and was beloved by all.

LORETTA S. JENDRITZA, Navajo
  (Military, Medicine 40)
  Born: 1920, Navajoland, Arizona
  Education: Nursing
  Significance: *Service through nursing*

Loretta S. Jendritza, Air Force Nurse Corps, Air Force Academy Hospital, Colorado Springs, Colorado, was promoted to rank of major. She is operating room supervisor at the Air Force Academy Hospital.

MARLENE JOHNSON, Tlingit
  (Community Service 37)
  Born: 1930, Hoonah, Alaska
  Education: Federal Indian schools
  Significance: *Assistance to Indians in projects to help themselves*

Mrs. Marlene Johnson believes that "community action programs offer Indian people one of the best opportunities for learning to help themselves." She is on the board of directors for the Hoonah Community Action Committee, Inc., and has served as a member of the board of directors of the Rural Alaska Community Action Programs (formerly ASCAP) since its inception. She has also served two terms as its president. She is chairman of the Southeast Alaska Community Action Advisory Board and a member of the Tlingit-Haida Central Council. In 1968 Mrs. Johnson was awarded the Rural Service Award by the Office of Economic Opportunity and was named winner of the 1968 Community Leaders of America Award. She has also served on the Hoonah Board of Education since 1961 and is a member of the Alaska Native Sisterhood and the Federation of Natives.

PAUL JONES, Navajo
  (Tribal Leadership 13)
  Born: 1895, Naschitti, New Mexico
  Education: Tohatchi Indian School, New Mexico; Englewood High School, New Jersey; Calvin College, Grand Rapids, Michigan; McLaughlin's Business

School, Grand Rapids, Michigan

Significance: *Untiring direction and stimulation for the betterment of life and education among his people*

Paul Jones, known among his people as Tl'aashchi'i Biye' of the Ta'neezahnii Clan (Scattered Tree Branches People), worked his way from humble and poor beginnings to positions of responsibility and dignity. Many important projects were begun or completed during his lifetime of service to his people. This was interrupted by World War I when he entered the army.

In 1955, Jones was elected chairman of the Navajo Tribal Council. As chairman, he assumed the responsibility of looking after the financial interests of his tribe. This involves millions of dollars, mostly from royalties from the natural resources found on the reservation, such as gas, oil, coal, timber, and uranium. Jones believes that the future of the Navajos lies in education, and five million dollars has been set aside for scholarship aid for the young people.

Jones, the man who got his start from firing a church furnace so that he could attend high school, is the inspiration for the upward march of the Navajos. He exerted tremendous influence in behalf of all Navajo people as district supervisor for the Bureau of Indian Affairs and as interpreter and liaison officer between the Navajo people and the Federal government. During his administration of the Tribal Council, he was one of two United States delegates to the fourth Inter-Indian Conference held in Guatemala. When the Navajo Community College at Many Farms, Arizona, a college planned, organized, directed and supported by the Navajo people, opened for classes in 1969, Jones was one of its professors. His life goal has been to earn happiness and prosperity for his people, for his family, and for himself.

JOSEPH (The Elder), Nez Percé
(Tribal Leadership 39)
Born: 1790, northwestern United States
Died: 1872
Education: Tribal

Significance: *Belief in peaceful co-existence*

Chief Joseph, The Elder, known as Tuekakas among his people, was a Christian convert dedicated to peace. He was a life-long friend of missionaries, settlers, and explorers. This traditional friendship was established as early as 1805 with the coming of Lewis and Clark. However, with the influx of white settlers, negotiations were necessary to maintain peace. Under the Walla Walla Treaty of 1855, the Nez Percé tribe of eastern Washington ceded most of its territory to the government and was resettled on lands in eastern Oregon and Idaho. With the discovery of gold on their Oregon holdings in the early 1860's, the area was immediately overrun by prospectors. To the demands of the Nez Percé for enforcement of treaty terms, Indian commissioners responded by calling another treaty council at Lapuai in the spring of 1863 to persuade the Nez Percé to "adjust the boundaries of the reservation."

As discussion of the new proposals continued, the Nez Percé divided into three groups. One group favored the treaty with its promises of cash, schools, shops, and other benefits. The second group, although demonstrating no enmity, refused to give up any more land and asked the government to remove the white trespassers. The third group objected to any treaty and demanded the return of all northwest lands to the Indians. The council dragged on with none of the rival chiefs willing to yield. Finally the tribe decided to disband leaving each leader free to negotiate separate treaties. One group then signed a treaty reducing the size of the Nez Percé reservation by three-fourths in return for cash and new building. In signing, the members had no intention of betraying the rest of the tribe, believing that those who did not sign would not be bound. The white officials, however, maintained that the treaty bound the entire Nez Percé tribe.

Chief Joseph, who for thirty years had been a friend to the white immigrants to his land, and who had always led his people in pursuit of peace and co-existence, tore up a copy of the treaty, destroyed his long-cherished copy of the

New Testament and declared that he would never again have anything to do with white men or their ways.

JOSEPH (The Young), Nez Percé
  (Tribal Leadership   23, 30)
  Born: 1840, Nez Percé Country
  Died: 1904
  Education: Tribal
  Significance: *Efforts to maintain peace and yet preserve the integrity of his people*

Chief Joseph, The Young, was known among his people as Hinmuttoo-Yatlatkekht (Thunder Rolling Over the Mountains). He was handsome and noble in appearance and became a combined national hero and military genius in attempting to continue his father's philosophy of peace and yet preserve his people's land.

In 1873, President Grant, by executive order, gave back to Chief Joseph and his followers the northern half of their own land. The tribe continued to peacefully ask for the removal of all settlers from the rest of their territory. The white settlers wanted all of the Nez Percé land so that in 1875 the earlier executive order was revoked and the Wallowa Valley was again declared open to homesteading.

In 1877, Chief Joseph was asked to move his tribe out of the Wallowa Valley within thirty days under threat of force. The Indians began rounding up their cattle and horses making ready to leave. Instead, because of unfortunate circumstances, there followed battle after battle. Rather than surrender, Chief Joseph decided to retreat. This move ranks as one of the most masterly in United States military history. In his retreat, Chief Joseph led his band toward Canada, a journey of more than 1,000 miles across the Rocky Mountains, through what is now Yellowstone Park and across the Missouri near its headwaters. The courageous chief, referred to as the Red Moses, was stopped just thirty miles south of the Canadian border by Colonel Nelson A. Miles whose soldiers outnumbered the Indians two to one. In surrendering, Chief Joseph spoke the now classic words of resignation:

Tell General Howard I know his heart. What he told me before, I have in my heart. I am tired of fighting. Our chiefs are killed. The old are all dead . . . It is cold and we have no blankets, the little children are freezing to death . . . I am tired, my heart is sick and sad. From where the sun now stands, I will fight no more forever.

So ended the most dramatic war of the many wars during the stand of the Indians against the unrelenting encroachment of white men.

FRED KABOTIE, Hopi
  (Art, Education   11, 27)
  Born: 1907, Shungopovi, Second Mesa, Arizona
  Education: Santa Fe Indian School, Santa Fe, New Mexico
  Significance: *Graphic expression of the way of life of his people*

Fred Kabotie, a distinguished artist, is the recipient of many national and international honors in art and the humanities. These include the Guggenheim Memorial Fellowship in 1945, the Indian Achievement Award in 1949, and the Palmes Academiques of the French government in 1954. He is field representative on the Indian Arts and Crafts Board of the United States Department of the Interior with his office at Second Mesa in Arizona. His murals depicting Hopi life and ceremonies appear in the School of American Research and the Archeological Society of New Mexico, in the Museum of the American Indian, New York City, and in the Indian Tower on the south rim of the Grand Canyon.

Kabotie wrote and illustrated *Designs From the Ancient Mimbrenos,* published in 1949. He reproduced the pre-Columbian Hopi paintings in the Awatobi ruins in Arizona when it was excavated by archaeologists from the Peabody Museum. In 1941, he sponsored the organization of the Hopi Silvercraft Cooperative Guild, a non-profit group of silver workers utilizing and adapting ancient Hopi designs in their products. He was art instructor at the Oraibi

High School, a position he held until his retirement.

BERNARD KATEXAC, Eskimo
(Handicrafts   16)
Born: 1922, King Island, Alaska
Education: University of Alaska
Significance: *Ability as a talented artist*
Bernard Katexac served in the National Guard and the Armed Forces of the United States during World War II. His much sought after work includes woodcuts, etching, jewelry, and wood sculpture.

WILLIAM W. KEELER, Cherokee
(Business, Tribal Leadership   16)
Education: LL.D., University of Kansas, Lawrence, Kansas
Significance: *Efforts to raise social and economic standards of his people*
William W. Keeler was appointed the principal chief of the Cherokee tribe of Oklahoma by Harry S. Truman in 1949. He is often referred to as the strongest tribal leader in more than 100 years and is often compared to John Ross, the Scotch-Cherokee, who unified the Cherokee Nation in 1828. He has been president of the National Association of Manufacturers, president of the National Phillips Petroleum Company and chairman of its Advisory Board.

During World War II, Keeler was stationed in Mexico as a Phillips representative where he worked on committees with the Petroleum Administration for War. In 1952, he was elected chairman of the Military Petroleum Advisory Board formed by the Department of Interior. He was busy with plans related to the White House Youth Conference in 1959 and 1960.

His civic activities include membership on the Board of Directors for the Gilcrease Museum of Tulsa; director of the First National Bank of Bartlesville, and membership on the Commission on the Rights, Liberties and Responsibilities of the American Indian. In 1961, he was chairman of the Presidential Task Force on Indian Affairs. Keeler received the All-American Indian Award in 1957 and, in 1961, the honorary LL.D., Distinguished Service Ci-

tation from the University of Kansas Alumni Association. He is the founder of the Cherokee Foundation, an organization to promote the welfare and culture of his tribe.

KEOKUK, Sauk
(Tribal Leadership   22)
Born: Late 1700's, area of Illinois
Died: Mid 1800's
Education: Tribal
Significance: *Ability to resettle his people peacefully*
Keokuk was appointed principal chief of the Sauk and Fox Nations by President Andrew Jackson in 1837 at the close of the Black Hawk War. Keokuk's public career began early in his life. His remarkable political sense, his knowledge of human nature, his tact, courage, prudence and eloquence, and his magnificent physical appearance commanded respect. In the Treaty of 1804, the closely related Sauk and Fox tribes agreed to leave their homeland in the rich prairie valleys of what are now Illinois and Wisconsin east of the Mississippi and settle on a reservation west of the Mississippi along the Des Moines River. This was to be accomplished as soon as the white settlements extended into their land.

In the 1820's, Keokuk led his people to their new land in Iowa, with the exception of the militant Chief Black Hawk who refused to leave his homeland. Keokuk directed the resettlement of his people with extraordinary skill and instilled in them a heritage of pride in discipline and management. His intercessions in Washington on behalf of Chief Black Hawk and his followers and of other warring tribes testified to the dignity, calm judgment, and superior intelligence of Keokuk.

JACK FREDERICK KILPATRICK, Cherokee
(Education, Literature, Music   16)
Born: 1915, Stillwell, Oklahoma
Education: Bacone College, Oklahoma;
    Northeastern State College, Oklahoma;
    B.Mus., University of Redlands,
    California; M.Mus., Catholic
    University of America, Washington,

D.C.; D.Mus., University of Redlands, California

Significance: *Preserving the culture of his people through writing*

Jack Frederick Kilpatrick is professor of music in the School of the Arts at Southern Methodist University in Dallas, Texas. He served in the Navy as instructor of music during World War II. His many honors and awards include grants from the National Science Foundation, the Danforth Foundation, the American Philosophical Society, and the Carnegie Foundation.

Kilpatrick's published works co-authored with Anna G. Kilpatrick include *Friends of Thunder,* published in 1964, *Walk in Your Soul,* in 1965, and *The Shadow of Sequoyah,* in 1965. His own work, *Sequoyah: Of Earth and Intellect,* was published in 1965.

KING PHILIP, Wampanoag
  (Tribal Leadership   35)
  Born: 1616, Warren, Rhode Island
  Died: 1676
  Education: Tribal
  Significance: *Valiant attempts to keep the peace*

King Philip, known to his people as Metacomet, was the youngest son of Massasoit and became chief or sachem of the Wampanoag tribe in 1661. For many years, he maintained inviolate a treaty of friendship with the colonists signed by his father, Massasoit.

The rapid spread of white settlements, however, and the encroachment of the colonists on Indian fishing and hunting grounds led to Philip's decision to war against them. On July 4, 1675, the Indian attack on the Quaker settlement at Swansea, Rhode Island, opened what came to be called King Philip's War. In alliance with the Narraganset and Nipmuck tribes, King Philip attacked settlements, burning houses and destroying crops in Rhode Island and Massachusetts. About 600 colonists were killed in battle or murdered, twelve towns were entirely destroyed and much of the countryside laid waste.

With all of central and southeastern New England up in arms against them, the Indians lost even more heavily. In a single battle, the Swamp Fight of December, 1675, the Indians lost over 1,000 warriors. The Indians were also weakened by famine and quarrels among themselves.

King Philip's allies, blaming their losses on his ambition, deserted him and surrendered. King Philip's War came to an end on August 12, 1676, when he was killed in his stronghold on Mount Hope, Rhode Island. It took many years before New England recovered from the devastation, ruin, and the economic and industrial setback occasioned by this war.

LEO JOHN LACLAIR, Muckleshoot
  (Tribal Affairs   16)
  Born: 1941, Auburn, Washington
  Education: B.A., Central Washington State College, Ellensburg; University of Colorado, Boulder; University of Utah, Salt Lake City
  Significance: *Leadership in Indian civic affairs*

Leo John LaClair is active on the committee for Educational Opportunities for American Indians and Alaska Natives. He is also an active member of the National Association of Intergroup Relations and the National Youth Council. He has been awarded a scholarship from the United Scholarship Service and a grant from the Eleanor Roosevelt Foundation to continue his education.

EDWARD LAPLANTE, Chippewa
  (Tribal Affairs   11)
  Born: ca. 1900, Minnesota
  Education: Reservation school; Carlisle Institute, Pennsylvania
  Significance: *Work for Indian self-determination*

Edward LaPlante, a descendant of a chief who signed the Chippewa Treaty of 1854, believes that Indians should maintain their racial identity. He has worked for the introduction of legislation to establish a standing Indian Committee in the Wisconsin State Legislature comprised of members of the five principal tribes of Wisconsin. In 1954, he addressed the United

Nations at the revision of the charter hearings. He had time to give leadership to an Indian education program and worked actively with the School Outdoor Activity Program. For his work in behalf of his people, LaPlante was named to the National Hall of Fame for Famous American Indians at Anadarko, Oklahoma. For many years, he was employed by a Milwaukee transport company.

CALVIN LARVIE, Brule Sioux
   (Painting   36)
   Born: 1920, Rosebud Reservation, South
     Dakota
   Died: 1969
   Education: Reservation school; Bacone
     College, Oklahoma
   Significance: *Preservation of the culture
     of his people through his art*

Calvin Larvie was a highly talented Sioux youth. His career as an artist began when he was young and was encouraged by the various public programs of the period. He was encouraged by Woodrow Wilson Crumbo, the famous Creek-Potawatomie artist with whom he studied for a time.

Larvie worked in highly formalized, stylized compositions in water-base media. His draftsmanship was sensitive with considerable charm. In 1939, he was commissioned by the Indian Arts and Crafts Board of the United States Department of Interior to execute a large mural depicting mounted Plains Indian hunters. This mural was featured in an extensive exhibition of historic and contemporary tribal arts in the United States Federal Pavilion at the Golden Gate International Exposition in San Francisco.

Larvie's promising career was cut short through serious disablement received in action in World War II. His paintings are museum pieces and prized in private collections.

GEORGE P. LAVATTA, Shoshone
   (Tribal Affairs   11)
   Born: ca. 1900, Idaho
   Education: Reservation school; Carlisle
     Institute, Pennsylvania

   Significance: *Inspiring his people to
     improve their economic condition
     through education*

George LaVatta was shocked to see the demoralizing effects of reservation life upon his people when he returned home from the Carlisle Institute. Believing strongly that work and self-determination are the salvation of any group or race, he hoped to strengthen weakened morale and to inspire members of his tribe toward greater efforts and industry. While working as a clerk in a store, he took night school courses.

After twelve years, LaVatta was appointed assistant guidance and placement officer for the Bureau of Indian Affairs. He was then advanced to the superintendency of the Taholah jurisdiction which comprised ten reservations. It was here that he initiated constructive programs in education and vocational training, assisting many Indian young people to gain profitable employment. LaVatta later served as area administration officer with headquarters in Portland, Oregon. In 1938 he was honored with the Indian Achievement Award of the Indian Council Fire. His activities included work with the National Congress of American Indians and the Optimist Club International.

LESCHI, Nisqually
   (Tribal Leadership   39)
   Born: Early 1800's, what is now western
     Washington
   Died: Late 1800's
   Education: Tribal
   Significance: *Attempts to negotiate peace*

Leschi was the chief of the Nisqually Indians. In 1854, territorial governors in the Pacific Northwest were instructed by the Federal government to buy out Indian rights. A period of treaty making began to relocate the different tribes on reservations. The Indians of western Washington were the first to be so relocated, peacefully. The situation changed as the Indians began to discover that reservations often did not include fishing or gathering grounds. Finding that the lands offered them were not as spacious nor as abundant in resources as the lands taken from them, the Indians threatened war. They were also angered by the methods used to obtain their signatures.

Finally, after frustrating attempts at negotiating for better conditions, the Nisqually and Puyallup tribes set upon the white immigrants in a series of bitter onslaughts including an attack on the pioneer town of Seattle. The Indians were outnumbered and defeated with heavy losses. Leschi and his small band of survivors retreated over the mountains.

Some coastal tribes had remained neutral. The large whaling tribes along the northwestern coast were fortunate since the white men did not want their beaches at the time. Many western Washington Indians, refusing to settle on reservations, roamed around the area, intermarried with the white settlers and were assimilated.

ROE B. LEWIS, Pima-Papago
(Religion   11, 40)
Born: ca. 1915, Arizona
Education: B.A., Arizona State College, Flagstaff; D.D., San Francisco Theological Seminary, California
Significance: *Service to his people through the ministry*

Reverend Roe B. Lewis of the Presbyterian Synod of Arizona is the son of an Indian missionary. In college, he majored in education. After his graduation, he organized and developed the modern school of agriculture at the Phoenix Indian School in Phoenix, Arizona. He was then sent to the Pima-Maricopa Reservation as school principal. Here he decided to further his own education in theology with special attention to sociology and economics. He returned to the Pima Reservation and later became associated with the Cook Christian Training School in Phoenix, where he organized a Department of the Rural Church. He became pastor of the Phoenix Indian Church. In 1966, he was granted an honorary doctorate by Dubuque University. He is the first Indian to be elected president of the Southwestern Regional Conference and is active in the National Fellowship of Indian Workers. He is also an education consultant to the Board of National Missions of the United States.

LITTLE CROW, Santee Sioux
(Tribal Leadership   30)
Born: ca. 1803, what is now St. Paul, Minnesota
Died: 1863
Education: Tribal
Significance: *Attempts to persuade his people to become farmers*

Chief Little Crow, a bold and persuasive orator, helped to sell the Mendota Treaty of 1851 to his people. The provisions of the treaty granted them eighty acres of land along the southwest side of the Minnesota River and $475,000 to defray the cost of moving. More than two-thirds of the money which was to have been divided among the chiefs of the various bands went instead to traders, fur companies, and self-styled "Indian agents." The little money that was distributed to Indians went to those who declared that they intended to become farmers.

The Santee Sioux had been roving hunters for hundreds of years. Now they were asked to settle in one place and work the soil for a living. Little Crow set the example by cutting his hair shoulder length and assuming the role of a farmer. He also attempted to stamp out liquor and immorality among his people. He had a mission established and attended services regularly in the mission chapel. By 1862, a decade later, the Santee Sioux had become quite disillusioned with the white man's ways. The agency trader, Andrew Myrick, had refused them credit saying, "If they are hungry, let them eat grass." This became the war cry that set off a swift and deadly surprise attack and the bloodiest massacre in the history of the long and bloody contest between the red man and the white man. Little Crow had tried to dissuade the chieftains, then said:

. . . Kill one, kill two, kill ten, and ten times ten will come to kill you. Fools! You will die like rabbits when the hungry wolves hunt them. Little Crow is no coward. He will die with you!

He did not realize that his action would be the first chapter in the great Sioux uprising that would continue for three decades until the Massacre of Wounded Knee in 1890. Little Crow's desperate decision meant that two thousand settlers and soldiers would be killed in one flaming month. Thirty-eight Sioux were tried, convicted and put to death in a mass hanging, having chanted their eerie, rhythmic, dissonant deathwail. Little Crow was shot a year later.

LITTLE THUNDER, Sioux
    (Tribal Leadership   6)
    Born: ca. 1800, Wyoming-South Dakota
      area
    Died: 1855
    Education: Tribal
    Significance: *Negotiation for and*
      maintenance of peace

Chief Little Thunder signed the treaty in 1851 between the Sioux people and the federal government, hoping that the 72,000,000 acres containing a Sioux population of 35,000 would be inviolate. This land extended from the Missouri River to the Big Horn Mountains and from the Platte River on the south to the Heart River to the north. The first treaty that had been signed in 1825 was hardly in effect when it was broken, not only by individuals but by groups, including the United States Army. Roads were laid out and railroads built through the heart of the Sioux hunting grounds. Sportsmen from all over the world came to hunt the buffalo, the mainstay of Indian life and culture. In spite of many deliberate provocations, Chief Little Thunder inspired constraint and patience among the Sioux.

LITTLE TURTLE, Miami-Mohican
    (Tribal Leadership   30)
    Born: 1752, what is now Ohio
    Died: 1812
    Education: Tribal
    Significance: *Fought to maintain the*
      homeland of his people

Chief Little Turtle, or Michikinikua, as he was called among his people, was a military genius. He was one of those rare leaders who could discipline his warriors to stand and fight against the white man in the white man's way. As a military tactician, he ranks with the best in any culture. In 1787, at the age of thirty-five, he was named war chief, inheriting the Pontiac Confederacy. This assembly of tribes, under Little Turtle called the Miami Confederacy, included the Miamis, Delawares, Shawnees, Potawatomis, Ottawas, Chippewas, and Wyandots. They were at home in what was then called the Northwest Territory. This was the land northwest of the Ohio River and east of the Mississippi River.

In a few years, however, the white settlers came crowding west across the Ohio River establishing homes and settlements. The Indians opposed the invasion. Under Chief Little Turtle the opposition grew into disastrous confrontations for the armies sent out by President Washington. The now historic "Battle of the Thousand Slain" on November 3, 1791 with General Arthur St. Clair in command was a final, brilliant victory for Little Turtle. Negotiations were attempted during the next few years. The peace commission offered the Indians an immediate cash sum for their land with regular annuity payments. Little Turtle answered in effect:

> We don't need the money, all we want is our native land. White men need the money more than we do. Divide the money among the settlers for abandoning their claims to our land. Then everyone will be happy and peace will be restored.

Indians would never understand the white man's hunger for owning a piece of land individually and completely. By 1794, the Miami Confederacy crumbled. During the peace negotiations of 1795, Little Turtle was the last to sign, saying, "I am the last to sign it. I will be the last to break it." He kept his word. When this great military leader died at Fort Wayne, Northwest Territory, he was buried with full military honors.

RONNIE LUPE, Apache
    (Tribal Affairs   40)
    Born: ca. 1930, Arizona
    Education: Reservation schools

Significance: *Direction to his people's future*

Ronnie Lupe, an active young leader of the White Mountain Apaches, is chairman of the Tribal Council. He has successfully implemented economic programs on the reservation which have kept his people in the forefront of his tribe's rapid move toward political and economic independence.

JUANA LYON, Mescalero Apache-Comanche
(Tribal Affairs, Government 37)
Born: ca. 1925, Arizona
Education: Federal Indian schools
Significance: *Work toward a better understanding of Indian needs*

Juana Lyon has been working in the best interests of her people for almost twenty years. Her early work was with the Bureau of Indian Affairs on the Navajo Reservation and then in the Phoenix area office. In 1952, she became executive secretary of the San Carlos Apache Tribal Council. In this capacity, she was responsible for the administration of various tribal functions. She also served as secretary of the Arizona Inter-Tribal Council and as relocation officer at the San Carlos Agency.

In 1967, she served simultaneously as Indian consultant for the Office of Economic Opportunity Job Corps and for the Northern Arizona Supplementary Education Center at Northern Arizona University. She is an active member of the National Congress of American Indians having served as its secretary. She is on the board of directors of the National Indian Training and Research Center. Mrs. Lyon is secretary of the Arizona Indian Association and executive secretary of the Governor's Commission on the Status of Women. She also serves on the Indian Coordinating Committee of Arizona, and the Indian Affairs Committee of the Phoenix Chamber of Commerce. Since 1967, she has been supervisor of services to Indians for the Arizona State Employment Service and has presented lectures, written articles, and appeared on television.

DANIEL M. MADRANO, Caddo
(Business, Government 11)
Born: ca. 1900, Oklahoma
Education: Sherman Institute, Riverside, California; Carlisle Institute, Pennsylvania; Wharton School of Finance and Commerce, Pennsylvania
Significance: *Work for the betterment of his people*

Daniel M. Madrano was born in a semi-dugout in the old Indian Territory of Oklahoma. He has forged ahead through his own determination and efforts. He is president and general manager of Madrano Enterprises, Incorporated, a land development company.

Madrano, with D'Arcy McNickle and others, founded the National Congress of American Indians in 1944, and was its first secretary. He is a former state legislator and a councilman of his tribe. National and state committee work for the Republican Party has taken much of his time since the 1920's. He was instrumental in influencing the United States Claims Commission to begin hearings on the Caddo Treaty Claim which was won in 1957. Madrano is the author of *Heap Big Laugh,* published in 1955. He firmly believes that the administration of Indian affairs should not be segregated because "Indians will learn by doing" when given equal opportunity. He is an active member of the Indian Council Fire, the Chamber of Commerce, the Masonic Order, and the Kiwanis Club.

MAHASKAH (THE YOUNG), Iowa
(Tribal Leadership 22)
Born: 1810, what is now Iowa
Died: Late 1800's
Education: Tribal
Significance: *Efforts to maintain the peace*

Chief Mahaskah, The Young, son of Mahaskah, The Elder, and his wife, the noted Rantchewime, was twenty-four years old when his father was assassinated. He was tall and finely proportioned with a striking resemblance to his father. Around his neck he wore the same bear claws which his father had long worn before him.

Although young Mahaskah inherited the title of chief by birth, he refused to occupy the place of his father unless called to that station by the majority of the people. A general council was called and he was elected chief without one dissenting voice. Upon his election, young Chief Mahaskah addressed his people: "My father taught the lessons of peace, and counseled me not to go to war except in my own defense. I have made up my mind to listen always to that talk. . . . I will live in peace."

He not only carried forward his father's peace policy, but he immediately engaged in agricultural pursuits, as his father before him had done as an example to his people. Young Chief Mahaskah had sixteen acres under cultivation on which he raised corn, pumpkins, beans, squash and potatoes, all well tended and cultivated. The hand plough, which he guided with his own hands was the principal tool. He distributed the surplus produce among his people, counseling them to look to the earth for their support.

In the years 1836 to 1837, Mahaskah went to Washington to talk with President Andrew Jackson about the great injustices of the United States government to his people. The stipulations of the Treaty of 1825 which had concluded a "talk" held between President James Monroe and Chief Mahaskah, The Elder, had been totally disregarded. The young chief told in his own simple but eloquent style the story of the wrongs. He was promised in reply that the grievances of his people would be made right. His portrait was made and hung in the Indian Gallery in the Department of War in Washington, D.C. where it can still be seen along with those of his father and his mother.

MANGOS COLORADOS, Mimbrenos Apache
(Tribal Leadership   14, 18)
Born: 1790, southwest, possibly Arizona
Died: 1863
Education: Tribal
Significance: *Fought for the rights of his people*
Mangos Colorados or Red Sleeves was a survivor of the Santa Rita Scalp Bounty Massacre of 1837. He was related by marriage to chiefs of the White Mountain and Chiricahua bands. An unusual Apache, he was a giant of a man with a massive head and comically bowed legs. In the 1850's, he was tied up by a group of miners in New Mexico and his massive back lashed to ribbons. For the rest of his life, he warred against "white eyes" and Mexicans without mercy. Mangos Colorados and Cochise laid waste the white settlements and promoted hatred of all Americans throughout Apache country. When the garrisons were recalled at the beginning of the Civil War, New Mexico and Arizona were virtually swept clean of white settlers by the triumphant Apache.

More than anything else, it was probably the incessant kidnapping and enslaving of Apache women and children that gave the Apache their bitter enmity toward the white newcomers from the earliest Spanish times onward. In 1866, after more than twenty years of American rule, it was officially estimated that more than 2,000 Indian slaves were held by white people in New Mexico and Arizona.

"Give them back to us," Apaches begged of an army officer in 1871, referring to twenty-nine children just stolen by Arizona citizens. "Our little boys will grow up slaves, and our girls, as soon as they are large enough will be diseased prostitutes to get money for whoever owns them. Our women work hard and are good women, and they and our children have no diseases."

After the Civil War, a campaign of Apache extermination was started, led by General James A. Carleton. Under pretext of "treaty" talks including the display of the white flag on the conference tent, old Mangos Colorados was one of the first to fall, dying with others of his band.

MANUELITO, Navajo
(Tribal Leadership   13)
Born: 1818, Bears Ears, Utah
Died: 1893
Education: Tribal
Significance: *Belief in education for Navajos*

Manuelito, a fiery and brave war chief, became leader of his people at the age of twenty-eight. He spent his lifetime trying to right the wrongs done to the Navajos and to stop his own people in their retaliatory raids on the livestock of the Mexicans and Americans. He suffered with his people through the years when they were taken from their homeland to the Bosque Redondo Reservation near Fort Sumner east of the Rio Grande River. He was one of the eleven major chiefs who negotiated the Treaty of 1868 for the opportunity to return the Navajos to their homeland.

Later, after the long, difficult walk home, he pleaded many times for more of the homeland to be restored to the rightful Navajo owners. His efforts to free Navajos who had been captured into slavery by Mexicans and Ute Indians were relentless. Manuelito encouraged his people to improve their condition through education. To this end, the young were urged to attend school. He died a disheartened man, but the Navajos had found strength in his strength, and regarded him as a strong and courageous leader.

MARIA MARTINEZ, San Ildefonso Pueblo
  (Handicrafts, Education   11, 27)
  Born: 1884, Santa Clara Reservation,
    New Mexico
  Education: Reservation Indian school
  Significance: *Rediscovery of the art of
    black pottery*

Maria Martinez, quite in the tradition of the women of her tribe, made pottery for utilitarian and economic reasons. In so doing, she revealed a particular skill in forming shapes and designs of high aesthetic quality. In the whole process, from the digging of the clay and the earth paints to the finished product, she followed the traditional customs of her people.

Mrs. Martinez has developed her art into an industry, the main occupation of a whole community. She worked for years to rediscover the secret of the highly polished black ware of which a few shards had been found in excavations. She finally learned that it was in the method of firing. Maria was not only a scientific researcher but a teacher. The women of her village are well tutored in her special technique of firing black pottery which has become the main source of income for the pueblo.

The beautiful artistry of her pots makes them collector's items. Her work is found in museums throughout the world and in private collections. Mrs. Martinez was the first woman to be honored by the Indian Council Fire with the Indian Achievement Award (1934). Her many honors include the Craftsman Medal from the American Institute of Architects in 1954, the Palmes Academiques of the French Government in 1954 and the Jane Addams Medal for Distinguished Service to Mankind from Rockford College in 1959. She received an honorary degree from the University of Colorado in 1954. Her life story can be read in *Maria, The Potter of San Ildefonso,* a monograph by Alice Marriott.

MASSASOIT, Wampanoag
  (Tribal Leadership   35)
  Born: Late 1500's in what is now Rhode
    Island
  Died: 1661
  Education: Tribal
  Significance: *Life-long friendship with the
    Pilgrims*

Massasoit, chief of the Wampanoag tribe, was known as Wasamegin (Yellow Feather) among his people. His home was at Sowams, now Warren, Rhode Island. His tribe numbered about 300 in 1620. On March 22, 1621, with sixty braves, he accompanied Samoset and Squanto of the Pawtucket tribe to the Plymouth Colony. Here he negotiated a treaty of peace and friendship with Governor John Carver. He never broke this treaty during his lifetime.

In 1623, he disclosed an Indian plot to destroy part of the white settlement. In 1635, Massasoit made a peace treaty with Roger Williams. He sold the site of Duxbury to the English in 1649. Metacomet, the youngest son of Massasoit, became the famous King Philip.

JOHN JOSEPH MATHEWS, Osage
  (Literature   16)
  Born: 1894, Pawhuska, Oklahoma

Education: B.A., University of
Oklahoma, Norman, Oklahoma; M.A.,
Oxford University, England
Significance: *Furthering of an
understanding of the culture of his
people through his writing*

John Mathews served in the United States
Air Force during World War I. He is a rancher
and an author. Some of his published works are
Wah'KonTah (1932); *Sundown* (1934); *Talking to the Moon* (1945); *Life and Death of an
Oilman* (1951); and *The Osages: Children of the
Middle Waters* (1961). His avocations are wildlife, photography, hunting, and ornithology.

Mathews was a member of the Oklahoma
State Board of Education and was active in the
Osage Indian Council from 1934 to 1942. His
books have won him much recognition and several awards. These include the American Association for State and Local History Merit
Award for *The Osages.* He was also honored
with the Distinguished Service Citation from
the University of Oklahoma.

W. E. "DODE" McINTOSH, Creek
(Tribal Leadership   40)
Born: 1893, Carthage, Tennessee
Education: Normal school
Significance: *Promoting of education for
Indian People*

W. E. "Dode" McIntosh became principal
chief of the Creek Nation. Formerly he had
been a real estate broker, county assessor, and
county treasurer. He served his country during
World War I. He was an active member of the
Oklahoma Historical Society, of the North
Tulsa Chamber of Commerce and was prominent not only in tribal affairs but also in statewide affairs. In these capacities, he had done
much to promote programs for the improvement of housing and education. He stressed education for "every Creek Indian, boy and girl,
and sanitation in every home." He traveled to
the Highlands of Scotland to attend the gathering of the McIntosh Clan. He is a collector of
rare books and a musician. In 1965, McIntosh
was honored with the Official Western Heritage
Award. He also won a place in the Cowboy

Gallery of the National Hall of Fame for Famous American Indians located in Anadarko,
Oklahoma for his lifetime of selfless work in
behalf of his people.

TAYLOR McKENZIE, Navajo
(Medicine   13)
Born: 1931, Rehoboth, New Mexico
Education: Navajo Methodist Mission
School, Farmington, New Mexico;
B.S., Wheaton College, Wheaton,
Illinois; M.D., Baylor University,
Houston, Texas
Significance: *Service to his people in the
field of health*

Dr. Taylor McKenzie is of the Kinlichii' nii
Clan (the Redhouse People). His father, Thilchee, died when Taylor was an infant. His maternal grandmother took care of him while his
mother worked as a housemaid in Shiprock,
Arizona, to help keep him and his grandmother
supplied with food and clothing. As did other
Navajo children, he cared for the sheep, carried
water, chopped wood and helped around the
hogan. Times were hard. His grandmother was
strict with him and expected perfection from
him. This helped develop the self-discipline and
determination necessary to reach his goal. Taylor says, "My grandmother was a midwife and
a skilled herbalist. It has been said that her
abilities and concern with health were transferred to me. In any case, I owe her much."

Shortly after his mother's marriage to Edwin
McKenzie in the late thirties, Dr. McKenzie's
long years of formal education began. His stepfather had a great influence on his life, instilling
the determination to get an education which
took courage, faith, and hard work. Finances
were always a problem, but he found employment and support throughout his long years of
study. In November of 1964, Dr. McKenzie
joined the United States Public Health Service
so that he could serve the Navajo people. He
was assigned to the Public Health Service Clinic
at Kayenta on the Navajo Reservation in New
Mexico and has been on duty there since July,
1967.

One of Dr. McKenzie's chief interests is to encourage young Navajo men and women to enter careers in management, paramedical, and medical services.

D'ARCY McNICKLE, Salish-Kootenai
    (Literature   16)
    Born: 1904, St. Ignatius, Montana
    Education: University of Montana,
        Missoula; Oxford University, England;
        University of Grenoble, France
    Significance: *Leadership in Indian affairs*
D'Arcy McNickle, Daniel M. Madrano and others founded the National Congress of American Indians in 1944. His attention was also given to Indian Development, Inc., of which he served as executive director. His memberships include the American Anthropological Association and the Society of Applied Anthropology. He is the author of the following books: *The Surrounded,* published in 1936; *They Came Here First* in 1949; *Runner in the Sun* in 1954; *Indians and Other Americans* with Harold E. Fey in 1959; *Indian Tribes of the United States - Ethnic and Cultural Survival* in 1962. He was co-author of an article "North American Indians" in the 1970 edition of the Encyclopaedia Britannica.

BILLY MILLS, Oglala Sioux
    (Track   40)
    Born: 1945, South Dakota
    Education: Federal schools
    Significance: *Success in athletics*
Billy Mills has achieved worldwide recognition for his prowess in athletics. In 1964, he won the Olympic Gold Medal in Tokyo for the 10,000 meter race. He is a United States Marine.

LORRAINE MISIASZEK, Colville
    (Tribal Affairs   37)
    Born: ca. 1930, Washington
    Education: B.A., Gonzaga University,
        Spokane, Washington
    Significance: *Belief in education for
        Indians*
Lorraine Misiaszek is a member of the Colville Confederated Tribes of Washington. She served on the Tribal Council from 1956 to 1960, as chairman of both the Economic Development and Planning Committee and the Health, Education and Welfare Committee. In this capacity, she helped formulate plans for an accelerated education program for both children and adults and for the development of tribal assets and natural resources. A strong advocate of greater educational opportunity for her people, she recommended an increase in the college scholarship program which is in effect today. She was instrumental in the development of an adult education program in 1960. Mrs. Misiaszek is also active in Indian organizations at the national level.

During her years of study, Mrs. Misiaszek found time to serve as president of the Western Inter-Tribal Coordinating Council. Upon graduation, she headed the Spokane office of the Washington State Board on Discrimination, concerned with civil rights. Since May of 1968, she has served as a consultant to the Intercultural Education Committee of the Washington State Office of Public Instruction.

N. SCOTT MOMADAY, Cherokee-Kiowa
    (Education, Literature   11, 27, 46)
    Born: 1934, Lawton, Oklahoma
    Education: B.A., University of New
        Mexico, Albuquerque, New Mexico;
        M.A., Ph.D., Stanford University,
        Stanford, California
    Significance: *Focusing world attention on
        the national abuse and alienation of
        the American Indian*
N. Scott Momaday is professor of English and comparative literature at Stanford University. In 1969, he won the Pulitzer Prize for his novel, *House Made of Dawn,* published in 1968. It is a magnificent, heart-breaking account of the American Indian, a proud stranger in his own land.

Momaday comes from a family of distinguished and varied accomplishments. His great grandfather was the first Indian judge when the Kiowa Agency was established in 1888. His father, Al Momaday, is an educator and artist of considerable note. The innovative programs which his father initiated at the Jemez Pueblo School in New Mexico brought the school international recognition. These programs concerned, for example, community involvement in activities for the development of creative ability through arts and crafts. His father has also received worldwide recognition and many honors for his paintings which sensitively depict the way of life of the Indians of the southern plains.

His mother, Natachee Scott Momaday, is a teacher, a former newspaper reporter, and an artist and author of renown. Her books are: *Woodland Princess,* a book of twenty-four poems (1931); *Big Ears* (1937); and *Owl in the Cedar Tree* (1965). Much of her efforts are directed to improving relationships between Indians and their white neighbors.

JACK MONTGOMERY, Cherokee
   (Military   38, 40)
   Born: ca. early 1900's, Oklahoma
   Education: Federal Indian schools
   Significance: *Bravery in the service of his country*

Lieutenant Jack Montgomery served his country during World War II and was honored with the Congressional Medal of Honor, the nation's highest award for "conspicuous gallantry at the risk of life above and beyond the call of duty."

GEORGE MORRISON, Chippewa
   (Art, Education   16)
   Born: 1919, Grand Marrais, Minnesota
   Education: Minneapolis School of Art, Minnesota; Art Students League
   Significance: *Talents as an artist and teacher*

George Morrison teaches art privately and is assistant professor of art in the Rhode Island School of Design. He is also an art therapist and a visiting art critic. He holds membership in various art galleries and associations. His work has been displayed in one, two, and three-man shows, invitational exhibitions, and group shows in the United States, France, Netherlands, South America and Japan. His work is found in many private, corporate, and museum collections in the United States and abroad. He has been honored with many scholarships and fellowships including the Fullbright Scholarship for study in France in 1952–53.

NAMPEYO, Hopi
   (Handicrafts   28)
   Born: Late 1800's, Hano, Arizona
   Education: Reservation school
   Significance: *Rediscovery of an ancient art form*

Nampeyo was a remarkably talented person. Her interest in the old pieces of pottery that were brought to light in the excavation of the ancient Hopi ruins at Sikyatki in 1897 led her to study the old traditional decorative designs. She then successfully revived this art giving it new meaning and life after a long period of decline. Her work is much prized and exhibited in museums.

NARBONA, Navajo
   (Tribal Leadership   13)   ·
   Born: 1766, Navajoland, Arizona
   Died: 1849
   Education: Tribal
   Significance: *Long years of negotiation for peace*

Narbona was born at the beginning of the bloodiest century the peace loving Navajos had ever known. He grew up to become a great leader of his people, a courageous warrior and the strongest peace advocate of his time. In 1773, when Narbona was scarcely seven years old, the Ute Indians and other tribes began a long series of bloody raids during which the Navajo men were killed, the women and children sold as slaves in Mexico, and the sheep and horses confiscated. These actions were promoted by the Spanish governor of the New Mexico Territory in the hope of getting new land for Spanish ranchers.

In 1819 through the efforts of Narbona, a treaty was concluded between the Navajos and the Spaniards. Peace lasted only a few years, however. In 1821 under Mexican rule the devastating raids were renewed. In 1846 Narbona was invited to Fort Macy in Santa Fe, the new seat for the United States government in the south-west, to sign a short-lived peace pact with General Stephen W. Kearney. Narbona and his headmen met together many times to find a solution to the Navajo situation. In 1849 on August 31, Narbona made his last, hopeful effort to achieve peace for his people. He promised to abide by the 1846 Treaty. As a reward for his effort, he and a number of his negotiating party were senselessly killed by white soldiers.

NESOUAQUOIT, Fox
    (Tribal Leadership   22)
    Born: 1791, area of southern Iowa
    Died: Late 1800's
    Education: Tribal
    Significance: *Promotion of his father's peace policy*

Nesouaquoit succeeded his famous father, Chief Chemakasee, in 1835, as chief of the Fox Indians who were at home in the rich, wooded country west and south of Lake Michigan. In the winter of 1837, Nesouaquoit traveled to Washington to talk with President Martin Van Buren regarding the Treaty of 1815, the provisions of which had been overlooked for over twenty years. Chief Nesouaquoit raised the money to pay for the trip through trading "furs and peltries" for three and one-half boxes of silver, the equivalent of 3,500 dollars. President Van Buren recognized the claim after Chief Nesouaquoit stated his case on behalf of his people firmly and eloquently.

Chief Nesouaquoit did not permit whiskey dealers to enter his country, nor traders and trappers to marry with the women of his band. His portrait hangs in the Indian Gallery in Washington, D.C.

LLOYD H. NEW, Cherokee
    (Fashion, Handicrafts   43)
    Born: 1916, Fairland, Oklahoma
    Education: Oklahoma State University, Stillwater; B.F.A., Chicago Art Institute, Illinois; B.A.E., University of Chicago, Illinois
    Significance: *Founding of cultural centers for the advancement of Indian arts and crafts*

Lloyd H. New, known professionaly as Lloyd Kiva, is a designer of international fame. His handwoven Oklahoma Cherokee tweeds and hand-dyed fabrics have brought new excitement in casual clothing for men and women. Top fashion publications have featured these from time to time. New has steadfastly championed the regional expression and use of native form in his designs.

Because of his faith in the future of Indian people, he organized the Arizona Craftsmen Council in Scottsdale, Arizona to promote Indian art. He also established, in partnership with Wes Segner, a new street in Scottsdale named Fifth Avenue. It was on this street that he and two Navajo friends developed a complex of buildings containing twenty-five arts and crafts studios. This was an influential factor in establishing Scottsdale as an important arts and crafts-centered community.

New's most significant accomplishment, however, is his innovative directorship of the famous Institute of American Indian Art in Santa Fe, New Mexico, which is shaping a talented force of new Indian leaders. He has directed art exhibits, instructed art classes, traveled and lectured. During World War II, he enlisted in the Sea Bees of the United States Navy, serving as deck officer in the Pacific. He now holds a lieutenant's commission in the U.S. Naval Reserve. He believes that the future of the Indian lies in the mainstream of American life, contributing that which is true and honest of the Indian culture. He is the author of *Using Cultural Differences as a Basis for Creative Expression,* published in 1964.

BARNEY OLD COYOTE, Crow
    (Government   16)
    Born: 1923, St. Xavier, Montana
    Education: Morningside College, Sioux City, Iowa
    Significance: *Promotion of education for all young people*

Barney Old Coyote has been special assistant to the Secretary of the United States Department of Interior since 1964. He has held positions with the Bureau of Indian Affairs in the following agencies: Fort Yates, North Dakota; Aberdeen, South Dakota; and Rosebud, South Dakota. He was in the National Park Service at the Crow Agency in Montana, and served in the United States Army Air Corps during World War II.

Old Coyote promotes education and participation in activities at the local, state, and national levels for Indians and the young people of all races. He is vitally interested in the conservation of human and natural resources. To achieve his ends, he takes an active part in civic affairs and gives leadership to such organizations in his community as the Congress of Parents and Teachers, the American Legion, and the Knights of Columbus.

FOREST D. OLDS, Miami
  (Agriculture, Tribal Leadership   16)
  Born: 1911, Miami, Oklahoma
  Education: Elementary school
  Significance: *Accomplishments in soil conservation*

Forest D. Olds is chief of the Miami tribe in Oklahoma. He is clerk of the North Fairview School Board, director of the Ottawa County Farm Bureau and the Ottawa County Soil and Water Conservation District. He is vice-president of the Miami Co-op Association, Inc., and of the Miami Metropolitan Area Planning Commission.

His interests are conservation, research into the history of the Miami tribe, and travel to former homesites of the Miamis in Indiana, Kansas, and Ohio. He went to Washington, D.C., to testify before Congressional committees as a representative of the Miami tribe. Olds serves as a resource contact for Dr. Bert Anson, Ball State University, in compiling a history of the Miamis. In 1964, he was honored for his outstanding accomplishments in soil conservation by the Goodyear Tire and Rubber Company.

ONGPATONGA, Omaha
  (Tribal Leadership   22)
  Born: 1760, north central plains
  Died: 1830

Education: Tribal
  Significance: *Adherence to peace and friendliness*

Ongpatonga, or Big Elk as he was known to the white settlers, was chief of the Omahas. This tribe lived along the Missouri River above its confluence with the Mississippi River. Ongpatonga was a distinguished orator. His most famous speech was delivered in 1811 at Portage des Sioux during a council between representatives of the American government and a number of Indian chiefs of different nations. Chief Black Buffalo, a Sioux, died suddenly during the conference and was given a full military burial. Ongpatonga delivered a eulogy that would have been a classic had it been uttered by a Greek or Roman orator.

At a later occasion, during an expedition from 1819 to 1820, he asserted that not one of his nation had ever stained his hands with the blood of a white man. He endeavored to live in peace with his neighbors and attempted to keep them on good terms with one another. He was kindly disposed toward the United States government and people. His portrait hangs in the Indian Gallery of the War Department in Washington, D.C.

CAROL ORR, Colville
  (Art   16)
  Born: 1943, Republic, Washington
  Education: B.A., University of Washington, Seattle
  Significance: *Depiction of the life and culture of her people*

Carol Orr, the wife of J. A. Maas, is a freelance artist specializing in illustrations, portraits, murals, and painting with Indian themes. Her mural commissions include a business mosaic at the University of Washington's Balmer Hall. She is a member of the Lambda Rho Honorary Art Fraternity, University of Washington.

Her work appears in the permanent collection of the United States Department of the Interior Office in Portland, Oregon, and at the Coulee Dam and the Fort Okanogan Museum, both in Washington. Her work is prized by many private collectors.

ALFONSO ORTIZ, Pueblo
  (Anthropology   26, 40)
  Born: 1930, San Juan Pueblo, New
    Mexico
  Education: M.A., Ph.D., University of
    Chicago, Illinois
  Significance: *Research on the Pueblo*
    Indian
Alfonso Ortiz is currently assistant professor of anthropology at Princeton University and has contributed much to the understanding of his people through his writing and lecturing. He is a member of the National Advisory Council on Indian Leadership in connection with the Navajo Community College at Many Farms, Arizona. He also serves on the Executive Committee and Board of Directors of the Association of American Indian Affairs, Inc. He is author of *The Tewa World – Space, Time, Being and Becoming in a Pueblo Society,* published in 1969.

OSCEOLA, Creek
  (Tribal Leadership   5, 21)
  Born: 1804, southeast, possibly Florida
  Died: 1838
  Education: Tribal
  Significance: *Belief in the*
    self-determination of his people
Osceola, referred to as the Swamp Fox by white officers and soldiers, was not a chief either by election or inheritance, but was an acknowledged leader. His great courage, intelligence, and leadership qualities were demonstrated during the First Seminole War, which began in 1819.

In 1832 the not yet defeated Seminole people were called together to sign a treaty with the United States government officials to end hostilities. This treaty known as the Treaty of Payne's Landing was to become hated among the Seminoles. Under this treaty, the Seminoles were to surrender all Florida lands and move to Indian territory in Oklahoma within three years. Escaped slaves from both Indian and white owners who had found refuge among the Seminoles were not permitted to leave, however. The no-Negro decree of the treaty would mean the breaking up of many families.

Although a few of the Seminoles signed, Osceola expressed open contempt for the treaty by furiously plunging his hunting knife into the paper, declaring that he would never agree to the terms. The Second Seminole War began at that moment and was to continue until 1841, four years after the death of Osceola at the age of thirty-four. Devastating guerrilla tactics had been used by Osceola during his years of opposition. Five United States generals under the direction of President Andrew Jackson had been defeated while he and his band had remained elusive deep in the Florida swamps.

In 1837 Osceola was captured by General Jesup through a violation of the truce flag. Osceola could not endure captivity and rapidly wasted away in prison. His portrait, painted while in prison by George Catlin, with whom he became good friends, hangs in the Smithsonian Institution.

JAMES C. OTTIPOBY, Comanche
  (Education, Religion   11)
  Born: 1910, Oklahoma
  Education: B.A., Hope College, Holland,
    Michigan; Western Theological
    Seminary, Holland, Michigan
  Significance: *Belief in the future of*
    Indians through education
James C. Ottipoby was the first Comanche to receive a college degree and the first Indian commissioned an Army Chaplain in World War II. As a boy, he led the nomadic life of the Plains Indian. He had a great fear of white people. Even more, he feared the Indian police who took the children to the "House of Writing." Now he encourages education for young and old alike.

Ottipoby has served on the Winnebago reservation and as a pastor at the Laguna Pueblo in New Mexico. He is pastor of a church in Albuquerque, New Mexico.

ROBERT L. OWEN, Cherokee
(Politics, Finance   4)
Born: 1856, Lynchburg, Virginia
Died: ca. 1940
Education: B.A., Washington and Lee
   University, Lexington, Virginia
Significance: *Service to his people
   through politics*

Robert Owen, after his graduation from Washington and Lee University in 1877, studied law and was admitted to the bar in 1880. He practiced law in the Indian Territory of what is now Oklahoma and organized a bank, of which he was president for ten years. From 1892 to 1896, he was a member of the Democratic National Committee. He was active in politics, and when Oklahoma was admitted as a state in 1907, he was elected to the United States Senate where he served from 1907 to 1925. After this, he returned to the practice of law in Washington, D.C.

ELI SAMUEL PARKER, Seneca
(Military, Government   40)
Born: 1825, Seneca Reservation
Died: Late 1800's
Education: Mission school
Significance: *Service to his country in
   war and peace*

Eli Samuel Parker was a Brigadier General in the Union Army. He drew up the articles of General Robert E. Lee's surrender at Appomattox Courthouse. He was then appointed as Commissioner of Indian Affairs with the Department of Interior.

LINN D. PAUAHTY, Kiowa
(Religion   16)
Born: 1905, Carnegie, Oklahoma
Education: Public school; B.S., Oklahoma
   Agricultural & Mechanical College,
   Stillwater, Oklahoma; B.D., Southern
   Methodist University, Dallas, Texas
Significance: *Research of native music
   and religions*

Linn D. Pauahty became a minister only by chance. Reservation born, he lived in a tepee the first nine years of his life, speaking only the Kiowa language. He was expected to become a medicine man, like his father, grandfather, and great grandfather before him. He had inherited their sacred medicine bag. With the death of his father, however, his mother became a Christian. Stories he read from the Bible gave direction to his life's work. He worked his way through college with scholarship assistance. He was ordained and served in churches among the Kiowa, Comanche, Apache, Osage, Creek, and Choctaw. Later, be became pastor of the Indian Methodist Church in Oneida, Wisconsin.

Because of his fluency in several different Indian languages, Pauahty has translated Christian hymns into these languages. He formed the American Indian Soundchief Company which now has the largest library of tape recorded Indian songs and chants in the country. Going from tribe to tribe among the various groups of Plains Indians, he has compiled their music including the music of the Sun Dance, an ancient rite. In 1960, he was named Outstanding Indian in Leadership Today by the Indian Council Fire, and is the first Indian to be listed in *Who's Who in Methodism.* He has also served on the Governor's Commission on Human Rights.

PEOPEO MOXMOX, Wallawalla
(Scouting   15)
Born: late 1700's, Washington
Died: 1855
Education: Tribal
Significance: *Promotion of peace*

Peopeo Moxmox was a friend of the fur traders and the father of the Christianized Elijah Hedding, who was slain in California. Moxmox served with Fremont and was murdered while a prisoner of the Oregon Volunteers, six months after the Walla Walla Council (June 7, 1855), in which he had participated.

FRANK PERATROVICH, Tlingit
(Politics   40)
Born: 1910, Alaska
Education: Federal schools
Significance: *Service to his people
   through politics*

Frank Peratrovich is an Alaskan lawmaker, having served in the Territorial and State Legislatures since 1944. He was president of the Senate and chairman of the Legislative Council. In 1955, he was vice-president of the Alaska Constitutional Statehood Convention. He was re-elected to the House of Representatives in 1968.

PETALASHARO, Skidi Pawnee
  (Civil Rights   30)
  Born: ca. 1800, area of Nebraska
  Died: ca. 1833
  Education: Tribal
  Significance: *Dispelling the myths surrounding the human sacrificial rites of his tribe*

Petalasharo was the son of Lachelesharo, chief of the Skidi Pawnee tribe. He later succeeded his father as chief. The Skidi Pawnee had long practiced the custom of sacrificing human victims to the Great Star, or the planet Venus, which in their belief controlled the spring growing season. Petalasharo rescued a victim, a kidnapped young Comanche girl, from this rite in the spring of 1817.

When the news reached Washington, D.C., he was invited to Miss White's elite school there. He was decorated and praised for his action. The girls presented him with a silver medal which bore the legend, "To the Bravest of the Brave." On one side of the medal was a figure of a man and woman in flight; on the other, a tree, some people and a scaffold. This medal was found in 1883 near Fullerton, Nebraska, at an Indian burial site.

Petalasharo later rescued another victim, a captured Spaniard, from the same fate by persuading the captors to "sell" him the victim, whom Petalasharo set free. No further efforts to immolate victims were made.

POCAHONTAS, Powhatan Algonquian
  (Diplomacy   35)
  Born: ca. 1595, in what is now Virginia
  Died: 1617
  Education: Tribal and Christian tutoring
  Significance: *Promotion of friendly relations with white settlers*

Pocahontas was the daughter of Powhatan, chief of the Powhatan Confederacy of Algonquian tribes living in what is now Virginia. In 1608 one year after the English had landed and established Jamestown, Captain John Smith, leader of the settlement, was reportedly saved from execution by Pocahontas. She was only thirteen at the time. In 1613 at the age of eighteen, Pocahontas was taken prisoner by the English as security for English prisoners and stolen arms. She was taken to Jamestown where she impressed the acting governor, Sir Thomas Dale. She was baptized with the Christian name Rebecca and was respected by the colonists.

In April of 1614, Pocahontas married John Rolfe, an Englishman, with the blessing of her father, Chief Powhatan, and the consent of Governor Dale. Both the English and the Indians regarded the marriage as a bond of friendship between the two cultures and from it dated a peace which continued during her lifetime.

In 1616 Pocahontas sailed for England with a retinue of young Indian girls. There she was received with the honors due a princess. She was entertained by the Bishop of London and presented at court. During her stay, Pocahontas endeared herself to the English people by her gracious manner and helped to build a bridge of understanding. In 1617 just prior to returning to her homeland, Pocahontas died, leaving her husband and son, Thomas Rolfe. Thomas Rolfe later returned to Virginia where many of his descendants still live.

PONTIAC, Ottawa
  (Tribal Leadership   35)
  Born: ca. 1720, in what is now Ohio
  Died: 1769
  Education: Tribal
  Significance: *Organization of one of the greatest alliances of Indians in American history*

Pontiac, a powerful and persuasive speaker, was the great chief of the Ottawa tribe. Their homeland was the Great Lakes country where the Ottawas and other Algonquian tribes had lived at peace with the French and had intermarried with them during the French occupation of the area. In 1760 the French were defeated by the English. Pontiac was still inclined to be friendly, but the Indians soon discovered that the English looked on them as unwelcome "squatters" on land that now "belonged" to the English. In 1763 Pontiac inspired the alliance of the great Algonquian tribes and became their military leader in the subsequent revolt against the British. This revolt is known as the "Pontiac Conspiracy."

Pontiac led coordinated attacks on British-held posts and within a few months nine forts had been captured and a tenth was later found abandoned. Pontiac was victorious in the bloody battle of Fort Detroit, the eleventh British fort. He was defeated, however, at the twelfth, Fort Pitt, in Pennsylvania. He had expected to be saved by the French, not knowing that a British-French Treaty had been signed in London the previous year. Pontiac had no choice but to abandon his sieges, which he did in 1765. He became a target of the jealousy and hostility of the Algonquian tribes which he had brought together. He was later murdered in Illinois by a Peoria Indian.

POPE, Pueblo
   (Military   35)
   Born: ca. 1640, in what is now New
      Mexico
   Died: 1688
   Education: Tribal
   Significance: *Organization of Indian
      resistance against the tyranny of the
      Spanish*
Pope was a medicine man from a Tewa Pueblo renamed "San Juan" by the Spanish. The Pueblo Indians had lived in villages along the Rio Grande River for hundreds of years before the coming of the Spanish. The Spanish found them to be successful farmers, potters, and weavers of fine cloth, living in permanent homes of heavy timber and adobe. Under Spanish rule, they suffered long. Their ceremonies and religious practices were forbidden. They had to pay heavy taxes in corn, cloth, or labor. However, under the leadership of Pope, the

Pueblo Indians began to resist Spanish rule and the intrusion of colonists.

Pope was imprisoned around 1675 by the Spanish under suspicion of witchcraft and the killing of several missionaries. After his release, Pope led the Pueblo people in an attack against the Spanish at Santa Fe on August 13, 1680. Four hundred "occupiers" were killed and the Spanish were forced to retreat to El Paso. Pope set about to erase all traces of the "Metal People," as the Spanish were called. He was received with great honor as he traveled from pueblo to pueblo.

POPOVI DA, San Ildefonso Pueblo
   (Handicrafts   40)
   Born: 1922, Santa Fe, New Mexico
   Education: Canyon School of Arts, New
      Mexico
   Significance: *Promotion of the culture
      and economy of his people through his
      art*
Popovi Da, the son of Maria Martinez, world famous potter, has carried on in his mother's tradition. He is a noted potter in his own right, teaching the art to his people. The black pottery unique to the San Ildefonso Pueblo is the major industry of the people. Popovi Da is in much demand as a lecturer. He served as chairman of the All-Indian Pueblo Council from 1950 to 1952, and was governor of his pueblo, the San Ildefonso, in 1959, 1960, and 1962.

SOFIA STRAND PORTER, Tlingit
   (Music, Education   37)
   Born: ca. 1935, Sitka, Alaska
   Education: B.Mus.Ed., College of
      Emporia, Kansas; University of
      Nevada, Reno
   Significance: *Involvement in the activities
      of her community*
Sofia Strand Porter has made a career in the performing arts. While in college, she received the highest award in the music department and won a graduate assistantship at the University of Nevada. Since 1961, Mrs. Porter has made her home in Sitka, Alaska, where she is musical director and accompanist for musical shows and

little theater productions. She is active in community affairs and is past president of Mu Phi Epsilon. She is a member of the American Association of University Women, the Sitka Concert Association, and the Barnof Little Theater Guild.

Mrs. Porter has appeared in the 1967 edition of *Outstanding Young Women of America,* and the 1968 edition of *Outstanding Personalities of the West and Midwest.* In June, 1968, she was one of six nominated by the Governor's Council on Arts to attend the Alaska Festival of Music in Achorage. Since 1967 Mrs. Porter has taught piano and chorus at Mt. Edgecumbe High School in Sitka, Alaska.

POWHATAN, Algonquian
(Tribal Leadership 35)
Born: ca. 1547, area of Virginia
Died: 1618
Education: Tribal
Significance: *Successful attempts to maintain peace with the first white settlers in America*

Powhatan, a tall and dignified man, known as Wahunsonacock among his people, was the chief of the giant Powhatan Confederacy which he had built during his lifetime. It was a union of the powerful Algonquian tribes and a number of separate tribes. It numbered over 200 villages. Powhatan and his people were generally friendly and helpful to the pioneers of John Smith's colony during their first difficult years. He could have easily stamped them out or left them to starve. Instead every effort was made to maintain peace and good will.

Legend has it that because of the pleas of Pocahontas, the daughter of Powhatan, John Smith was pardoned even though he had intruded too far into Indian territory. With the increased intrusion of settlers and with broken promises on each side, several years of minor warfare developed. Chief Powhatan asked at one point, "Why should you take by force from us that which you can obtain by law?" Due to the marriage of his daughter to the Englishman, John Rolfe, Powhatan maintained peace with the English until his death.

PUSHMATAHA, Choctaw
(Tribal Leadership 22)
Born: 1764, area of Mississippi
Died: 1824
Education: Tribal
Significance: *Support of the colonists in the Revolutionary War*

Pushmataha was a distinguished chief of the Choctaw Nation. Their homeland was the area which is now the State of Mississippi. He was a war chief of great prowess at the age of twenty. During the Revolutionary War, he led parties against the British and their Indian allies. His vengefulness against his enemies was in strict adherence to the Indian code of honor. He was invited to visit Washington, D.C., in 1824. He met Lafayette, who was on a triumphal tour of the United States at the time. Pushmataha visited the Secretary of War, and was to have addressed Congress, but his sudden death from croup intervened. The celebrated John Randolph eulogized Pushmataha from the Senate floor. His attachment to the American government had been steady and unshaken. He was awarded a posthumous medal by President James Monroe as a testimony of respect to his memory.

QUANAH PARKER, Comanche
(Tribal Leadership 35)
Born: 1845, Southwest Plains, possibly Texas
Died: 1911
Education: Tribal
Significance: *Helping his people adjust to reservation life*

Quanah Parker was the oldest son of Chief Nokoni and Cynthia Ann Parker, who had been kidnapped from her home in east Texas in 1835, when she was about ten years old. She had grown up with the Comanche and married Chief Nokoni. The Comanche had been generally friendly with the white settlers, but became their bitter enemies when the Texas settlers took over their best buffalo hunting grounds. Then, for many years, the word "Comanche" meant terror on the Texas frontier. The fiercest of the Comanches was the Kwahadi band in which

Quanah Parker grew up. When his father died, he became chief, a tribute to the young man's ability and intelligence since chieftainships were not ordinarily inherited among the Comanche.

The Medicine Lodge Treaty of 1867 assigned the Comanche with other tribes to reservations, but Quanah Parker refused to sign the treaty. He continued to hunt buffalo on the plains and to plunder Texas settlements and the camps of the illegal buffalo hunters until 1875, when he surrendered. He resolved to adjust to the dominant civilization, and he did. His real career began at this point.

Quanah Parker influenced the remaining renegade Comanche bands to come to the southwestern Oklahoma reservation and for the next thirty years, he was the industrious organizer and able leader of the Confederation of the Comanches, Apaches, and Kiowas. He was their influential businessman and their guide to white civilization. He encouraged home building, agriculture, and education, yet held fast to important Indian beliefs and ceremonies. He spoke both English and Spanish fluently and traveled frequently to Washington on behalf of his people. In 1957, Quanah Parker was re-buried at Fort Sill, Oklahoma, with full military honors.

JOHN C. RAINER, Taos Pueblo
   (Education, Tribal Affairs   11)
   Born: ca. 1920, Taos Pueblo, New
     Mexico
   Education: Santa Fe Indian School, New
     Mexico; Bacone College, Oklahoma;
     B.A., University of Redlands,
     California; M.Ed., University of
     Southern California, Los Angeles
   Significance: *Promotion of good*
    education for Indians

John Rainer spoke only the language of his tribe until the age of thirteen. His schooling was pursued in the face of the bitter resentment of the Taos Pueblo people who are inclined to be resistant to infiltration from the outside world. The Taos Pueblo is virtually a walled fortress and the people remain aloof. They have successfully coped with the raids of other Indian tribes,

the invasion of the Spanish, the occupation of the Mexicans and then the Americans who finally gave them full citizenship.

Wanting to return to his people, Rainer concentrated on a career in education. He taught in reservation schools, served as principal in others, and then became principal of the school in his own village of Taos. In 1950, he was appointed executive secretary of the National Congress of American Indians. This work was interrupted on receipt of a scholarship for graduate study from the John Hay Whitney Foundation.

Following this, he was appointed director of the rehabilitation program for the Ute Mountain Indians, tribally financed from oil royalties and a thirty-two million dollar claim award. Rainer was then elected to represent the 22,000 Pueblo Indians of New Mexico at a conference in Washington, D.C., concerning jurisdiction of state and civil authorities. He was later elected as chairman of the All Pueblo Council comprising the eighteen pueblos of northern New Mexico. In addition, he maintains a mercantile store in the Taos Pueblo and manages a cattle ranch. His civic activities are many, extending to the state and national levels.

RANTCHEWAIME, Iowa
   (Civil Rights   22)
   Born: ca. 1750, area of what is now Iowa
   Died: ca. 1790
   Education: Tribal
   Significance: *Support of the peace policies*
    of her husband

Rantchewaime, translated Female Flying Pigeon, was a beautiful Iowa woman, the wife of Chief Mahaskah, The Elder, and the mother of Chief Mahaskah, The Young. Her portrait is displayed in the Indian Gallery of the Department of War in Washington, D.C. She was gentle, generous, and devoted to her husband. She promoted harmony and peaceful pursuits among the women of the tribe, and contributed to the welfare of the people by giving them food and blankets. She was extremely religious, praying and fasting often. She was accustomed to assembling hundreds of the women of her tribe to preach morality to them. By her virtues and good works, she aspired to reach the Indian version of heaven.

RED CLOUD, Oglala Sioux
  (Tribal Leadership   35)
  Born: 1821, what is now Wyoming
  Died: 1909
  Education: Tribal
  Significance: *Fighting for the land and rights of his people*

Red Cloud, one of the greatest of all Sioux chiefs, stands alone in the history of the American West as the chief who won a war with the United States. General George Crook described him as "a magnificent specimen of physical manhood, as full of action as a tiger." In 1865, the Dakotas, more commonly known as the Sioux, bitterly opposed the building of the Bozeman Trail, a major route with protective forts across the Sioux hunting grounds to the newly found gold mines of Montana. The Sioux found a powerful voice of opposition in Red Cloud. Through all attempts at negotiation, he remained adamant with great force and dignity.

In 1866 troops began to occupy Wyoming's Powder River country. This marked the beginning of Red Cloud's War which was to continue with relentless harassment for two years. In 1868 in another attempt at negotiation, Red Cloud's ultimatum was complete abandonment of all posts and of all further attempts to open the Bozeman Trail. The garrisons were withdrawn and the forts burned to the ground before Red Cloud signed the Fort Laramie Treaty which created the vast area known as the Great Dakota, or Sioux, Reservation. Red Cloud traveled to Washington, D.C., on several occasions, and his views became known to newspaper readers throughout the country.

He kept his promise to live peacefully and would not join the other Sioux chiefs in a declaration of war after the deliberate 1875 and 1876 provocations by the United States government. The Sioux Indians realized that the die was cast when General Sheridan was given orders to reduce the Sioux to complete subjugation. At this time, the words of Red Cloud were, "I have signed the Treaty of 1868, and I intend to keep it." Through this statement, as a point of honor, Chief Red Cloud towered far above the five generals who had signed the treaty with him. His portrait hangs in the Smithsonian Institution in Washington, D.C.

The Treaty of 1868 had given the Black Hills of the Dakotas to the Sioux "for as long as grass shall grow and waters flow," but the discovery of gold in the Black Hills put a dramatic end to that.

RED JACKET, Seneca
  (Tribal Leadership   22)
  Born: 1756, Seneca, New York
  Died: 1830
  Education: Tribal
  Significance: *Support of the colonists during the Revolutionary War*

Red Jacket was an eminent chief of the Senecas, the most important and powerful tribe of the celebrated League of the Iroquois. He was known to his people as Sagoyouwath, translated Keeper Awake, which was most appropriate to the vigilance of his character. His more familiar name of Red Jacket was acquired when he was given a richly embroidered scarlet jacket for the service of his tribe to the British. His running ability and keen memory led to his employment as a dispatch carrier for the colonists during the Revolutionary War, even though his tribe fought under the British during that war. In 1792 he was decorated by General George Washington for his service in the Revolution.

He was the counselor, negotiator, and orator of his tribe and was considered the perfect man in every respect. Later in life, he and his tribe became true and faithful allies of the Americans. Red Jacket continued his life-long opposition to war and tried through peaceful means to halt the encroachment of the white man upon the Indians and to preserve the independence of his people.

BENJAMIN REIFEL, Brule Sioux
  (Politics   1, 11, 40)
  Born: 1906, Parmellee, South Dakota

Education: B.S., M.S., South Dakota
   State University, Brookings; Ph.D.,
   Harvard University, Cambridge,
   Massachusetts
Significance: *Service to his people
   through politics*

Benjamin Reifel is a member of the United States House of Representatives from South Dakota. From his early boyhood, Reifel had an intense interest in his home area and wanted to do something about the improvement of ranching and farming practices. He attended agricultural school during the winter months and worked at home the remainder of the year. His mother, a full-blooded Indian without formal education, spoke broken English only when necessary. His white father had settled in Indian country as a young cowhand. The family lived on a ranch. Reifel says that "Our mother, in spite of her limitations, was instrumental in shaping our lives to meet the challenge of an integrated life. She had the foresight to know that education was essential to bridge the gap from the old to the new."

Reifel has contributed much to the betterment of his people through active leadership among them and through his office on the national level. He believes that Indians can have a meaningful part in the life of America today but that it must evolve through Indian planning and struggle. He was honored in 1956 with the Outstanding Indian Award at the All American Indian Days in Sheridan, Wyoming. He is a member of the National Congress of American Indians and president of the National Fellowship of Indian Workers. He saw military service in Europe during World War II.

His brothers, Alexander and Albert, also "caught the spark that set off the will to learn." Alexander is a civil engineer with the Corps of Engineers of the Southwest Pacific Division with offices in Los Angeles. He is responsible for contract plans and specifications in connection with channel improvement for flood control projects. He served as an Infantry Unit Commander in Europe during World War II. The GI Bill and supplementary work enabled him to secure his professional training.

Albert, the youngest of the three Reifel brothers, is a member of the medical staff at the Veteran's Hospital in Sioux Falls, Iowa. Dr. Reifel learned to fear tuberculosis when he was a child. It was the leading cause of death among Indians. His interest in this problem deepened with his own fight against the invasion of tuberculosis. He determined early on a medical career in the face of many serious obstacles. With the help of scholarships, work, and dedicated determination, he achieved his goal.

ALLIE REYNOLDS, Creek
   (Baseball   40)
   Born: ca. 1920, Oklahoma
   Education: Oklahoma State University,
      Stillwater
   Significance: *Singular achievement in
      baseball*

Allie Reynolds, perhaps the most noted of living Indian athletes, retired from Major League baseball in 1954. He was selected for the Oklahoma State University's Hall of Fame in 1958. He had also won the Sid Mercer Player of the Year Award from the New York Sports Writers Guild in 1951. He is a sports writer, president of the Atlas Mud Company of Oklahoma City, and sports director for state and national organizations.

In 1951, he pitched two no-hit games, the first in the history of the American League, and he was second among modern players to have thirty-seven shutouts. He was a member of the American League All-Star Team seven years. In 1938, he captained the college baseball team and pitched a no-hit game that year. Reynolds entered professional baseball in the Minor Leagues in 1939. He moved to the Major Leagues in 1942 with the Cleveland Indians. He was traded to the New York Yankees in 1947.

JOHN RIDGE, Cherokee
   (Journalism, Education   44)
   Born: ca. 1790, Cherokee Territory East,
      now Georgia
   Died: 1836
   Education: Mission schools

Significance: *Promotion of education and self-determination*

John Ridge, whose Indian name meant "Walking the Mountain Tops," was a full-blooded Cherokee, the second son of the popular, distinguished Cherokee chief, Major Ridge, so named by General Andrew Jackson. His parents believed that the principles of civilization were grounded in education, so his schooling began early in the home of a missionary. During his four years at the Foreign Mission School in Cornwall, Connecticut, Ridge met and married Sarah Northrup, a young white woman.

After graduation from college, Ridge returned home with his young bride to take an active part in the affairs of his people at a time when they were being stirred by the winds of change. The Cherokee were developing an independent nation. Sequoyah, known also as George Guess, had invented the alphabet which gave the Cherokees a written language. This resulted in the establishment of schools, missions, and a newspaper.

Ridge had youth, enthusiasm, education, and piety. Immediately, he became the writer for the Cherokee newspaper, *The Cherokee Phoenix,* and a leader in the new government which was patterned after the United State government. In 1838, however, the eastern Cherokee Nation of Georgia was forcibly moved to the reservation west of the Mississippi. Here the internationally acclaimed Cherokee government was continued, but the leadership of Ridge was cut short by assassination.

HOWARD ROCK, Eskimo
(Journalism 16)
Born: 1911, Point Hope, Alaska
Education: University of Washington, Seattle
Significance: *Promotion of education and welfare*

Howard Rock is the editor of the *Tundra Times* in Fairbanks, Alaska. He served in the United States Army Airways Communication System during World War II. He is actively involved with the Inupiat Paitot, an Eskimo organization in northern Alaska, having served as

its executive secretary. He is interested in painting and in designing Alaskan scenes in ivory.

EDWARD ROGERS, Chippewa
(Law 11)
Born: 1885, Minnesota
Education: Carlisle Institute, Pennsylvania; Dickinson College, Carlisle, Pennsylvania; LL.B., University of Minnesota, Minneapolis
Significance: *Dedication to the progress of his people*

Edward Rogers practiced law for two years after which he became a Probate Judge. He was subsequently elected county attorney, a position he held for forty years. Rogers is the son of an early day logger who operated a number of logging camps in northern Minnesota. He was born when his mother was making maple sugar in an Indian camp.

Keeping in close touch with Indian matters, Rogers was tribal attorney from 1941 to 1945. He has materially assisted his people to self-realization and determination. He believes that wardship under government supervision diminishes industry and resourcefulness. He also believes that discriminatory laws with respect to Indians should be repealed.

Rogers, former president of the District Bar Association and former vice-president of the National Congress of American Indians, received the Outstanding County Attorney of the United States Award in 1962.

HAROLD E. ROGERS, Seneca
(Military 38)
Born: early 1900's, Miami, Oklahoma
Died: 1944
Education: Haskell Institute, Lawrence, Kansas; Sherman Institute, Riverside, California; Riverside Junior College, California
Significance: *Valor in service to his country*

T-Sgt. Harold E. Rogers served with the 8th Air Force based in England during World War II. He flew twenty-five missions and was awarded the highest honor in aviation, the Distinguished Flying Cross and the Air Medal with nine oak leaf clusters. T-Sgt. Rogers then served as instructor in the United States for six months after which he returned to action with the 15th Air Force based in Italy. He was reported missing in action in 1944 while on a mission over Budapest. The Purple Heart was awarded to him posthumously. His wife, a Potawatomi from Kansas, was a student at Haskell Institute with her husband. He was studying law at the time he was called into service.

WILL ROGERS, Cherokee
  (Entertainment   16)
  Born: 1879, Oologah, Oklahoma
  Died: 1935
  Education: Kemper Military Academy,
    Booneville, Missouri
  Significance: *Ability to make a nation
    laugh during the Depression years of
    the 1930's*

Will Rogers was a noted homespun philosopher of international fame and is still regarded as one of the greatest humorists of all time. He was a talented writer, and his news commentaries appeared in over 350 daily newspapers. In 1926, he toured Europe as President Calvin Coolidge's ambassador of good will. The following year, 1927, a nation of admirers chuckled about his *Letters of A Self-Made Diplomat to His President.*

Of his two years at the Military Academy, Will Rogers said "I spent one in the guard house and the other in the 4th grade." He left school in 1898 and became a cowboy in the Texas Panhandle. Then he drifted to Argentina and turned up in South Africa a few years later as a member of Texas Jack's Wild West Circus. Rogers made his first stage appearance in New York City in 1905. He reached fame in the Ziegfeld Follies of 1916. In 1918 he began his motion picture career. In 1934 he made his first appearance in a stage play, in Eugene O'Neill's *Ah, Wilderness.*

Rogers married Betty Blake, an Arkansas school teacher, in 1908. They had four children. Rogers' death came suddenly in a tragic plane crash near Point Barrow, Alaska, while on a flight to the Orient with Wiley Post.

JOHN ROSS, Cherokee
  (Civil Rights   44)
  Born: 1790, Turkeytown, Alabama
  Died: 1866
  Education: First school of the Cherokee
    Nation
  Significance: *Fight for the rights of his
    people*

John Ross was born near the Coosa River in Alabama of a Scotch father, Daniel Ross, and a Cherokee-Scotch mother, Mollie McDonald. He was privately tutored and then educated in the first school of the Cherokee Nation and still later in the popular school in Kingston, Tennessee. He was mediator in the Treaty of 1817, followed by constant untiring effort to secure justice and relief for his suffering people.

In 1828 at the age of thirty-eight, the blue-eyed Ross became the principal chief of the Eastern Cherokees. He did his best to prevent the removal of his people from Georgia, but in 1838 with all hope gone, all he could do was to get his people west as safely as possible. The forced journey westward known as the "Trail of Tears" took over six months in the hardest part of the year with a loss of one-fourth of the Cherokee Nation, 4,000 of the 16,000 who started the walk west. In the new land, Ross continued as chief until his death, beloved by his people. He had never given up his dream of seeing his people elevated to a place of equality in the white man's society.

RAMON A. ROUBIDEAUX, Brule Sioux
  (Law   11)
  Born: 1922, Rosebud Reservation, South
    Dakota
  Education: Mission schools; Haskell
    Institute, Lawrence, Kansas; B.A.,
    LL.B., George Washington University,
    Washington, D.C.
  Significance: *Protection of the civil rights
    of Indians*

Ramon A. Roubideaux enlisted in the Army Air Corps shortly after he became eighteen. He was commissioned second lieutenant and served overseas in World War II as a Radar Observer-Navigator in a night fighter squadron. After twenty-four missions, he was promoted to first lieutenant and was awarded the Air Medal with oak leaf clusters and two battle stars. The turning point in his life came while on leave. He was not permitted to enter a public dance hall because he was an Indian. Unsuccessfully attempting to secure legal counsel to prosecute the dance hall manager for violation of civil rights, Roubideaux was so infuriated that he vowed to become an attorney in order to right such injustices.

Congressman Francis Case of South Dakota, on hearing about the incident, offered Roubideaux employment in his Washington office. With help from the GI Bill, he took up his law studies. He is now state's attorney for Stanley County, South Dakota. He was elected to this post in 1954, after a period as private and city attorney in Pierre, South Dakota. Roubideaux believes that the future of the Indian lies within himself and that independence will be reached when programs and policies necessary to improve conditions come from Indians themselves.

SACAGAWEA, Shoshone
(Interpreting   2, 32, 35)
Born: 1788, area of what is now Idaho
Died: 1884
Education: Tribal
Significance: *Participation in the Lewis and Clark Expedition*

Sacagawea was captured as a young girl by the Minnetaree or Hidatsa Indians who gave her the name Tsakakawias, meaning Bird Woman. She was sold to Toussaint Charbonneau, a French trapper and trader. Sacagawea and her newborn son, Baptiste, accompanied her husband on the expedition.

Sacagawea was not an official guide of the expedition, as has been claimed, but she did act as interpreter. She taught the men how to find edible roots and medicinal herbs. She pointed out occasional landmarks familiar from her childhood, made buckskins and moccasins, and

in general was of invaluable aid particularly as a symbol of the peaceful intentions of the expedition. In the Rocky Mountains, the Lewis and Clark party encountered a band of Shoshones. Sacagawea was overjoyed when she recognized her brother, Cameahwait, chief of the band. He provided horses, supplies, and a respite to the weary travelers. Sacagawea has become an American heroine. There are more monuments to her than any other American woman.

BUFFY SAINTE-MARIE, Cree
(Entertainment   1)
Born: 1942, Craven, Saskatchewan, Canada
Education: B.A., University of Massachusetts, Amherst
Significance: *Crusade for a better understanding of all Indians and giving them the proper place in the historical records*

Buffy Sainte-Marie is a well-known recording artist and contemporary folk singer. She grew up in Wakefield, Massachusetts and in 1963 moved into the folk places of New York. She began recording in 1964. She is also a freelance writer and the associate editor of *The Native Voice,* a Vancouver, British Columbia publication. As a folk singer, she is best known for songs and poems directly related to past and present American Indians, the best known of which is her bitter protest song, "My Country 'Tis of Thy People You're Dying." She is an authority on North American Indian music and folklore and has contributed to *The Native Voice, American Indian Horizons,* and *Boston Broadside.* She is active in Indian affairs.

Miss Sainte-Marie has lived on or visited reservations in fifteen states and four provinces. She has traveled, lectured and sung in England, France, Canada, Italy, and Mexico. She performs in concert and on television internationally and in major American cities.

JOE SIMMON SANDO, Jemez Pueblo
(Tribal Affairs, Education   40)
Born: ca. 1920, New Mexico

Education: B.A., University of New
Mexico, Albuquerque
Significance: *Leadership in Indian
education*

Joe Simmon Sando is the director of the Pueblo Indian Education Talent Search Project for the University of New Mexico. He is chairman of the All Indian Pueblo Housing Authority and of the Education Committee of the All Indian Pueblo Council. He is a member of the executive board of the Northern New Mexico Economic Development District. Sando is a World War II Navy veteran. He is also the author of numerous articles on Indian problems and history.

ALBERT GEORGE (CHIC) SANDOVAL,
Navajo
(Tribal Affairs   13)
Born: 1892, Cabezon, New Mexico
Died: 1968
Education: Albuquerque Indian School,
New Mexico
Significance: *Dedication to improving the
conditions of his people*

Albert George Sandoval of the Kinlichii'nii Clan (the Red House People) learned English in the elementary school in Albuquerque, New Mexico. This knowledge later led to a job as interpreter at the mission in Chinle, Arizona. In 1914 he became a teacher at the Chinle Indian School. For many years, Sandoval alternated between work for the Franciscan Fathers and for the United States Bureau of Indian Affairs. He interpreted for those who had no knowledge of the Navajo language. In the late 1920's and early 1930's, he worked as a researcher at Yale, Harvard, and Chicago Universities. He was a district supervisor for the Bureau of Indian Affairs as well as a member of the Navajo Tribal Council. After retirement in 1960, he was consulted by people from all parts of the United States for information regarding Navajo customs, ceremonials, legends, and myths. He was a man of ability and humility and worked for his people with energy, faith, and devotion.

ANTONIO CEBOLLA SANDOVAL, Navajo
(Tribal Affairs   13)
Born: 1807, near Mt. Taylor, New
Mexico
Died: 1859
Education: Tribal
Significance: *Cooperation with the
Americans while maintaining his
loyalty to his people*

Antonio Cebolla Sandoval of the Totsohnii Clan (People of the Big Water) learned Spanish when he was very young and the southwest was under Spanish rule. In 1821 things changed for the peace loving Navajo people. The Mexicans overthrew the Spanish government. A bounty was put on the scalp of every Navajo, and Navajos were considered the best of all the Indians in the southwest for the slave markets of Mexico. Because of his knowledge of Spanish, Sandoval became the interpreter of the great Navajo leader, Narbona, who tried to negotiate peace with the Mexican government. After the Mexican-American War of 1846–48, Sandoval was invaluable as an interpreter to new American officials. Sandoval was considered a traitor by some Navajos for cooperating with the Americans, but he did lead a band of over 400 Navajos for years, in freedom from both Mexicans and Americans. Though many Navajos distrusted him, he worked, fought, and suffered to take care of his people.

AGNES SAVILLA, Mohave
(Tribal Affairs   11, 37)
Born: ca. 1905, Arizona
Education: Federal Schools
Significance: *Lifetime of service to Indian
people*

Mrs. Agnes Savilla, chairman of the Colorado River Tribal Health, Education and Welfare Committee since 1955, is a well-known tribal historian and genealogist. She is active in developing and encouraging the preservation of arts and crafts on the Colorado River Reservation in Arizona. She served continuously on the Tribal Council from December, 1950, until her retirement in December of 1968. She was selected Arizona Fair Lady in 1964, for personal and career achievements, a tribute to Arizona working women. She is a member of the National Congress of American Indians, serving as regional vice-president from 1967 to 1968. Mrs. Savilla was one of the United States delegates to the Inter-American Congress on Indians in Quito, Ecuador in 1964.

SEATHL, Suquamish
   (Tribal Leadership   24, 35)
   Born: 1786, area of Seattle, Washington
   Died: 1866
   Education: Tribal and Catholic
      missionary schools
   Significance: *Devotion to the promotion
      of peace*
Seathl was the great chief of the Duwamish Confederacy, an alliance of tribes of northwestern Washington, formed by his father, the famous peace loving Chief Schweabe. In 1792, as a boy, Seathl witnessed the arrival in Puget Sound of Vancouver's "immense white-winged bird ship," the Discovery. The wonderful new riches and the friendliness of the first white men he had ever seen impressed young Seathl, who became convinced as he grew up that peace, not war, was the right path for all men to follow. It was a revolutionary belief because battle and pillaging were long established in the life of Pacific Coast Indians. When Catholic missionaries entered the northwest in the 1830's, he became a convert to Christianity and inaugurated regular morning and evening prayer meetings among his people, a practice they continued after his death.

White settlers from Boston who founded present day Seattle on the shores of Puget Sound in 1851, received unlimited friendship and help from chief Seathl. By 1855, with more and more white immigrants settling in the Pacific Northwest, it was necessary for Isaac I. Stevens, the first Governor of the Washington Territory, to call the leaders of the Duwamish Confederacy together to negotiate plans for the removal of all Indians to a reservation. Chief Seathl, over six feet tall, broad shouldered, deep chested, an impressive and powerful orator, made his reply in a resounding voice which all

the people assembled along the beach could hear. The dignified old leader's words, now classic, were beautifully poetic, touched with sadness and resignation. He was the first to sign the Port Elliott Treaty of 1855, which meant evacuation by canoes and sloops from their traditional coastal home to the Port Madison Reservation. Here Seathl faithfully supported the white cause, at the same time continuing to be a true and powerful leader of his own people.

SEQUOYAH, Cherokee
   (Invention, Education   20, 35)
   Born: late 1700's, Willstown, Alabama
   Died: 1843
   Education: Tribal
   Significance: *Inventive genius which
      included the Cherokee alphabet*
Sequoyah, or George Guess, as he was more commonly called, was the son of a white father named Gist and a Cherokee mother who gave him the name Sequoyah. From early childhood, Sequoyah showed his inventive genius which flowered at the time that the Cherokee had reached a remarkable level of civilization. They were good farmers, owned plows, wagons, and thousands of livestock. They wove their own cloth from cotton raised in their own fields for clothing of their own fashioning. They operated saw mills, grist mills, blacksmith shops, and ferries, and built roads, schools, and churches. They governed themselves with a constitutional system patterned after that of the United States.

Sequoyah was amiable, accommodating, unassuming, and industrious. He was a renowed woodsman and hunter until crippled by an accident. This, however, did not deter him from enlisting in the War of 1812, during which he fought under Andrew Jackson. His inventiveness knew no limits in labor-saving devices and implements. He mastered silversmithing and the art of drawing and engraving. Later, he became fascinated with writing in English and set out to develop a Cherokee alphabet. His tribesmen became frightened of his strange symbols and suspected him of witchcraft. His cabin and all of his working papers were burned, whereupon Sequoyah left his home and went

west to Arkansas to live with the Western Cherokees who had emigrated there earlier.

Here, after twelve years, in 1821, Sequoyah
had developed an alphabet called "The Talking
Leaves," the first Indian writing system north of
Mexico. It was a brilliant achievement that rev-
olutionalized Cherokee education. Within a
year, thousands of Cherokee Indians of all ages
learned to read and write in their own language.
By 1824, parts of the Bible were printed in Cherokee, and in 1828, the tribe published a weekly
newspaper, the *Cherokee Phoenix,* both in
Cherokee and in English.

Sequoyah was honored by the Cherokee Legislature with a silver medal and a lifetime pension, the first ever given by an Indian tribe. The
medal bore on one side two pipes and on the
other a head with the inscription: "Presented to
George Gist, by the General Council of the
Cherokee Nation for his ingenuity in the invention of the Cherokee alphabet." The same inscription appeared on both sides, on one side in
English and on the other in Cherokee. A portrait of Sequoyah hangs in the Smithsonian Institution in Washington, D.C.

SHAHAKA, Mandan (Chief)
   (Tribal Leadership   22)
   Born: mid 1700's
   Died: Early 1800's
   Education: Tribal
   Significance: *Aid to the Lewis and Clark
     Expedition*

Shahaka, or Big White, was the chief of the
Mandans, who lived on the upper reaches of the
Missouri River far beyond the frontier settlements. He received the Lewis and Clark party
with kindness in 1804. The Mandans had had
no direct contact with the white man. On the
arrival of Lewis and Clark, a council was held.
After smoking the pipe of peace, Lewis and
Clark explained the object of the exploring
party and assured friendship and trade. The explorers spent a harmonious winter with the
Mandans, who supplied the party with fresh
meat.

Lewis and Clark were again received with
friendliness on their return to the Mandan villages after an interval of about eighteen months,
during which time they had crossed the Rocky
Mountains and penetrated to the shores of the
Pacific Ocean.

Chief Shahaka accompanied Lewis and
Clark on their return to Washington, D.C. He
visited with President Thomas Jefferson, after
which he returned safely to his people, maintaining a lasting peace.

SHINGABA W'OSSIN, Chippewa
   (Tribal Leadership   22)
   Born: Late 1700's, Lake Superior area
   Died: Early 1800's
   Education: Tribal
   Significance: *Establishment of an Indian
     school*

Shingaba W'Ossin, translated Image Stone,
was also known among his people as Waab-
Ojeeg. He was head chief of the Chippewas and
was a strong advocate of peace yet his bravery
was never questioned. This extraordinary chief
was a man of discretion and far in advance of his
people in ideas and insightfulness, for which he
commanded respect. He attended the peace
councils held in 1825, 1826, and 1827, to adjust
boundaries between warring tribes. He was the
first of the chiefs to speak eloquently in behalf
of peace and the first to sign the treaties resulting from each council. These were held respectively at Prairie du Chien on the upper
Mississippi, at Fond du Lac Superior, and at the
Butte des Morts, on the Fox River near Lake
Michigan.

He advised the Chippewas that the annuity
received by the tribe should go to support the
school for Indian children which had been established in Sault St. Marie on Lake Superior.
He was beloved for his kindness and benevolent
policies.

JAY SILVERHEELS, Mohawk
   (Acting, Sports   11)
   Born: ca. 1920, southeastern Canada
   Education: Federal and public schools
   Significance: *Success as an athlete and an
     actor*

Jay Silverheels, who for many years played Tonto, the indispensable friend of the Lone Ranger, was born Harry Smith. He is the son of Captain A. G. E. Smith, said to be the most decorated Canadian Indian soldier of World War I.

Silverheels became a star lacrosse player while still a boy and distinguished himself in lacrosse, hockey, football, and track. He also won honors in boxing and wrestling. He was the Western States Golden Glove Champion in 1937 and Niagara District Middleweight Champion in 1937 and 1938. He was in the Western States Golden Glove Champion in 1937 and Niagara District Middleweight Champion in 1937 and 1938. He was in Hollywood with a lacrosse team when Joe E. Brown persuaded him to join the Screen Actors Guild. He made his mark in *Broken Arrow, Brave Warrior,* and other westerns and accepted the part of Tonto in 1949. He has established the Jay Silverheels Scholarship Foundation for the education of Indians.

SITTING BULL, Sioux
(Tribal Leadership   10, 35)
Born: 1834, Northwestern Plains
Died: 1890
Education: Tribal
Significance: *One of the greatest Indian leaders of all times*

Sitting Bull is a name known throughout the world. Today he is still ranked as the greatest Sioux chief who ever lived. He distinguished himself within his tribe as a child, hunting buffalo at the age of ten and achieving his first war honor at fourteen. He believed that he was divinely chosen to lead his people. He was a shaman (medicine man) with extraordinary ability to organize and plan. By 1876, about 3,000 warriors had joined the camp of Sitting Bull, who was supreme commander. He defeated the army of General George Crook at the Battle of the Rosebud on June 16, 1876, a war which Sitting Bull had a vision of many white people falling upon his people from the sky. He knew that his battles with the white soldiers and settlers were not finished.

On June 25, 1876, Sitting Bull achieved his greatest triumph at the Battle of the Little Big Horn, also referred to as Custer's Last Stand. General Custer and his 224 men were swiftly annihilated during this spectacular Indian triumph. No trap had been laid for Custer and his forces, and no special strategy had been planned. The battle was a sudden defensive action and a sudden victory.

American troops continued to harass Sitting Bull thereafter. Many of Sitting Bull's followers gradually surrendered but Sitting Bull and his band escaped to Canada. He pled in vain for a reservation there. He finally surrendered on July 19, 1881, and remained a war prisoner for two years. Later, he toured for a year with Buffalo Bill's Wild West Show. He was a legend in his own time and deluged by fan mail. A granite monument marks his final resting place in Mobridge, South Dakota. Sitting Bull remains in the annals of history as the "Sioux of Siouxs" with the highest Sioux virtues of courage, generosity, and steadfast loyalty to tribal ideals. Few, if any, Indian chiefs achieved his glory and fame.

SAM SIXKILLER, Cherokee
(Law Enforcement   34, 37)
Born: ca. 1840, Going Snake District, Oklahoma
Died: 1886
Education: Tribal
Significance: *Service to his nation in maintaining the law*

Sam Sixkiller was appointed in 1875 as high sheriff of Tahlequah, Oklahoma, the capital of the Cherokee Reservation. He was warden of his nation's new prison there. He discharged his duties in an exemplary manner under the wild conditions prevailing at the time. Five years later, he became captain of the Union Agency police, with the town of Muskogee, Oklahoma, as his principal responsibility. Concurrently, he was a deputy United States Marshal and a special agent for the Missouri Pacific Railroad. Again he proved his competence as a lawman, his work putting him in contact with the dangerous elements of a frontier society in which lawbreakers abounded. On Christmas Eve of 1886, he was ambushed, shot and killed. He was eulogized in the press, and it was his murder that led to legislation extending the protection of federal law to Indian police.

KEELY SMITH, Cherokee
   (Entertainment   16)
   Born: 1932, Norfolk, Virginia
   Education: Public schools
   Significance: *Successful performance as a vocalist*

Keely Smith was born Dorothy Jacqueline Keely of Cherokee-English-Scotch-Irish lineage. Her father was a carpenter. We "never had much except a house full of love." At the age of eleven, she began to sing with the Joe Brown Radio Gang in Norfolk, Virginia, and remained with the group from 1943 to 1949. Following this, she sang with the Saxie Dowell Navy Band from 1949 to 1950, with the Louis Prima Orchestra from 1950 to 1954, and co-starred with Louis Prima as entertainer-singer in nightclubs from 1955 to 1961.

Her television appearances included the Dinah Shore, Frank Sinatra, and Dean Martin shows. She co-starred with Robert Mitchum in the motion picture, *Thunder Road,* and has recorded for Capitol and Dot Records. She is the president of the Enterprise Music Corporation. In 1958, she was honored with the Disc Jockey's Favorite Female Award, the Most Promising TV Performer Award given by the National Academy of Musical Arts, the Grammy Award given by the National Academy of Recording Arts and Sciences, and the Number One Female Vocalist Award given by Billboard and Variety magazines. In 1959 she received the Playboy Jazz Award; in 1960 the Joey Award for the Best Variety Act; and in 1962 she was named Woman of the Year in the World of Entertainment. She is the author of *Half Child, Half Woman.*

MILDRED HOTCH SPARKS, Tlingit
   (Community Service   37)
   Born: ca. 1920, Alaska
   Education: Federal schools
   Significance: *Work for the betterment of her people*

Mildred Hotch Sparks is an active member of the Alaska Native Sisterhood, having served as chapter president for twenty-five years, past grand president and grand treasurer for thirteen years. As a member of the Haines Health Council, she was largely instrumental in obtaining the services of a resident doctor and dentist for the community. She helped form a youth dance group now known nationally as the Chikat Dancers. She is a key figure in a move to revive Tlingit art. Mrs. Sparks was selected Alaska's Mother of the Year in 1968. She is department chairman of The Home Life Committee of the Alaska Federation of Women's Clubs, and chaplain of the local post of the American Legion Auxiliary.

SQUANTO, Pawtuxet
   (Interpreting   14)
   Born: ca. 1580, area of the New England States
   Died: 1622
   Education: Tribal
   Significance: *Friendship with the Pilgrims*

Squanto, also known as Tisquantum, is the legendary friend of the Pilgrims whom he met in 1621 when he acted as an interpreter during the negotiation between Governor John Carver of the Plymouth Colony and Massasoit, chief of the Wampanoag tribe. The negotiations ended in the Treaty of Plymouth which tied both parties to peaceful relations.

Squanto was taken to London in 1605 with one of the early explorers and lived there for nine years. He was kidnapped and sold as a slave to Spain but escaped back to England. An English sea captain returned him to Cape Cod. He lived with the Pilgrims, showing them where to fish and how to plant corn. Plymouth Colony might have failed, if it had not been for Squanto's help.

STANDING BEAR, Oglala Sioux
   (Tribal Leadership, Literature   25)
   Born: 1868, Pine Ridge, South Dakota
   Died: ca. 1945

Education: Tribal

Significance: *Recording of the history of his people*

Standing Bear, hereditary chief of the Oglala Sioux, was also an artist and storyteller. He depicted events that have significance in the life and culture of his people. As an oral contributor to the life story of Black Elk in the book, *Black Elk Speaks - Being a Life Story of a Holy Man of the Oglala Sioux,* by John G. Neihardt, Chief Standing Bear made graphic contributions. His illustrations speak eloquently of historic events in the westward expansion of our nation.

In 1939 he commissioned sculptor Korczah Ziolkowski, then assistant sculptor on the Mount Rushmore Memorial, to create a monument to Chief Crazy Horse so that "the people may know we also have great heroes." Ziolkowski started this lifetime, herculean task in 1948, carving an equestrian statue of Chief Crazy Horse into the solid granite of Thunderhead Mountain in the Black Hills of South Dakota. When finished, it will be 641 feet high and 563 feet wide. Chief Standing Bear is author of *My People the Sioux,* 1928, and *Land of the Spotted Eagle,* 1933.

JOHN STANDS IN TIMBER, Cheyenne

(Literature   33)

Born: 1884, possibly Montana

Died 1967

Education: Reservation and federal schools

Significance: *Preservation of the culture of his people*

John Stands In Timber was born a few years after his grandfather was killed in the Battle of the Little Big Horn in 1876. The recounting of Cheyenne traditions formed an important part of his life from early childhood. Upon his return from school in 1905, he became the tribe's historian and the keeper of the oral literature of his people, seeking out every oldtimer who could contribute personal memories to Cheyenne lore. He died while his book, *Cheyenne Memories,* was in press. This book, published by Yale University, was co-authored by Liberty Margot, a teacher-anthropologist, who inspired Stands In Timber during his ten years of research. The words of one of his favorite warrior songs, "My friends, only stones stay on earth forever. Use your best ability," appear as a dedication in his book.

FRED STEVENS, JR., Navajo

(Painting   27)

Born: 1922, Sheep Springs, New Mexico

Education: Fort Wingate High School, New Mexico

Significance: *Perpetuation of his culture through unique art*

Fred Stevens, Jr. has developed his patient skill as a sandpainter to the extent that he is known worldwide. He is much in demand as a teacher and demonstrator of the art. He maintains a studio in Chinle, Arizona, but spends much time in travels throughout the world to demonstrate his unique art. He takes time to interpret the meaning of the intricate patterns he forms with fine sand of different colors on a floor of sand. He obtains these colors by grinding stones found in the environment. He also explains the ritual significance of sandpainting in the culture of his people, particularly as part of the healing rites of the medicine man. His designs are made freehand and from memory and are destroyed after the demonstration.

JOHN W. STEVENS, Passamaquoddy

(Tribal Leadership   16)

Born: 1933, Washington County, Maine

Education: High school

Significance: *Defense of Indian rights*

John W. Stevens is a tribal chief. He served in the United States Marines from 1951 to 1954, and received the Presidential Unit Citation, the Korean Presidential Unit Citation, and the United Nations Medal. He is a member of Local 26, International Brotherhood of Firemen and Oilers, A.F.L. and C.I.O. Stevens writes, "Being chief of an Indian tribe of about a thousand members who are struggling in court and on all fronts to overcome local discrimination and poverty, and to have reservation treaty rights respected by the State of Maine is enough of a task, and doesn't leave much time for anything else."

ALBERT STEWART, Chickasaw
(Music   11)
Born: ca. 1925, Oklahoma
Education: Chicago Musical College,
    Illinois; Roosevelt University, Chicago,
    Illinois
Significance: *Preservation of his culture
    through song*

Albert Stewart is a successful concert and platform artist with a rich bass-baritone voice of remarkable range and power. He earned his way through college largely by his singing. He devotes much time to the study of Indian song and lore. His work in this field has been featured by Encyclopaedia Britannica Films. Through the International Platform Association of Lecturers and Concert Artists, he tours the country with an educational-musical program. He is active in the Indian Council Fire, having served as its president. During the summer he is the featured singer in the Indian ceremonials held at the Wisconsin Dells near Madison, Wisconsin.

MARIA TALLCHIEF, Osage
(Dancing   11)
Born: 1925, Fairfax, Oklahoma
Education: Public schools in California
Significance: *Success as a prima ballerina*

Maria Tallchief, a ballerina of international fame, was born on a reservation but lived in Los Angeles from the age of seven. Her mother was Scotch-Irish and her father Osage. She and her younger sister, Marjorie, also a ballerina of international fame, began to study ballet as very young children. When she was fifteen, Miss Tallchief made her debut in classical ballet in the Hollywood Bowl. In 1942, after graduation from Beverly Hills High School, she joined the Ballet Russe de Monte Carlo. Toward the end of the season, as an understudy, she danced the premier role.

In 1947, she joined the New York City Center Ballet Company as ranking soloist, and later became the prima ballerina. She has danced as guest ballerina with the Ballet Theater in this country, and in Paris with the Paris Opera Ballet. She has appeared in most countries of Europe and in Japan as well as in all the principal cities of the United States. Her sister has also reached a high pinnacle of success. She lives in Paris where she dances with the Paris Opera Ballet. The sisters have received many honors. Both are married.

TE ATA, Chickasaw
(Acting   11)
Born: ca. 1925, Oklahoma
Education: Reservation schools; A.B.,
    Oklahoma College for Women,
    Chickasha, Oklahoma; Theater School
    of the Carnegie Institute of
    Technology, Pittsburgh, Pennsylvania
Significance: *Interpretations of Indian life
    and culture*

Te Ata, translated Bearer of the Morning, is considered the foremost interpreter of the Indian on the stage today. After a number of roles on the Broadway stage, Te Ata found that her deepest interest lay in the folklore and traditions of her race. Using her dramatic training, she prepared a program of folklore and rituals which she has presented in every state in this country, in many countries of Europe, Central America, and South America, and on every large Indian reservation in the United States.

Te Ata was invited by President and Mrs. Franklin D. Roosevelt to entertain at their first official dinner in the White House in honor of Prime Minister Ramsay McDonald of England and again at Hyde Park when King George VI and Queen Elizabeth visited this country. Lake Te Ata in the Palisade Interstate Park of New York and New Jersey was named in her honor. In 1957 Te Ata was named to the National Hall of Fame for Famous American Indians at Anadarko, Oklahoma.

JOHN TEBBEL, Ojibwa
(Education, Literature   16)
Born: 1912, Boyne City, Michigan
Education: B.A., Central Michigan
    University, Mount Pleasant, Michigan;
    M.S., School of Journalism, Columbia
    University, New York

Significance: *Promotion of an
understanding of his people*

John Tebbel is a professor of journalism at New York University. He received the Columbia University School of Journalism Alumni Medal in 1964, and has been an honorary member of the National Association of Book Editors since 1965, the first Indian so honored. Among his many published books are *An American Dynasty* (1947), *George Washington's America* (1954), *The American Indian Wars* (1960), *The Inheritors* (1962), and *From Rags to Riches* (1963). He is a contributor to the *Saturday Review* and other magazines.

TECUMSEH, Shawnee
(Tribal Leadership   35)
Born: 1765, Ohio River country
Died: 1813
Education: Tribal
Significance: *Work in behalf of the rights
of his people*

Chief Tecumseh, Shawnee warrior and statesman, is considered one of the greatest of American Indian leaders. He was a famed fighter against white settlers while still a young man in the Ohio River country.

By 1780 Tecumseh, a bold, eloquent and fearless speaker, was acknowledged as the leading Indian statesman of the Ohio area. Profoundly disturbed by the growing menace to Indian lands and life through the expansion of white settlers, Tecumseh worked out a great plan for his people's future. The only Indian hope, he believed, lay in uniting into a powerful confederation of tribes which would create a great Indian state centered around the Ohio Valley and the Great Lakes.

With his brother, Tenskwatawa the Prophet, Tecumseh established an Indian settlement on the Wabash River near the mouth of the Tippecanoe River. More than 1,000 Indians from Shawnee, Delaware, Wyandot, Ottawa, Ojibwa, and Kickapoo tribes settled there, forming the beginning of Tecumseh's great alliance. Liquor was forbidden in the Indian villages and the tribesmen lived according to ancient patterns.

Tecumseh continued to travel from Florida to St. Louis urging the Indians to unite. He was away in 1811 when Tenskwatawa allowed himself to be maneuvered into the disastrous battle with William Henry Harrison at Tippecanoe.

Tecumseh was a magnificent figure whose impact was felt by Indian and non-Indian alike. A white observer reported that Tecumseh's voice "resounded over the multitude—hurling out his words like a succession of thunderbolts." Harrison himself described Tecumseh as "one of those uncommon geniuses which spring up occasionally to produce revolutions." Tecumseh was a brigadier general with the British armies in the War of 1812 and died in battle covering the retreat of the British from Detroit.

LOUIS TEWANIMA, Hopi
(Track   40)
Born: ca. 1885, Arizona
Died: Mid 1900's
Education: Carlisle Institute, Carlisle,
Pennsylvania
Significance: *Excellence in sports*

Louis Tewanima attended Carlisle Institute at the same time as Jim Thorpe. He competed in the 1908 Olympics in London. Four years later at Stockholm, he was second to Kannes Kolehmainen, the Flying Finn, who was one of the greatest runners the world has ever seen. Tewanima was one of the Olympic Games' most colorful stars, earning many medals. He was triple medal winner in the 1908 and 1912 Olympics, running in the 5,000 meter, 10,000 meter, and marathon races. He was the first athlete to be named to the Arizona Hall of Fame.

JIM (JAMES F.) THORPE, Sauk and Fox
(Sports   1)
Born: 1888, near Prague, Oklahoma
Died: 1953
Education: Carlisle Institute, Carlisle,
Pennsylvania
Significance: *World renown as an
all-around athlete*

Jim Thorpe was one of the greatest American athletes. He was Coach Warner's most outstanding football player while at Carlisle, He weighed 190 pounds, was six feet tall, and an incredibly powerful runner who helped to make Carlisle the football scourge of the east. An All-American football player from 1911 to 1912, he once drop-kicked four field goals against Harvard.

King Gustaf V of Sweden called him "The greatest athlete in the world." During the 1912 Olympics, he became the first person ever to win both the decathlon and pentathlon. Later, officials took back his medals charging that he had previously played professional baseball. In 1913, shortly after he signed with the Giants, Thorpe married Iva Miller, the daughter of a hotel man in Muskogee, Oklahoma. She had attended the Chilocco Indian School in Oklahoma.

In 1933, Universal Studios in Hollywood hired Thorpe to play Chief Black Crow in a routine movie. He also did some work in a baseball picture for Metro Goldwyn Mayer.

BOYCE D. TIMMONS, Cherokee
(Community Service, Education   16)
Born: 1911, Pawhuska, Oklahoma
Education: B.S., Oklahoma State
    University, Stillwater; LL.B.,
    University of Oklahoma, Norman
Significance: *Dedication to the education
    of Indians*

Boyce D. Timmons is the director of registration at the University of Oklahoma and consultant on Indian affairs at the Southwest Center on Human Relations. He is interested in the welfare of Indians, and sponsors a weekly radio program, "Indians for Indians." He is also sponsor of the Sequoyah Club at the University of Oklahoma and a member of the University Scholarship Committee. Timmons, the former editor of *Oklahoma Indian Newsletter,* is active in the Junior Chamber of Commerce and the Boy Scouts of America. He is a former president of the Oklahoma Association of Collegiate Registrars and Admissions Officers and belongs to the Oklahoma Bar Association. Over the years, he has been presented with many honors and awards including the Achievement Plaque from the National Independent Students Association and the Outstanding Citizen Award from the Junior Chamber of Commerce.

THOMAS TOMMANEY, Creek
(Education, Government   16)
Born: 1913, Eufala, Oklahoma
Education: Chilocco Indian School,
    Oklahoma; B.A., University of
    Kansas, Lawrence; M.S., Oklahoma
    State University, Stillwater
Significance: *Assistance to other Indians
    in educational endeavors*

Thomas Tommaney is presently the superintendent of Haskell Institute at Lawrence, Kansas, long an institution of higher education for Indians. Before this, he was the superintendent of the Intermountain Indian School, the largest boarding school ever established by the government for Indian education, located near Brigham City, Utah. Tommaney entered the Indian Service of the Bureau of Indian Affairs when he graduated from college and has continued in Indian education with distinction except for two year's service in the Air Corps during World War II.

Tommaney says, "My blood has helped me to advance. I have never found it to be a hindrance. I was helped with scholarships during the lean years of the 1930's, and I have since tried to repay this debt by helping other Indian young people." He enjoys speaking to non-Indian groups about the Indian people.

ROGER JOHN TSABETSAYE, Zuñi
(Handicrafts   16)
Born: 1941, Zuñi, New Mexico
Education: Institute of American Indian
    Arts, Santa Fe, New Mexico; School
    for American Craftsmen; Rochester
    Institute of Technology, Rochester,
    New York
Significance: *Creation of silver jewelry in
    Indian design*

Roger Tsabetsaye is a silversmith of renown. He produces and markets his jewelry and silver work. He was commissioned by President and Mrs. Lyndon Johnson to design a silver necklace which was presented to the wife of a Costa

Rican official. In 1965 he traveled with the Zuñi Performing Dance Group as the official representative of the Governor of the Zuñi Pueblo. He has received many honors and awards for his beautiful creations.

ANDY TSINAJINNIE, Navajo
  (Painting   16)
  Born: 1919, Chinle, Arizona
  Education: Fort Apache Indian School, New Mexico; Santa Fe Indian Art School, New Mexico; College of Arts and Crafts, Oakland, California
  Significance: *Picturing Navajo life and folkways*

Andy Tsinajinnie ranks as one of the five best known painters among the Navajos, with a style distinct from the other members of the "Big Five." He is extremely original and the follower of no tradition. His murals are found in California, New Mexico, Oklahoma, and in many of the new buildings around Phoenix, Arizona. His imaginative full color illustrations of Van Clark's *Peetie the Pack Rat* are authentic examples of the fine detail that is characteristic of Indian art. Tsinajinnie's early works, done as a small boy, were of the sheep he was herding and were drawn on nearby rocks. He has also illustrated *Who Wants to be a Prairie Dog?* and *Spirit Rocks and Silver Magic.*

He served with the Fifth Air Force in the South Pacific and with the Navajo Signal Corps during World War II. Today, he has a studio at Scottsdale, Arizona. His paintings are much sought after and highly prized.

LEGORIA VELARDE (Tafoya), Tewa Pueblo
  (Handicrafts   27)
  Born: 1911, Tewa Pueblo, near Española, New Mexico
  Education: St. Catherine's Indian school, Sante Fe, New Mexico
  Significance: *Perpetuation of Indian art*

Legoria Velarde is a world renowned potter. She has brought fame to herself and to her people with her skill and artistry. Her creations are collector's items, and examples of her work are found in museums throughout the world and prized by private collectors. The other women of her pueblo have been taught her craft. She has given both inspiration and a valuable source of income to her people.

Legoria was married while quite young to a fellow tribesman, Pasqual Tafoya. She became interested in making pottery to supplement the family income, and for aesthetic expression, as many of the Tewa women do. Pottery making is still a living art in many of the pueblos, the most familiar being the polished blackware which is the specialty of Legoria. She demonstrates her art and explains that the black is produced in the firing process. The blazing mass is smothered with powdered manure, and the smoke, impregnated with carbon from the burnt fuel, envelopes the red-hot pottery, coloring it permanently throughout.

She has many awards to her credit. Educational films featuring her pottery making are available through the National Park Service and the University of Ohio.

PABLITA VELARDE (HARDIN), Santa Clara Pueblo
  (Painting, Literature   11)
  Born: 1918, Santa Clara Pueblo, north of Sante Fe, New Mexico
  Education: St. Catherine's Mission School, Sante Fe, New Mexico; Sante Fe Indian High School, New Mexico
  Significance: *Perpetuation of her culture through art*

Pablita Velarde is recognized as the most outstanding Indian woman artist of today. Her unusual gift as an artist was recognized and nurtured at an early age. After her graduation from the Santa Fe Indian School, Pablita spent two years as an assistant art teacher at the Santa Clara Pueblo Day School. In 1938, Pablita built her own studio and continued to paint in the traditional technique of her people, always expressing basic integrity and faithfulness to her culture. From 1939 to 1941, Pablita was employed by the government in a CCC project to paint murals for the museum at Bandelier, New Mexico.

Among her greatest achievements are the paintings she did at Bandelier National Monument in New Mexico. These reveal her detailed knowledge and depth of vision of the daily life and crafts of her people. In 1956 she was commissioned to do a Corn Dance mural for a building in Houston, Texas. In 1960 Pablita completed a large mural in oils of the Santa Clara Buffalo Dance for the First National Bank in Los Alamos, New Mexico. Her paintings are in permanent collections of several museums and in private collections throughout the country.

One of Pablita's most significant achievements is the writing and illustrating of a book of tribal legends entitled *Old Father, the Story Teller,* published in 1960. She is recognized for reviving the ancient art of earth painting. Although modest and retiring, her warm personality is reflected in her wide smile, keen wit, and fine sense of humor. She is in great demand as a lecturer. She lives in Albuquerque, New Mexico, near her two children and a granddaughter.

WILMA L. VICTOR, Choctaw
   (Education   11)
   Born: 1919, Idabel, Oklahoma
   Education: University of Kansas,
      Lawrence; B.S., Wisconsin State
      College; M.Ed., University of
      Oklahoma, Norman, Oklahoma
   Significance: *Leadership in the education
      of Indians*
Wilma L. Victor began her career in education during her second year in college when she was given a scholarship grant and encouraged to prepare herself for a teaching career. Immediately after her graduation, she was given a position as teacher at Shiprock, Arizona. Her teaching career was interrupted during World War II, when she enlisted in the Women's Army Corps. After her basic training and officer's training, she was commissioned second lieutenant. She worked in military intelligence and finally as company commander at Camp Campbell, Kentucky.

After the war, she completed her master's degree and became the academic head of the elementary department of the Intermountain Indian School near Brigham City, Utah. She became the superintendent of this same school and a spokesman for Indian education at the national level. In 1970, Miss Victor was appointed deputy area director of the Phoenix office of the Bureau of Indian Affairs. This position includes jurisdiction over the B.I.A. Schools in all of the western states.

Miss Victor is a member of the American Association of School Administrators and the Northern Utah Chapter of the Council for Exceptional Children. She is active in the Governor's Committee on Indian Affairs in Utah. She was honored by the United States Department of Interior in 1958 with the Incentive Award for Sustained Superior Performance.

GERALD ROBERT VIZENOR, Chippewa
   (Literature   16)
   Born: 1934, Minneapolis, Minnesota
   Education: B.A., University of
      Minnesota, Minneapolis
   Significance: *Poetry which reflects the
      Indian culture*
Gerald Robert Vizenor is a guidance director with the Department of Corrections in Minneapolis, Minnesota. He is also a poet with the following publications to his credit: *Seventeen Chirps* (1964), *Raising the Moon Vines* (1964), and *Summer in the Spring: Ojibway Lyric Poems* (1965). Vizenor served in the United States Army from 1952 to 1955. He is a member of Delta Phi Lambda, honorary writers' fraternity.

MARIE LUCILLE WADLEY,
   Cherokee-Shawnee
   (Tribal Affairs, Literature   16)
   Born: 1906, Pensacola, Oklahoma
   Education: Muskogee College, Oklahoma;
      Draughon's Business College,
      Muskogee, Oklahoma
   Significance: *Author and active civic
      leader*
Marie Lucille Wadley, a speaker and writer on Indian subjects, was tribal operations officer in the Muskogee Area Office of the Bureau of Indian Affairs from 1925. She also had time to

serve as the first president of the board of directors of the Five Civilized Tribes Museum. She worked actively as a member of the advisory board of the National Hall of Fame for Famous Indians in Anadarko, Oklahoma, of the Murrow Indian Children's Home, and of the Great Foreman Centennial Scholarship Fund. She was executive secretary of the Inter-Tribal Council of the Five Civilized Tribes and of the Cherokee Nation of Oklahoma. She was chairman of the Human Relations Institute in Muskogee, Oklahoma, and served on the Governor's Committee to Further Employment of the Handicapped.

Her awards include the Distinguished Service Award for Services Beyond the Call of Duty and the Certificate of Special Recognition for Outstanding Service from the Cherokee Nation of Oklahoma in 1954 and 1964 respectively. She received a citation for superior performance from the Bureau of Indian Affairs in 1965, the Distinguished Service Award from the United States Department of the Interior in 1966, the Order of the Rose Degree for Outstanding Service to Beta Sigma Phi in 1966, and the citation for Community Services from the Muskogee Elks Club. Her published works include *A Biographical Sketch of Houston Benge Tehee* (1959), and *The Five Civilized Tribes: Their Contributions to Our Civilization* (1962).

WAKAWN, Winnebago
(Tribal Leadership   22)
Born: 1788, near Green Bay, Michigan
Died: 1838
Education: Federal school at Prairie du
    Chien, Wisconsin
Significance: *Belief in the need for
    education*
Wakawn, translated the Snake, was a war chief of the Winnebagoes. He was in the famous battle of Tippecanoe after which he was unfailingly friendly to the white settlers. He studied at the government school which was opened at Prairie du Chien in 1834, and urged his family and other Indians to study, also. Agriculture, English, and religion were offered as subjects. On one occasion Wakawn risked his life to defend his benevolent views of the United States Government and his affirmative opinions regarding the importance of education. He clung to the customs of his forefathers, but he urged the young Indians of the upcoming generation to learn civilized ways from the white man and to attend school.

AMOS LEWIS WALLACE, Eskimo
(Handicrafts   16)
Born: 1920, Juneau, Alaska
Education: Federal schools
Significance: *Portrayal of Eskimo culture
    through his craft*
Amos Lewis Wallace is a highly skilled craftsman specializing in handcarved totem poles. His work is displayed in the Brooklyn Children's Museum, the Boston Children's Museum, the Indian Village at Disneyland, and the University of Alaska. He served in the United States Army and has been active in the Alaska Native Brotherhood since 1958.

ERMA WALZ, Cherokee
(Tribal Affairs   37)
Born: 1915, Hulbert, Oklahoma
Education: Haskell Institute, Lawrence,
    Kansas; Northwestern University,
    Evanston, Illinois
Significance: *Solving tribal government
    problems*
Mrs. Erma Walz has built an outstanding career in the field of tribal government and tribal claims, two subjects likely to cause dissension. As chief of the Division of Tribal Operations with the Bureau of Indian Affairs, Mrs. Walz has won the respect of Indian groups across the nation for her fairness in solving knotty tribal problems and for her ability to find solutions that are in the best interests of all concerned. Tribal groups now frequently seek her advice in complex tribal situations.

In 1934 under the Indian Reorganization Act, Mrs. Walz began as a typist clerk with the Organization Division of the Bureau of Indian Affairs. She participated in the formation of tribal constitutions. Today she leads the effort to make those same tribal constitutions effective in instruments in the upward journey of Indian peoples. Since her appointment as division chief, she has supervised the payment of more than one hundred million dollars in Claims Commission awards to more than thirty tribes.

WASHAKIE, Shoshone
(Tribal Leadership   14)
Born: Early 1800's, Bitterroot Valley,
    Montana
Died: 1900
Education: Tribal
Significance: *Leadership in coexistence*

Washakie was an illustrious chief of an eastern band of Shoshone. He was respected by his people and the white settlers alike. He could see the fate in store for the red man and guided his people along the path of peaceful coexistence.

In the early 1840's, he began the climb to leadership over all the Shoshones. Washakie is unique by virtue of his connection with successive eras of white expansion over an extended period of time. He had intimate contact with scouts, trappers, traders, explorers, immigrants, Mormons, miners, settlers, and soldiers. These he befriended unfailingly, and he assisted all newcomers over the course of many years.

He attended the council of 1851 at Fort Laramie, Wyoming, witnessed the Army's Mormon Expedition of 1857, and signed the Treaty of 1868 that gave him a long-desired reservation in Wyoming's Wind River Region. Fort Washakie was named for him.

He served with General George Crook in 1876 against Chief Crazy Horse and with General Ronald Mackenzie against Chief Dull Knife. On his death, Washakie was buried with full military honors at Fort Washakie. The greatest tribute came in the memorial of gratitude signed by some 9,000 pioneers whom Chief Washakie and his people had helped cross different fords or for whom they had recovered straying stock. He was also honored for keeping his people out of quarrels even when an occasional unruly immigrant seemed bent on provoking one.

CHABAH DAVIS WATSON, Navajo
(Education   13)
Born: 1906, Wheatfield,
    Arizona
Education: Fort Defiance Indian School,
    New Mexico; Albuquerque Indian
    School, New Mexico
Significance: *Belief in education and
    self-determination*

Chabah Davis Watson was born in a hogan on the Navajo reservation. When she was five years old, her mother died. Her father enrolled her and her brothers in a boarding school. With her first school experience, life took on a new meaning. She was born Chabah, but at school, she was given the name Davis. Early she showed a special interest in the piano, which she learned to play without help. With lessons from a skilled teacher, she was soon playing for assemblies, school plays, operettas, and recitals. At this same time, she became a teacher without being conscious of it. When she was in tenth grade, although she had neither a diploma nor a teaching certificate, she substituted in music classes and in regular classes.

After completing high school, her father would not permit her to fulfill her cherished dream of further education at the University of New Mexico, but this did not deter her from her ambition to teach. She began her teaching in a hogan supported by the Navajo parents. Her life's work in education has brought her national and international fame. The remarkable Rough Rock Demonstration School which is operated by an all Navajo Board of Education is a monument to her endeavors as is Diné, Inc., a related private corporation, whose title is an acronym for Demonstration in Navajo Education. "Diné" is also the Navajo word meaning "the people." The three directors of Diné are all Navajos.

In 1966 Mrs. Watson was honored by the United States Bureau of Indian Affairs with the Continuous Service Award for her thirty years of dedicated work with the Navajos. At the same time, she received the special Commendation Medal. Although retired since 1967, she is an active member of a resource team for kindergarten education and has made trips to Washington, D.C., in connection with this work.

ANNIE DODGE WAUNEKA, Navajo
  (Health   13)
  Born: 1910, Navajo Reservation in
    Arizona
  Education: Federal schools, Fort
    Defiance, New Mexico, and
    Albuquerque, New Mexico
  Significance: *Promotion of Indian health
    and education*

Annie Dodge Wauneka is the daughter of
Henry Chee Dodge, the last chief of the Navajos. As soon as she could walk and run, Annie
Dodge helped herd her father's sheep. Her
school experience was not too satisfying because
of health interruptions. She did continue her
formal schooling through the eleventh grade,
however. Her informal education continued
throughout her life, much of it coming from her
father who managed the large ranches and who
was chairman of the Tribal Council from 1923
to 1928.

Annie Dodge married George Wauneka at
nineteen in 1929. She became the first woman
member of the Navajo Tribal Council in 1951.
She is nationally known for her fight against
tuberculosis. She is a member of the United
States Advisory Committee on Indian Health
and had a popular radio program on Indian
Affairs. In 1958 she was honored by the Arizona
Women's Press Club as Arizona Woman of
Achievement. In 1963 Mrs. Wauneka was the
recipient of the highest civil honor that can be
presented to individuals in peace time, the Presidential Medal of Freedom, for her dedicated
leadership and service to her people.

CLARENCE WESLEY, San Carlos Apache
  (Tribal Affairs   11)
  Born: 1912, Bylas, Arizona
  Education: Federal schools, Phoenix,
    Arizona, and Albuquerque, New
    Mexico
  Significance: *Direction of citizenship
    education for Indian people*

Clarence Wesley is a successful farmer and
cattleman. In addition, he provides leadership
for the betterment of his people. He is called
upon to represent the Indian viewpoint to local,
state, and national organizations and universities interested in the affairs of Indians. He has
taken part in public assistance litigations, has
helped in removing local discriminatory laws,
and has created a public relations program both
on and off the reservation. Wesley is the chairman of the San Carlos Apache Tribal Council
and in this capacity has initiated a program to
help his people take more responsibility in managing their own affairs. He is the founder of the
Junior Chamber of Commerce on the reservation. This is the only Indian J. C. in existence.

WALTER RICHARD WEST, Cheyenne
  (Art, Education   11)
  Born: 1912, Darlington, Oklahoma
  Education: Haskell Institute, Lawrence,
    Kansas; Bacone College, Oklahoma;
    B.F.A., M.F.A., University of
    Oklahoma, Norman; University of
    Redlands, California; Tulsa University
  Significance: *Promotion of Indian culture
    through art*

Walter West developed his natural talents in
art while in elementary school. He is among the
foremost of the present day Indian artists and
quite versatile. He was art instructor at the
Phoenix Indian School in Arizona, and with an
interruption for military service in World War
II, worked toward his Master's degree. He is
possibly the first member of his tribe to receive
higher degrees in art.

West became the director of the Art Department at Bacone College in Muskogee, Oklahoma. He is a member of the Muskogee Rotary
Club, the Muskogee Art Guild, the Southwestern Art Association, and president of the Education Association at Bacone College. He has
received many awards and honors for his work,
which has been shown in exhibitions and one-
man shows throughout the United States and
South America. His illustrations appear in *The
Thankful People, Tales of the Cheyennes,* and
Indian Legends. West has also won renown as
a ceramist, wood carver, and maker of Indian
flutes.

WHITE ANTELOPE, Southern Cheyenne
(Tribal Leadership   3)
Born: 1784, possibly southwestern
   Wyoming
Died: 1864
Education: Tribal
Significance: *Pursuit of peace*
White Antelope was a distinguished chief of
the southern Cheyenne, who had lived in peace
among the white settlers. In 1864, he went to
Denver for "peace talks" which were called to
persuade the Indians to live on reservations
away from land desired by the white settlers.
Upon their arrival in Denver, on the advice of
the military commandant at Fort Lyon, White
Antelope established his temporary village on
Sand Creek, thirty miles from the fort. The village was then destroyed in a stealthy, sudden
attack by Colonel Chivington and a force of
about 1,000 troops. Colonel Chivington gave
the orders to "Kill and scalp all, big and little;
nits make lice." White Antelope refused to run
or fight. He stood in front of his lodge with
folded arms, singing his death song, "Nothing
lives long except the earth and the mountains."

THOMAS S. WHITECLOUD, Chippewa
(Medicine   11)
Born: ca. 1910, Wisconsin
Education: Federal schools, Albuquerque
   and Santa Fe, New Mexico; B.S.,
   University of Redlands, California;
   M.D., Tulane University Medical
   School, New Orleans, Louisiana
Significance: *Concern for community
   health*
Dr. Thomas S. Whitecloud served as Battalion Surgeon in the United States Army Para-
chute Infantry when he graduated from medical
school. He was a qualified parachutist and saw
combat in Europe during World War II. After
the war, he was a physician with the Bureau of
Indian Affairs, first in Montana and then in
Minnesota. He opened his own practice in Newton, Texas, where for over seven years he was
the only physician in the county. He maintained
a thirty-five bed county hospital with no outside
aid or county funds. He delivered a total of

2,000 babies. He was also county coroner,
health officer, deputy sheriff, and active in boys'
work. He is now engaged in limited practice in
Pascagoula, Mississippi.
   While in college, he wrote "Blue Winds
Dancing," which appeared in *Scribner's Magazine* in 1938. He writes for his local newspapers,
particularly on sports and athletic injuries. He
owns his own plane and is keenly interested in
all aspects of aviation.

ROLAND WHITEHORSE, Kiowa
(Art   16)
Born: 1920, Carnegie, Oklahoma
Education: Bacone College, Oklahoma;
   Dallas Art Institute, Texas
Significance: *Preservation of Indian
   culture through art*
Roland Whitehorse is an illustrator and art-
ist. He is graphics supervisor for the 4th United
States Army of North Texas, Oklahoma, and
Arkansas. He served as the art director at the
American Indian Exposition in Anardarko,
Oklahoma. During World War II, he served in
the United States Army in the European The-
ater of Operations with the 9th Infantry Divi-
sion. He is a member of the Southwestern
Artists Association, the American Indian Art-
ists Association, and the Great Plains Historical
Association in Lawton, Oklahoma. White-
horse's illustrations appear in *Winter Telling
Stories,* by Alice Lee Marriott and in *Heap Big
Laugh,* by Daniel M. Madrano.

DAVID WILLIAMS, SR., Tlingit
(Handicrafts   16)
Born: 1905, Douglas, Alaska
Education: Elementary school
Significance: *Skill as a carver*
David Williams, Sr. is a renowned totem
carver. He demonstrates his work and relates
the cultural significance of the totem found
among the Pacific coast and Alaska Indians. He
explains that totems are the symbol for a tribe,
clan, family, or person. The clan totem may be
a bird, fish, animal, plant, or other natural object. Some groups consider the totem as an ancestor of the clan and may have rules against

killing or eating the species to which the totem belongs. Some clans consider the totem holy and pray to it. When the totem pole is put up, a potlatch is held. This is a ceremonial feast of the Indians of the Pacific northwest and Alaska. Clan members are often known by the name of the totem.

EMMA WILLOYA, Eskimo
(Tribal Affairs   16)
Born: 1898, Fort Barrow, Alaska
Education: Brevig Mission School, Teller, Alaska
Significance: *Dedication to the betterment of her people*

Emma Willoya, now retired, was the manager of the Nome Skin Sewers Association from 1945 to 1960. She also served as the Nome, Alaska, agent for the Office of Price Administration. For this work, she was honored with citations from Presidents Franklin D. Roosevelt and Harry S. Truman.

Mrs. Willoya has dedicated her life to helping her people toward economic independence through hand-made products. Whenever possible, she served on boards and committees where the needs and the problems of the Eskimo could be presented. In 1950, she represented the Eskimos in the Nome area at the invitation of the Legislative Reference Service of the Library of Congress. In 1951, she was invited to attend the annual Arts and Crafts Board Conference and in 1961 assisted Dorothy Jean Ray in the research for her book, *Artists of the Tundra and the Sea.* She also served as the supervisor of a highly creative project in which skins were sewn to make symbolic plaques for the Air Force Chapel in Fairbanks, Alaska, and for Our Savior's Lutheran Church in Nome, Alaska.

WINEMA, Modoc
(Interpreting   34)
Born: ca. 1840, northern California
Died: ca. 1900
Education: Tribal
Significance: *Acts of diplomacy*

Princess Winema, also known as Tobey Riddles, was the wife of a white man, Frank Riddles, and a relative of the Modoc leader, Captain Jack. In 1873, during the Modoc War, Princess Winema arranged a parley hoping to save her people from extermination. Learning of probable Indian treachery at the scheduled peace council, Winema warned General Canby and the white peace negotiators. General Canby, however, proceeded with Winema and her husband, Frank Riddles, acting as interpreter. As she had predicted, the Indians suddenly rose up during the conference and murdered General Canby and several others. One was saved by Winema's intervention.

SARAH WINNEMUCCA, Paiute
(Interpreting   9)
Born: 1844, Nevada
Died: ca. 1905
Education: Mission schools, California
Significance: *Mediating for peace*

Sarah Winnemucca was the granddaughter of the legendary leader of the Paiutes, Chief Winnemucca, who remained at peace with the white man and who served as guide to John Charles Fremont in 1845. Her grandfather was also known as Captain Truckee, a name bestowed upon him by Fremont. Sarah was educated in California as a result of her famous grandfather's travels there with Fremont.

Speaking both English and Paiute, Sarah became an interpreter and later won concessions from state officials for her people. Under white pressure, the tribe was moved to a reservation in Oregon. Being dissatisfied, they were receptive to pleas by the Bannock tribe to join them in forays against white settlers. The army was called in. Sarah pleaded with the commander not to attack until she could convince her people that they should withdraw from the alliance. Sarah and her brother crept into the Indian camp at night and led their people out. She then served as scout and interpreter with Brigadier General O. O. Howard. She was instrumental in establishing schools for the education of her people. Later, she traveled in the east, lecturing and writing. Her book, *Life Among the Paiutes: Their Wrongs and Claims,* was published in 1883.

WAYNE WOLF ROBE HUNT, Acoma Pueblo
(Art   11)
Born: early 1900's, Acoma Pueblo, New
    Mexico
Education: Albuquerque Indian School,
    New Mexico; Public school
Significance: *Promotion of the culture of
    his people*

Wayne Wolf Robe Hunt, the son of a noted leader of his pueblo, is a silversmith, artist, author-illustrator, lecturer, Indian dancer, and businessman. He operates a craft shop in Tulsa, Oklahoma, featuring his silver and turquoise jewelry. He also owns and operates The Grotto, a thirty-one unit motel in Tulsa.

Wolf Robe Hunt was one of the first of his people to attend high school. He participated in sports and equaled the state record in the discus. With his background and knowledge of Indian lore and customs, he became a highly successful interpreter of Indian songs and dances. He appeared before school and educational groups across the country and abroad. For a time, he worked for the Bureau of American Ethnology of the Smithsonian Institution as interpreter of Pueblo material. His birthplace, known as the "city in the sky," is the oldest continuously inhabited village in the United States, built long before the coming of the Spanish.

JOHN WOODENLEGS, Northern Cheyenne
(Tribal Affairs   16)
Born: 1912, Lame Deer, Montana
Education: Federal schools and public
    high school
Significance: *Dedication to the betterment
    of Indian people*

John Woodenlegs has been the president of the Northern Cheyenne Tribal Council since 1955. He is also the manager of the Northern Cheyenne Steer Enterprise. As the official leader of his tribe, he uses every source available on the federal, state, and local levels to help his people to greater responsibilities and self-determination. He travels throughout the United States and Europe to promote an understanding of the culture of his people. He is a member of the Montana Inter-Tribal Policy Board and has been president of the Northern Cheyenne Native American Church since 1950. In 1965, he was awarded the Northern Cheyenne Tribal Council Achievement Award. He has appeared as one of the principal actors in the Warner Brothers movie, *Forgotten Cheyennes.*

WOVOKA, Paiute
(Religion   35)
Born: 1858, Valley, Nevada
Died: 1932
Education: Tribal
Significance: *Founding of the historic
    Indian Messiah Movement*

Wovoka, or Jack Wilson as he was known among the white people, was the son of Tavibo, a medicine man. When Wovoka was fourteen years old, his father died. He was then taken into the family of a local rancher, David Wilson. The spiritual leanings Wovoka inherited from his father were strengthened by the practice of reading the Bible aloud in the Wilson family. The young Indian was strongly impressed by accounts of Jesus and his miracles. Seriously ill with a fever in 1888, and during a total eclipse of the sun, Wovoka had a vision. Recovering, he told of a revelation from the Great Spirit, "God told me to come back and tell my people they must be good and love one another and not fight or steal or lie."

Wovoka's message began a cult known as the Ghost Dance which spread like wildfire among Indians from the Rocky Mountains to the Missouri River. Wovoka became a Messiah whose doctrine, an explicitly peaceful one, promised that Indian lands would be restored, that Indian dead would arise, that buffalo, deer, elk, and other game would once again roam the plains in abundance, and that all Indians would be saved by dancing the Ghost Dance.

Wovoka's message was perfectly timed to appeal to western Indians confined on reservations. The revitalized stirring of the Indians, particularly the Sioux, made the white people nervous, coming so soon after the Battle of the Little Big Horn of 1876. The infamous Massacre of Wounded Knee on December 29, 1890, resulted. Wovoka was dismayed. His message had never counseled bloodshed. Although his messianic doctrine persisted, Wovoka altered his prophecies exhorting his people that their salvation rested in following the white man's road.

BEATIEN YAZZ, Navajo
(Painting   12, 38)
Born: 1932, Navajoland, Wide Ruins near Chambers, Arizona
Education: Sante Fe and Fort Wingate Indian Schools, New Mexico; Sherman Institute, California; Mills College, Oakland, California
Significance: *Artistic interpretation of the Navajo culture*

Beatien Yazz, born Jimmy Toddy, is considered the greatest living Indian primitive painter. When he was still a small boy, his artistic talent was discovered and sensitively nourished by Bill and Sally Lippincott of the Wide Ruins Trading Post in Arizona. His first pictures were delightful drawings of the animals he knew on the desert. Yazz is the appealing "Little No Shirt" in *Spin a Silver Dollar,* the story of his childhood written by Alberta Hannum and illustrated with his own drawings. It was published in 1945; *Paint the Wind,* published in 1958, continues the story of "Little No Shirt" after his return to the reservation following his discharge from service in World War II.

Yazz enlisted by subterfuge in the Marines when he was not quite sixteen. He served in the Navajo Code Unit of the Signal Corps as one of the famous Navajo Code Talkers, an extremely valuable branch of the service. Yazz now has a studio at the Wide Ruins Trading Post.

EVELYN YELLOW ROBE, Brule Sioux
(Education   11)
Born: ca. 1920, Rosebud Reservation, South Dakota
Education: Public schools; B.A., *Magna cum laude,* Mount Holyoke College, South Hadley, Massachusetts; M.A., Ph.D., Northwestern University,

Evanston, Illinois
Significance: *Research in speech pathology*

Evelyn Yellow Robe was born on an Indian reservation but grew up in New York, where she went to live with an older sister upon the death of her parents. While in high school, she was elected the first girl president of Arista, a citywide honor society. In college, she majored in speech and psychology. In recognition for her excellence in scholarship, she was honored with several scholarships and awards which enabled her to complete the requirements for a master's degree in speech pathology.

For the next eight years, Evelyn Yellow Robe was a member of the faculty of Vassar College. She then began her doctoral studies in speech pathology and audiology with the help of a John Hay Whitney Fellowship and a Ford Foundation Fellowship. The research for her doctoral dissertation relating to postlaryngectomy speech was sponsored by the Illinois Division of the American Cancer Society.

In 1954 Evelyn Yellow Robe was the recipient of a Fulbright Award for study in Paris under the direction of Dr. Jean Tarneaud, internationally known for his work in the field of voice research and the treatment of voice disorders. Evelyn Yellow Robe visited ear, nose, and throat clinics throughout Europe and was asked to report on her research. She was then invited to join the staff of the Northwestern University Medical School. In 1959 she married Hans Finkbeiner, professor of obstetrics and gynecology at the Free University of Berlin in Germany, where she now lives.

In 1946 Evelyn Yellow Robe was honored with the Indian Achievement Award of the Indian Council Fire.

ZARCILLOS LARGOS, Navajo
(Tribal Affairs   13)
Born: ca. 1800, Arizona
Died: 1860
Education: Tribal
Significance: *Promoting a philosophy of peace*

Zarcillos Largos, a medicine man for his tribe, prevented Navajo-Mexican and Navajo-American wars many times. He knew that the Navajos were destined to be driven from their land, but he worked for peace even when war appeared inevitable. He became spokesman for the Navajo Nation during the peace negotiation with the American Army at Bear Springs in 1846, at the beginning of the Mexican-American War. Narbona, his friend and leader, was weak and ailing at the time. Zarcillos Largos carried forward the peace policies of Narbona and always kept his promises to strive for peace in spite of the continual harassment by the Mexicans, the provocations of American soldiers and Navajo warriors, and the demands of the American officials to reduce the boundaries of their land. He was honest and courageous throughout and was killed on the peace trail.

JOSÉ A. ZUNI, Isleta Pueblo
(Tribal Affairs   16)
Born: 1921, Isleta Pueblo, New Mexico
Education: University of New Mexico, Albuquerque, New Mexico
Significance: *Dedication to the education of Indians*

José Zuni is the superintendent of the Stewart Indian Agency near Carson City, Nevada. This agency includes the Stewart Indian School, one of the large boarding schools designated for the education of Navajo young people. He served in the United States Army Air Force from 1943 to 1945, and received the Air Medal and four oak leaf clusters. In addition to his administrative duties at the agency in Nevada, Zuni is lieutenant governor and tribal judge in his own pueblo. He is also a member of the Isleta Tribal Council.

BIBLIOGRAPHY OF SOURCES USED

1   "American Indians: Strangers in Their Own Homeland," *Senior Scholastic,* (March 7, 1969), pp. 13-15; 23.

2   Andrist, Ralph K. *To The Pacific With Lewis and Clark.* Scranton, Pennsylvania: American Heritage Publishing Co., Inc., 1967.

3   Berthrong, Donald J. *The Southern Cheyennes.* Norman, Oklahoma: University of Oklahoma Press, 1963.

4   *Biographical Directory of the American Congress, 1774–1961.* Washington, D.C.: Government Printing Office, 1961.

5   Blassingame, Wyatt. *Osceola: Seminole War Chief.* Champaign, Illinois: Garrard Publishing Company, 1967.

6   Chief Eagle, D. *Winter Count.* Denver, Colorado: Golden Bell Press, 1967.

7   Cobe, Albert. *Great Spirit.* Chicago: Children's Press, 1970.

8   *Current Biography.* New York: H. W. Wilson Company, 1969.

9   Forbes, Jack D. *Nevada Indians Speak.* Reno, Nevada: University of Nevada Press, 1967.

10 Garst, Shannon. *Sitting Bull, Champion of His People.* New York: Julian Messner, Inc., 1946.

11 Gridley, Marion E. (ed.). *Indians of Today.* Chicago: Towerton Press, 1960.

12 Hannum, Alberta. *Spin a Silver Dollar.* New York: The Viking Press, 1958.

13 Hoffman, Virginia, and Johnson, Broderick H. *Navajo Biographies.* Rough Rock, Arizona: Diné, and the Board of Education, the Navajo Curriculum Center, 1970.

14 Josephy, Alvin M., Jr. (ed.). *The American Heritage Book of Indians.* Scranton, Pennsylvania: American Heritage Publishing Co., Inc., 1961.

15 _____. *The Nez Percé Indians and the Opening of the Northwest.* New Haven: Yale University Press, 1965.

16 Klein, Bernard, and Icolari, Daniel (eds.). *Encyclopedia of the American Indian.* New York: B. Klein and Company, 1967.

17 Kroeber, Theodora. *Ishi in Two Worlds.* Berkeley: University of California Press, 1961.

18 Langley, Dama. "The Indestructibles," *Arizona Highways,* (August, 1968), pp. 8-13.

19 [Magnuson, Ed, and Johnson, Keith]. "The Angry American Indian: Starting Down the Protest Trail," *Time,* (February 9, 1970), pp. 14-20.

20 Marriott, Alice. *Sequoyah, Leader of the Cherokees.* New York: Random House, 1956.

21 McGovern, Ann. *The Defenders: Osceola, Tecumseh, Cochise.* New York: Scholastic Magazines, Inc., 1970.

22 McKenney, Thomas L. and Hall, James. *Biographical Sketches and Anecdotes of Ninety-five of the 120 Principal Chiefs From the Indian Tribes of North America.* Washington, D.C.: United States Department of Interior - Bureau of Indian Affairs, 1967.

23   Montgomery, Elizabeth Rider. *Chief Joseph: Guardian of His People.* Champaign, Illinois: Garrard Publishing Company, 1969.

24   _____. *Chief Seattle: Great Statesman.* Champaign, Illinois: Garrard Publishing Company, 1966.

25   Neihardt, John G. (Flaming Rainbow). *Black Elk Speaks: Being a Life Story of a Holy Man of the Ogalala Sioux.* Lincoln, Nebraska: University of Nebraska Press, 1961.

26   Ortiz, Alfonso. *The Tewa World: Space, Time, Being, and Becoming In a Pueblo Society.* Chicago: The University of Chicago Press, 1969.

27   Personal Interview.

28   Personal research and viewing of paintings at the Heard Museum, Phoenix, Arizona.

29   "Philip Cassadore Sings Apache Songs." Record Album Number 6056. Phoenix, Arizona: Canyon Records, 1968.

30   Porter, C. Fayne. *Our Indian Heritage: Profiles of 12 Great Leaders.* Philadelphia: Chilton Books, 1924.

31   Richardson, Bernard E. "A Wind Is Rising," *Library Journal,* (February 1, 1970), pp. 463-467.

32   Seymour, Flora Warren. *Bird Girl: Sacagawea.* Indianapolis: The Bobbs-Merrill Company, 1945.

33   Stands In Timber, John, and Liberty, Margot. *Cheyenne Memories.* New Haven: Yale University Press, 1967.

34   United States Department of the Army. Office of the Chief of Military History. *Military Connected Contributions of American Indians.* Washington, D.C.: Government Printing Office, December, 1969.

35   United States Department of the Interior. Bureau of Indian Affairs. *Famous Indians: A Collection of Short Biographies.* Washington, D.C.: Government Printing Office, 1966.

36   _____. Indian Arts and Crafts Board. *Contemporary Sioux Painting.* Rapid City, South Dakota: Simpson's Creative Printers, 1970.

37   United States Department of the Interior. Bureau of Indian Affairs. *Indian Record.* (February, 1969). Washington, D.C.: Government Printing Office, 1969.

38   _____. *Indians in the War.* (November, 1945). Lawrence, Kansas: Haskell Institute Printing Department, 1946.

39   _____. *Indians of the Northwest.* Washington, D.C.: Government Printing Office, 1968.

40   _____. *You Asked About Prominent American Indians.* Washington, D.C.: Government Printing Office, 1969.

41   United States Department of the Navy. Office of the Chief of Naval Operations, Washington, D.C. Correspondence.

42   Waters, Frank. *Book of the Hopi.* Based on source materials recorded and interpreted by White Bear Fredericks. New York: Viking Press, 1963.

43   Waugh, John and Waugh, Lynne. "Renaissance of the Indian Spirit," *American Education,* (July, 1970), pp. 15-20.

44   White, Ann Terry. *The False Treaty: The Removal of the Cherokees From Georgia.* New York: Scholastic Magazines, Inc., 1970.

INDIAN AMERICANS

OTHER REFERENCES

BOOKS FOR TEACHERS

Blassingame, Wyatt. *Sacagawea: Indian Guide.* Champaign, Illinois: Garrard Publishing Company, 1965.

Cahn, Edgar S. (ed.). *Our Brother's Keeper: The Indian in White America.* Washington, D.C.: New Community Press, Inc., 1969.

Clark, Ann Nolan. *Journey to the People.* New York: The Viking Press, 1969.

Clark, Van. *Peetie The Pack Rat and Other Desert Stories.* Illustrated by Andy Tsinajinnie. Caldwell, Idaho: The Caxton Printers, 1960.

Collier, John. *The Indians of the Americas.* New York: W. W. Norton and Company, 1947.

Dunn, Dorothy. *American Indian Painting.* The University of New Mexico Press, 1968.

Gridley, Marion E. *Indian Legends of American Scenes.* Chicago: M. A. Donohue and Company, 1939.

Josephy, Alvin M., Jr. *The Indian Heritage of America.* New York: Bantam Books, 1968.

Kelly, William. *Indians of the Southwest. A Survey of Indian Tribes and Indian Administration in Arizona.* Tucson, Arizona: University of Arizona, 1953.

Kennedy, Michael S. (ed.). *The Red Man's West: True Stories of the Frontier Indians.* New York: Hastings House, 1965.

Kroeber, A. L. *Handbook of the Indians of California.* Berkeley: California Book Company, Ltd., 1953.

Kroeber, Theodora, and Heizer, Robert E. *Almost Ancestors, The First Californians.* San Francisco: Sierra Club, 1968.

Marriott, Alice, and Rachlin, Carol K. *American Indian Mythology.* New York: Thomas Y. Crowell Co., 1968.

Marriott, Alice. *Indians of the Four Corners. A Book About the Anasazi Indians and Their Modern Descendants.* New York: Thomas Y. Crowell Co., 1952.

Momaday, N. Scott. *House Made of Dawn.* New York: New American Library, A Signet Book Publication, 1966.

Place, Marian T. *Comanches and Other Indians of Texas.* New York: Harcourt, Brace and World, 1970.

Seton, Julia M. *American Indian Arts, A Way of Life.* New York, The Ronald Press Company, 1962.

Skinner, Alanson. *Indians of Manhattan Island and Vicinity.* New York: The American Museum of Natural History, 1947.

Wilke, Katharine E. *Pocahontas: Indian Princess.* Champaign, Illinois: Garrard Publishing Company, 1969.
Wissler, Clark. *Indians of The United States.* New York: Doubleday and Company, Inc., 1940.

PERIODICALS AND AIDS FOR TEACHERS

Alexander, Shana. "The Sad Lot of the Sioux," *Life,* (February 7, 1969).
"Apache Songs by Philip and Patsy Cassadore," Record Album Number 6053. Phoenix, Arizona: Canyon Records, 1966.
Bongartz, Roy. "Three Meanies: 1. The New Indian . . ." *Esquire,* (August, 1970), pp. 107-108, 125-126.
Hendrick, J. Robert, and Metos, Thomas H. "Outstanding Amerindians," *Instructor,* (February, 1970), pp. 98-101.
Josephy, Alvin M., Jr. "Indians in History," *Atlantic,* (June, 1970).
Parker, Charles Franklin. "The Peace Treaty With the Navajos," *Arizona Highways,* (August, 1968), pp. 2-7.
Wingell, Bill. "Indians on Alcatraz," *Youth,* (May 24, 1970).

BOOKS FOR CHILDREN

Appell, Claude. *Indians.* Chicago: Follett Publishing Company, 1965.
Beatty, Patricia. *Indian Canoe-Maker.* Idaho: The Caxton Printers, 1960.
Bleeker, Sonia. *Horseman of the Western Plateaus.* New York: William Morrow and Company, 1957.
_____. *The Sea Hunters.* New York: William Morrow and Company, 1951.
Brandt, Rose K. (ed.). *The Colored Land.* San Francisco: Charles Scribner's Sons, 1937.
Brindze, Ruth. *The Story of the Totem Pole.* New York: The Vanguard Press, Inc., 1951.
Brewster, Benjamin. *The First Book of Indians.* New York: Franklin Watts, Inc., 1950.
Butterfield, Marguerite, and Brown, Dorothy Lothrop. *Morning Star.* Pasadena: Lyons and Carnahan, 1963.
Clark, Ann Nolan. *Along Sandy Trails.* New York: The Viking Press, 1969.
_____. *Blue Canyon Horse.* New York: The Viking Press, 1954.
_____. *The Desert People.* New York: The Viking Press, 1962.
_____. *In My Mother's House.* New York: The Viking Press, 1962.
D'Aulaire, Edgar Parin, and D'Aulaire, Ingri. *Pocahontas.* Garden City, New York: Doubleday & Co., 1946.
Dines, Glen, and Price, Raymond. *Dog Soldiers.* New York: Macmillan Co., 1961.
Dorian, Edith, and Wilson, V. N. *Hokahey!: American Indians Then and Now.* New York: Whittlesey House, 1957.
Embree, Edwin R. *Indians of the Americas.* Boston: Houghton Mifflin Co., 1961.
Estep, Irene. *Iroquois.* Chicago: Melmont Publishers, Inc., 1961.
_____. *Seminoles.* Chicago: Melmont Publishers, Inc., 1963.
Farnsworth, Frances Joyce. *Winged Moccasins: The Story of Sacajawea.* New York: The Junior Literary Guild and Julian Messner, 1954.
Farquhar, Margaret C. *A Book to Begin On The Indians of Mexico.* San Francisco: Holt, Rinehart and Winston, 1967.

Fletcher, Sydney E. *The American Indians.* New York: Grosset & Dunlap, 1950.

Floethe, Richard, and Floethe, Louise Lee. *The Indian and His Pueblo.* New York: Charles Scribner's Sons, 1960.

Glubok, Shirley. *The Art of the North American Indian.* Evanston, Illinois: Harper and Row, Publishers, 1964.

Graff, Stewart, and Graff, Polly Anne. *Squanto Indian Adventurer.* Champaign, Illinois: Garrard Publishing Company, 1965.

Grant, Bruce. *American Indians Yesterday and Today.* New York: E. P. Dutton & Co., Inc., 1960.

Gridley, Marion E. *Indians of Yesterday.* Chicago: M. A. Donohue & Company, 1940.

Hodges, C. Walter. *Columbus Sails.* New York: Coward-McCann, Inc., 1939.

Hofsinde, Robert. *The Indian and the Buffalo.* New York: William Morrow and Company, 1961.

_____. *Indian Picture Writing.* New York: William Morrow and Company, 1959.

_____. *Indians At Home.* New York: William Morrow and Company, 1964.

Israel, Marion. *Cherokees.* Chicago: Melmont Publishers, Inc., 1961.

_____. *Dakotas.* Chicago: Melmont Publishers, Inc., 1959.

James, Harry C. *Ovada an Indian: Boy of the Grand Canyon.* Los Angeles: The Ward Ritchie Press, 1969.

Marcus, Rebecca B. *The First Book of The Cliff Dwellers.* New York: Franklin Watts, Inc., 1968.

Meadowcroft, Enid LaMonte. *Crazy Horse, Sioux Warrior.* Champaign: Garrard Publishing Company, 1965.

Morcomb, Margaret E. *Red Feather, A Book of Indian Life and Tales.* Pasadena: Lyons and Carnahan, 1963.

Morris, Loverne. *The American Indian As Farmer.* Chicago: Melmont Publishers, Inc., 1963.

Payne, Elizabeth. *Meet The North American Indians.* New York: Random House, 1965.

Payne, George E., and Driggs, Howard R. *Red Feather's Home Coming.* Pasadena: Lyons and Carnahan, 1963.

Rachlis, Eugene. *Indians of the Plains.* New York: American Heritage Publishing Co., Inc., 1960.

Russell, Solveig. *Navajo Land - Yesterday and Today.* Chicago: Melmont Publishers, Inc., 1961.

Salomon, Julian Harris. *The Book of Indian Crafts and Indian Lore.* New York: Harper and Brothers Publishers, 1928.

Shannon, Terry. *Stones, Bones and Arrowheads.* Chicago: Albert Whitman and Company, 1962.

Sutton, Felix. *North American Indians.* New York: Grosset and Dunlap Publishers, 1965.

Thompson, Hildegard. *Getting to Know American Indians Today.* New York: Coward-McCann, Inc., 1965.

Tunis, Edwin. *Indians.* Cleveland: The World Publishing Company, 1959.

Velarde, Pablita. *Old Father, the Storyteller.* Globe, Arizona: Dale Stuart King, Publisher, 1960.

Williams, Barbara. *Let's Go To an Indian Dwelling.* New York: G. P. Putnam's Sons, 1965.

Worthylake, Mary M. *Moolack: Young Salmon Fisherman.* Chicago: Melmont Publishers, Inc., 1963.

_____. *Nika Illahee.* (My Homeland). Chicago: Melmont Publishers, Inc., 1962.

PART FOUR

MEXICAN AMERICANS

... The truest act of courage,
the strongest act of manliness
is to sacrifice ourselves for others in a
totally non-violent struggle for justice.
To be a man is to suffer for others.
God help us to be men.

CÉSAR CHÁVEZ

MEXICAN AMERICANS

HISTORICAL PERSPECTIVE

THE PROUD NORTH AMERICAN HERITAGE of the Mexican American today dates beyond the Mayan calendar, which is considered more precise than that in use today and was in use 300 years before Christ. Also, prior to 1492, an estimated fifteen million Indians, speaking about 1,700 languages, inhabited the Western Hemisphere. More than ninety percent lived below the Rio Grande. Alfred Sandel writes that the most advanced Indians were those along the Pacific Coast in northern South America, and those of Mexico, Yucatan, and Guatemala. Their engineering, art, architecture, textiles and astronomy were of a high order, on a level with those of ancient Egypt and Mesopotamia.*

Today in the southwest there are nearly 6,000,000 people with cultural ties to Mexico and Spain. It has been estimated that there may be up to 9,000,000 Spanish-speaking persons in the United States. It is impossible to arrive at a single name that will be suitable to all of these. They call themselves, and are called, Mexicans, Mexican Americans, Hispanos, Americans of Mexican descent, Latinos, Manitos, and others. Each of these names, in part, indicates the degree of ethnocultural identification felt toward Mexican and Spanish societies. Most recently, a growing movement of young people call themselves Chicanos and assert they are not foreigners, but descendants of the original and the second societies to settle the American southwest. Through education and community involvement they are determined to change the economic poverty of the Mexican community and instill a strong pride in being of Mexican ancestry. In tracing their heritage, many Chicanos prefer to trace it to the Mexica tribe, known in our historical accounts as the Aztecs. The legends of the Mexicas tell of a great migration of the tribe from Atzlán to a final stop at Teotihuacán, which is now Mexico City. Other Chicanos identify with a heritage that claims each of the great Indian civilizations of Mexico, among which are the Olmec, Maya, and Toltec.

Dr. Julian Samora has written of the Mexican American that [they were here] before there was a British Jamestown; and [they are] as recent as tomorrow's immigrants who will walk across the border, visa in hand, to join relatives in East Los Angeles or Denver.

They are as rural and rooted as a mountain villager of Trampas, New Mexico, and as mobile and urban as a United States congressman.

Their early ancestors contributed to the area, and consequently to American culture, the domesticated animals of the region: horses, cattle, sheep, and goats. They brought the fruits and most of the vegetables that have made agri-business what it is in the southwest today. They brought the knowledge and the means to extract the minerals of the earth.

*Alfred Sandel, *A History of the Aztec and the Mayas and their Conquest,* (New York: Collier Books, 1967).

209

The livestock industry and its concomitant cowboy mystique are their legacy. Irrigation and present-day water laws derive from them.*

As a matter of interest, Jack D. Forbes says that about 500 A.D., southwestern Indians began to develop the Pueblo Indian civilization. This advanced way of life, which still flourishes in Arizona and New Mexico, was largely based upon Mexican influences in architecture, pottery-making, clothing, religion, government, and agriculture.**

Perhaps most significant is the fact that a United States citizen of Mexican descent or the most recent immigrant from Mexico can pridefully proclaim a viable North American heritage and one in which Mexicans were active in significant developments in what is now the United States. For example, gold was discovered in California in 1842 by Francisco Lopez. Juan DeAnza was the leader of the longest overland migration of a colony in North American history before the settlement of Oregon. Isidoro Aguilar supervised the building of San Juan Capistrano Mission, "Jewel of the Missions." Schools were founded. About twenty-two teachers were brought to California in the 1830's and a seminary was established at Santa Ynez. New towns were established, such as Sonoma, California. Printing presses were set up in 1835. Northern California was a frontier region and, therefore, not in the forefront of Mexican cultural progress, but there were benefits from developments originating further south.

Gradually the way of life brought to America by the Europeans became mixed with native Mexican influences, until the life of the common people became a blend of Spanish-Arabic and Indian traits, much as the culture of England after 1066 became a blend of French-Latin and Anglo-Celtic traditions. The Spaniards modified their language for governmental, scholarly, and religious purposes for several generations by incorporating many Mexican words, such as coyote, jicara, tamal, chile, chocolate, jacal, ocelote, and hundeds of other words which became part of Spanish as spoken in Mexico. Roman Catholic religious practice was modified by many Indian customs and devotion to the Virgin of Guadalupe has had a lasting impact upon the Catholic faith and the Mexican people.

The peoples of what is now Mexico intermixed with diverse tribes and eventually began to absorb both the non-Mexican Indian and the Spaniard himself. This process of migration and mixture made possible the creation of the independent Mexican republic in 1821, after a ten-year struggle for freedom.

The Mexican American community and its Spanish heritage was established on the North American continent on September 5, 1598, when Don Juan De Onate founded the settlement of Chamita, New Mexico. Since then, the Spanish/Mexican culture has continued to have a substantial influence on the development of the southwestern area of the United States in regard to architecture, religion, law, agriculture, mining, industry, and art. The Mexican people, approximately ninety-five percent of whom are part Indian, have absorbed the Spanish culture and maintained their ancient native heritage as well. Close proximity to Mexico has enabled the Mexican American to perpetuate his ties with the past. Mexican Americans today represent both the earliest settler and the most recent immigrant to the United States. Border crossings are a daily occurrence.

With the onset of the war between the United States and Mexico in 1846, the intensity of cultural alienation began, due to the demise of bilingually written legislation, and a halt to the use of the

---

*Julian Samora (ed.), *La Raza: Forgotten Americans,* (Notre Dame, Indiana: University of Notre Dame Press, 1966).

**Jack D. Forbes, *Mexican Americans - A Handbook for Educators,* (Berkeley, California: Far West Laboratory for Educational Research and Development, 1966).

children's native language of Spanish in the schools. In California this officially occurred in 1879, at which time a new constitution was adopted which eliminated Spanish as an official second language of the state.

The migratory process in agriculture made opportunities for education, social advancement, and assimilation into the Anglo-American cultural pattern more difficult. In 1910 immigration from Mexico increased. By 1920 it had reached tremendous proportions, thereby alarming the North Americans who exerted pressures to have many Mexicans deported. Although Spanish-speaking people were indigenous to the southwest region, even comprising the majority population in some areas, they nevertheless were subjected to the will of the Anglo-American population. They were either sent to segregated schools or to Anglo schools where the curriculum was devoid of any Spanish language or cultural influence.

Occupational opportunities for Mexican Americans today continue to be limited. Of those not engaged in farm labor, over eighty percent engage in hand labor and service occupations, such as construction work, clothing trades, domestic services, building maintenance, restaurant and hotel work, gardening and landscaping, trucking and retail selling.

The Mexican American has a far greater percentage of the poor than any other segment of the total population. The historic role of the Mexican has been to keep the supply of manual labor well ahead of demand. The continuing inflow of job seekers like himself, and mechanization in canneries, farming and other areas have served to keep the Mexican American among the lowest paid members of society. Characteristically, in the southwest, the Mexican American has created his own community within the greater American Society. In contemporary literature, this community has been referred to as the *barrio*. There are Mexican American entrepreneurs; typically they are the restaurant keeper, the grocer, the publisher of a newspaper, almost all of whom operate within the barrio. They have even become numerous enough to create their own chambers of commerce.

Educational opportunity for the Mexican American has always been limited. The schools in general have failed to consider bilingualism as a cultural asset and have insisted that children be schooled in a language which is unfamiliar and at times completely unknown to the child prior to starting school. Only recently, since 1967, has the Mexican American child been allowed to speak Spanish anywhere on school grounds other than in Spanish instruction classes. Teachers, unfamiliar with the language or the cultural values of the Mexican American, have at times unwittingly and at other times with open prejudice engendered in the child a poor self-image. As an ethnic group the Mexican American has an educational handicap of from four to seven years in comparison with the rest of the population.

After World War II most Mexican American organizations, organized by young war veterans, focused their interests on neighborhood improvement, protest of police harassment and brutality, election reforms, citizenship and naturalization, and funeral insurance protection.

An emerging trend in the Mexican American community began in the 1960's with the widespread support by students and adults for the Delano and Rio Grande Valley strikes by farm workers against the denials of social legislation and collective bargaining. This trend resulted in a growing unity among the Mexican American people. Identity labels were dropped in order to further *La Causa*. In addition, this movement has generated a growing bicultural awareness and support from many areas of American life.

The Mexican American has been type-cast as an itinerant, uneducated, unskilled worker whose position in life is unalterable. Gradually, this myth is being dispelled by leaders in the Mexican American community by men who have attained acceptance and esteem through education, business, political involvement, and through artistic accomplishments. Many Mexican Americans have been awarded medals for valor in combat and distinguished service in the various branches of the armed forces. In seeking to dispel prejudice and become assimilated, but not at the expense of abandoning their heritage, the Mexican Americans have founded such organizations as the Mexican Liberal Party, the Order of Sons of America, the League of United Latin-American Citizens, Community Service Organization, American G. I. Forum, Mexican American Political Association, and Political Association of Spanish-Speaking Organizations. These groups have professed allegiance to the United States, sought to advance understanding and mutual respect, advocated political participation and responsibility, and encouraged equality in education, in law and in employment for the Mexican American.

This section of *The Emerging Minorities in America* is planned to provide the classroom teacher with selected personal models from the Mexican American community with whom the Spanish-speaking student can identify whether he considers himself to be Chicano, Mexican, Mexican American or of Mexican descent.

It is a very small but, hopefully, a significant step in helping the American school system to cope with the challenge of educating our Chicano youth without requiring him to sacrifice his culture in the process. Indeed, as the schools accept this challenge then we will truly fulfill an age-old maxim of American education: *We teach to the individual differences of children.*

MEXICAN AMERICANS

BIOGRAPHICAL SUMMARIES

ROBERT J. ACOSTA
   (Education   15*)
   Born: 1939, Los Angeles, California
   Education: B.A. (Social Studies), B.A.
      (English), California State College, Los
      Angeles
   Significance: *Inspiration to other blind
      persons*

Robert J. Acosta was born into a family whose history in California goes back several generations. They once owned vast sections of what is now the Pomona Valley in southern California. Due to a congenital condition, Acosta is completely blind, but his parents wisely urged him to participate in as many normal activities as possible. He rode horseback, played a number of outdoor sports and attended summer camp. Acosta's accomplishments are the result of his own energy and determination, aided by the positive atmosphere created by his family as he was growing up. One of Acosta's favorite activities is sponsoring the Future Teachers of America at Chatsworth High School in the San Fernando Valley, California, where he is presently teaching.

RUDOLPH ACUÑA
   (Education   13)
   Born: 1932, Los Angeles, California
   Education: B.A., M.A., California State
      College, Los Angeles; Ph.D.,

*These numbers refer to the *Bibliography of Sources Used,* found at the end of this section.

University of Southern California, Los
   Angeles
Significance: *Leadership in the
   development of Mexican American
   Studies Programs*

Rudolph Acuña emigrated with his parents to the United States from Mexico in the 1920's. He served in the army from 1953 to 1955.

Dr. Acuña is chairman of the Mexican American Studies Program at San Fernando Valley State College and is a member of the National Laboratory of Inter-American Studies. His book entitled *The Story of the Mexican American: The Men and The Land* for use by children and teachers was published in 1969.

ISIDRO AGUILAR
   (Construction   11)
   Born: Culiacan, Mexico
   Died: 1803
   Significance: *Work in building the San
      Juan Capistrano Mission*

Isidro Aguilar, of Spanish and Aztec blood, was a stone mason and builder. He supervised the building of the "Jewel of the Missions," San Juan Capistrano, from 1799 until his death in 1803. The mission was not completed until three years after his death.

LUÍS VALENTINE AMADOR
   (Medicine   10)
   Born: Las Cruces, New Mexico
   Education: B.S., New Mexico State
      University, Las Cruces; M.D.,

213

Northwestern University, Evanston, Illinois

Significance: *Leadership in spastic paralysis research*

Dr. Luís Valentine Amador was a captain in the army and served at the Letterman Army Hospital in San Francisco. Later, he was a Fellow in Neuropathology at the University of Illinois and Senior Resident Neurosurgeon for the Illinois Research and Educational Hospitals and the Illinois Neuropsychiatric Institute. Subsequently in 1950 he was appointed Research Associate in Neurophysiology for the Rockefeller Institute for Research in Europe; in 1954 he became a Guggenheim Fellow in Neurosurgery.

Dr. Amador has lectured for the Scandinavian Neurological Society in 1952, the University of Freiburg, Germany in 1954, the New England Neurosurgical Society in 1954, the Academy of Neurological Surgeons in 1958, the New York University - Bellevue Medical Center in 1959, and the Second International Congress of Neurological Surgeons. The professional societies to which he belongs include the Harvey Cushing Society and the Congress of Neurological Surgeons.

JOHN A. ARGUELLES

(Law 7)

Education: University of California at Los Angeles

Significance: *Judiciary leadership*

John Arguelles is a judge of the Municipal Court in the East Los Angeles District. He served as a presiding judge and was re-elected without opposition to a six-year term. He has served nine years in all areas of criminal and civil work at trial and appellate levels of the state courts and at the trial level in the federal courts. He was elected councilman for the City of Montebello in 1962 and served as its mayor during 1964.

SANTIAGO ARGUELLO

(Government 11)

Born: 1791, Monterey, California

Died: 1862

Significance: *Leadership through government service*

Captain Arguello can be cited for setting up a militia for protection from the pirate Hippolyte de Bouchard. He was made commander and governor of San Diego about 1825. Later, he was appointed administrator of San Juan Capistrano. Arguello died at his beloved Rancho Tia Juana, which had been granted to him in 1829.

FRANCISCO BRAVO

(Medicine 9)

Born: 1910, Santa Paula, California

Education: Ph.D., Stanford University, California; M.D., University of Southern California, Los Angeles

Significance: *Concern for medical treatment of the poor*

Francisco Bravo founded a free medical clinic in Los Angeles soon after he completed his medical education. He was with the Army in the Pacific during World War II, and returned to his work with the Bravo Clinic in 1946. His father and mother and other members of his family were agricultural laborers. His continuing concern for the disadvantaged was demonstrated by his clinic activities; his role as the director and organizer of the Medical Program for Mexican Braceros; membership in the Governor's Committee on the Employment of the Handicapped, and continuing work with the East Los Angeles Commission. He has also been medical examiner for the state athletic commission, Los Angeles health commissioner, member of the board of police commissioners, and on the city charter revision committee. He is also president and chairman of the board of the Pan American National Bank and active in cattlemen's organizations.

ARTURO Y. CABRERA

(Education 13)

Born: Pittsburg, California

Education: B.S., M.A., Ed.D., University of Colorado, Boulder; D.F., Fresno State College, California; and, University of Autonoma, Mexico

Significance: *Belief in the importance of education*

Dr. Arturo Y. Cabrera's parents came from Mexico. The family in which he grew up was large and poor. For many years they lived in a small California town where his father worked as an unskilled laborer. The entire family worked regularly in the crops, especially during the summer periods. He and his sisters and brothers stayed in high school and graduated. The war gave them the advantage of the G.I. Education Bill. He and his brothers and sisters attended college and four have graduated. They found that the hardest part of going to the university was the strangeness of it and feeling so far behind everyone else. In time gains were made.

Dr. Cabrera is convinced that education has made it possible for him to be of service to his total community in a way not otherwise possible. Every Chicano who moves ahead makes a contribution by that fact alone. The many Mexican Americans in the barrios, however, need understanding and support. He has found that the Mexican American bicultural and bilingual heritage is an asset. This great gift should be cultivated through education, community service and political participation. He says that the way is at times rough, but one can do it. Chicanos can count on a better tomorrow.

Dr. Cabrera is professor of education at California State College at San Jose. He is also author of *Schizophrenia in the Southwest* and *Chicano Voice is Being Heard.*

VIKKI CARR
(Entertainment   7)
Born: Texas
Education: Rosemead High School, Rosemead, California
Significance: *Outstanding singer*

Vikki Carr was named Florencia Bisenta de Casillas Martínez Cardona. She grew up in Rosemead, California. While in high school she took all the music courses she couid and sang the lead roles in the school musicals. Upon graduation she won the solo spot on he Pepe Callahan Mexican-Irish Band and traveled to Reno, Lake Tahoe and Hawaii. She has been featured on television with the Ray Anthony Show, the Danny Kaye Show, and she has appeared with Steve Allen, Johnny Carson and Jerry Lewis. She has starred in five TV specials in England.

REYNALDO J. CARREÓN, JR.
(Medicine   7)
Born: 1900
Education: D.O., Los Angeles College of Optometry; D.O., Los Angeles College of Osteopathic Physicians and Surgeons; M.D., University of California, Los Angeles
Significance: *Activities in civic affairs*

Dr. Reynaldo J. Carreón, Jr. is a staff director of the Pan American Medical Eye Group at the Los Angeles County Hospital and director of the Parkview Hospital in Los Angeles.

In 1959 he was appointed as a Los Angeles Police Commissioner and served again in 1965. He has been active in his community as past president of the Civil Defense Board, a member of the Board of Police Commissioners, and of the Los Angeles Mexican Chamber of Commerce. He is a member of the Elks Club, and has served as coordinator of Latin American Affairs for Los Angeles. He founded the United States Committee of the World Medical Association.

JOSÉ ANTONIO CARRILLO
(Government   1)
Born: 1796, Santa Barbara, California
Died: 1862
Significance: *Leadership in retaining Mexican culture in California*

José Antonio Carrillo, along with his brother Carlos, was extremely active in the complex politics of Alta California during the Spanish and Mexican periods. He was a leader of determined resistance by the Californios—Spanish-speaking citizens of the Mexican province of Alta California—to the American conquest of California in 1846. The Californios under Carrillo's leadership routed U.S. forces in several skirmishes near Los Angeles before the conquest was finally secured. He accommodated himself to the new order and was one of eight Spanish-speaking delegates to the constitutional convention of 1849, taking a leading part in the convention's deliberations. He retired soon after to his home in Santa Barbara and private business.

ANDRÉS CASTILLERO
(Metallurgy   8)
Born: ca. 1820, Mexico
Died: late 1800's
Significance: *Discovery of the first quicksilver mine in the western hemisphere*

In 1845, the Mexican government sent Captain Andrés Castillero, a young cavalry officer, on a military mission to Fort Sutter. Castillero had been trained in metallurgy earlier in his life. A priest at the San Jose Mission told Castillero of a famous vermillion cave. (Vermillion is a color pigment found in cinnabar which in turn is the most significant source of quicksilver.) He became very interested.

By putting some of the cinnabar clay in his gun, Castillero discovered that drops of quicksilver gathered in the gun barrel after the gun was fired. The mine was named New Almaden. The discovery of the New Almaden quicksilver mine near San Jose, California, unlocked the gold and silver resources of California and changed the course of American economic history. Prior to this discovery, it had been necessary to import quicksilver from Europe. Quicksilver is essential in the process of separating the metal from the waste in the gold and silver extraction process.

RAUL H. CASTRO
(Government   9)
Born: 1916, Cananea, Mexico
Education: B.A., Arizona State University; LL.B., University of Arizona, Tucson
Significance: *Service to his country at many leadership levels*

Raul Castro came to the United States in 1926 and was naturalized in 1939, the same year he took his bachelor's degree. He worked as a State Department clerk and as an instructor in Spanish until he got his law degree. After some years in private practice and as a deputy county attorney in Tucson, he became county attorney in 1954. He was a judge in the superior court and in the juvenile courts of Tucson until 1964, when he was appointed U.S. ambassador to El Salvador. In 1968 he became ambassador to Bolivia.

CÉSAR CHÁVEZ
(Civil Rights   9)
Born: 1927, Yuma, Arizona
Significance: *Leadership toward achieving better working conditions and legal protection for farm workers*

César Chávez was active in several organizational efforts in the Mexican-American community in Los Angeles in the 1950's and in 1958 he was appointed general director of the Los Angeles Community Service Organization. He decided to put his organizational talent and experience into an effort to organize farm workers, an enterprise that had frustrated many predecessors, including his own father. Accordingly, in 1962 he moved to Delano, California, where he founded the National Farm Workers Association. The merger of several California agricultural organizing efforts resulted in the formation of the United Farm Workers Organizing Committee (UFWOC) with AFL-CIO support, and Chávez became the new union's most important leader. The UFWOC's epochal strike against growers in the San Joaquin Valley began in 1966. Chávez orchestrated a nationwide boycott in support of the farm strikers that eventually helped them to win union contracts. UFWOC soon established itself in fields from the Salinas Valley to the Rio Grande, and its struggle is a central theme in the cultural awakening among Spanish-speaking Americans of the Southwest.

DENNIS CHÁVEZ
(Politics   9)
Born: 1888, New Mexico
Died: 1962
Significance: *Championship of civil rights*

Dennis Chávez addressed the people of New Mexico by saying, "Soy de ustedes" which means *I am one of you.* He was elected to the United States Senate from New Mexico and served in this capacity for over twenty-five years.

Chávez was one of eight children of an old family of New Mexico. In 1930, he became a clerk in the House of Representatives. Four years later he ran for office, but lost. However, when Senator Bronson Cutter died in 1935, Chávez was appointed to complete the term. He then became a leader in the United States Senate and was chairman of the Public Works Committee and a member of the powerful Appropriations Committee. Senator Chávez was a firm believer in full equality for everyone.

BERT N. CORONA
   (Civil Rights   15)
   Born: 1918
   Education: El Paso City Schools;
      University of Southern California, Los
      Angeles; University of California at
      Los Angeles
   Significance: *Leadership in the Mexican
      American cause*
Bert N. Corona has been, from his teen-aged years, a pioneer in the areas of social reform and educational opportunity for Mexican Americans. The Mexican Youth Conference, which he helped to start, grew into a high school and college student movement throughout the southwestern states and became known as the Mexican American Movement.

Corona has demonstrated his qualities of leadership by organizing such groups as the Mexican American workers in the Los Angeles area, and the National Congress of the Spanish Speaking People which is the first national organization for the civic, political, and civil rights of the Mexican population in the southwest. He founded the Mexican American Political Association (MAPA) in Phoenix, Arizona, and has been quite active as a member of the organization, holding offices of importance.

   (Used by permission of Educational Consulting Associates, Menlo Park, California.)

JUAN BAUTISTA DE ANZA
   (Exploration   11)
   Born: 1736, Fronteras, Arizona (near
      Douglas)
   Died: ca. 1800
   Significance: *Leadership in the settlement
      and development of California*
Juan Bautista De Anza, born of an aristocratic family, joined the army at sixteen. In 1760 he was made lieutenant. Fourteen years later he became a captain. Then in 1782 he was promoted to colonel.

On January 8, 1774, De Anza and a group of Indians began a journey which eventually led them to Monterey, California. This march became famous in history. De Anza is spoken of as the leader of the longest overland migration of a colony in North American history before the settlement of Oregon.

ELIGIO DE LA GARZA
   (Politics   9)
   Born: 1927, Mercedes, Texas
   Education: LL.B., Saint Mary's Law
      School
   Significance: *Service as a legislator*
Eligio De La Garza served for twelve years in the Texas House of Representatives and was elected to Congress in 1964. He had a long struggle to gain an education, but did receive his law degree in 1952. His experiences in both the United States Navy and Army encouraged him to serve the public in civilian life as well.

Garza has been an active member of the League of United Latin American Citizens (LULAC).

DANIEL FERNÁNDEZ
   (Military   9)
   Born: 1944, Albuquerque, New Mexico
   Died: 1966
   Education: High school
   Significance: *Valor in military service*
Daniel Fernández was the first Mexican-American to win the Congressional Medal of Honor in the Vietnam War. His unit was surrounded while on patrol in 1966, and Sp4 Fernández threw himself on a grenade to save the

lives of the men around him. Sixteen Mexican-American Medal of Honor winners preceded him, and at least four more have followed.

JOSÉ FIGUEROA
(Government   18)
Born: Mid 1700's
Died: 1835
Significance: *Humane approach in implementing laws*

José Figueroa was the sixth governor of California under Mexican rule from 1833 to 1835. He was an able man and sincerely interested in bettering California. When the National Congress of Mexico passed the famous Act of Secularization in 1833, Governor Figueroa put the new law into immediate effect. The Secularization Act provided that the missions would become pueblo churches and that the vast land holdings of the missions would be divided among the Indians and opened for settlement. He felt, however, that a gradual policy of emancipation would be better for the Indians. In 1834 ten missions were secularized, six in 1835, and the remaining five were secularized in 1836.

FRED G. FIMBRES
(Law   7)
Born: 1917, Tucson, Arizona
Education: B.A. University of Southern California, Los Angeles
Significance: *Leadership through law enforcement agencies*

Fred G. Fimbres served as a captain in the infantry of the United States Army, winning the Bronze Star, Combat Infantry Badge and Army Commendation Medal during World War II.

In 1940 he had joined the Sheriff's Department, first working as a patrol officer and then serving in the Juvenile Bureau in East Los Angeles. He became a lieutenant and then commander of the Public and Foreign Relations Bureau. Later he became captain and commanded the Narcotic and Vice Details. In 1955 he was appointed chief and placed in charge of the Administrative Division of the Los Angeles County Sheriff's Department.

MANUEL FLORES
(Government   7)
Born: 1927, San Fernando, California
Education: University of Idaho, Moscow; University of Southern California, Los Angeles; University of California at Los Angeles
Significance: *Political achievement through community involvement*

Manuel Flores is an industrial engineer. In 1966 he ran for councilman in San Fernando, California, stressing the rights of all people and speaking for a better education for Spanish-speaking Americans. In 1968 he was elected mayor of San Fernando, California.

ERNESTO GALARZA
(Civil Rights   1)
Born: ca. 1900, Jalcocotan, Nayarít, Mexico
Education: Sacramento City schools; B.A., Occidental College, California; M.A., Stanford University, California; Ph.D., Columbia University, New York
Significance: *Activities in behalf of the Mexican farm laborer*

Ernesto Galarza came to the southwest from Mexico as a small boy. At an early age, he worked with a band of harvesters and later he worked in a cannery and at many other jobs to help pay his way through school. His determination to seek an education carried him through a doctoral program in history.

After graduation, he held many important jobs, including Chief of the Division of Labor of the Pan American Union. In this capacity he was able to exert leadership in bringing about change for farm laborers. He quit this important post, however, to return to the southwest to lead farm workers in a more direct way.

Dr. Galarza also found time to write and to publish many articles. He is the author of *Strangers in Our Fields, Merchants of Labor, Spider in the House,* and *Workers in the Field.* He is writing a children's literature series in Spanish of which *Zoo-Risa* is the first to be published.

He has also written his autobiography which takes him through his high school years. He has given much time in working with teacher groups on the education of the Mexican American.

EUGENE GONZALES
(Education   13)
Born: 1925, Anaheim, California
Education: B.A., Whittier College, California; M.S., University of Southern California, Los Angeles; Honorary LL.D., Whittier College
Significance: *Leadership in the development of educational programs for Mexican American youth and adults*

Dr. Eugene Gonzales began his career in education in 1950 in the schools of Whittier, California. From the beginning, his interest in the problems and education of the recalcitrants, the disadvantaged, and the dropouts was paramount. In those early days of teaching in the seventh and eighth grades, his innovative practices with these young people and their parents and his knowledge of school law led to his assignment as Supervisor of Child Welfare and Attendance. In this capacity he became a member of the professional staff of the Santa Barbara County Schools Office, in Santa Barbara, California. His creativity in the interest of children flourished there. He organized councils in strategic parts of the county made up of community agencies involved with the welfare of children. This was to facilitate action in the best interest of children and youth. Later, as Coordinator of Special Education, he assisted districts throughout the county to establish innovative programs for children with special educational needs.

In 1964 Gonzales was named assistant to the California State Superintendent of Public Instruction with offices in Los Angeles. In this capacity he exerted considerable influence on the education of minority groups and in solving problems of inter-group, and public relations. For this service he received the honorary degree of Doctor of Laws from Whittier College in 1968. In this same year he was appointed Associate Superintendent of Education for the State of California.

In 1969 Gonzales was honored again by the California Council for Adult Education with a Special Recognition Award "for his continuous and vigorous support of adult and vocational education, especially in the formulation of programs for the Mexican American: Bilingual Education for the non-English speaking and Reading Programs for the Migrant Workers."

More recently, in June of 1970, President Nixon asked Dr. Gonzales to serve on the Presidential Commission on School Finance.

HENRY B. GONZALEZ
(Politics   9)
Born: 1916, San Antonio, Texas
Education: LL.B., Saint Mary's University School of Law, San Antonio, Texas
Significance: *Sponsorship of many bills ending segregation*

Henry Gonzalez was with military intelligence during World War I and worked for his father's translating firm and as a public relations counselor for an insurance company before he became a probation officer for Bexar County (San Antonio), Texas, in 1945. He was elected to the San Antonio city council in 1953 and subsequently became mayor pro-tem, state senator (the first Mexican-American in the Texas Senate since 1846), and congressman (1961). With Eligio de la Garza, elected in 1964, he is one of only two Texas congressmen of Spanish surname.

RICHARD "PANCHO" GONZALES
(Tennis   7)
Born: 1928, Los Angeles, California
Significance: *Athletic achievements*

Richard "Pancho" Gonzales' interest in tennis started when he was thirteen. He practiced at Exposition Park in Los Angeles, winning his first championship when he was nineteen. He won again in 1950 and became a member of the United States team that won the Davis Cup by defeating Australia. He was the World's Professional Champion in tennis from 1954 to 1962.

He owns the Pancho Gonzales Tennis Ranch in Malibu, California. Gonzales is also interested in racing cars.

RALPH GUZMAN
(Education 13)
Born: 1924, Mexico
Education: B.A., M.A., California State College, Los Angeles; Ph.D., University of California at Los Angeles
Significance: *Author and lecturer in Mexican American affairs*

Dr. Ralph Guzman has been active in Mexican American educational affairs since 1952 when he taught bilingual classes in United States citizenship for elderly Mexican Americans. Since that time he has lectured at major universities and colleges in California on topics related to the Mexican American community in education, political participation and community involvement.

Dr. Guzman has served as a consultant to Secretary John Gardner of the Department of Health, Education, and Welfare on the educational problems of the Mexican American people; to Secretary Robert C. Weaver of the Department of Housing and Urban Affairs; and to the Office of Economic Opportunity regarding problems of community development. He has held other major government and private consultancy positions requiring a high level of expertise, knowledge and professional competence.

In international affairs Dr. Guzman served as associate director to the United States Peace Corps for the Republics of Venezuela and Peru. As assistant director of the Mexican American Study Project at the University of California at Los Angeles, from 1964 to 1968, he has prepared various reports and papers dealing with contemporary problems faced by Mexican Americans. Two of his most significant papers are "The Role of the Mexican American Voter and the Democratic Party" and "The Political Potential of Mexicans and Negroes in California." Among his published books is *The Mexi-can American People: The Nation's Second Largest Minority.*

WILLIAM G. HERRERA
(Law 7)
Born: ca. 1920, Albuquerque, New Mexico
Education: University of New Mexico, Albuquerque; Brigham Young University, Provo, Utah
Significance: *Leadership in law enforcement*

William G. Herrera, a deputy district attorney, is on the District Attorney's Crime Prevention Staff and is active in law enforcement in the League of California Cities. In addition, he serves as a councilman in Pomona, California, is on the Mayor's Traffic Safety Committee and the committee for the development of a civic center.

Herrera has worked with the Boy Scouts, Young Men's Christian Association, Pop Warner's Football League and the Pony League. He has been a member of the Board of Directors of the Boy's Clubs of America and has been active in a variety of civic affairs including the PTA, March of Dimes, Concert Music Fund Drive and the Cal Poly Booster Club. In 1965, the City of Pomona honored him as "Father of the Year."

Herrera was the charter chairman of the Mexican American Political Association (MAPA).

EMMA JIMÉNEZ
(Education 7)
Born: ca. 1930, New Mexico
Education: B.A., California State College, Los Angeles
Significance: *Career in teaching*

Emma Jiménez moved to California with her family while she was still in elementary school. She has taught in elementary schools and in special classes. She has worked in educational television on such programs as "Wonderful World of Children." She is helping to write books in Spanish for very young children, which include *Cancioncitas Para Chiquitines* and *Versitos Para Chiquitines.*

JOHN F. LEÓN
(Education   7)
Born: 1924, Tucson, Arizona
Education: Pepperdine College, Los
    Angeles; M.A., University of Southern
    California, Los Angeles
Significance: *Leadership in instructional
    planning*
John F. León came to Los Angeles while very young. Early in life he made up his mind to become a teacher. After serving in the United States Army in the Solomon and Philippine Islands, he began teaching at the elementary school level. He then became a school principal and has also worked as a consultant, supervisor and coordinator. He is now director of the East Los Angeles Instructional Planning Center.

FRANCISCO LOPEZ
(Exploration   1, 8)
Born: ca. 1800, Sonora, Mexico
Significance: *Discovery of gold in
    California*
Francisco Lopez, a herdsman, discovered gold in 1842 in the Santa Feliciana Canyon forty miles from Los Angeles. While riding near today's city of San Fernando he became hungry and decided to eat some of the wild onions which grew in the canyon. As he dug the onions he noticed some flakes and nuggets clinging to their roots. Lopez had in fact discovered gold which he then mined in paying quantities several years before James W. Marshall made his famous discovery in 1849. Mexicans had been mining various locations along the coast range between Los Angeles and Santa Cruz. Jack Forbes states in his publication, *Mexican-Americans; A Handbook for Educators,* that Mexicans were often experienced miners and their techniques were used during the California Gold Rush until the advent of steam powered machinery.

HENRY LÓPEZ
(Law   1)

Born: ca. 1915, Denver, Colorado
Education: University of Denver,
    Colorado; LL.B., Harvard Law
    School, Cambridge, Massachusetts
Significance: *Career as a lawyer and
    author*
Henry López is a leading international lawyer. He is also an author, having published articles in leading American magazines. For many years López lived in Mexico where he edited a Mexican literary magazine.

López's parents came from Chihuahua, Mexico and settled in Denver, Colorado. As a small boy, López worked in the beet fields of Colorado with his father. Later he worked his way through high school and the university. He now lives in New York City and continues to work in behalf of the Mexican Americans. He encourages students to attend law school. He is a member of the Mexican American Legal Defense Fund.

TRINI LÓPEZ
(Entertainment   7)
Born: 1937, Dallas, Texas
Significance: *Success in entertainment*
Trini López is a world famous Mexican American entertainer whose skill with the guitar and warm singing style have brought him success. He began entertaining at the age of eleven in a small combo formed with his friends.

In 1960 López came to Los Angeles. His style was immediately popular and he was signed with a record company. Some of his top hits are "Trini López at P. J.'s," "If I Had a Hammer," "La Bamba," and "A-me-re-ca." He has toured many countries, has appeared in many TV shows and has begun an acting career in films.

IGNACIO E. LOZANO, JR.
(Journalism   12, 15)
Born: 1927, San Antonio, Texas
Education: B.A., University of Notre
    Dame, Notre Dame, Indiana
Significance: *Career as an influential
    publisher*

Ignacio Lozano comes from a family prominent in the world of publishing. His father founded the well known newspaper, *La Opinion,* the only Spanish language daily serving the southwestern states. At the age of twenty, Lozano became assistant to the publisher, and for the next six years he learned the newspaper business. In 1953 he became publisher of *La Opinion* and has succeeded in maintaining its wide influence among the Spanish speaking people of the southwest. In addition, Lozano has been active in civic affairs, and has served on the California State Advisory Committee to the United States Commission on Civil Rights. He has been a consultant to the Bureau of Educational and Cultural Affairs of the United States Department of State.

(Used by permission of Educational Consulting Associates, Menlo Park, California.)

MANUEL MICHELTORENA
(Government   5)
Born: ca. 1790
Died: ca. 1860
Significance: *Governorship of California under Mexican rule*

Manuel Micheltorena was the twelfth governor of California during the years 1842 to 1845. He was friendly toward the American settlers and impartial in his dealings with them. He expected them to conduct themselves properly and to comply with the colonization laws of Mexico. Micheltorena gave California land to American settlers as readily as to native born citizens.

RICARDO MONTALBÁN
(Entertainment   7)
Born: 1920, Mexico City, Mexico
Education: High school; Drama school
Significance: *Career in acting*

Ricardo Montalbán left Los Angeles to go to New York where he studied drama. He has played singing roles in many stage plays and in movies. Among these are *Sweet Charity, Battleground, Border Incident,* and *Sayonara.*

PHILIP MONTEZ
(Education   12)
Born: 1931, Los Angeles, California
Education: B.A., M.A., University of Southern California, Los Angeles
Significance: *Work for the Mexican American people*

Philip Montez has served in California as director of psychological services for the Palos Verdes School District, research psychologist for the El Rancho Unified School District, research associate at the University of Southern California and professor at San Fernando State College. He has served as executive director for the Foundation of Mexican American Studies. He is the founding president of the Association of Mexican American Educators.

In 1967 Montez was appointed director of the western field office of the United States Commission on Civil Rights. He has been on the board of directors for the Council of Mexican American Affairs. He is the author of "Bicultural Problems," "A Need for Bicultural Programs," "Cultural Differences," "The Psychology of the Mexican American Student," and "Remarks by Philip Montez."

ALFREDO MORALES
(Education   7)
Born: ca. 1925, Veracruz, Mexico
Education: Elementary and high school, Mexico; California State College at Long Beach; M.A., Ph.D., University of Southern California, Los Angeles
Significance: *Work with Peace Corps*

Dr. Alfredo Morales has been a teacher and lecturer at the University of Southern California. He is a professor of Foreign Languages at California State College at Los Angeles. He worked in the language training program for members of the Peace Corps assigned to Central and South American countries. He is interested in Latin American Theater and has helped to compile a collection of Mexican one-act plays.

JULIÁN NAVA
(Education   13)
Born: 1927, Los Angeles, California

Education: B.A., Pomona College, Claremont, California; M.A., Ph.D., Harvard University, Cambridge, Massachusetts

Significance: *Encouragement of good education for all children*

Dr. Julián Nava is a professor in the history department at San Fernando Valley State College and serves as a member of the Board of Education of the Los Angeles City Schools. His early home life was typical of other Mexican Americans. He attended public schools in Los Angeles. During the summer he picked fruit with the entire family. When war came, he volunteered for the navy as did his older brother. Military service opened his eyes to realities beyond the barrio. He met people who did not see him as a "Mexican." He found that he could choose what he wanted to be.

After his military service, he worked in auto and truck shops with his older brother. He had learned this work when he was fourteen years old. Shop courses in school helped him and his teachers encouraged him.

He never imagined going to college, but when a new junior college was opened between the barrio and the Anglo neighborhood, he enrolled. College work was hard, but his teachers were understanding and helpful. Soon his grades were mostly "A's" and "B's". A group of students at East Los Angeles Junior College worked out a plan with their professors. Instead of giving speeches to each other in class, they talked to groups of high school students in the barrio. The purpose was to encourage students to look beyond high school in their educational careers.

After graduation, Dr. Nava went to Pomona College where standards were so high that only about one out of a hundred applicants gained entrance. He competed with students who had been preparing for Pomona College while he had been picking apricots and straightening fenders.

Dr. Nava went on to Harvard University for his doctorate degree in history, which he gained in four years. He taught in Puerto Rico, in Spanish, for two years and in 1957 joined the staff of San Fernando Valley State College. He has taken leaves to teach in Spain as a Fulbright lecturer. In 1967 he was persuaded to run for public office. The "experts" said that it was impossible to elect a Mexican American to the school board. Dr. Nava was accustomed to facing big challenges. He concentrated on the need for the kind of good schools that would serve all young people. He stressed the main elements that unite all Americans. Now, as one of seven board members, he serves over 800,000 pupils from kindergarten to junior college.

Dr. Nava is the author of *Mexican Americans: Past, Present and Future* published in 1969.

ESTEVAN OCHOA

(Business 8)

Born: 1831, Chihuahua, Mexico

Died: ca. 1900

Significance: *Leadership in the development of the southwest*

As a young man, Estevan Ochoa went to Independence, Missouri to learn English. In 1859 he returned to the southwest by way of the Santa Fe Trail and established a chain of stores and a well-organized packtrain system to supply them. The freighting firm of Tully and Ochoa was famous throughout the southwest and deep into Mexican territory.

Ochoa was instrumental in the establishment of the first public school system in the Arizona Territory. He was a member of the territorial legislature and mayor of Tucson. When the railroad finally reached Tucson, in 1880, Ochoa presented Charles Crocker with the silver spike used in the dedication ceremonies. The coming of the railroad spelled the end of the packtrains.

UVALDO H. PALOMARES

(Education 13)

Born: 1936, Indio, California

Education: B.A., Chapman College, Orange, California; M.A., San Diego State College, California; Ed.D., University of Southern California, Los Angeles

Significance: *Concern for the education of children*

Dr. Uvaldo Palomares is president of the Institute for Personal Effectiveness in Children and its related Human Development Program. A clinical psychologist, Dr. Palomares is nationally acclaimed as a lecturer on effective education and minority group problems. He serves on numerous national committees and is a consultant to the United States Office of Education, the United States Office of Housing and Urban Development and the United States Office of Civil Rights.

Dr. Palomares was born and reared in a Spanish-speaking environment. His family traveled a great deal throughout Arizona and California while engaged in picking crops. This accounts for his interests in the Mexican American as a sociological group, the education of the migrant and the culturally disadvantaged and his work in early childhood guidance.

HILARIO PEÑA

(Education   7)

Born: ca. 1925, Deming, New Mexico
Education: B.A., M.A., Pasadena
    Nazarene College, California; Ed.D.,
    University of Mexico; Ph.D.,
    University of Madrid, Spain
Significance: *Contributions to the
    education of his people*

Dr. Hilario Peña worked his way through school. His wit and humor made him a favorite as master of ceremonies during his college years. He has taught at Santa Monica and Pasadena City Colleges. He is co-author of several foreign language textbooks. Some of his more prominent works are *Galeria Hispanico, Tesoro Hispanico,* and *Rumbas de España.*

Dr. Peña is supervisor of foreign languages in the Los Angeles City School District. He has worked to improve understanding among people and has been chairman of the Human Relations Council of the Los Angeles City Schools. He is a member of Phi Beta Kappa and is listed in *Who's Who in American Colleges and Universities.*

ANDRES PICO

(Politics   11)

Born: 1810, San Diego, California
Died: 1876
Significance: *Military service*

Andres Pico, brother of Pio Pico, was an honored soldier. In 1847 he and General Fremont signed the Capitulation of Cahuenga, bringing Mexico's rule in California to an end. He served as California State Senator in 1860 and 1861.

PIO PICO

(Government   11)

Born: 1801, Los Angeles, California
Died: 1894
Significance: *Governorship of California
    under Mexican Rule*

Pio Pico was the fifth governor of California from 1832 to 1833 and the thirteenth from 1845 to 1846. He was the last of the thirteen governors who served during the twenty-four years of Mexican rule.

Pio Pico and his brother, Andres, were among the largest landowners of southern California. Their holdings included the vast Rancho Santa Margarita y Las Flores near the mission of San Juan Capistrano. In 1832 Pico, a powerful and ambitious man, led a revolution to depose the hot-tempered Manuel Victoria, who was serving as the fourth Mexican governor of California from 1831 to 1832. Such influential landowners as José Antonio Carrillo, Don Juan Bandini, José Maria Echeandia, who had served as the third Mexican governor from 1825 to 1831, and Abel Stearns joined Pico in forcing Manuel Victoria out of office.

The second governorship of Pico was brought to an end, however, when the Departmental Assembly was dissolved because of the Mexican American War of 1846 to 1848. Pico went to Mexico until he learned that the Americans had taken political control of California. Returning to San Diego, he continued to manage his land and maintain his prestige.

ANTHONY RUDOLPH QUINN

(Acting   17)

Born: 1916, Chihuahua, Mexico
Education: Los Angeles public schools
Significance: *Outstanding actor*

Anthony Rudolph Quinn became a naturalized citizen of the United States in 1947. He has acted in plays such as *Clean Beds, Gentlemen from Athens, Street Car Named Desire, Let Me Hear the Melody, Beckett,* and *Tchin-Tchin.* He has appeared in many motion pictures, including *Buccaneer, Viva Zapata, Lust for Life, La Strada, Man from Del Rio, The Black Orchid, Warlock, Last Train from Gun Hill, Guns of Navarrone, Barabbas, Lawrence of Arabia, Zorba the Greek* and others. He won Academy Awards in *Viva Zapata* in 1952 and in *Lust for Life* as the best supporting actor in 1956.

FRANCISCO P. RAMIREZ
(Journalism   14)
Born: ca. 1840, Mexico
Died: ca. 1900
Education: Mexican schools
Significance: *Publisher of frontier newspaper for Spanish-speaking Americans*

Francisco P. Ramirez published one of the first Spanish language newspapers specifically devoted to the cause of meeting the needs of Spanish-speaking Californians. He dedicated his paper to political independence, moral and material progress, and the furtherance of a regime of law and order. He paid homage to the ideals of the United States Constitution, the Declaration of Independence and to the nation's dedication to popular government, economic progress, civil rights and the arts of peace. In his own way, Ramirez expressed the liberal-democratic philosophy of Jefferson and Jackson.

Ramirez sought to educate both Yankee and Spanish-speaking Americans about the progress of Latin American liberalism. He served his people in many ways. As their chronicler, he revived little-known historical facts, such as how Sonorans had discovered gold in Mexican California long before the advent of James Marshall. As their public defender, he chronicled all their expulsions from the mines, lynchings, and courtroom difficulties. As moral critic, he presumed to tell his fellow youths how to conduct themselves. As instructor in civics, he did what he could to initiate novice citizens into the workings and traditions of their new government. He published thumbnail sketches of the American presidents, the full Declaration of Independence, texts of state laws pertinent to the Spanish-speaking people and reports of current affairs in the nation at large.

CARLOS RIVERA
(Education   13)
Born: 1916, El Paso, Texas
Education: B.A., University of Texas, El Paso; M.A., University of Texas, Austin; Sorbonne University, Paris; Johns Hopkins University, Baltimore, Maryland; University of Pennsylvania, Philadelphia
Significance: *Pioneer work in the field of bilingual education*

Carlos Rivera was born in El Paso, Texas. His father was a pioneer cattleman who opened the Apache Trail from Presidio, Texas, to Kansas City, Missouri. Growing up in a home of strictly Mexican heritage and customs, he did not speak English until the age of seven. He went through El Paso High School during the years of the depression, working part-time after school. He was encouraged by his mother, who believed in education for her children. While in college he worked as assistant in the Foreign Language Department under a student aid program. Upon graduation he taught English and Spanish until 1942, when he joined the Defense Department as a translator.

During World War II, Rivera was drafted and assigned to War Crimes in Heidelberg, Germany as investigator and translator. He was able to attend Heidelberg University and was given a scholarship to the Sorbonne University in Paris, France. In 1951, he returned to El Paso schools to direct the teaching of Spanish in the elementary grades. Rivera is now Coordinator of Bilingual Education for the El Paso Public Schools. Since 1952 he has directed workshops in bilingual education at various universities.

He was chosen chairman of the International Relations Committee for the Texas PTA. He was elected to Phi Delta Kappa and appointed to its National Committee on Human Rights in Education. Later he was named to the Committee for the expansion of Phi Delta Kappa into Mexico.

Rivera says, "Everyone has a right to an education; but it is our duty to be prepared through education in order to take our rightful places in society. If we are to make demands, then we must be responsible to meet the challenge brought about by such demands."

VIDAL RIVERA, JR.
(Education 2)
Born: 1930, Los Angeles, California
Education: B.A., Arizona State
    University, Tempe, Arizona
Significance: *Leadership in improving the*
    educational plight of Mexican
    Americans

Vidal Rivera, Jr. entered the teaching profession in Phoenix Elementary School District #1. During his teaching experience there he also conducted a Spanish class and promoted an educational television program.

As director of the Division of Migrant Child Education with the State Department of Public Instruction in Arizona, he developed migrant education programs which received national recognition. His leadership led to his present position as chief of the Migrant Programs Section of the United States Office of Education. His continuous efforts to improve educational opportunities for migrant children throughout the United States have met with national approval.

ARMANDO M. RODRIGUEZ
(Education 15)
Born: 1921, Gomez Palacio, Durango,
    Mexico
Education: B.A., M.A., San Diego State
    College, California
Significance: *Leadership at the national*
    level in education for the Mexican
    American

Armando M. Rodriguez rose through the ranks in teaching and administration until today he is one of the most influential educational leaders in the United States. As director of the Office for Mexican American Affairs in the United States Office of Education, Rodriguez regards his role as that of a "sounding board" for the ideas and hopes of school and community leaders at the local level. From his extensive travels across the country, Rodriguez believes that there are three main obstacles to educational equality for Mexican Americans: scarcity of bilingual teachers, lack of well-integrated curricula, and too small a number of heroes to whom the Mexican American students can look for inspiration.

(Used by permission of Educational Consulting Associates, Menlo Park, California.)

JOHN A. ROSALES
(Education 13)
Born: ca. 1925
Education: B.A., M.A., Colorado State
    College, Greeley, Colorado
Significance: *Work for the Mexican*
    Americans in Colorado

John A. Rosales was the first Mexican American to be elected to any public office in Pueblo, Colorado. Rosales was elected councilman-at-large in 1965 and 1967 he became vice-president of the council. Many ordinances which were unfavorable to the disadvantaged were reviewed and through the efforts of Rosales have been repealed. He is presently a member of the Southwest Council of LA RAZA, representing Colorado.

EDWARD R. ROYBAL
(Politics 7, 9, 15)
Born: 1916, Albuquerque, New Mexico
Education: University of California, Los
    Angeles
Significance: *Legislative service*

Edward R. Roybal was with the Civilian Conservation Corps in the thirties and was a social worker and health education worker before his Army service in 1944–45. He was health education director for the Los Angeles Tuberculosis and Health Association from 1942–49, when he was elected to the Los Angeles City council on his second try. He was the Community Service Organization's first chairman and has since then been active in almost every effort to organize the Mexican-American community's political voice. He was elected to Congress in 1962 and successively reelected.

RUBEN SALAZAR
  (Journalism   13)
  Born: 1928, Juarez, Mexico
  Died: 1970
  Education: B.A., Texas Western
    University, El Paso
  Significance: *Champion of Mexican
    American civil rights*
Ruben Salazar, in the words of United States Senator for California, Alan Cranston, was a peaceful and compassionate man who dedicated his life to the eradication of poverty, injustice, prejudice and ignorance.

Soon after graduation from college he joined the Los Angeles Times in 1959. He began writing stories that were the highlights of his career. Salazar spotlighted injustices against Mexican Americans and other minorities. Through his news columns, he was especially instrumental in alleviating the plight of Mexican American children by publicizing the fact that they were placed in special education programs in California schools without fair consideration of their bilingualism. He researched the founding of Los Angeles, California, and published a statement that the original founders were Indians, Negroes and Mexicans rather than dashing Spanish Dons.

He served as a correspondent during the revolutionary outbreak in the Dominican Republic and covered the war in South Vietnam. As the Los Angeles Times Bureau Chief for Mexico City, he was an eyewitness to the student riots during the 1968 Olympics. Throughout his career, Salazar remained an objective observer in reporting current strife, relying on first-hand information through personal involvement.

JULIAN SAMORA
  (Education   12, 15)
  Born: 1920, Pagosa Springs, Colorado
  Education: B.A., Adams State College,
    Colorado; M.S., Colorado State
    University, Fort Collins; Ph.D.,
    Washington University, St. Louis,
    Missouri
  Significance: *Author, educator and
    champion of the Mexican American
    cause*
Julian Samora, as a member of the Department of Sociology at Notre Dame University, has engaged in extensive field work on problems of acculturation and health attitudes among the Spanish speaking population of Michigan and the southwest. In addition, he has written numerous articles on the subjects of sociology, anthropology, and rural health in Spanish speaking communities in the United States. Dr. Samora has served as a consultant to several important agencies, including the Ford Foundation which sent him on assignment to Mexico as an advisor on population problems. One of his most recent publications is *La Raza: Forgotten Americans* which depicts some of the more significant problems of the Mexican American community.

(Used by permission of Educational Consulting Associates, Menlo Park, California.)

GEORGE I. SANCHEZ
  (Education   1, 15)
  Born: 1906, Albuquerque, New Mexico
  Education: B.A., University of New
    Mexico, Albuquerque; M.S.,
    University of Texas, Austin; Ed.D.,
    University of California, Berkeley,
    California
  Significance: *Efforts to further knowledge
    and understanding of the Mexican
    American*
George I. Sanchez began as a rural school teacher in New Mexico, where he established himself during the following forty years as one of the nation's foremost experts on the educational and social problems of Spanish-Mexican minority groups in the United States. He is also an authority on these problems in Latin America. Dr. Sanchez has been director of numerous

teachers' workshops and institutes on bilingual-migrant problems, education in Latin America, and English as a second language sponsored by schools of higher education in the United States, Mexico, and Central and South America.

While studying education in Mexico, he discovered the Mayan mathematical code. He was author and editor of the Inter-American Series published by the Macmillan Co., as well as books, articles, and reports. One of his best known books is *Forgotten People*. He has participated in United States government, community, and professional activities.

(Used by permission of Educational Consulting Associates, Menlo Park, California.)

LEOPOLDO G. SANCHEZ

(Law   9)

Born: 1926, Los Angeles, California

Education: LL.B., Southwestern
   University, Georgetown, Texas

Significance: *Judiciary service*

Leopoldo G. Sanchez won his law degree in 1949, was elected to the Los Angeles municipal court bench in 1960 and to the superior court in 1966. He started school unable to speak a word of English and failed the first two grades, but subsequently became an honor student. He was in the army in 1945–46 and worked in steel mills while a student. He has won several awards for community activities and writes frequently for professional and general publications.

ANTONIO SEPULVEDA

(Law   11)

Born: 1842, San Juan Capistrano

Died: 1916

Education: Harvard University,
   Cambridge, Massachusetts

Significance: *Service as a judge of the
   Superior Court*

The most famous of the Sepulvedas, Antonio attended Harvard University from which he received a law degree. In 1863 he became a member of the District Court Bar, and a State Legislator in 1864. He was judge of the Superior Court in Los Angeles from 1879 to 1882.

JOSÉ SEPULVEDA

(Agriculture   16)

Born: ca. 1814, San Diego, California

Died: ca. 1870

Significance: *Prominent early California
   rancher*

José Sepulveda was one of the native Californian ranchers prominent in the cattle industry during the California Rancho period. His holdings included thousands of acres of grazing land inherited from his father, José Delores Sepulveda, in 1824. These holdings included the famous San Joaquin Rancho.

CARLOS MENDOZA TERAN

(Law   7)

Born: 1915, California

Education: A.B., LL.B., University of
   Southern California, Los Angeles

Significance: *Judiciary service*

Carlos Mendoza Teran has lived in California all his life. He was a captain in the service during World War II. Awarded the Bronze Star for bravery, he also received three Battle Stars.

Teran practiced law privately until his appointment to the Municipal Court. Two years later, in December of 1969, Governor Edmund G. Brown of California elevated him to the Superior Court. He is now serving as judge of the Juvenile Court in Los Angeles.

LEE TREVINO

(Golf   1)

Born: 1940, Vickery, Texas

Significance: *Success as a golfer*

Lee Trevino is one of the top golfers of the world. He gained fame in 1968 when he won the United States Open, one of the most important tournaments in the world of golf.

EDWARD E. TRIVIZ

(Law   10)

Born: ca. 1915, Las Cruces, New Mexico

Education: B.A., New Mexico State
   University, Las Cruces; M.A., George
   Washington University, Washington,
   D.C.

Significance: *Judiciary service*

Edward E. Triviz served in the Army Adjutant General Corps during World War II, in England, France and Germany. He entered the armed forces as an enlisted man and was discharged as a captain. He practiced law in Las Cruces, New Mexico from 1953 until 1966 when he was appointed a district judge. He is a member of the New Mexico Revision Commission and has served as its chairman. He has been a leader in studying the problems of juvenile delinquency and in organizing volunteers for probationary counseling.

DANNY VILLANUEVA
(Football   9)
Born: 1937, Tucumcari, New Mexico
Education: New Mexico State University,
    Las Cruces
Significance: *Athletic skill*

Since his career with the Dallas Cowboys and the Los Angeles Rams, Danny Villanueva has undertaken creative experiments in bilingual broadcasting, and has devoted himself to public service and education. He served on the California State Park and Recreation Commission under Governors Edmund G. Brown and Ronald Reagan.

Villanueva belongs to several civic organizations.

VINCENTE T. XIMENES
(Government   15)
Born: 1919, Floresville, Texas
Education: B.A., M.A., University of
    New Mexico, Albuquerque
Significance: *Leadership in Mexican
    American affairs*

Vincente T. Ximenes became affiliated with the United States government in 1939. He worked as a company clerk with the Civilian Conservation Corps (C.C.C.), an agency created during the depression of the 1930's to employ young people to conserve natural resources. He taught for a year in the elementary school in Wilson County, Texas, before entering college. Ten years later, having earned two degrees in the meantime, he was appointed as research economist at the University of New Mexico, where he stayed another decade.

During World War II, Ximenes flew some fifty missions as a lead bombardier with the United States Air Force. He won both the Distinguished Flying Cross and Air Medal. He was honorably discharged with the rank of Major. On June 9, 1967, Ximenes took his oath of office as Commissioner of the Equal Employment Opportunity Commission. He formerly held the chairmanship of the Inter-agency Committee on Mexican American Affairs.

(Used by permission of Educational Consulting Associates, Menlo Park, California.)

MEXICAN AMERICANS

Bibliography of Sources Used

1   Acuña, Rudolph. *The Story of the Mexican Americans: the Men and the Land.* New York: American Book Co., 1969.
2   Arizona. University. Alumni Association Files.
3   California. University. San Francisco Medical Center. Information Files.
4   Forbes, Jack D. *Mexican-Americans, a Handbook for Educators.* Berkeley, California: Far West Laboratory for Educational Research, 1966.
5   *In California Before the Gold Rush Days.* Los Angeles: Ward Ritchie Press, 1948.
6   Johnson, Kenneth R. *Teaching Culturally Disadvantaged Pupils.* Chicago: Science Research Associates, 1967.
7   Los Angeles City Schools. Audio-Visual Section. *Mexican Americans Today.* 25 study prints. Los Angeles: Los Angeles City Schools, 1968.
8   McWilliams, Carey. *North From Mexico: The Spanish-Speaking People of the United States.* Westport, Connecticut: Greenwood Press, Inc., 1968.
9   Nava, Julian. *Mexican Americans: Past, Present and Future.* New York: American Book Co., 1969.
10 New Mexico. State University. Alumni Association Files.
11 Orange County, California, Genealogical Society. *Saddleback Ancestors.* Orange County, California: The Genealogical Society, 1969.
12 Palacios, Arturo (ed.). *The Mexican-American Directory.* Washington, D.C.: Executive Systems Corp., 1969.
13 Personal Summary.
14 Pitt, Leonard. *Decline of the Californios.* Berkeley, California: University of California Press, 1968.
15 Rivera, Feliciano. *A Mexican American Source Book with Study Guide Outline.* Menlo Park, California: Educational Consulting Associates, 1970.
16 Ward, Don, and Dykes, J. C. *Cowboys and Cattle Country.* "American Heritage Junior Library." New York: American Heritage Publishing Co., 1961.
17 *Who's Who in America.* Chicago: Marquis-Who's Who, Inc., 1965.
18 Wood, Richard Coke. *The California Story.* San Francisco: Fearon Publishers, 1967.

OTHER REFERENCES

BOOKS FOR TEACHERS

Allen, Steve. *The Gound Is Our Table.* New York: Doubleday and Co., 1966.

Burma, John H. *Spanish-Speaking Groups in the United States.* Durham, North Carolina: Duke University Press, 1954.

Covarrubias, Miguel. *Indian Art of Mexico and Central America.* New York: Alfred A. Knopf, Inc., 1957.

Galarza, Ernesto. *Merchants of Labor: The Mexican Bracero Story.* Santa Barbara, California: McNally and Loftin, 1964.

Gamio, Manuel. *Mexican Immigration to the United States.* Chicago: University of Chicago Press, 1930.

Griffith, Beatrice. *American Me.* Boston: Houghton-Mifflin Co., 1948.

Heller, Cecillia S. *Mexican-American Youth: Forgotten Youth at the Crossroads.* New York: Random House, 1966.

Lado, Robert. *Linguistics Across Cultures.* Ann Arbor, Michigan: University of Michigan Press, 1957.

McWilliams, Carey. *Brothers Under the Skin.* Boston: Little, Brown & Co., 1942.

_____. *Factories in the Field: the Story of Migratory Farm Labor in California.* Boston: Little, Brown & Co., 1942.

_____. *Ill Fares the Land: Migrants and Migratory Labor in the United States.* Boston: Little, Brown & Co., 1942.

_____. *Mexicans in America.* A Student's Guide to Localized History. New York: Teachers College Press, 1968.

_____. *Southern California Country.* Des Moines, Iowa: Duell, Sloan, & Pearce (Meridith Press), 1946.

Olguin, Leonard. *Shuck Loves Chirley.* Huntington Beach, California: Golden West Publishing House, 1968.

Olivia, Leo E. *Soldiers on the Santa Fe Trail.* Norman, Oklahoma: University of Oklahoma Press, 1967.

Paz, Octavio. *The Labyrinth of Solitude: Life and Thought in Mexico.* New York: Grove Press, 1961.

Ramos, Manuel. *Profile of Man and Culture in Mexico.* Translated by Peter C. Earle. Austin, Texas: University of Texas Press, 1962.

Robinson, Cecil. *With the Ears of Strangers: The Mexican in American Literature.* Tucson, Arizona: University of Arizona Press, 1963.

Rubel, Arthur. *Across the Tracks.* Austin, Texas: University of Texas Press, 1966.

Ruiz, Ramon (ed.). *The Mexican War: Was it Manifest Destiny?* New York: Rinehart & Winston, Inc., 1963.

Samora, Julian (ed.). *La Raza: Forgotten Americans.* Notre Dame, Indiana: University of Notre Dame Press, 1966.

Solutions in Communications. Film. 25 minutes each, sound, b/w. A series of eight T.V. programs and an introductory lesson by Leonard Olguin. For teachers working with Mexican American children experiencing language difficulties. Sacramento, California: State Department of Education, Mexican American Education Research Project, 1968.

BOOKS FOR CHILDREN

Appel, Benjamin. *We Were There With Cortez and Montezuma.* New York: Grosset & Dunlap, 1959.

Atkins, Elizabeth Howare. *Treasures of the Medranos.* Berkeley, California: Parnassus Press, 1957.

Baker, Nina. *Juarez, Hero of Mexico.* New York: Vanguard Press, 1951.

Bleeker, Sonia. *Aztec Indians of Mexico.* New York: William Morrow & Co., 1963.

Buehr, Walter. *Spanish Conquistadores in North America.* New York: G. P. Putnam's Sons, 1962.

Bulla, Clyde. *Poppy Seeds.* New York: Thomas Y. Crowell Company, 1955.

Downey, Fairfax, *Texas and the War With Mexico.* New York: Harper and Row, Publishers, 1961.

Freeman, Dorothy Rhodes. *Home for Memo.* Encino, California: Elk Grove Press, 1968.

Glubok, Shirley. *Art of Ancient Mexico.* New York: Harper and Row, Publishers, 1968.

Krumgold, Joseph. *. . . and now Miguel.* New York: Thomas Y. Crowell Company, 1953.

Marshall, Helen Laughlin. *New Mexican Boy.* New York: Holiday House, 1940.

Politi, Leo. *Juanita.* New York: Charles Scribner's Sons, 1948.

————. *Pedro, the Angel of Olvera Street.* New York: Charles Scribner's Sons, 1946.

PART FIVE

APPENDICES

A: HISTORICAL PERIODS

B: SUBJECT OR
   OCCUPATIONAL
   CLASSIFICATION

APPENDIX A

HISTORICAL PERIODS

1861–1878
CIVIL WAR AND
RECONSTRUCTION PERIOD

1941–1970
WORLD WAR II
TO THE PRESENT

Mexican American

APPENDIX B

SUBJECT OR
OCCUPATIONAL CLASSIFICATION

ACTING

Afro American
Aldridge, Ira 6
Bailey, Pearl 8
Belafonte, Harry, Jr. 11
Cole, Nat "King" 22
Davis, Ossie 25
Duncan, Todd 30
Harrison, Richard B. 37
Horne, Lena 42
Hyman, Earle 42
Jones, James Earl 48
McDaniel, Hattie 56
O'Neal, Frederick 59
Poitier, Sidney 62
Robeson, Paul 66
Silvera, Frank Alvin 70
Waters, Ethel 77

Indian American
Silverheels, Jay 185
Te Ata 189

Mexican American
Quinn, Anthony Rudolph 224

AGRICULTURE

Afro American
Carver, George Washington 19
Pinder, Frank Edward 62

Asian American
Lue, Gim Gong 113

Minami, Harry Yaemon 102
Sawada, Kosaku 103
Shima, George 103
Suto, Kotaro 104

Indian American
Olds, Forest D. 171

Mexican American
Sepulveda, José 228

ANTHROPOLOGY

Afro American
Cobb, William Montague 22

Indian American
Dockstader, Frederick J. 146
Fredericks, Oswald White Bear 148
Garner, Beatrice Medicine 150
Ishi 156
Ortiz, Alfonso 172

ARCHITECTURE

Afro American
Downs, Thomas E. 28
Williams, Paul Revere 80

Asian American
Matsumoto, George 101
Pei, Ieoh Ming 114
Wong, Worley K. 115
Yamasaki, Minoru 106

ART

Afro American
Campbell, Elmer Simms   18
Douglas, Aaron   27

Asian American
Lee, Chingwah   111
Wong, Jade Snow   114

Indian American
Amiotte, Arthur Douglas   131
Begay, Harrison   132
Cochran, George McKee   142
Crumbo, Woodrow   144
Echohawk, Brummett   147
Gorman, R. C.   150
Houser, Allan   155
Howe, Oscar   155
Howling Wolf   155
Kabotie, Fred   158
Morrison, George   169
Orr, Carol   171
West, Walter Richard   196
Whitehouse, Roland   197
Wolf Robe Hunt, Wayne   199

ASTRONOMY

Afro American
Banneker, Benjamin   9

BASEBALL

Afro American
Aaron, Henry   5
Campanella, Roy   18
Mays, Willie   55
Paige, Satchel   60
Robinson, Jackie   67

Indian American
Reynolds, Allie   179

BASKETBALL

Afro American
Alcindor, F. Lewis, Jr.   6

Chamberlain, Wilt   20
Russell, Bill   68

BOXING

Afro American
Johnson, Jack   45
Louis, Joe   53

BUSINESS

Afro American
Cuffe, Paul   23
Jones, John (b. 1817)   48
Jones, John (b. 1829)   48
Spaulding, Asa T.   72
Walker, C. J.   76

Asian American
Chow, David Ta Wei   109
Ho, Chinn   110
Hsu, Leonard Shih Lien   111
Shoong, Joe   114
Yasui, Masuo   106

Indian American
Cobe, Albert   141
Cochran, George McKee   142
Florendo, Alice   147
Garcia, David   149
Keeler, William W.   159
Madrano, Daniel M.   164

Mexican American
Ochoa, Estevan   223

CINEMATOGRAPHY

Asian American
Howe, James Wong   110

CIVIL RIGHTS

Afro American
Bond, Julian   12
Carmichael, Stokley   19
Douglass, Frederick   28
DuBois, William E. B.   29

INVENTION

Afro American
Beard, Andrew J.   10
Blair, Henry   12
Latimer, Lewis H.   51
Matzeliger, Jan Ernest   55
McCoy, Elija   56
Morgan, Garrett   57
Rillieux, Norbert   65
Robertson, Elbert R. "Doc"   66
Temple, Lewis   74
Woods, Granville T.   80

Asian American
Guey, Fung Joe   110

Indian American
Sequoyah   184

JAZZ

Afro American
Armstrong, Louis   7
Basie, William (Count)   9
Charles, Ray   20
Coltrane, John   22
Davis, Miles   25
Fitzgerald, Ella   33
Gillespie, Dizzy   35
Hawkins, Coleman   37
Holiday, Billie   41
Morton, Ferdinand   58
Parker, Charlie (Bird)   60
Waller, Thomas   76

JOURNALISM

Afro American
Abbott, Robert S.   5
Bennett, Lerone   11
Fortune, T. Thomas   33
Johnson, John Harold   46
Lomax, Louis E.   53
Russwurm, John B.   68
Thompson, Era Bell   74
Vann, Robert L.   75
Wells, Ida B.   78

Asian American
Abiko, Kyutaro   97
Hosokawa, William   98
Tajiri, Larry   104
Tanaka, Togo William   104

Indian American
Ridge, John   179
Rock, Howard   180

Mexican American
Lozano, Ignacio E., Jr.   221
Ramirez, Francisco P.   225
Salazar, Ruben   227

LABOR

Afro American
Myers, Isaac   58
Randolph, A. Philip   64
Rapier, James T.   64

LANGUAGES

Asian American
Chan, Shau Wing   107

LAW

Afro American
Dudley, Edward R.   29
Gibbs, Mifflin W.   35
Hastie, William H.   37
Marshall, Thurgood   54
Motley, Constance Baker   58
Rivers, Francis E.   66
Sampson, Edith   69
Vann, Robert L.   75

Asian American
Aiso, John   97
Lum, Emma Ping   113
Marutani, William   100
Mau, Chuck   113
Tang, Thomas   114
Tsukiyama, Wilfred   105

Indian American
  Garcia, David   149
  Rogers, Edward   180
  Roubideaux, Ramon A.   181

Mexican American
  Arguelles, John   214
  Fimbres, Fred G.   218
  Herrera, William G.   220
  López, Henry   221
  Sanchez, Leopoldo G.   228
  Sepulveda, Antonio   228
  Teran, Carlos Mendoza   228
  Triviz, Edward E.   228

LAW ENFORCEMENT

Indian American
  Sixkiller, Sam   186

LIBRARY SCIENCE

Afro American
  Bontemps, Arna   13
  Jones, Clara   48
  Jones, Virginia Lacy   49
  Newsome, Effie Lee   59

LIFE SCIENCE

Afro American
  Buggs, Charles W.   16
  Just, Ernest E.   49
Asian American
  Li, Choh Hao   112

LITERATURE

Afro American
  Baldwin, James   8
  Bontemps, Arna   13
  Brooks, Gwendolyn   14
  Brown, Sterling   16
  Brown, William W.   16
  Bullins, Ed   17
  Chesnutt, Charles W.   21
  Cullen, Countee   24
  DuBois, William E. B.   29

  Dunbar, Paul L.   29
  Ellison, Ralph   31
  Emanuel, James A.   32
  Graham, Shirley   35
  Hansberry, Lorraine   37
  Hughes, Langston   42
  Johnson, James Weldon   45
  Jones, Le Roi   49
  Locke, Alain Leroy   52
  Motley, Willard   58
  Newsome, Effie Lee   59
  Wheatley, Phillis   78
  Wright, Richard   81

Asian American
  Aruego, Jose   115
  Lee, Chin Yang   111
  Uchida, Yoshiko   105

Indian American
  Belindo, John   133
  Berrigan, Ted   133
  Chief Eagle, D.   140
  Davis, Russell G.   144
  Kilpatrick, Jack F.   159
  Mathews, John Joseph   166
  McNickle, D'Arcy   168
  Momaday, N. Scott   168
  Standing Bear   187
  Stands in Timber, John   188
  Tebbel, John   189
  Velarde, Pablita   192
  Vizenor, Gerald Robert   193
  Wadley, Marie Lucille   193

MATHEMATICS

Afro American
  Banneker, Benjamin   9
  Blackwell, David H.   12

MEDICINE

Afro American
  Dailey, Ulysses Grant   24
  Derham, James   27
  Drew, Charles R.   28
  Lewis, Julian   52

MERCHANT MARINE

METALLURGY

MILITARY

MUSIC

SPORTS

Asian American
Cheng, Chi   108
Kono, Tommy   100

Indian American
Silverheels, Jay   185
Thorpe, Jim   190

TENNIS

Afro American
Ashe, Arthur   7
Gibson, Althea   35

Mexican American
Gonzales, Richard "Pancho"   219

TRACK

Afro American
Hayes, Bob   38
Johnson, Rafer   47
Owens, Jesse   60
Rudolph, Wilma   68

Indian American
Mills, Billy   168
Tewanima, Louis   190

TRIBAL AFFAIRS

Indian American
Bronson, Ruth Muskrat   137
Deganawidah   145
LaClair, Leo John   160
LaPlante, Edward   160
LaVatta, George P.   161
Lupe, Ronnie   163
Lyon, Juana   164
Misiaszek, Lorraine   168
Rainer, John C.   177
Sando, Joe Simmon   182
Sandoval, Albert George   183
Sandoval, Antonio Cebolla   183
Savilla, Agnes   183
Wadley, Marie Lucille   193
Walz, Erma   194

Wesley, Clarence   196
Willoya, Emma   198
Woodenlegs, John   199
Zarcillos Largos   200
Zuni, José A.   201

TRIBAL LEADERSHIP

Indian American
Ahkeah, Sam   130
Barboncito   132
Black Hawk   135
Black Kettle   135
Brant, Joseph   136
Buffalo Horn   138
Butterfield, Angela P.   138
Captain Jack   138
Cochise   142
Cornplanter   142
Crazy Horse   143
Dodge, Henry Chee   146
Ganado Mucho   149
Geronimo   150
Hoowanneka   154
Jones, Paul   156
Joseph (The Elder)   157
Joseph (The Young)   158
Keeler, William W.   159
Keokuk   159
King Philip   160
Leschi   161
Little Crow   162
Little Thunder   163
Little Turtle   163
Mahaskah (The Young)   164
Mangos Colorados   165
Manuelito   165
Massasoit   166
McIntosh, W. E. "Dode"   167
Narbona   169
Nesouaquoit   170
Olds, Forest D.   171
Ongpatonga   171
Osceola   172
Pontiac   174
Powhatan   176
Pushmataha   176
Quanah Parker   176